The ZOMBIE ADVENTURES of SARAH BELLUM

Lisa Scullard

The Zombie Adventures of Sarah Bellum

ISBN 9781481194730

Formatted and edited with U.K. spelling

Also by the author:

LIVING HELL (eBook & paperback)

TALES OF THE DEATHRUNNERS series:
DEATH & THE CITY: Book One (eBook & paperback)

DEATH & THE CITY: Book Two (eBook & paperback)

DEATH & THE CITY: Heavy Duty Edition (eBook)
DEATH & THE CITY: Cut to the Chase Edition (eBook, paperback edit)

THE ZOMBIE CHRONICLES OF OZ:
THE TERRIBLE ZOMBIE OF OZ with L. Frank Baum (eBook & paperback)

CONTENTS

INTRODUCTION
ABOUT THE AUTHOR
CEMETERY ~ FILTHY SHAVINGS OF GRAY MATTER 1
NINE AND HALF REAPS 10
NINE AND A HALF REAPS, CONTINUED 14
BODY OF CONDIMENTS 18
PRETTY WARM ONE 22
SCAR WARS 27
PHANTOM OF THE OPERATING THEATRE 32
TOMB BATHER 37
DANGEROUS LACERATIONS 45
BADMAN 50
BLADE RUSTER 54
E.T. ~ HOMER LONE 58
THE GROANIES 62
RADIALS OF THE LOST ARM 68
GOBBLINGS OF THE LARYNX 73
NECROMANCING THE BONES 78
SLIPPED DISCLOSURE 84
THE COCKERELS OF HERNIA 88
STARGRAVE 93
DROOL OF THE NILE 97
REFLEX OF THE JEJUNUM 102
QUIM OF THE DAMNED 106
PRUDE AND PREPUTIUM 109
THE GRANULATE 113
PUMP FRICTION 118
DIRTY HARRIDAN 121

PYGANGLION	125
UNDEATH ON THE NILE	128
OCTOPULPY	133
THE MAGNIFICENT SEPTUM	138
THE LIFE OF BRAINS	142
BIG TROUBLE IN RECEPTACULUM CHYLI	147
THE MEN WHO STARE AT GLUTES	151
THE LOST BONES	156
INDEFINABLE BONES & THE TEMPLES OF GLOOM	159
CROUCHING TIBIA, HIDDEN DUODENUM	162
THE MALPIGHIAN'S NEPHRITIS	167
SHALLOW GRAVY	173
THE LEG OF EXTRANEOUS GENITO-URINARY MEDICINE	179
THE HUNT FOR RECTAL OEDEMA	184
CREMASTER TIED	190
20,000 LEGS UNDER THE SEA	195
SPLAT	202
THE UVULA STRIKES BACK	205
ILIUM RESURRECTION	208
GNASHER NAIL TREASURE	215
BEETLEJUGULAR	219
HAIRY PALATE & THE CHAMBER OF SECRETIONS	223
LOBULES OF AREOLA	228
SECTS AND THE CITADEL, TOO	233
CASABLADDER	238
DIURETIC 13	243
CARUNCULA ROYALE	248
SORE	252

FERMAT'S WOMB 257
PARANODULE 261
MEDIASTINUM IMPOSSIBLE 266
GURNEY TO THE CENTER OF THE EARTH 271
A TOWN CALLED PANCREAS 275
JURASSIC PRICK 279
DEATH FACE 284
MENOPAUSE IN BLACK 290
M*A*S*H*E*D 298
GOOD MOANING, VERAMONTANUM 304
DAD'S ARMLESS 309
FULL METACARPAL JACKET 315
APOPHYSIS NOW 322
IT AIN'T HALF ARSED, MUM 330
CHYME BANDITS 340
THE WONDERFUL WRISBERG OF OESOPHAGUS 348
SCARDUSK 357
THE TOURNIQUET 366
CHYLE & THE CHOCOLATE FASCIA 373
TOMB BATHER ~ CRADLE OF AFTERLIFE 377
COWBOYS AND ILEUMS 383
FRANKENMINKY 390
IRON MANDIBLE 398
TRANSMOGRIFIERS 405
PROSTATES OF THE CARIBBEAN 411
THE RIDICULES OF CHRONIC 418
BIG KNOBS AND BROOM CLOSETS 425
TRUE LICE 432
DÉJÀ VOODOO ~ FIFTY SHALLOW GRAVES 436

INTRODUCTION

"You'll be hearing from our lawyers." *W.D, film artisan empire.*

"And mine." *Mr. Steven S, purveyor of moving pictures.*

"Our author has never read your books…" *R.H, publisher.*

"Lisa who?" *Q.T, film fanatic, writer and bon viveur.*

"I'll never hear the end of it…" *Anonymous.*

"What's her name and Social Security Number?" *A.J, United Nations Ambassador.*

"There better be stuff in it worth stealing…" *A.L.S. Esq, lawyer.*

"I knew it was just a uniform thing." *P. Harry, on tour.*

"More." *Swaggers, Hastings.*

LIKED *Mr. D. Hedgehog, on Facebook via BlackBerry.*

"I must finish my blog…" *S. Neville, backpacker extraordinaire.*

"Delicious." *Patricia Morgan, paintbrush wielder, 10th Dan.*

"Bums on seats." *O. Cinemas, popcorn and hot-dog distributor.*

(The above quote widely misinterpreted in the United States).

"Looks interesting…" *P.E, satirist and commentator.*

"Which book is this one?" *DS-10, demonic stats expert.*

"I was making it up as I went along." *H. Gray, F.R.S.*

"We can confirm that 'Miss X.' worked for us between October 1996 and January 1997. However, we do not take responsibility for any loss or damage incurred by your relying on this as a reference." *Safeways, no longer trading as a U.K. supermarket.*

"Carlsberg don't make nightclub bouncers. But if they did…" *A. Customer, Southampton.*

ABOUT THE AUTHOR

The Zombie Adventures of Sarah Bellum started out as a blog parody of copyright law, having read something that gave me about three months' worth of uninterrupted *déjà-vu* and pattern-matching.

The blog gathered momentum and fell into a great sucking vortex of movie scenes, dialogue, characters and settings, that folk had conveniently posted on YouTube for me to reference.

It has been the most fun I have ever had on this sofa.

I'd like to thank all those talented people who not only made the original films, but also the fans who posted their own edits, alternative trailers, and mashed-up tunes, which I featured in my blog posts while writing this bloodthirsty monster.

And also the professionals in writing, film, law, publishing and journalism whom I met and corresponded with this year – your time was much appreciated. Thanks for clarifying everything…

When not enjoying long walks off short cliffs and walks on the wild side, I like to walk the path of least resistance. I have found that this involves a lot more effort than just sitting on the fence.

lisascullard.wordpress.com

voodoo-spice.blogspot.com

www.screenkiss.co.uk

on Twitter: aka_VoodooSpice

For Caitlin

at Brighton 'Beach of the Dead' 2012

CHAPTER ONE:
CEMETERY ~
FILTHY SHAVINGS OF GRAY MATTER

I look in the mirror. I do it every day. Pretty much most people look in the mirror every day.

I see a girl. That's a relief. A girl with hair, two eyes, a nose, one mouth, and as I push the hair back as I'm brushing it to check – yes, still got two ears. *Phew.*

My housemate, whose name escapes me most days, has forced me into this, the reason I'm awake and brushing my hair at the ungodly hour of ten a.m. How dare she go for her abortion today, and pack me off instead to do her media studies homework? Couldn't she have had her termination some other time?

"Mr. Dry," I say to my reflection, giving myself a momentary identity-crisis. I see the panic in my two eyes, and pull myself together. *Rehearse, dammit!* "I'm Sarah Bellum. Pleased to meet you..."

I have to go for an interview with some vending machine business mogul. The company is called Dry Goods, Inc, and the owner, Crispin Dry, supplies our University with all of its vending machines. He's notoriously hard to get appointments with. When you ring his office, you have to press so many buttons on the phone to finally get through – only to be told that your selection is no longer available, and to choose an alternative.

Miss Whatsername, my housemate, says that she's got to get this interview for the University paper. I don't know why, they only use it to wrap take-out cartons in the refectory. Maybe it's to promote a new drinks machine range.

I think she's secretly fishing for a job too, as she's insisted I take along her school yearbook, and a set of twelve professional head-shots – which must have been taken some time between tooth-braces, and her recent foray into fertilisation.

So I'm having to forgo my weekly visits to the Body Farm and the morgue for my own research project. I don't even know if I'll be back in time for work later.

She's going to owe me big-time for this. If I don't get to see a corpse this week, I don't know what I'll do. There's one I'm rather fond of in a wheelie-bin under a silver birch tree at the Body Farm, where I like to sit and eat my sandwiches.

He'll have changed so much the next time I see him…

I leave Whatserface, my best friend, packing her nightdress for the clinic.

"Good luck!" says Thingummyjig, as I head out. "Don't forget my C.V!"

I struggle to guess what she means… Cervical Vacuum? Crazy Voodoo? Crotch Visor? Copulation Venom? Crinoline Vagina? Contraceptive Velcro? What kind of prophylactic is called a *C.V?*

Perhaps if she'd remembered some of that sooner, she wouldn't be heading for a *D&C* now…

"I'll bring you back some sanitary towels," I concede, and slam the front door.

It's a long drive to Seafront West Industrial Estate, but luckily I have my father's trusty bullet-proof Hummer in which to navigate the rain-soaked roads. I don't think my *Pizza Heaven* scooter would have made it. When I put my books in the insulated top-box, it always skids over in the wet. And sometimes nasty people put other things in there, when I'm doing a delivery.

Dry Goods House is a huge monolith of connected storage containers, converted into offices on the seafront industrial park, an illegal immigrant's fantasy. Mirrored glass windows inserted into the corrugated steel keep out any prying eyes.

The revolving doors swish as I enter the Customer Enquiries lobby. A brain-dead-looking blonde is sitting at the stainless surgical steel counter.

"I'm here for the interview with Mr. Crispin Dry," I announce. "I'm Sarah Bellum. Miss Thing from the University sent me."

"I'll text him," says Miss Brain-Dead, picking up her phone. "Have a seat."

She eyes me as I sit down on the plastic chair between two vending machines, one for hot drinks, the other for snacks. I feel over-dressed. Maybe stealing my housemate's *Christian Louboutin* studded Pigalle pumps and Chanel suit had been taking it too far. The receptionist looks cool and comfortable, in turquoise blue overalls and a neon yellow hi-visibility industrial vest.

"He's on his way down," she says, after a moment. She reaches under the desk. "You'll have to put this on."

I get up again to accept the hi-visibility yellow vest she hands me, which has *VISITOR* stencilled on the back. I pull it on grudgingly over my borrowed Chanel.

The adjoining door creaks, and I turn, still adjusting my Velcro.

I know, the moment I see him.

The black suit. The pallor of his skin. The attractively tousled, unkempt bed-hair. The drool. That limp… oh, God, that limp…!

"Crispin Dry?" My voice catches in my throat.

"Miss… *Bellllummmm*," he moans softly, extending a dirt-encrusted hand.

My heart palpitates wildly, noting his ragged cuticles, and the long, gray, prehensile fingers.

"My housemate," I begin. "Miss Shitface – she couldn't make it today. Got the uterine bailiffs in…"

I grasp his outstretched hand in greeting. *So cold… and yet so mobile…* a tingle crawls deliciously up my forearm, and I snatch my hand away quickly, scared of showing myself up. His jet-black eyes glitter, equally cold, and his upper lip seems to curl in the faintest suggestion of a smirk, like a slow, private spasm.

"Were you offered a refreshment, Miss *Bellumm?*" He gestures towards the famous vending machines.

I shake my head, and he turns to glare at the receptionist. She cowers visibly, and I'm sure I hear him emit a long, low, guttural sound. The receptionist scrabbles in her drawer and holds out a handful of coin-shaped metal tokens.

"I'm fine, really…" I croak, although in all honesty, my throat does feel terribly dry.

"Very *wellll…*"

My knees feel weak as he holds the door open, and beckons, his head at a quirked angle.

"This way, Miss… *Bellummm.*"

How he rolls my name around his mouth makes my own feel drier than ever. I stumble hazily through into the corridor, hearing the door creak closed again behind me, and the shuffling, shambling sound of his footfalls in my wake.

"Straight ahead, Miss *Bellumm.*"

His voice is like sandpaper being rasped over a headstone. It tickles my inner ear and the back of my throat, sends chills down my vertebrae. It resonates with my deepest darkest thoughts.

Things I had not even entertained notions of while eating sandwiches under the silver birch tree, beside my dear Mr. Wheelie-Bin…

His arm extends past me to swipe his security card in the lock of the next door, and a waft of his moss-like scent washes over my strangely heightened senses.

"Go through, Miss *Bellumm,*" he practically whispers in my ear.

The door clicks open, and I do as bidden. Murky grey daylight filters through the tinted windows from the seafront, and I gasp.

Another brain-dead blonde is banging her head repeatedly on the steel wall, not three feet away from the door.

"Debbie," Mr. Dry says. Is that a tinge of disappointment, or disapproval in his voice? "Take Miss *Bellummm's* coat. You will not need the yellow site vest either while you are with me, Miss *Bellummm.*"

Debbie turns to look at us, her flat bleached-out bloodshot eyes registering nothing. She holds out her arms to accept the navy-blue Chanel and hi-visibility vest as I shrug them off, feeling exposed now in my Andy Warhol *Marilyn Monroe* t-shirt.

Miss Brain-Dead Mark II takes my jacket with a soft grunt, but goes nowhere, turning back to face the wall instead, contemplating the smear where her head had been rebounding off it just a moment before.

Crispin Dry takes my arm to steer me past, the unexpected contact eliciting another gasp from me. *Those long cold prehensile fingers, closing around the soft warm flesh of my tricep!* I trip along the next corridor, trying to keep pace with his rolling, loping gait, like that of a wounded panther.

"My office…" he hisses, swiping his security pass a second time, and ushering me through.

It is black. Everything is black, from the desk, to the leather seating, to the vertical blinds. The only colour in the room is a giant white canvas, on the wall facing the long window, upon which a modern meditation in red is represented.

"You like my art, Miss *Bellummm?*" he murmurs, seeing my open gape at the piece.

"It's yours?" Wow – now I'm really intimidated. I swallow. "It's, er – beautiful…"

"I call this one… *'High-Velocity Spatter'*," he confides in a husky voice. "Sit."

I plant my quivering haunches onto the soft leather, and start to take out my notes. The only sound otherwise in his office is the eerie call of gulls, from the windswept pebble beach outside.

Crispin Dry watches me, calculatingly. He circles around the sofa opposite, not yet seated.

"Would you like something to drink, *Sarah Bellumm*?" He moves languidly towards the huge, black, state-of-the-art vending machine in the corner.

The sound of my full name on his lips is like the opening of a beautiful white lily…

"I am a little parched," I admit. "Yes, please, Mr. Dry. Thank you."

"What would you like?" His hand hovers over the illuminated keypad. "Tea, coffee, hot chocolate? Iced water? Chicken soup? Gin and tonic? Bubblegum? Breath mints?"

Mmmm – a vending machine with everything!

"A chicken soup would be lovely," I hear myself say, and my stomach grumbles in agreement, recalling the last slice of cold *Pizza Heaven* pizza I ate for breakfast, many hours ago.

"Chicken noodle, chicken and sweetcorn, Thai chicken and lemongrass…?"

"Yes please – the last one…"

I watch as his clever fingers dance over the keys. There is the faintest hum from the machine. In a trice, a large fine china mug appears, steaming, on its own saucer, garnished with fresh chives and coriander. There is even the traditional porcelain soup-spoon on the side, intricately decorated.

I wonder what sort of businesses he supplies this particular machine to? All that the University ones dispense, is various colours and temperatures of pond-water *à la* Styrofoam. We must be at the very bottom of their budget range.

He brings it to the low onyx table in front of me, and presents it with the gallant flourish of a red napkin. Something of the gesture, and the way he arranges himself laconically on the sofa opposite, makes my heart sink slightly.

Oh no. He's so gay…the way he's fidgeting his earlobe in that *I'm-ready-to-listen* way and stroking his knee with his other hand – that's throwing at least fifty shapes of gay…

I struggle to focus on the list of questions that Knobhead has written out for me. I'm starting to worry that maybe I won't enjoy finding out the answers to some of them.

"It's very hot," he says, in a warning tone. It startles me.

"Hmmm?" Am I always this jumpy? Well – to be honest… yes.

"The soup, Miss *Bellummm*." His mouth twitches in the corner, and his black eyes crinkle slightly. It's as if he can see into the dark shadows at the back of my own mind.

"I can get started with the questions while it cools down," I say, brightly, batting away the shadows in my head at his curt nod. *Definitely gay*. I look down at the sheet of paper. "Now… the first question. Is it true that you employ foreign child labour in the construction of your vending machines?"

"No." The answer is as cold as ice, and as solid. "There are other ways of manufacturing our machines to a budget that is mutually beneficial, to the product consumers, and the workforce."

"Right…" I scribble this down, in my best pizza-order shorthand. "And is it also true that you sub-contract your perishable goods supplies, for human consumption, out to companies who deal in black market foodstuffs and out-of-date stock?"

"Our sub-contractors are fully vetted," he assures me. "If any sub-standard products are finding their way into my machines, it is usually the fault of the site owners, outsourcing to cut-price vandals who access the machines without our endorsement. Quality control is of paramount importance in this business."

The aroma drifting up from the soup is certainly backing up his argument. *But still...*

"Are you saying that the recorded cases of food poisoning at Cramps University, and at other sites, is the faculty's fault?" I ask.

"I am not saying anything, Miss *Bellumm*," he muses, his eyes still faintly entertained, his neck still quirked. "But you are, it seems."

I stare down at the page. That wasn't one of Miss Fucktard's questions! My stomach growls, guiltily. Damn food-poisoning…

"I am disappointed in you, Miss *Bellummm*," he continues. "I hoped perhaps that your agenda for this little 'interview' was more personally – *ambitiousss*… in a secretarial direction?"

Stupid Twat's next question, coincidentally, had originally been: *'How likely are you to give me a job in exchange for keeping all this stuff quiet?'*

But it had been crossed out, and replaced with something else.

"Moving on," I say swiftly, aware that his eyes are mentally dismembering me. I look at the revised Question Number Three. "How do you explain your current one thousand percent increase in profits in the current financial climate, Mr. Dry?"

"With excellent book-keeping."

I look up at him, uncertain as to whether this is merely a stab at humour.

He is still lounging on the sofa, the jet black of his eyes resting on me steadily. My own eyes follow the line of his jaw, and the rumpled Bohemian mane of hair, still intact. His square shoulders in that black suit make me feel weak.

What's wrong with you, girl? He's still walking around and talking! You'd be bored sick of him within minutes, same as all the others...

I press on with the questions, covering the various charges of tax evasion, pollution, carbon footprint, and illegal immigration, and he has a cool answer for every single one. I'm relieved to turn the page, and find the closing questions are brief.

"…Finally, Mr. Dry. Can you tell me your favourite colour?"

He indicates the décor of the office.

"Black," he confirms. "With a fetish for red, occasionally. And sometimes…"

His face darkens. He looks away.

"White?" I suggest, thinking of the painting.

"When black meets white, there is a certain shade – a very delicate and vulnerable shade – that illustrates humanity in its most primitive state."

"You mean gr…"

He puts his finger to his lips.

"Best left unspoken." Those black eyes burrow into my head. "A colour for the mind. Not for the lips. Only… under very special circumstances… should the matter pass the lips."

He's bonkers. Just what we need right now. Another gay eccentric. I return to the final questions.

"And what music do you listen to?"

"Soul."

"And last question. What car do you drive?"

"I have a number of cars, all black, and a chauffeur, who drives very sedately. You must allow me to take you on a tour of the rest of my complex some time. I still have an opening for a new cemetery… I mean… a new *secretary*."

My lips part like the Red Sea. How *blatant* was that? That was no slip – that was a whole Freudian tripwire!

Is he psychic? No… *psychotic*, more likely…

Outside the window behind him, something turquoise blue and neon yellow crashes wetly onto the pebble beach from above. Without looking around, he produces a remote control, and closes the vertical blinds. Automatic halogen lights phase on overhead, so there is no change in illumination inside the office.

"Thank you, Mr. Dry." I'm on my feet in that instant, suddenly wary of being in an enclosed office alone with him. Those dark shadows have all sprung to attention in the back of my mind, at the closing of those blinds. "You have been very accommodating, but really I mustn't keep you any longer."

"Indeed?" he asks in turn, rising out of his seat. For the first time I notice how tall and manly he is… *was*, I correct myself angrily. "Keep me for what purpose, I wonder?"

So arrogant!

I just nod, blushing fiercely, and head for the door.

"I will have to show you out," he reminds me, taking out the security pass again, and lurching forward to accompany me. "It has been a pleasure, Miss *Belllummm*."

His voice is driving me crazy. And his hand on my arm again, guiding me out of the door and into the corridor. I practically scamper ahead, snatching my coat back from Brain-Dead Blonde Mark II.

"Thank you for your time, Mr. Dry," I say, back in the near-safety of the lobby. There is no sign of Brain-Dead Blonde the receptionist, and I can't wait to get away. "It has been very educational."

"I'm sure it will be," he agrees, with a courteous nod. "*Au revoir*, Miss *Belllummm*."

I run to the Hummer in my pointy Pigalle pumps, and lock myself in. I can see gulls flocking to the spot on the beach outside his office, on the far side of the building.

Those shadows in my head – I fight to control them.

How dare he hijack my fantasies, my pure and innocent thoughts of the dead? How dare he make a mockery of it all by *walking around* in *broad daylight* and *touching me??!*

There ought to be a law against that sort of thing…

As I drive home again, all I can see through the rain bouncing off the road in front of me, is his gray and amused, sardonic and demonically attractive face.

CHAPTER TWO:

NINE AND A HALF REAPS

My *Pizza Heaven* scooter is protesting as I ride up the mile-long driveway to the enormous stately home. I've never been called out here before. The little two-stroke engine is making those annoying little noises, only slightly more annoying than the noises that the gorgeous Ace Bumgang at *Bumgang & Sons' Breaker's Yard* makes when I ask him to take a look at it for me – on the occasions that I've ridden it through gravel, or a puddle more than three inches deep.

Good Lord, the house is huge. Like one of those 'brownsigns' in England, that have most of the rooms sectioned off with gilt corded rope, and that the public are allowed to wander around in at the weekends. So long as they don't stray from the carpet and into the electric fencing, preventing them from leaving with more shiny heirloom helmets hidden down their trousers than they came in with.

A black stretch Cadillac limo is parked at the foot of the steps, the engine and exhaust still ticking quietly as it cools, as if the owner has only recently arrived home. I pull in at a respectable distance behind.

Swallowing my nerves, I take the pizza bag out of the top-box after parking up, and scale the enormous marble steps. I was rather hoping there would be a delivery slot, or at least a cat-door big enough to push the box through and run, which is my preferred tactic when also delivering to the rough end of town. I'd rather lose one pizza's worth of payment, than my whole bike while my back is turned. Still smarting from the occasion when I returned to the kerb just in time to see it being towed away around the far corner of the block, by four small children on a Fisher-Price musical push-along cart. Playing *Old MacDonald Had a Farm*… I cannot listen to that nursery rhyme since. It gives me terrible PTSD flashbacks.

But no. Just an entryphone beside the studded oak door. I press the buzzer, wondering if there is a camera as well, and if they'll insist I remove my *George and Mildred* peaked crash helmet before responding. The one I still wear because I love Ace Bumgang's face as he tells me the horrors of fixed-peak open-face headwear in an RTA. Sort of a mixture of caring, considerate, concerned, and 'get out of my site office, you deluded stalker…' While he pulls a sweater over his tight t-shirt, hiding those delicious-looking biceps and pectorals from my hungry gaze…

Expecting an intercom reply to my buzz, I get a shock when the door is opened silently in front of me – and for the first time I fully understand the meaning of the famous phrase 'the world dropped out of my bottom.'

For standing in front of me, his matt-black tie undone and just-dead hair hypnotically dishevelled, is Crispin Dry – vending machine magnate, entrepreneur, and the sexiest corpse I've recently seen – since *4:23p.m.* last Thursday, in a wheelie-bin under the silver birch tree at the Body Farm…

"Mr. Dry!" I squeak, terrified – and immediately thrust the pizza box under his nose. Hoping to avert the smell of nervous pizza-delivery girl.

"Miss… *Belllummm…*" he slurs. "What a pleasant surprise. Do come inside. The kitchen is just this way."

And he turns in the doorway and shambles off into the opulent entrance hall, beckoning for me to follow. It looks as though I have no choice. I pull the gigantic door closed behind me, feeling as though I now know how *Gretel* felt, upon entering the gingerbread house…

The kitchen is vast – like a bowling alley. When he opens the giant refrigerator, and starts selecting his condiments, I half expect to see the bottles deposited mechanically onto the shelf in front of him, like a set of ten-pins.

"I'll just leave it right here, shall I?" I suggest, sliding the box onto the glassy-smooth granite counter-top. It sparkles with quartz and mica – not superheat-treated granite then, I find myself thinking… my mind wanders like this unpredictably at times…

"Join me, Sarah *Bellummm*," he says, unexpectedly. "I believe you might be famished, after your long day…"

Damn. That will scupper my usual Friday plans, of waiting outside *Bumgang & Sons' Breaker's Yard* with a Chinese Meat Feast. Ace always pretends to be surprised, which is sweet, and sometimes he even takes it with him. He's usually in a big hurry to meet up with his friends at the boys' club, *Gentlemen Prefer Poledancers* – which is endearing, as it means he's telling me in his own special way that he's not settled for anyone important yet…

"Well – I think the last thing I ate, was a sip of chicken soup, from the vending machine at your office earlier…" I admit timidly.

"*Toooo* long," he agrees, with a devastatingly wonky nod. "Take a seat. And close your eyes. I have a surprise for you."

I slip off my *George and Mildred* and try to make the most of my helmet-hair as I arrange myself on the seat at the counter. He darts me a meaningful look, still foraging in the refrigerator, and obligingly I close my eyes.

Gosh, I hope this means a big tip.

"Is that your Cadillac outside?" I ask, to pass the time with small-talk, while I hear him putting dishes on the counter in front of me.

"It is just a courtesy car," he says, dismissively. "The Bugatti and the Maserati are away for servicing, and I only use the Diablo on holiday weekends, when I go hot-air ballooning."

"Hmm," I murmur, only half-believing him. Probably only got a Ford Out-of-Focus, or a common-or-garden Vorsprung Dork Technique in his garage… I make a private bet that the Cadillac is rented, just for show – utilised to pick up innocent girls when he's in town. I mean, guys like Ace Bumgang, you expect them to have a couple of sports cars, a racing bike and a speedboat, I mean, petrolhead mechanics always do… but not a businessman. A fleet of cheap *1.2L* commuter compacts, if anything…

"I hope you are hungry," Crispin Dry says, rather darkly, interrupting my fantasy that Ace Bumgang is *The Stig*, which would explain why he's always so elusive. "I have an idea of your tastes already. Open wide."

I promptly rearrange myself on the seat.

"I meant your mouth," he croons, and I slam my knees together again, like a barn door in a tornado.

Nervously, I let my mouth fall open, in a textbook Q.

"Put your tongue in, *pleeeaase*," he moans softly.

The Q becomes an O, as requested.

Something tickles my lower lip, sticky, and fragrantly barbecued. Mmm – chicken wings! My stomach rumbles immediately in response, and I chew enthusiastically.

"You approve?" he asks, and he sounds hopeful.

"Yum," I nod. "Is there more?"

"Nine more, I believe," he confirms, as I run my tongue around my teeth to dislodge any gristly bits. I cough on something dry, and remove something curved, cartilaginous, almost fingernail-shaped from my cheek, which he quickly brushes aside from my own fingertips. "I think we have found your acquired taste exactly."

"Do you have anything to drink?" I ask. My eyes are still rapturously closed, all thoughts of the tanned, toned and droolworthy Ace Bumgang forgotten.

"Be patient, Sarah *Bellummm*," my dream zombie whispers. "I am sure I have a cocktail worthy of you."

I am shocked by his intimate tone.

"It's as if you were expecting me," I gasp, feeling myself blush.

"But of course," he says, so close to my ear, I nearly swoon off the chair. "I do still need a new secretary, of which I'm sure you must be aware. Which means we have our interview process to complete. I even made sure to re-stock the vending machine in my bedroom, right before you arrived…"

CHAPTER THREE:

NINE AND A HALF REAPS, CONTINUED…

The intensity in the atmosphere is excruciating. I can hear Crispin Dry (vending machine CEO of Dry Goods Inc., *nouveau morte* and *bonne bouche*) still moving around me in the vast kitchenette of his Grade II-listed mansion. Chopping, dicing, blending, and possibly mixing up the previously-mentioned cocktail, which he says is tailored especially for me.

Me: Sarah Bellum – mild-mannered pizza delivery girl by night, ambitious Forensic Anthropology student by day, and incurable romantic. Apart from the very much alive Ace Bumgang, who I like to watch from a distance through the chicken-wire fencing of *Bumgang & Sons' Breaker's Yard* – especially when he's outside his site office with his shirt off – the only male bodies I ever see are in various stages of decay, on the Body Farm.

I'm lucky if I get five minutes a week there to study, recently. Or at the Body Farm. What with Miss Wotsit, my best friend and housemate, being so demanding – with her delayed birth control plans, and electronically-tagged boyfriend, with whom she seems to be smitten.

Actually, her situation would be more accurately described thus: *'By whom she seems to be smashed up, on a regular basis.'*

No wonder I never even remember her name. She comes home with a different face every few days.

With a great pang of loss I wonder how much my dearest one at the Body Farm, Mr. Wheelie-Bin Under The Silver Birch Tree, will have progressed the next time I see him. Apparently he was a domestic violence victim too. You could tell particularly in the early stages, by the way his scalp was hanging off like a bad toupée…

…But the sound of Crispin Dry sliding something along the counter towards me dissolves that thought, as quickly as an acid bath.

"No peeping," he murmurs, and I nod, confirming that my eyes are still obediently closed. "Perhaps we should retire to the other room, where you will be more comfortable. Take my arm."

"Where are we going?" I ask, sliding off the seat at the counter.

I had been enjoying the food game. My stomach was still hinting that it had room for more. I feel the cold cloth of his sleeve under my fingers as I reach out, and the even colder press of his flesh underneath, as he tucks my arm into his side to guide me along.

"Just across the hall," he confides. "There is a very nice late evening lounge."

"You have a lounge for different times of day?" I ask, making careful effort to keep pace with his attractive, undead pimp-limp. *What do they call it? Crap walk? Crabstick walk?* I'm glad Ace Bumgang can't hear my thoughts, sometimes. Although the look he gives me when he espies me through the boundary fence of the breaker's yard suggests he does know exactly what I'm thinking, and it comes with the words 'restraining order' attached. He's so cute. He just knows I'm a sucker for threats like that… *Cripple walk…?* Hmm. Maybe I made it up…

"I have a room for every time of day, Miss *Bellummm*," Crispin Dry assures me, heavy with implied meaning.

My kneecaps try to switch places, while my tongue tries to hide behind my epiglottis and escape up the back of my nasal cavity.

"Turn around," Crispin's voice whispers against my ear, his other hand on my shoulder, pivoting me to face him. I feel him testing the sleeve of my *Pizza Heaven* work fleece. "Would you like to take this off?"

"Er, well, actually…" I cough, trying to sound nonchalant. "I kind of had a nap before work tonight, so this is all I have on. Er. Underneath. Just me."

"Intriguing," he says, and I can hear his approval. I gulp.

He moves forward just enough to help me take a backward step, and I feel the soft give of a cushioned seat at the back of my legs.

"Make yourself comfortable," he says, and for my wandering kneecaps' sake, I plop thankfully onto the velvet cushions. "I will return with the drinks. And still no peeping."

"I promise," I nod, my anticipation at his own promise of *drinks* already building again. I'm parched. I could go for a fish-tank cocktail right now, never mind a fish-bowl cocktail.

"I think I will take out a little insurance on your promise," he remarks, and I hear the swish of silk. "I will use my tie to blindfold you. Do you mind?"

"Is it another game?" I ask, accepting the strip of material as he places it gently across my eyes.

"Another sensory game," he agrees. "Not taste, this time. I think your tastes are well-established."

"Good," I say, relaxing a little. "Because blindfolds and food combined could create a potential choking hazard."

As he departs, I wonder what he could possibly mean. *Smell?* I take a few experimental sniffs once I hear his footfalls crossing the marble hall floor again, receding away back to that food-court of a kitchen. I don't smell anything in this room. Not even a joss stick, or deodoriser designed to mask the scent of a personal hygiene problem, or anti-social habit. Strange. *Sound?* I strain to hear anything other than the clink of glassware on a tray, and before I know it, the shambling footfalls are approaching again.

I lean into the embrace of the couch, trying to appear relaxed. It's only slightly spoiled by the fact that the back of the couch is a lot further away than I thought, so I fall through the loosely-heaped pillows in slow-motion, until I am nearly prone.

"I see you are getting comfortable, Sarah *Bellummm*."

He teases me with the sound of my own name. Maybe he knows that all I get called at work is 'Cheese-Bag' or at University, 'Bell-End'. I never thought that the ink printed on my birth certificate could sound so sexy.

I feel the couch dip beside me, as he sits down.

"We are going to play a game of touch," he says.

"Soccer?" I ask, puzzled. "Blindfolded?"

"No, the sensation of touch. With your permission I will draw some different objects across the surface of your skin, and you will guess what they are."

"Oh, like *Draw My Thing*?" I conclude. One of my favourite pursuits on the internet in the evenings, while not doing homework assignments, is to try and get Ace Bumgang to *Draw* his *Thing* and email it to me. "Do I get three clues as to what you're drawing?"

"If you relax, we shall start," he says at last. "And the game will explain itself as we go along."

"Sure," I shrug, and roll up my sleeve. "Nothing on the face. Or below the wrist, in case it doesn't wash off. People don't appreciate seeing knobs drawn on your hand when you're delivering their pizza…"

I break off with a gasp, as I feel something icy cold slide up the sensitive skin of my inner arm.

"What do you think this is?" he asks, as the tingling cold sensation slides slowly all the way down again, and back up.

"Er…" The cold has alerted parts of me I that didn't even know were peckish. I could use another bucket of chicken wings, never mind that cocktail, wherever it is. "Um, can I ask for a clue?"

"If you ask a question, it must be in the form of a question with a Yes/No answer."

Phew… I feel the icy cold sliding, torturously, all the way back down from my shoulder to my wrist. *So* different from playing online…

"Okay," I say at last, my mouth almost like sandpaper by now. Mostly in trepidation of what the answer to my question might be. "Is it to scale?"

CHAPTER FOUR:
BODY OF CONDIMENTS

I got to grips with the rules of the blindfold touch game eventually. It was the object that Crispin Dry was drawing on me with that I was supposed to guess, not the *Thing* he was drawing. That made it much easier, to my vast relief.

So obviously the first object was an ice cube. The second was also easy – I've handled enough human scalps in my time at University to recognise the tickle of tanned hide and hair. The third was harder – I hazarded an Ugli fruit, a cauliflower floret, a sock full of marbles, a stitched leather catcher's mitt, and even an artichoke, before giving up. I was kicking myself when Crispin told me it was a shrunken human head. I should have known that one.

The fourth object was another easy guess, but it was the noise that gave it away. I felt the dig of something sharp clustered against my belly, through my *Pizza Heaven* work fleece, and the soft feathery tickle against my bare arm. There was an unmistakable crooning sound, followed by an uncertain cluck.

"A live chicken," I announce, triumphantly. I hear Crispin's echoing undead chuckle.

"I see I will have to be more creative, Sarah *Bellummm*," he says, in his now-familiar zombie moan.

Still blindfolded, I hear him moving things around on the tray. I wonder if there's any danger of that drink appearing any time soon. Typical male. They invite you in for a coffee, and it turns out they have no coffee in the house after all, just a waxworks dungeon and a complete box-set of *Playboy Mansion*.

I jump out of my skin, as the next sensation I feel is a mechanical vibration against my hip. My sudden movement seems to startle Crispin also, because I hear something metallic clatter on the tray.

"What is the matter, Sarah?" he asks.

"It's okay, it's just my mobile phone," I say, feeling the rhythmic buzz a second time.

I squirm around to reach my pocket, and prop myself up on my elbow, pulling the blindfold up to see the number. *Caller ID* informs me that it's Cramps University Hospital. *Yes!*

"It's the hospital," I tell him, and he looks disappointed. "They've promised me an autopsy session if a suitable research donor is found… maybe there is a fresh one in that has the right paperwork."

"You must answer, by all means," he says, and replaces the forceps regretfully on the tray.

He picks up a hi-ball glass instead, containing an iced pink liquid garnished with mint and lime, and I hold my free hand out eagerly to accept it as I press Connect. Ooohh – Sloe Gin Sling! My favourite…

"Hello?" I say into the phone, and take a huge gulp of Gin Sling before the sting of alcohol on my tongue reminds me that I'm not allowed into the morgue under the influence. *Damn!* I hope I have breath mints on me.

"Sarah, it's me," says Miss Blah-blah-blah, my housemate.

"Hello – what are you doing calling me, *hombre*?" I ask. "I'm working, I hope you realise."

"Sarah, I'm in Cramps Hospital. My boyfriend didn't believe me when I said I had the termination today. He came round and we had a fight. We started to have make-up sex but then he said he was still angry with me, and bit my thumb off. They're going to try and reattach it. I'm in the Emergency Room now, will you come and sit with me? I'll make sure you get paid for the rest of your shift."

"Oh, you mean now?" I grumble. "I'm with a customer…"

"I will take you wherever you need to go, Sarah *Bellummmm*," says the perfect zombie gentleman beside me, deftly tidying the tray.

I nod, and swallow the rest of the Sloe Gin Sling. Phew. I could use a few more of those.

"I'd really appreciate it, Sarah…" Dumb-Ass whines in my ear, over the phone.

"Yeah, yeah, I'll see what I can do," I say, and hang up. "That girl gives retards a bad name. I need to get to the hospital. She's had another bedroom mishap with that delightful human butcher she calls a boyfriend."

"We must go immediately," Crispin nods, getting to his feet and offering his gray-skinned hand to help me up. "I will take you in the Cadillac."

I allow him to lead on, wondering hopefully if that means there will be more cocktails to look forward to on our return… At least now I don't need to worry about the breath mints.

We enter the hospital via the rear transport entrance on the lower ground floor, and make our way to the elevators that will take us up to the *Accident & Emergency* department at the front. Two porters and a nurse pass us, wheeling a cadaver wrapped in white sheets on a trolley, and I hear a low guttural sound from my delectable zombie companion. It hotwires my adrenal glands directly to my heart rate.

"Is it the smell?" I whisper, wondering what has caused his reaction.

"The rigor," he murmurs. The elevator doors open in front of us. "This way."

We head into the elevator, and the doors close, sealing us alone together in the bare metal cell. I press the button, and the lift grinds into life.

The atmosphere is suddenly electric.

"What is it?" I squeak, aware that his eyes are drilling holes into me.

"I cannot go out in public like this," he tells me.

No!

"You should have said," I complain, my heart now sinking. "Why did you offer to come? You could have stayed behind, out of sight…"

"No – not like that…" He flaps his hands a little awkwardly, reminding me of a forlorn *Edward Scissorhands*. "The hospital – that corpse – it is too much…"

What could he mean? I stare bewildered into his jet-black eyes, willing him to open up to me. He casts his eyes hopelessly down at himself.

"I have a Zomboner," he admits.

"What?" I look down at his fly, horrified, and hurriedly look away again. "Is that all? Er, I mean, not in that way, I mean to say – it's very impressive, in fact – but what I actually mean – why don't you just style it, dude?"

"It is my first," he says, wretchedly. "Since passing… I would hate for it to fall off…"

I close my eyes and heave a sigh. All that mental rehearsal (with frankfurters in coat pockets while thinking about Ace Bumgang) is going to come in handy now, I tell myself.

"I'm an expert in handling dead bodies, at any stage," I tell him, summoning up all of my confidence. "And I haven't lost an extremity yet. You will just have to trust me."

He looks imploringly and awkwardly at me.

"We can kiss," I suggest, in barely a whisper. "If it will make you feel better at the time…"

He turns slowly towards me. For some reason I wonder, at the back of my mind, if those breath mints would help me now…

CHAPTER FIVE:
PRETTY WARM ONE

I jolt awake, at the sensation of sliding helplessly down off the washable hospital-hospitality chair. Quickly catching myself, and prising my eyes open, I'd much rather be in a hospital-hospitalised bed right now, the way I feel at the moment.

Blimey. Did I actually kiss the zombified Crispin Dry in the elevator, while helping him with his little (okay, not so little) localised *rigor mortis* problem, or did I dream it?

I run my tongue over my teeth, thankful to find that there are no bits of zombie tongue left lodged in there. I remember that overwhelming mossy scent, of old black wool suit, and even older *Old Spice*. The sensation of falling into those two hypnotic pools of jet that his eyes had become…

My stomach feels strangely empty, and even my head feels weightless. I feel as though if I try to stand up and walk anywhere too soon, I'll be lurching uncontrollably all over the place.

Slowly, bits of my memory return. Oh yeah. I'm here to sit with my dear housemate, er… fuck… maybe I never even knew her name in the first place. How does she expect people to remember her anyway? She'll be a statistic sooner than a bride, with the ones she can pick. What was it today? *He bit her thumb off during sex!* I grin triumphantly, as my brain gets something right for once.

I look across towards where her gurney should be, but there's just a space in the bay. Odd.

Maybe she went to surgery already.

I think she was pleased to see me. Hard to tell with her head being the shape of a football at the moment. The only expression she could do being 'half-finished Halloween Pumpkin.'

"Don't you think it's time you dumped him?" I remember saying to her, when I was shown through. Crispin excused himself to find a vending machine that would meet his exacting requirements, leaving us to our girls' talk.

"Oh, *noooo*," Dufus-Features protested, waving her bandaged club-hand, in defence of the sadist currently fulfilling the job-spec of 'abusive boyfriend' in her life. "He really loves me. And I can handle him. You have no idea how bad he used to be. He's really making an effort to change. I'm his best therapy, he says."

"By which you mean, he uses you as his punch-bag?" I remarked. My stomach growled weirdly and horribly at the sight of all the blood-soaked gauze, and I had to sit down on the horrible *Health & Safety* hazard of a chair, more slippy and slidey than trying to ride an eel. I was feeling dizzy already. I wondered if I should have asked Crispin to sneak some more booze in with us. It looked like being a long night, on only one Sloe Gin Sling. "I hear his last dumb slut, Chelsea, now has a smile to match her name that he gave her. As a parting gift."

"Exactly. He's SO much better now, you have no idea," Brainwashed Prick said, her one bloodshot eye (that I could still just about see) all misty with delusional erotomania. Or maybe it was only the Chloramphenicol. "Remember, you have to kiss a lot of frogs, before one starts to turn into a prince."

"I really don't want to know about your Batrachiphilia as well," I replied. "Don't you ever watch *CSI?* Guys like him don't get better. They're serial offenders. They get worse. Soon as you're trapped in a false sense of security with them, you think everything's hunky-dory because he hasn't slammed your head in the washing-machine for a few days, and the next thing you know you're flying out of the woodchipper all over the garage ceiling."

"Oh, Sarah, you're so melodramatic," Miss Dunce's Cap of the Year told me.

"One in three," I warned her. "The statistics say one in three murders isn't a domestic. The two in three are the ones that don't get on the news. The open-and-shut cases. Phone call to the police, confession, arrest. Is that how you want to end up?"

"Now I think you're just being mean. Because if you're a woman too, really you're only jealous," Shithead snapped. "Don't deny it. Every girl I see is secretly eyeing him up. You could never handle a bad boy. You're going to end up a lonely old spinster, with a room full of eyeballs in jars. Whereas I've been designing my wedding dress, Googling honeymoon locations, and planning baby names."

"Really?" I asked, not feeling the slightest inclination to prove my gender to her current state of mind. Which seems to include the fantasy that every other woman around fancies a bit of assault and battery. "What did you name the one you had sucked out at the clinic this morning, because your Mr. Perfect was about to cut off your ears and nose and feed them to you for forgetting to take the Pill?"

Maybe I was a bit harsh on her. But seriously, the guy doesn't even deserve the honour of ending up pinned out as an actual anatomical diagram on the Body Farm. If something happens to him, I hope it comes with the label *Body Never Recovered*. Maybe I'll ask Ace Bumgang whether they have one of those things that crushes cars into a small cube at the breaker's yard. Then Miss Fucktard could get herself referred to a hostel or refuge, or for counselling (instead of the morgue) by the police or her doctor or whatever – to stop her hooking up with the next optimistic slimeball psycho who stalks her with the best intention of adding her to the notches on his shovel-handle. They must think all their Christmases have come at once when she stumbles half-deliberately into their laps, having spiked her own drink to make it that bit easier for them. I'd have to get another housemate, but the way things are going in Super-Twat's life, that eventuality doesn't look too far off anyway.

Hmm. Crispin Dry is taking a while. I can see a nurse and a receptionist at the far end of *Accident & Emergency*, but otherwise it's strangely quiet. What on Earth could there be to take up a zombie's time in a hospital?

I slide off the slippery chair and decide to have a stretch, and a wander around. I do feel a bit of vertigo as I stand. Yeah – one drink and then fall asleep, always a sign of a crap night. I lurch slightly as I aim for the nearest door into the corridor, and follow the *EXIT* signs, meaning to get a nip of fresh air.

The doors are still open, as the Emergency department is 24-hour here, what with the plethora of brain-dead hopeless romantics getting methodically dismembered by their choice of partners these days. So it's a relief to step outside into the front car-park, and feel the cool night air blow away the cobwebs between my own ears, taking my housemate's idiotic illusions with them.

The breeze also brings the sound of a distant piano from across the main road. Feeling in need of a musical ear-worm (to remove the remaining irritating echoes of Douchebag's recital of gross sexual perversions she chooses to list as her boyfriend's 'good points') I head over there, to get a better listen.

It's *Hookah's*, the Cypriot restaurant. The waiters are just starting to clear and re-dress tables for the next day, while one couple still sit at the bar, finishing their coffee.

And in the corner, through the window, I see the grand piano. My breath stops altogether as I see the pianist is none other than my new zombie acquaintance, Crispin Dry.

I push the door timidly, and bells tinkle to announce my entrance. He stops playing abruptly, and turns.

"No, it was good," I say, encouragingly. "I love Franz Ferdinand…"

A takeaway box is by his feet, and I see him nudge it under the piano, embarrassed. As I get closer, I think I see a restaurant logo I'm not familiar with… *Yuman Tisseus*, or something exotic like that.

"I came back earlier, but you were asleep, Sarah *Bellummm*," he says, reproachfully. "They took your friend to surgery…"

"I guessed as much," I nod. "Budge up. More music, Maestro, please."

He fondles the piano keys lovingly, as I park my still decidedly dizzy butt on the tapestry seat beside him.

"I remember… learning," he ponders aloud. "While I was alive. But it's so hard to tell now. Memories after death are not the same as living memories. They are mixed up with the total memory of Universal life. So they may not be my memories at all."

"I agree. I think you may be channelling *Blade Runner* right now, in fact," I remark.

"I was worried that you might not be happy, after the elevator thing earlier," he says sadly, not meeting my gaze.

"What?" I reply, amazed. "No! You give great elevator thing. No complaints there." I'm secretly relieved, as I'd been worrying about the same. My advantage in handling corpses regularly, seems to have made up for my lack of relationship experience in that department. I mentally notch another one up on my list of skills. I decide to push for yet one more, while the mood is right. "Do you think the waiters would mind if we make out on this piano?"

The strains of *Do Ya Wanna* hesitate slightly, as his prehensile gray fingers seem to lose track of the keys.

"I think perhaps it would be an idea if we close the lid first, Miss *Bellummm*," he nods, eventually. "No point tempting Fate…"

CHAPTER SIX:

SCAR WARS

I gaze helplessly into the dark stars of his eyes, as Crispin closes the piano-lid softly down over the keys. The final few bars of his piece are still fading away. Is he going to make the first move?

But before either of us can make that idea a reality, through the windows of the restaurant I see the lights of Cramps University Hospital suddenly flicker, and then go out.

"Oh no!" I cry. "A power-cut!"

Crispin turns to look. After a few seconds, it is evident that there is no emergency power to save the day. Even the street-lighting over the car-park starts to fizzle out, one by one.

"My housemate!" I gibber. "Whatsername… Cock-hazard… she's in surgery!"

"We must go back, Sarah *Bellummm*," Crispin groans sympathetically. "To ensure that all is well."

He grabs his take-out box from under the piano, and helps me to my feet. The waiters barely take notice, as we hurry out of *Hookah's* Restaurant.

We shamble as quickly as we can across the road, back into the hospital grounds. They are eerie and forbidding, without the phosphorescent lights.

The electronic doors are no longer functioning. But no matter – the glass in them has already been smashed – into a million pieces.

"What the f…?" I begin to say, thoughts of a siege appearing, uninvited. Crispin's hand on my arm stops me.

"Emergency shatter," he remarks – pointing to a device in the doorframe.

"What does it do?"

"It fires high-velocity metal ball-bearings into each panel of glass, from inside the double-glazed unit," he shrugs. "It is old technology now, but effective, in corporate building fire safety."

Aha. Clever. I seem to recall something like that having been patented, on *Tomorrow's World*…

We step through the empty frames, feet crunching on the shattered fragments. I take another piece of old technology – by Trevor Baylis – out of my pocket, kept attached to my keyring. Wind it up with its tiny handle for a few seconds to charge the battery, and switch it on. The bright LED torch beam illuminates the pale walls of the hospital corridor.

We head for the Emergency Room. Distant cries, and groans of distressed patients echo in the building. I wonder how many life-support systems have just been abruptly cut off.

More torchlight greets us, as we find the Reception desk, exactly where we left it.

"My housemate," I pant, my nerves making me breathless. "Er… you know… looks like she lost a fight with a bulldozer. Bad taste in men. Talks like she still reads too much *Brothers Grimm* for her age. Miss Fuck-Knows. Went to have her thumb reattached…"

"Oh, yes," the receptionist nods, her spectacles reflecting the torchlight. "The psychiatric biohazard case. Her bloods and swabs came back as positive for syphilis, gonnorrhea, chlamydia, T-parasites, ringworm, impetigo, herpes, HPV, and HIV – so she's been put in the Isolation Ward following her surgery."

"What?" I make a mental note to keep my toothbrush and toothpaste separate from hers in the bathroom, from now on. Preferably locked in a strongbox, somewhere else. Like Switzerland. "How on Earth could she have EVERYTHING?"

"Well, apparently, she never went to the GUM clinic, and always just took her boyfriend's word for it when he said he didn't have anything infectious, before having unprotected sex with him. Including the boyfriends who admitted to paying for sex, and to group sex in the past," the receptionist shrugs, with an expression of 'what a stupid twat' that I fully understand. "You can go and check up on her – it's at the far end of the hospital, lower ground floor, next to the morgue. You'll have to use the stairs."

Of course. Corpses aren't at risk of catching anything. Makes sense to put the biohazard cases down there.

"Will you be all right on your own here, ladies?" Crispin asks, his voice concerned. The receptionist, and uniformed HCA on duty, look at each other and smirk.

"Sure," says the receptionist. "Any trouble comes looking for us, they'll be met with the almighty force of this armed and fully operational nursing station."

The assistant twangs the fingertips of her latex gloves meaningfully. *Ouch.*

I think they'll be just fine.

We avoid the *WET FLOOR* warning signs and head through the swing doors, down the stairwell. High above us, I can hear shuffling and groaning, about three floors up.

"Maybe a sleepwalker?" I suggest in a whisper.

"One can only hope," Crispin admits, hugging his take-out box close to his chest.

We emerge next to the elevators – I blush in the darkness at the memory, glad that no-one can see – and follow the markers directing us past the morgue.

Crispin stops abruptly in front of me, so that I nearly bump straight into him. His head turns, angles questingly, and he sniffs the air.

"Not now, Crispy!" I hiss, startling myself at my own disapproving tone. As if I'm talking to a giant, upright, shaggy dog. "Stop thinking with your stomach!"

"It is not my stomach we need to worry about," he remarks, still in his beautiful, resonating monotone. "They are on the move…"

"Who are on the move?" I ask, my heart trying to join my tongue, at the back of my mouth.

He raises the box briefly.

"Perhaps they objected to my carry-out," he sighs.

I shine the torch beam on the box's logo.

Human Tissues!

Fuck! I am SO stupid!

Even my housemate Shithead can read! At least, read juvenile stuff, like *Beauty and the Beast…*

"You didn't go to research the vending machines here?" I explode. "You went stealing actual parts of other people? What the fuck for? Are you *Dr Frankenstein* or something, as well as a zombie?"

He hangs his head, a little more than usual.

"They will only look for replacements," he says. "The nearest."

He glances towards the darkness at the end of the corridor, after the morgue.

To the Isolation Ward.

"So now we're going to have biohazard zombies carrying infectious diseases too?" I ask. "Well, that's just lovely, knowing that everyone's going to have to insist on prophylactics as well, before having their brains sucked out."

He nods, sheepishly.

"You are going to tell me what you planned to do, with all those parts you've stolen," I remind him. "But first, we're going to check up on Miss Sperm-Bank Deposit Box down there, and see if there's anything left of her to pay the rent that she owes me!"

But – as we turn towards the Isolation Ward, the sudden squeal of gurney wheels reaches our ears. Crispin Dry reacts, leaping and pinning me to the wall – just as an occupied trolley hurtles past, narrowly missing us. Several draped white shapes seem to be pushing it at once.

"Sarah – help me…!" a faint, weak voice cries, *Doppler*-ing away out of the transport entrance, at the other end.

"That's her!" I shout, my adrenaline rendering me immune to his current proximity. "They're kidnapping her!"

"To the Cadillac!" Crispin says, releasing me – and we lurch in pursuit.

Oh, no…

The car park is a zombie convention. We watch helplessly as my housemate's gurney is loaded into an abandoned ambulance. The engine starts.

"We'll never make it to the car," I tell him.

A zombie corpse flies past us at head-height, landing upside-down in a box topiary sculpture, and a local taxi brakes abruptly at the kerb. Its windscreen-wipers activate, trying to move the entrail smear out of the driver's direct eye-line.

We exchange a look, and amble over.

"Follow that ambulance!" I order, as we squeeze into the back, the *Human Tissues* box between us on the seat. "Don't let him out of your sight!"

"Yes, Ma'am," the driver replies, and switches on his *In Service* tracker. He sounds oddly calm. "Is it a relative?"

"My housemate," I say, choking up a little, at the thought of having to invent a name to go on her headstone, at the end of the day. Or maybe I'll just find an excuse to rifle through her wallet at some point, and check her I.D.

"These patient transfers are always stressful," he says, soothingly. "I'll try and get us all there in one piece."

"Quickly, would be preferable," I gulp.

"Yes, Ma'am," the driver chuckles, enjoying my little melodrama. My zombie companion squeezes my hand reassuringly.

"Stay on his tail, Luke," Crispin orders.

"Luke? How do you know his name?" I ask.

Crispin points to the Nigerian Work Permit in the corner of the courtesy window, between the driver and ourselves.

Oh.

GAYLORD LUKAN. WORKING LEGALLY SINCE 1971.

Our taxi rockets sickeningly after the hijacked ambulance, weaving in and out of the garbage-collection-night rubbish, piled up at intervals along the road.

"Go around the next crescent – see if you can cut them off," Crispin adds, his monotone never changing. "Luke – trust me…"

CHAPTER SEVEN: PHANTOM OF THE OPERATING THEATRE

Our driver takes Crispin's advice, scattering street-garbage as we cut to the right. Faced with a deserted residential crescent ahead, and flooring it. With any luck we'll beat the ambulance-jackers to the next junction, and head them off.

I wonder how my housemate is holding up in there, with her reattached thumb, and record-breaking collection of boyfriend-imparted abuse injuries and STDs. Being kidnapped by spare-parts-hungry zombies and rattling around in a stolen ambulance is probably an improvement, for her.

Knowing her as well as I do, she'll have *Stockholm Syndrome* by the time we catch up with them. Hmmm. Maybe they'll give her a new Zombie name. That would help things along, at any rate. I'll have something to put on her tombstone. Something to identify her, before the engraved words *'Feel free to wipe your feet on this Doormat'*.

I must have known her name at some point…

We hurtle out of the junction, just missing the rear of the passing ambulance – by a gnat's twat.

"Dammit!" I shout, frustrated.

"Which hospital are they transferring your friend to?" Mr. Lukan – the taxi-driver – asks us.

"They will require somewhere with surgical or dissection facilities," Crispin Dry muses, and I feel his cold zombie fingers squeeze my own more tightly.

I'm glad I'm sitting down, because my hamstrings are suddenly akin to soggy spaghetti. I've never heard the word 'dissection' sound so attractive. Considering that to me, it's already right up there with 'Forensics' and 'Pathology'.

"The University campus?" the driver suggests. "It's the Masquerade Summer Ball tonight – all the buildings will be open for showcase presentations…"

"Yesss," Crispin hisses, in his hypnotic monotone, causing my buttocks to clench sympathetically to my jellied hamstrings. The ambulance, rocking along the road in front of us, abruptly takes a turning indicated by a Cramps University road-sign. "Go with your feelings, Luke…"

Sure enough, the ambulance heads straight for the Science buildings. It is allowed directly through the barriers, by the night security team.

"They must have been alerted to the power cut at the main hospital already," I say. "What about us?"

"You just stay quiet," says Luke. "Let me worry about the guards."

Before I can worry about what that might entail, we pull up at the barrier, and Luke rolls his window down.

"Where are you driving this – thing?" the night security guard demands, eyeing the zombie-entrail-smeared windshield, and shreds of garbage clinging to the bodywork.

"Patient transfer from Cramps University Hospital," says Luke, briskly. "We're with them."

"I wasn't notified," the guard responds, deadpan, and his one glance at the two of us huddled in the back seems to seal our fate. "And no partygoers under the influence allowed in the Science buildings. You'll have to go back across the street to the public car park for the Masked Summer Ball, folks."

"My mistake," says Luke smoothly, putting the taxi into reverse. "Thanks for your help."

"No!" I cry, as we turn in the road. "My housemate – she's here!"

"We won't help her by charging in on our own, tearing the place up," Crispin reasons – although it sounds like perfect zombie retribution to me. "We'll be better off mingling with the crowd, and waiting for reinforcements."

"What? I've never heard of an escape plan like that before!" I shout. I rack my brains. Or have I? Was it Steven Seagal? Oh no, wait – I think that was the takeover scene in *Under Siege*… they all hung out pretending to be part of the crew, and then some more flew in by helicopter, and then…

"It's cool, man," Luke interrupts my procrastinating thoughts. "You two hang out here at the party, and I'll find a way to distract the guards. Give me ten minutes, then you can stroll right through."

"Ten minutes? She'll be hamburger by then!" I rant.

"But you forget, Sarah *Bellummm*," Crispin says, soothingly. "I have all the necessary spare parts."

And he pats the lid of the *Human Tissues* container, still on the seat between us.

I just manage to stop myself from yelling at him, that if he hadn't stolen them in the first place, we wouldn't even be in this predicament…

Luke drops us in the car-park of the main campus, circles around, gives us a brief salute, and heads off on his mysterious mission, pulling up the brown hood of his *Christian Audigier* skull-logo jacket.

Students and faculty staff are converging on the Conference Hall, in a dazzling array of costumes and masks. Fireworks in the night sky scatter rainbow light, reflecting off all the glitz and glitter.

"We're not in costume!" I whisper, in panic. "They'll think we're gatecrashers!"

Crispin turns and looks at me, appraisingly.

"I see a perfectly attractive young woman, dressed for the occasion as a pizza-delivery girl," he says, quite calmly. I look down at my *Pizza Heaven* work fleece, wondering if he still recalls what I said earlier about having nothing on underneath. It's certainly starting to feel a bit itchy, in a couple of specific places. "And I have come as a zombie Crispin Dry, the famous vending machine entrepreneur. I do not see anything about either of us to arouse suspicion. Just try to avoid stealing too many magnums of Champagne."

I flush scarlet. My thinly-disguised alcoholism is obviously doing me no favours. But he's right. I've thought of pretty much little else but that next Sloe Gin Sling awaiting me, when we get back to his place at some point.

"As if!" I scoff instead though, trying to feign hurt feelings. Idly, I wonder how big the wine cellar might be, under that huge mansion of his.

Crispin takes my hand with his free one, the other carrying the *Human Tissues* transport box (now relegated to the role of fancy-dress prop) and leads me up the grand steps, into the Conference Hall.

The décor is breathtaking. No expense has been spared on lighting and effects. I take in the gold drapery and red carpet in the giant lobby, set off with full-size potted palms, and ten-metre plasma screen displays. I gaze around, open-mouthed, momentarily forgetting my dear housemate, Fuckwit, currently being demolished by zombie surgeons in the Science block across the road…

"Sarah?"

The familiar voice brings me back to planet Earth with a clang. I lower my eyes from the gaudy fabric-swirly in the ceiling, to meet the startled gaze of my own reflection, in a fancy-dress welding mask. The wearer pushes it up, sharply – but I've already identified the owner of those to-die-for pectorals, in the deliberately charred workman's coveralls…

"Ace!" I squeal, terrified.

Ace Bumgang!

Here???!! NO!

My dream encounter shatters into a million pieces. For not only am I here in my work clothes, on a mission to save my housemate-slash-best friend, Name-That-Smell – I'm here with Someone Else. Whose hand I'm still holding…

Wrong, wrong, wrong!!!

This isn't the way it was meant to happen…!!

Ace's fabulously dark brown eyes look me up and down.

"Tight budget on the costume front, huh?" he remarks.

"Could say the same for you, petrol-head," I shoot back, trying to disguise the tremor in my voice.

My knees are knocking, and trying to switch places in time with the music.

"Or did you spend the budget on your date for the night?" he teases, nodding towards my zombie companion, Crispin. "That's a pretty good look-alike. Does he do Strip-a-Grams, as well as escorting?"

"I don't know," I say, tersely, ignoring the zombie's low growl. "I'll have to ask him later, when I'm negotiating my after-party extras."

"No need to boast," Ace grins. Oh Em Gee. Looks as good as his should come with CPR instructions, for faint-hearted females. "I brought a date too, you know…"

My failing heart sinks as he turns slightly to look behind him, and another familiar face atop an Adonis body swivels to gaze at me.

NO…

"Hello, Sarah," says the human butcher and bulldozer, his eyes half-hidden, *American Psycho*-style, behind an *Avon* anti-stress refrigerator mask.

It's him. Miss Fucktard's assault and rechargeable battery-powered boyfriend.

CHAPTER EIGHT:
TOMB BATHER

"How nice to see you," the psychopath continues, dripping sarcasm like hydrochloric acid. Which I bet he already keeps stockpiled, in his own bathroom. "Are you still stalking guys, pretending to deliver pizzas for a living?"

"Carvery," I greet him coldly. "And are you still pretending to be the love of my housemate's life?"

"You look a little bit worse for wear, Sarah," Ace Bumgang says, tilting his nearly-full pint glass towards me. "How many have you had so far?"

"Not enough to have my beer goggles on yet," I answer haughtily.

Even though, confronted by Ace Bumgang and the equally delicious-looking Carvery Slaughter – my forgettably doomed housemate's current psycho-with-benefits – I feel as though both of my ovaries are racing to hatch the first available egg.

Damn my traitorous hormones! Faced with the two most pheromone-loaded specimens of live masculinity at the University's Masquerade Summer Ball, my eligible dream zombie Crispin Dry, lurking silently at my side, seems no more than a cardboard cut-out in comparison.

"You could have fooled me," Carvery cuts in slyly, indicating my companion, on cue.

I wish Crispin would do something to defend my honour, fly into zombie rage action… but he's too genteel, too eccentric. *Edward Scissorhands* meets Michael Keaton's *Batman* incarnation, without the art of a director like Tim Burton to hold it together. Those 'fifty shades of gay' that I suspected earlier are looming again – in contrast to the overwhelming testosterone now evident in the room.

"Seriously," Ace continues, to my own surprise, with a hint of concern in his voice. "You're actually drooling, Sarah. It's kind of creepy. And your right eye is all wandering and squinty. I'm sure you were limping as you walked in. To be fair, I thought it looked like you'd had a stroke. I remember what it was like when my old dear had one. You should go to the hospital, get checked out – if it's honestly not the alcohol this time."

"No, I'm fine, really." I shudder, ignoring my ongoing light-headedness, and the numbness now obvious in my right hip. The hospital is the last place I want to be right now…

"Or maybe your pay-as-you-go date is just more lively in the sack than he looks?" Carvery suggests. "I've seen more than a few girls hobbling around and dribbling, after a good session in my company."

"And the rest are under your floorboards, I imagine?" I reply, trying to match him, snark for snark.

He shakes his head.

"That's the benefit of having my own paving business," he smiles nastily. "They're all under everyone else's property."

My mouth drops open, like an unsecured loft hatch. The nerve! He could get sued for use of sub-standard foundation materials… everyone knows that human remains don't retain their structural integrity, even when buried in concrete…

My voice refuses to co-operate, as some announcement comes over the Conference Hall tannoy, about an imminent World Poverty lecture by Bono from *U2*, in the main amphitheatre. Partygoers in fancy-dress costume and masks start to gravitate towards the theatre doors.

"Ten minutes have passed, Sarah *Bellummm*." Finally! Crispin interrupts, coming to my rescue – like a Speaking Clock in shining armour.

"I'm afraid I will have to leave you, gentlemen," I say, striking out for the use of courtesy as a weapon. But the way I'm currently slurring, I note it sounds more as though I was declaring my undying love to them both, in drunken Bavaria-dialect German.

At least I have the satisfaction of seeing some disappointment mingled with their repulsion. Although disappointment at what, I'm not sure – depending on what they just heard me say.

"Not staying for a drink, then?" Ace observes, as I link my arm with Crispin once more.

I hesitate.

"Perhaps you're right," I say, rebelliously.

I take Ace Bumgang's pint of Snakebite & Black out of his hand, and down it almost as fast as stand-up comic Billy Stephens. Christ. *How does he do that?* It feels as though it's going to whoosh straight out of my ears…

I act as if to hand the empty glass back, letting it slip through my fingers before Ace can grasp it, intending it to smash dramatically on the floor. But I'd forgotten the red carpet laid out especially for the Masked Summer Ball. The pint glass merely bounces, and delivers me a crack on the shin.

Ow…

"Are you sure you're okay?" Ace queries, sounding even more doubtful.

"Of course," I retort. "And you shouldn't be drinking anyway. I'm sure they can find a new *Stig* to replace you, on *Top Gear.*"

"Well, would you drive that fast sober?" Ace calls after me, as I turn away, head in the air – now finding out what it's like to limp with both feet.

I wish I had a clever parting shot to deliver over my shoulder… Jeremy Clarkson would have thought of one… instead I allow Crispin Dry to guide me back down the many steps of the Conference Hall, to the magnificently-decorated, open-air quad outside, still ringing with the sound of the fireworks display. Where I promptly join several Freshers in their celebrations, by throwing up the Snakebite & Black all over my own feet.

I don't know how Luke did it, but there is no sign of the night security guard at the gates of the Science block. We hurry through, and I point out the abandoned ambulance by the Anatomy & Physiology Department.

"They must have taken her up to Pathology," I say. The thought of my housemate being subjected to zombie torture isn't as terrifying as it had been, just fifteen minutes earlier. Perhaps seeing her current real live psychopath, who attempts to put her through the meat-grinder on a regular basis, has put the idea into subjective context.

She'd probably compare a zombie rampage to having a Swedish Massage, measured up against one of her booty-calls from him.

At least here the electricity is still functioning, unlike at the hospital. We rush past signs directing us to the laboratory, although they're kind of negated by the trail of blood, and infrequent bits of abandoned zombie.

At last, we find the dissection bay, and burst in.

"Oh, no!" I cry. Both my eyes and mouth are competing with each other, over who wants to be covered up first. "We're too late…!"

Crispin lurches over to the gurney and puts the *Human Tissues* box onto the steel counter, suddenly all businesslike and professional. My housemate, Zero-for-Brains (pretty accurate description, right now) is lying there with all her incisions exposed, and bloodied instruments scattered around, some of them still half-inside her like a game of *Operation*.

The zombies themselves have apparently long gone…

"It is just a matter of replacing the components in the right order," says Crispin, the epitome of calm confidence. "And not crossing the streams."

"Not crossing the what?" I ask, bewildered. So much gore – it can't be possible…

"The bloodstreams, Sarah *Bellummm*," says Crispin. "You have to ensure that you don't confuse the veins and the arteries."

"I knew that," I snap, irritated, wondering why I'm suddenly craving giant marshmallows. "You insert, and I'll stitch up."

We work feverishly. Or maybe I just work feverishly. Crispin works methodically, as if servicing and replenishing any old vending machine. In due course, we have a complete and watertight cadaver on the gurney between us. A cadaver that used to be my housemate. My best friend. Aaargh! I'll have to think of a pet-name for her. This is ridiculous.

"Well?" I say. "How do we wake her up?"

Crispin stares at me, with his inky black eyes.

"Oh," he says, crestfallen. "You wanted her alive?"

"Of course ALIVE!" I yell. "What do we have to do? Invoke a special god? Say some magic words? Take her to a forbidden temple? Sacrifice an illegal immigrant? Tell me how we bring her back to life, dammit!"

"I can do that," interrupts a sardonic voice, and the evil outline of Carvery Slaughter appears in the doorway. "Wondered where you had to be in such a hurry."

He saunters in, the laboratory spotlights glistening off his hard, unyielding musculature. Oh boy. Would I sperm-jack him… Posthumously, of course. After I'd bumped him off, and figured out how to dispose of the body.

"So," he continues, looking impassively down at the shape of his hitherto punch-bag. At least most of the swelling has gone down, since being shanghaied and pillaged by zombies. She's barely recognisable from how I usually see her, except for being black-and-blue still. "What trouble did Wank-Tits get herself into this time?"

Phew. At least it's not just me, who never remembers her real name.

"She became a live organ-donor," I say, scowling at Crispin, who has the sense to look suitably pensive. "We've fixed her up, but I don't know how to re-animate her. I only perform on dead people."

"Yeah, I had heard that about you," Carvery sighs, and peels up one of Miss Numb Nut's eyelids. "Yeah, it's not too late. I have to carry one of these. Girls conk out on me all the time. It's a tough life, being such a stud."

He walks around to the foot of the gurney, and takes out a Taser. I'm just quick enough to leap away from the metal flat-bed, as he stabs the contacts into the sole of her foot.

Her whole body arches off the trolley. After a few seconds, the psychopath disconnects the current, and she slams back down again, scattering the remaining instruments.

After what seems like a millennium, she suddenly takes a long, shuddering breath.

"She's alive!" I cry, relief flooding through me, like the effect of mild bladder weakness on the underpants.

"Yay," says Carvery Slaughter, deadpan. He twirls the Taser in his hand, and puts it away again.

Crispin takes the professional attitude. He prods her shoulder.

"Can you open your eyes, Miss…?" He looks at me for a prompt. Carvery and I exchange a look, and both shrug.

"My eyes are open," she mumbles. Phew. At least she can still talk. That tongue was very fiddly to insert.

"I think you have your eyes wide shut at the moment, Miss," Crispin confirms. "Can you tell me your name?"

We all lean in, hopefully.

"Er…" *Fuck.* Maybe that was too much to hope for. "My boyfriend… I think he knows. Something beginning with N… Nim… Nymph… I think it might be Nymphette…"

"Nympho," Carvery corrects her. "But only if you're good, then I call you Nympho."

She bolts upright on the trolley, tears streaming down her face, her bloodstained arms outstretched.

"Carver!" she cries. "I knew you'd come to my res… res… resuscitation…"

"Yeah, yeah," he grumbles, and helps her off the trolley. "Come on, Punk. I'll take you home. Unless you want to come back to the party with me first. You make a good Autopsy costume impression, in your current state…"

"Punk…?" I query, wondering if it's something I'd recognise as printed on our tenancy agreement. "Is that an abbreviation?"

"Short for Pumpkin, I guess," Carvery tells me. "Because usually she looks like one, if you get my drift."

With an unpleasantly meaningful wink, which puts thoughts into my head of both sex and shovels, he leads her out. I hear her apologising to him for being so useless as usual, as their footsteps fade away down the passage.

"We should go too, Sarah *Bellummm*," Crispin says, interrupting my thoughts of sperm-jacking and justice.

Dumbly, I nod. Maybe there'll be another Gin Sling in it for me tonight, after all.

Luke, the taxi-driver, meets us outside.

"Back to the hospital," Crispin orders. "My Cadillac is there."

"Sure thing," Luke nods.

"What happened with the security guards?" I ask. We go over a speed-bump leaving the Science block, and I hear a thud and a knocking sound coming from the trunk. "Is your car all right? It's making a bit of a funny noise back here…"

"I just pretended to need a little roadside assistance," Luke chuckles. "They were very co-operative. I didn't even need to use the force."

The zombies had moved on from the hospital car-park, so we were able to retrieve the Caddy easily, and drive back to Crispin Dry's mansion, in silence. My *Pizza Heaven* scooter is still where I left it, on the palatial driveway.

He turns to me, and sighs. It has been a long night.

"Can I offer you a nightcap, Sarah *Bellummm*?" Crispin says quietly.

"Thought you'd never ask!" I leap promptly out of the passenger door. I'm parched.

"You can use the bathroom and shower, if you wish," he says, as we enter the huge abode. I look down at my housemate's blood all over my work uniform. Good point. Some of this might be infectious. "I will make the drinks."

There is a large gold-and-marble *en-suite* bathroom in an apartment on the first floor. I scrub my skin all over with a loofah until I am bright red, then turn the water to cold and wait until I am pale blue.

Hopefully nothing serious could survive that. I wonder if I should get myself checked for radiation at the Physics department as well tomorrow, just in case. You never know what else Twat-Face might be carrying, a little voice says in my head.

I emerge from the shower in a white towel. Strange. My uniform isn't where I left it. I head out of the bathroom, into the bedroom of the luxurious suite of rooms.

"I put your uniform in the incinerator," Crispin greets me apologetically. Thank goodness, he is standing there with a tray of drinks. I grab the nearest glass and knock the contents back in one, before reaching for the second. "Only your underwear was free of bloodstains. I can lend you some clean ones belonging to my household staff, along with some other clothes…"

"No thanks," I say, plonking the second empty hi-ball glass back on the tray. "I don't think I want to wear any of your other tarts' trophy knickers."

I turn away, summoning all of my pride, and hear him gasp as I drop the towel on the floor dismissively, in a blatant impersonation of Angelina Jolie in *Lara Croft: Tomb Raider.* Even though she didn't win an Oscar for that one, it's still one of her most-Googled scenes. Hah! He's not immune to my charms either, then…

I give him a triumphant glance over my shoulder, before striding over to the bed, and reaching for my own underwear.

The effect is completely ruined, when his pet cockerel runs flapping across the duvet. Meaning I have to spend the next hour and forty-five minutes chasing it around the suite, while it panics, the gusset of my knickers wrapped around its leg.

CHAPTER NINE: DANGEROUS LACERATIONS

Finally dressed once more – having retrieved my underwear from the escaped pet cockerel, and been loaned a set of Paisley pyjamas by the ever-gentlemanly zombie Crispin Dry – I assert my decision to head home.

His mansion feels so large, so empty – so imposing… I feel the need for my home comforts – like cold pizza, and even colder, slippery, undergraduate sleeping bag.

"But you have had too much to drink to ride your scooter, Sarah *Bellummm*," Crispin moans.

"I'll push it if I have to," I reply, rolling up the over-long pyjama sleeves. "No offence, but I've seen quite enough undead action for one night."

…Not to mention Ace Bumgang action, the thought creeps up on me.

I shiver involuntarily under the thin silk.

I wonder if he's still at the University Masquerade Summer Ball?

If I push the scooter halfway, until I'm near-sober, and ride the other half, could I make it back there in time to catch the end, and see if he leaves with anyone…?

Although of course, that would also risk the possibility of running into my stupid housemate, Miss Ladygargle, and her GBH-qualified boyfriend, the lethally charismatic Carvery Slaughter. And maybe the likelihood of more zombies, along the way…

I realise that Crispin is looking yearningly at his nightwear, on my comparatively alive frame.

"There does not have to be undead action, as you say," he says, a little sensitively.

"Really?" I remark. "Then why offer me just pyjamas to wear? And I don't have a headache as an excuse either, if that's what you're hiding those painkillers in your hand for."

I just about spot the pharmacy box, as Crispin swiftly moves it behind his back.

"I would feel much better if you stayed, Sarah *Bellummm…*" he says, hopefully.

"I think we've done plenty enough for one night," I tell him. "We've played blind-tasting food games, and *Draw My Thing With Something* on my own skin, been to hospital, nearly made out in an elevator – and on a grand piano – had a close encounter of the reckless kind with an immigrant taxi-driver, found my housemate kidnapped by zombie surgeons, performed a reverse autopsy, and bumped into probably the last two fit guys alive on Earth – one of whom is most definitely carrying a jaw-dropping collection of STDs and a chainsaw in the trunk of his car. If I have any more excitement tonight, I'll probably explode with life-affirming overindulgence."

"It was life-affirming indulgence that I was thinking of, certainly," Crispin muses, taking a step closer.

I take one back in turn, pointing at what he's attempting to conceal in his other hand.

"And you can put that camera down for a start," I warn him. "I don't know what cruel intentions you had on your mind by trying to sneak up on me with that… but there's enough porn on *Facebuddy* already, without adding zombie-necrophilia to the mix."

"I was worried you might not come back again, if I let you leave so early." Crispin sighs, and puts the camera and the pharmacy box down on the bed, showing me his empty hands, in supplication. "I just wanted a little souvenir of your visit."

"I hope by that, you mean a photo of me wearing your jammies," I say warily, thinking of the empty *Human Tissues* transport box, left abandoned back at the University. "And not any actual physical parts of me. You still haven't explained what you were doing, stealing those organs from the hospital…"

He reaches out and takes hold of my hands, in his cold gray ones.

"No, no, Miss *Bellummm*," he says. "I was thinking of your needs… and of mine…"

"You're thinking of Gin Sling cocktails… and human brain vending machines?" I hazard, confused by his change of tack.

He shakes his head, in that endearing, wonky fashion.

"No, Sarah," he groans. "Not that…"

I hear the hiss and rattle of his lungs, as he inches that little bit closer. The tension in the bedroom cranks up another notch.

"You can depend on me to keep your confidentiality," he continues. "If you are honest with me."

"About what?" I ask, wondering what I might want kept secret. And if I've been inappropriately disclosing information about myself, all my life so far.

"Would I be right in believing that you are… a virgin, Sarah *Bellummm*?"

Shocked, I laugh.

This reaction has got me into trouble many a time. In fact, without the nervous laughter reflex, I might not even still be a… whatever he's implying.

And there'd be a few less grouchy pizza-delivery boys around, carrying inferiority complexes.

"A what?" I chuckle, trying to use the laugh to brush the accurate assumption off. "Don't be silly! Those guys we bumped into earlier? I've had them both. At once, in fact. Lots of times. Before the violent one caught all sorts of lurgy off his girlfriend…"

Crispin leans in a little closer still, causing me to stop, and gulp my giggles back down. I hear him sniff slowly, at my throat.

"Hmmm," he muses. "I think you may be wrong, Sarah *Bellummm*. And I am correct, in this instance."

"What about it?" I shrug. "Nothing wrong with waiting for Mister Right."

"Supposing…" he begins thoughtfully. "Supposing your Mister Right, as you call him… had a certain condition, that could be cured, by your own – condition?"

Oh, no. This sounds familiar. It's been addressed in our Anthropology lectures, for a start.

"Have you been taking sexual health advice from West African witch-doctors?" I ask, disapprovingly.

He looks surprised, then down at himself resignedly, with a broad sweeping gesture of both arms.

"You think?" he says, and it's the first time I've detected sarcasm in his tone. "You're talking to a damned zombie, may I remind you?"

"You can't cure diseases by sleeping with virgins!" I shout at him. "That's the kind of stupid dumb-ass Medieval thinking that starts pandemics! Do you see people in the third world bouncing around on TV, the picture of health? Do you see academics heading over there to find out why they live so long, instead of going to do their research in Okinawa? No! It's because it's not the cure! For anything!"

"I don't have a disease, Sarah," he says, quietly. "I'm dead."

"In which case, how about I call up my retard housemate's boyfriend Mister Slaughter, and ask if he'll give YOU the Taser treatment as well?" I snap. A mental image of Carvery Slaughter with his shirt off arrives uninvited into my mind, which makes me wonder immediately where I could get a hole dug, six feet deep, at short notice. "Because I can assure you, a massive electric shock is more likely to affect your current situation, than my considerably debatable cherry is!"

"You don't understand," he moans. "Where do you think all those rumours started? Because it IS the cure for a zombie…"

God, I've heard some bad pick-up lines in my time, but this one takes the biscuit. It takes the whole barrel…

"No, it's not a cure for zombies. It's a cure for princes, who have been turned into frogs and hideous beasts, by the *Brothers Grimm* and *Hans Christian Anderson*," I correct him. "And those were all fantasy too. Probably to persuade pretty girls to date ugly dudes in the first place."

"So think of me, as such a cursed prince," Crispin murmurs. His hand brushes my cheek lightly, rather like the tickle of a falling autumnal leaf.

"I was thinking more along the lines of 'depraved' than cursed," I scoff.

"As a zombie, I assure you that depravity is something I can only aspire to, in my current situation." He echoes my own words again, in typical NLP brainwashing-style.

"You're going about this entirely the wrong way, I hope you realise," I tell him. I move to one side, aiming to get a clear run to the doorway. "What self-respecting woman wants an emasculated hero with a sob-story? Most women would just see the sob-story, and worry that if he was stupid enough to get himself into such a mess in the first place, he isn't likely to be able to help out if she's ever in a crisis herself. It's like guys on dating sites, who don't drive. They might as well put on their profiles *'Kicked out by Mother aged forty-seven, needs regular clean laundry and taxi service'*."

Crispin heaves a sigh, and looks at the floor. He knows he's losing the argument.

What an idiot.

If he'd only kept the drinks coming, and said a few choice things like *"You're very pretty"* and *"You smell nice"* – this could all be going so differently right now…

I catch myself before I start to feel any sorrow for the poor dead guy, and sidle a little more towards the door.

I remind myself that Ace Bumgang is probably still at the Summer Ball, getting himself drunk.

He and Carvery Slaughter probably have an entertaining wager on, regarding the outcome of their night. Which I could be making interesting use of, instead of hanging around this place.

"You are right, Sarah *Bellummm*," Crispin agrees, at last. "I see I will have to prove myself in many ways, before becoming worthy of your… charms. I will lend you a coat."

I nod, dignity regained. Before I can turn away, he takes my hand again, gently.

"Before you leave…" he says, and I glance back at him. Something seems to flare in his hypnotically black eyes. "Just one kiss."

"Sure," I concede, warily, and offer him my cheek.

He strokes it with a fingertip.

"Not here," he whispers. "But… here…"

And his fingertip continues to trail, downwards…

CHAPTER TEN:
BADMAN

"Er…" I interrupt, before he gets any further. "I don't think my organs are ready for that sort of intimate contact yet. I don't carry a donor card, for one thing… and I'm sure I read somewhere that a tongue is not a recommended substitute for an organ temperature probe."

Crispin straightens again in front of me, while I do up the one pyjama button that his wandering hands had managed to dislodge.

"I see you will need a little more convincing," he says. "Allow me to show you something of interest – about my house."

"A tour?" I ask, puzzled. What has a tour of his mansion got to do with him poking around at me like an unqualified masseur?

"*Yesss*," he hisses, and his zombie fingers curl around my own. "This way, Sarah *Bellummm*."

I allow him to lead me out of the opulent suite, leaving the disgruntled cockerel behind, and we go back down the grand marble staircase to the ground floor. Behind the stairs, next to the library, two doors are set into the oak panelling.

He takes out a set of keys, selecting one for the nearest door.

"This better be either the *Bat-Cave*, or a REALLY impressive wine cellar," I warn him. "And not some kinky dungeon full of whips and chains – where you keep all your other delivery-boys and girls, because you're too tight to pay for the pizza…"

He hesitates, the door half-open.

"Wrong door," he says smoothly, closing it again, with barely a cough of embarrassment. "That was the broom closet."

"Closet, being the operative word," I mutter.

He checks his keys again, and unlocks the second door. A light illuminates the stone steps, heading down.

"After you?" he offers.

"Wine cellar?" I repeat, meaningfully.

"Better," he tells me.

"You first, I think," I suggest, wary. "Then if I trip on the way down, at least I'll have a soft landing."

"Semi-soft, I think you'll find," he smirks, and takes the lead.

We go down the winding subterranean route, around and around, until I've almost completely lost my sense of direction. Eventually, we emerge onto an underground landing. He stops at the railings, and I join him, peering into the gloom.

Lights start to flicker on automatically, the nearest first.

"Oh," I say, surprised. "It's your garage…"

So he wasn't lying about the Lamborghini Diablo… or the others… there's a top-of-the-range Hummer, but the rest are all performance cars. Why did I assume all high-earning billionaire CEOs only drove touring car models, like Quattro and Ford, as if they're imitating plain-clothes police speed traps? I must have read it in some badly-researched Cinderella-based novel… Now I think about it, even my housemate Thingummyjig's boyfriend, the psychopath Carvery Slaughter, has the latest Ferrari as his regular commuter run-around – and he just does paving and concreting for a living…

But the lights continue to flicker on, far into the distance…

"How big is this place?" I gasp.

"How big can you handle, Sarah *Bellummm*?" he chuckles, with that incredible sandpaper-rasping-a-headstone sound. "As big as it needs to be. More that just a garage, I think you'll find. Follow me."

We go down the remaining stairs, and walk between the many vehicles, glinting under the spotlights. It's like the garage in *Lara Croft: Tomb Raider* – only a hundred times larger.

This cellar is definitely bigger than the footprint of his mansion. It must cover half of the grounds as well…

"It's like an ancient military bunker," I remark. "Have you got your own subway down here?"

"If I did, I wouldn't have to order in pizza," he stops and says, a little coldly.

"No, I meant subway – as in, underground railway," I explain.

"Oh." He looks a little flustered, then shrugs, and continues trudging ahead. "Perhaps."

The cars on show eventually end, but the underground bunker doesn't. Suits of strange armour and battle-dress follow, along with displays of old weapons.

"You have a Gatling gun!" I exclaim, pointing at the wheeled military apparatus. "Goodness. All I've ever handled is a potato-pistol."

"You like to shoot, Sarah?" he asks me.

"Well, the most I shot was a spider," I admit. "I tried hunting rabbits, but with a spud-gun, they just thought I was feeding them. Especially when I ran out of potato, and resorted to using carrots as ammunition. They still come out and follow me around, whenever I'm in my parents' field."

After the armoury, the cavern suddenly takes on more of a science laboratory feel. Computers and technical equipment are set up everywhere.

Crispin takes down a transparent PVC lab coat from a hook, and hands it to me to put on over the Paisley pyjamas, before taking one himself. As he shrugs it on over his fine black wool suit, I imagine Carvery Slaughter wears one too, when he's disposing of his ex-girlfriends' bodies that he's failed to resuscitate, for the last time. *Hmmm*. Still got to come up with a suitable plan to deal with him…

"As you can see, my interests go beyond the world of vending machines," Crispin Dry tells me. "And the advice of West African witch-doctors, as you so insightfully noted… I too had a problem with the old wives' tales of 'sex with virgins' being the cure for zombification. But unlike you, not from the point of view that such stories are medically implausible. My issue with those notions, was the shortage in supply."

"That's quite offensive and chauvinistic," I observe, wondering where this exposition is heading. "But go on."

"I decided to find out for myself if there could be better medical cures for zombies," he explains. "Perhaps with transfusions – or transplants. You wondered why I was collecting organs at the hospital… well – this is why…"

We go through a double-seal air-locked quarantine door, and into a vast – store-room.

Refrigerated cabinets line the walls. Most containing sealed medical crates. But some – containing entire people…

"You were experimenting on zombies?" I whisper, shocked.

"*Yesss*," he hisses, resignedly. "And that was when I myself became infected. Only two weeks ago… I had almost revived a subject – but his first instinct was to bite. I woke up dead, here on this very floor – and my patient had long gone."

"They're not your patients!" I say, horrified. "You're not a doctor – or a surgeon – you're a vending machine designer! Okay, a multi-billionaire vending machine magnate… but what on Earth were you doing interfering with zombies in the first place?!"

He looks at me sadly, but before he can respond, a red light flashes over our heads, and a low siren sounds, intermittently.

"What is that?" I cry out.

"My security system," he says, and beckons urgently. "But we are relatively safe – down here. We must check the CCTV immediately. Come with me – if you want to live…"

CHAPTER ELEVEN: BLADE RUSTER

We leave the quarantine area, and Crispin heads directly for one of the computer workstations, where a number of virtual monitors display live feed from various locations on his property. A 3-D walk-through image of the house and underground bunker on a projection interface shows where each image is taken from. It looks as though there are no blind spots at all.

"How many cameras do you have in this place?" I ask, in awe.

It's like being in the control room of an *Oceana* nightclub. Only tidier, without the detritus of Starbuck's cups and McDonald's wrappers, or stripper's thongs pinned to the notice-board.

I notice that the one solitary thing in the zombie businessman's waste basket, is a single screwed-up ball of paper.

"Over three thousand, Sarah *Bellummm*," Crispin tells me, tapping quickly on his interactive screen. "As well as six thousand hidden microphones, motion and pressure sensors, temperature gauges, light-sensitive triggers, laser-interrupter switches, automatic deadbolts, emergency power back-up, automated instant police and fire control call-out, intercom, sound-system, and mood-lighting throughout. There is also a chicken-feeding station and egg-laying coop in every room, should one of my pets accidentally be shut in."

"You have thought of everything," I nod. I glance at the screen, where I notice the cockerel chasing one of his harem along an unknown corridor. "Do you keep any other pets, besides chickens?" I gesture back at the quarantine bay. "…And dormant zombies…?"

"I used to have homing pigeons on the estate," he reminisces distantly. "But one day, they failed to come back. I was informed that they had landed at the nuclear power-plant, and were all shot by the Hazardous Waste Regulation snipers. I was too sad to replace them."

"Ah," I say, realisation dawning. "So that's why you keep the birds indoors now…"

"Oh, no." He shakes his head, in that attractively arrhythmic, wonky fashion. "The chickens have special… scientific significance. They are allowed anywhere they please."

"Scientific significance?" I repeat. "What significance does a chicken have to a Zom… oh. Of course. West African witch-doctors. I suppose you're trying to distil the essence of *Voodoo*, to help with your research for a cure?"

He shuffles awkwardly, in his seat at the console.

"Here," he says, avoiding the subject, pointing to a segment of the 3-D image in the main house. One of the rooms in the interactive graphic is glowing red. "We have the location of our breach."

He taps on the virtual model, and the camera views pop up, on a giant ether screen in front of us. The room of interest is in complete darkness.

"Initiate emergency lighting," he orders.

The model room glows green, but nothing happens on the monitor.

"He has covered the cameras," Crispin murmurs. "Go to heat sensor view…"

A white line of light scans back and forth over the 3-D model, but again – nothing on the screen.

"All the equipment is functioning," Crispin murmurs. "Which means only one thing…"

"What?"

"That room," he remarks, tapping on the screen again. "It also has significance."

I wonder what he could mean.

"Is it a shrine?" I ask, nervously.

It hadn't occurred to me that the enigmatic entrepreneur Crispin Dry might be religious.

Or what that might entail.

Never mind the wonderful world of *Voodoo*, it's the other sorts of religion that scare me. The religions that come with men in long dresses, fancy headgear, and spending a lot of time on one's knees for no useful purpose… not even a bit of *'wax-on, wax-off'* while you're down there…

"A shrine would indeed be one way of describing it," he murmurs, stiffly. "Show footage from two weeks ago today, *06:00* hours."

The screen clears, and reveals what to my relief looks like a normal, ordinary – if somewhat large and elegant bedroom. Within a few seconds, something dark moves over the screen, rendering it black again.

"Run sequence again," says Crispin. "Zoom in on reflection, upper left."

The image reappears. The footage expands, increasing the size of a large vanity-unit mirror, on the far side of the room.

A shape moves across it swiftly, causing me to jump and gasp.

"Stop!" Crispin snaps, and I nearly swallow my poor tongue, before realising he's still talking to the computer. "Run again, quarter-speed…"

The image of the mirror refreshes. Expecting it this time, I wait for the anticipated shape – and sure enough – the side-view of another zombie steps into frame, reflected in the glass.

No wonder there was no heat signature detected…

"So…" Crispin whispers, as the frame freezes. "It is him…"

"Who?" I ask. There is a long pause.

"The zombie I revived," he sighs, staring at the image. "He must have remained hidden in this house for the last two weeks – possibly recuperating and convalescing – until the motion sensors detected his movements in the room just now."

"How would he know about the cameras?" I demand. "Do zombies have incredible intuition?"

Crispin shakes his head, and moves the footage forward, one frame at a time. The zombie's head turns, with slow precision, to look directly into camera – via its reflection in the mirror.

And it *grins*.

"No," Crispin says, grimly. "He knows about the cameras, because they are in his bedroom."

"His bedroom?" My brain can't keep up.

Is he sub-letting to zombies as well?

"It has always been his bedroom," Crispin nods. "That is my brother… Homer N. Dry."

I have to grip the edge of the console. My knees have handed in their notice, both at the same time.

Crispin continues to stare impassively, at the grinning image of his brother's face on the giant screen.

He was experimenting on his own family… *his own flesh and blood…*

"Print me a hard copy," he says at last, and the appropriate equipment hums into life. "Right there."

CHAPTER TWELVE:
E.T. ~ HOMER LONE

"Keep this," my zombie host says, handing me the CCTV image, from the printer. "Remember that face. He must come to no harm."

"Of course," I agree, studying the hard copy, before pocketing it. "He's your brother…"

"Not only that," Crispin interrupts. "He is the first zombie to respond – at least partly – to treatment. He is thinking and plotting… see how he concealed himself in the mansion? We must find him – and ascertain how much of his faculties have recovered."

"Sure," I remark. I'm relieved. Perhaps now something else seems to be effective, that rumour about virgins as medical therapy will finally go away… it's not as if we're living in the Middle Ages. Although by the behaviour of some of the men I know, you'd think it still was.

He gets to his feet, starting to shamble back through the vast underground cavern.

"Come, Sarah *Bellummm*," he hails me, over his shoulder.

"Yes," I respond, but not before bending to retrieve the other piece of paper, balled-up in the waste basket. Curiosity having got the better of me, I unravel it, flattening out the creases, and turn it over.

Oh.

TAKE OUT TRASH.

Well, that was an insight that could have been left undisturbed. I toss the piece of paper into the basket again, and head after him.

"We must be cautious, Sarah," he warns me, as we go back up the stone steps, out of the deep echoing basement, and into the slightly less enormous house. "My brother Homer has always been nervous in company. He may go to great lengths, to maintain his privacy."

"I can tell, by the way he covered up the cameras in his room," I say, thoughtfully. "Will he lock himself in there indefinitely, do you think?"

"It is not his ability to covert himself away that is of concern." Crispin stops and turns to face me in the grand entrance hall, his hands on my shoulders. Those fathomless black eyes seem to burrow into my skull once more. "It is what he may do in order to protect his concealment."

I get a familiar chill in my veins, at his words.

"Is your brother violent?" I dare to ask.

Thoughts of my housemate, Miss No-Knickers, and her ABH-on-legs boyfriend, Carvery Slaughter, flit across my mind. I wonder if she's managed to keep all of her stitches intact in the last few hours, in his company?

"He is – creative," Crispin Dry admits. "Stay close. If I give you an order, or tell you to move, act immediately. Without question."

Hmmm. I can see where this might be open to abuse…

"So long as you're not just grabbing me to try and cop a feel," I say, pointedly shifting slightly away from his hands, which seem to be heading for the direction of buttons and buttonholes again. "I know all about those guys who get reported on TV, for telling girls they're in imaginary mortal danger – so they can be persuaded to hide in the trunk of an unlicensed car, and be driven to cheap motels in the middle of nowhere."

"Be vigilant," my zombie says in warning, and turns away, to lead me upstairs.

"Exactly my meaning," I mutter, but hang close behind, anyway.

You never know. In my housemate Wossname's case, quite literally. She falls for that macho bullshit game every time…

As we scale the next flight, up to the second floor, the lights start to flicker in the entrance-hall chandeliers, at our eye-line from the gallery. Although aiming for steely determination in our climb, I still jump.

"He will not be successful in disabling the lighting," Crispin assures me. "It is all supplied with back-up reserves…"

Then he hesitates, and a faint clicking noise reaches our ears – gradually getting closer…

"Against the wall, Sarah *Bellummm*!" he hisses. "Do not step on the carpet!"

"What is this, nursery games now?" I ask, incredulous.

"You could say that," he nods.

To my alarm, he looks terrified. I press myself likewise, against the flock wallpaper.

The clicking becomes louder. I look down at my feet.

Dozens of glass marbles suddenly roll past, in a steady stream. They carry on with their own momentum, and start bouncing down the ostentatious staircase, smacking and cracking loudly where they strike the actual marble, either side of the carpet-runner.

"We will proceed with caution," he says at last, as the last few Dobbers and a Thumbelina Milky trickle by. "Be careful to step only where I step…"

There is a sudden twang, and he is flat on his face, prostrate on the rug.

"…Except there," he amends, as I help him up. "Hah! Tripwires… a spell in cold storage has evidently done nothing to improve his tactics…"

At which point we both have to duck abruptly, as a remote-control Spitfire zooms down the corridor towards us. I feel my hair flatten in the downdraft, as it whines overhead.

"His aircraft are occasionally armed," Crispin announces, as dumbstruck, I watch the Spitfire do a circuit of the biggest chandelier, and hightail it back, for a second assault. "Now, I suggest, we should run…!"

He doesn't need to repeat the idea. I hurtle after him, down the long corridor, lined with doors. The cockerel bursts out of a cat-flap in one of them as we pass, and joins us in our escape, flapping its panic-stricken wings, squawking and scattering loosened feathers.

"He has been attacking my chickens!" Crispin rages. The Spitfire's high-pitched whine seems to get higher, as it approaches from behind. "One of these doors will be safe – the rest will be booby-trapped…"

"In what way?" I pant, limping to keep up. I stumble, to the sound of a strangled cluck. "I think I tripped over your cock…"

Crispin yanks open a door at random, and leaps aside as a large ironing-board pops out, with a clang. Seizing it, he wrenches it loose, and hefts it in both hands.

"Duck, Sarah *Bellummm*," he orders.

"No, definitely a cock. I thought you only kept chickens?" I say, confused.

He swings the ironing board with a grunt, and I do indeed duck. There is the dull smack of ironing-board cover against RC Spitfire, and the whine stops dead. Bits of *Airfix* kit land in my hair, and slide down the collar of my borrowed pyjamas.

"I know where he will be hiding," Crispin says, tossing the ironing board aside, and offering his gray hand to help me up. "It is the same, since we were children. Quickly – this way…"

He drags me to the turning at the end of the corridor, and we hurry into another glamorous, expansive suite of rooms.

They are decadently decorated in pink and white silk, with a rose motif, and the scent of lavender hangs in the air.

"This isn't your bedroom, is it?" I gulp, thinking about those 'fifty shades of gay' again.

"No," he says, to my relief. He lets go of my hand, and almost strides into the walk-in closet. "It is – or rather WAS – our mother's room."

He stops by the slatted white wooden doors of the built-in wardrobes, running the length of the wall. Seems to pause, to sniff out the immediate area – and flings the doors of the closet wide.

"Homer…" croaks a strange voice. "Home… home…"

A single, gray finger points out from the depths of the closet, reaching up to Crispin's face in an unearthly appeal – for help, perhaps?

"Yes, you are home, Homer," Crispin sighs. "And you are in Mother's closet, dressing up in her clothes, as you have done for the past forty years."

Shocked, I cannot resist a peek past him, into the wardrobe.

There indeed, is the poor emaciated gray zombie – the billionaire Crispin Dry's brother, Homer N. Dry – resplendent in a pink dress, white crochet shawl, a blonde wig, and a rather fetching summer hat.

CHAPTER THIRTEEN: THE GROANIES

"Mrs Frittata is going to be very annoyed that you've taken her Sunday wig as well," Crispin scolds his brother, while the transvestite zombie cowers in the closet, attempting to hide his face in shame, behind a bejewelled clutch-purse.

"Who's Mrs Frittata?" I ask, wondering if they refer to their mother so formally in this house.

"The housekeeper," Crispin groans. "She and her two sons, the Frittatas, form the main hub of my staff here. Jerry Frittata is my driver, while Ben Frittata is the gardener. There was a third Frittata brother, who did odd jobs as handyman on the estate – but he fell down a well in the sunken garden some years ago, and has never been quite the same since."

"Is he in care?"

"No, still down the well. He likes to try and entice female visitors to climb down and kiss him, impersonating a cursed frog. Honestly. Like you say, as if women persist in believing that you have to kiss a lot of frogs before a prince appears, these days."

"Quite," I agree stiffly, thinking of my brainwashed housemate, Insert-Name-Here – who was virtually born with a glass slipper between her legs – and had been discussing the very same myth with me (in her usual deluded fashion) earlier this evening. Before having her boyfriend-amputated thumb reattached.

The reminiscing is interrupted by the *'DONNNGGG'* of the impressive doorbell, reverberating through the mansion.

"Strange…" hisses my host for the night so far. "Who would call at this hour? I only ordered the one pizza…"

"Er – which you still haven't paid for!" I point out, hurrying after him, as he leaves his mother's boudoir.

With a squeak of abandonment, I hear his brother Homer disentangling himself from coat-hangers and designer footwear on the floor of the closet, and shuffling quickly to keep up – jabbering *'Home... home...'* as he scuttles after us along the corridor, to the second-floor landing.

I risk a glance behind. His progress is hindered, Pippa-Middleton-style, by the pink fishtail wiggle dress.

Well – he doesn't look too dangerous... At least, not to humans, I think, as he burps a chicken feather.

We descend the two flights of stairs to the ground floor again. Reaching the doors first, Crispin answers it himself – just as he did when I first arrived, with that pizza.

I wonder how I'm meant to ride the *Pizza Heaven* scooter back, now I'm only wearing his loaned pyjamas.

"Luke," Crispin greets our *Legally-entitled-to-work-since-1971* Nigerian taxi-driver, from the hospital. "What brings you here?"

"The young lady left her mobile phone on the seat of my cab," Luke announces, holding it out to me. "I was passing by on another passenger route, thought I would see if you folk were home."

"How kind!" I say, although I'd barely missed it. The only calls I get are from my housemate Twatface, when she has some new drama with Carvery Slaughter...

I pocket the phone, and look up again, just in time to see another movement in the doorway behind the taxi-driver...

Fuck.

Speak of the Devil...

"Hey, this doesn't look like *The Astoria*," Miss Novelty-Tricks slurs, staggering in behind Luke.

"No – this is way better," says another familiar voice, and – oh, no – Ace Bumgang lopes in as well. "Where's the bar in this place?"

Last and definitely least, Mister Slaughterhouse himself walks in, and spots me immediately.

"Don't know about the bar, but I've found the toilet," he says, meaningfully. "Hello again, Sarah."

"I'm sorry." Luke apologises to Crispin, trying to herd the three of them back outside. "Drunk customers. Always leaping out of the cab if you so much as stop at a traffic light. Let's get you nice people home..."

"Home!" shrieks Homer N. Dry, tripping over his skirts, at the bottom of the stairs.

"Oh, do we have to?" complains Whatsername, pointing at the fallen zombie. "It's fancy dress here as well, look…"

"Please," Crispin steps aside, gesturing into the grand hall. "Make yourselves *all* at home. It is the least I can do to thank you, for returning my friend's property. You will find a drinks bar in the Three a.m. Lounge – straight ahead to your left."

"Very kind of you," Luke grins, and strolls jauntily after the others.

I grab Crispin Dry's sleeve.

"None of them are virgins," I warn him, under my breath. "If you were thinking of including them in your little *experiments* in the basement!"

"Not at all," he smiles. "Why would I need them, when I still have you, Sarah *Bellummm*?"

And he limps after them. Homer manages to get to his feet in turn, and hobbles along in pursuit.

A moment later, the cockerel appears in the kitchen doorway, gives me a sidelong glance, and flutters in the same direction.

"Et tu, Brute?" I sigh. "Looks like everyone wants to go and play with the big boys tonight…"

I hesitate, wondering whether to just go back to my scooter, taking my chances with the unknown zombies out there, and my boss at *Pizza Heaven* instead. It would beat the company of two very definite zombies, and one certified girlfriend-battering psychopath, right here in this house. Although the thought of Ace Bumgang getting himself approachably drunk in the same vicinity is hard to resist…

But with escape resolutely in mind, as I'm aiming for the kitchen to retrieve my crash helmet and keys, I'm alerted by the creak of floorboards overhead – and the unmistakeable sound of someone moving around upstairs…

"Someone else is in the house!" I cry, bursting into the Three a.m. Lounge. Miss Tosspot has somehow ended up wearing Homer's hat, and Crispin is mixing up cocktails. He looks at me and holds out a Sloe Gin Sling in his gray-skinned hand. My legs betray me immediately, carrying me in a bee-line to the bar.

"Didn't you hear me? There's someone in the room above the kitchen! I heard them moving around!"

"Ah," Crispin muses, as I drain the cocktail in one gulp. "Our antics have awoken the housekeeper, Mrs Frittata. Homer, I hope you have prepared your apologies regarding her Sunday wig?"

"Homer!" cries Homer, clamping the wig to his ears, with both hands.

"What will she do?" Ace queries.

"Well, as she usually does when roused by strange noises in the early hours, she will wake up her two sons, Ben and Jerry, arm themselves with shotguns, and scour the property looking for interlopers." Crispin leans idly on the bar, twirling a paper cocktail umbrella between his fingers. "Oh. I haven't introduced any of you to the Frittatas, have I? How remiss of me."

"We should go," I announce, putting the hi-ball glass back down regretfully, and wishing there was a full one right next to it.

"No need," says Crispin, smoothly. "The mansion is full of secret passageways. It is rather fun to play at avoiding the persistently dogged Mrs Frittata and her sons for a few hours."

He pulls a lever under the bar, and a wall of bookshelves abruptly disappears. I'm disappointed to see that Carvery Slaughter, who was leaning nonchalantly against it, doesn't follow through, but merely straightens up with the slightest acknowledgement of one eyebrow.

Grrrr… that butcher is going to pay in blood one day… and maybe sperm, given the opportunity.

"Shall we?" Crispin suggests. "And quickly? The Frittatas are always bad-tempered before breakfast."

The others shrug and follow. I take out my *Trevor Baylis* wind-up torch again, and duck into the narrow passageway behind them. I hear the shelves grind back into place, after I've gone less than ten feet into the walls of the great mansion.

"There are some minor hazards *en route* in these passages, designed to prevent misuse," Crispin's voice intones, from the front. "Just be careful to only follow my lead. Now – here we have pit of spikes. The ladies – yes, that includes you, Homer – will need assistance to step across…"

"This is scary," I hear Miss Fuck-Nose whining, somewhere in front of me. "I can't see a thing down here!"

"NOW you're complaining of being scared?" Carvery mutters, in disbelief – much closer than I like to think.

Bringing up the rear, I approach cautiously, and shine my torch downwards. My toes are at the edge of a pit so deep and dark, even the torchlight fails to illuminate the bottom.

"When you're ready, Sarah," says a grim voice.

I look up into the evil eyes of Carvery Slaughter, feet braced across the abyss, holding out his hand to help me bridge the gap. Oh boy. I know where I'd like those spikes to end up…

I put my torch in my pocket, and allow him to take my shaking hand. But my feet panic, both wanting to go first – and my heels skid off the edge of the precipice.

I'm left dangling by one wrist, held at arm's length by the monster Carvery Slaughter.

"Thinking of dropping me?" I challenge, numb with terror.

His amber eyes bore into my brain, faintly disgusted.

"You wish," he replies. "Pervert."

"I know what you're like!" I hiss at him.

"No you don't," he says. And with barely a flick of his elbow, deposits me on the other side.

What? He didn't try *anything*??

"You're the kind of guy who'd break into my room, and wank on my diary!" I hiss again, and cover my mouth, horrified. Did I say that out loud?

"Only if it was full of stuff about cars and firearms," he shrugs, easing himself over the gap, and falling into step again. "But I've read it already, when you've been at work. It's all about dead guys at the Body Farm, and your fantasy notion about Ace Bumgang being *The Stig*. And if I wanted to, I could just wank on him when he crashes out at my place, so your diary is kind of a poor substitute. You don't even talk about your tits or touching yourself in it."

Outraged, I can't even speak, let alone think of a response.

"Up ahead," Crispin's impeccable monotone breaks the fuming silence, ringing in my ears. "There is a giant pendulum. But it may be quite rusty now – and is a little unpredictable…"

Behind me, I hear a distant clatter, and the grumbling of three apparently male voices.

"Aha, Mrs Frittata and Sons have joined us," Crispin continues. Odd. I thought the third son lived in the well? But Crispin seems to sense our communal doubt. "…Hers is the bass voice with the hacking cough, that you can hear. It might be an idea for the seven of us to split up at some point."

"Hmmm…" I hear Carvery's voice, right by my ear again. "That *would* make things more interesting…"

CHAPTER FOURTEEN:
RADIALS OF THE LOST ARM

We catch up with the others, where the zombie businessman Crispin Dry is waiting at the edge of an even larger pit.

"As you can all see, demonstrated by my brother Homer," he says. "And I use the word 'brother' in the loosest of terms – the pendulum, installed over four hundred years ago by a previous owner of the estate, has a mind of its own. There may also be a family of giant monitor lizards still living in the pit underneath, but no-one visiting the site from the Animal Cruelty Department has reported back on their welfare for quite some time."

The rush of air above the pit is interceded by Homer N. Dry, petrified, clinging to the shaft above the inverted crescent blade, as it whooshes past us. Remarkably, his stolen blonde wig and pink dress are still intact – although the white crochet shawl, fluttering in the draft, now looks a little tattered, and worse for wear.

"Ouuuuch..." groans Homer, his yellow zombie eyes enormous in his ravaged gray face, passing again on the return swing.

"There is a lever to stop the blade," Crispin informs us. "But it is on the far side. One of us has to make it over there in order to operate it. Homer, unfortunately, has only made it halfway."

"Easy enough," Ace remarks.

"Yeah," Carvery agrees, cocking his head, as if sizing up the distance. "Even easier to throw one of the girls across."

"I'm too pissed to throw anything straight," Ace tells him, and exaggerates a crossed squint. "Check out my eyes, buddy."

"You look fine to me," says Carvery. "Let's throw Sarah."

I only resent being volunteered, because I was thinking of giving Carvery Slaughter a meaty shove over the edge first, in the name of domestic justice.

"Hasn't this property always been in your family, then?" I ask Crispin, to change the subject, and avoid showing myself up. "I assumed it was."

"Sadly no, Sarah *Bellummm*," Crispin sighs. "It was bought by my grandfather, a designer of weapons of modern warfare of the time, and then passed on to my father, also in munitions. But before he too died, my father said that neither of his sons had earned the honour to take their place at his right hand – my brother being the flamboyant wastrel you see before you now – and I had not only forgone the family business tradition, but I had also failed to marry and produce the next in line. On his death, it was stipulated that we still had to earn that right hand status, within the decade – or the property will be turned over to the National Trust."

"But you're rich – you're the owner of Dry Goods Inc," I say. "Surely you've earned it by now?"

"Financially, it is possible," Crispin nods, gloomily. "But finding my father's right hand has proved less simple. It was a clockwork hand, made by the finest Swiss watchmakers, passed down in the family for many generations. It holds the key to our family's true knowledge and wealth. The selfish bastard hid it, somewhere on the estate. And so far, neither my satellite land surveys, nor Homer's rummaging in Mother's closets, has been able to unearth it."

"He didn't leave a map or anything?" I demand, and he shakes his head, unevenly.

"No clues?" Luke chips in, enthralled. "That's what I came here for, from Nigeria. To seek a fortune."

"I hate to butt into the history lesson, but there still seems to be a trio of gun-toting household staff on our tail," Carvery points out. He's right. The grumbling and coughing of the Frittata family seems to be getting closer. I can hear them scolding one another, over the earlier pit of spikes. "Is this conversation getting us anywhere, or am I going to have to take drastic action?"

"Action with extreme prejudice, I suppose?" I suggest, and let out a squeak of fear, as he grabs the back of my collar.

"Remind me – what do you weigh?" he asks, and dangles me again experimentally, by the scruff of the pyjamas. "Thought so – you two fellas. Grab her legs."

"What?!" I yell, as Luke and Ace each get hold of an ankle, and suspend me, between them and Carvery Slaughter, like a human skipping-rope.

"If you survive, it'll be something exciting to write in your diary, won't it?" says Carvery. "On three… no, two… fuck it. Now!"

The three of them swing me back, and then violently into the air over the pit. I feel myself spin on release, seeing a brief flash of blackness below, and the terrifying face of Homer N. Dry swinging towards me on the pendulum above – and I continue to rotate in midair.

Is this what it's like to fly?

Until after what seems like an age, I crash onto a gritty stone surface, on the far side, still rolling over and over, my forearms instinctively shielding my face.

"Home…!" cries Homer weakly, hurtling by, in my wake. It sounds as though he is deteriorating…

"The lever, Sarah *Bellummm*!" Crispin calls out to me, authoritatively. "Push it back into the wall in front of you!"

The noise of the Frittatas in the distance takes a new turn. Now, they seem to be *chanting*. I can't understand what they're saying, but the atmosphere is suddenly ominous. It's almost monastic in tone, putting images of *Voodoo* priests and strange blood-letting rituals into my head.

"What's that noise?" Ace Bumgang wants to know. "Sounds like those Tibetan throat-singers, on *Youtube*."

"Mrs Frittata and her sons are a little superstitious," says Crispin, vaguely. "But in a jolly way – translated, it's all just a bit of *Hi-ho, hi-ho, off to work we go*, kind of thing… Concentrate, Miss *Bellummm*!"

I get to my hands and knees in agony, and crawl forwards. True enough, a large lever sticks up out of the floor, at about thirty degrees to the wall, where a recess in the stonework shows its intended position.

I push on it hard, but nothing happens.

"It's stuck!" I shout back.

"The compression switch at the top!" he tells me. "You have to squeeze it, as it goes in!"

"No comment…" Ace coughs.

Luke's hands go to cover his groin automatically, as if out of nervous habit.

I glance angrily at Carvery for *his* reaction, but there is no expression in his face or body language at all – just the usual endemic evil, as he watches, arms folded.

Not even another rude remark?? It's as if he knows what I believe about his personality, and deliberately acts the opposite, to thwart me, making me doubt my own sanity…

I get to my feet to provide more leverage of my own, and find the smaller lever at the top of the big one. It clicks shut as I close all of my fingers around the handgrip, and with my weight behind it, the larger lever starts to shift upright, back into the wall.

A horrible metallic grinding and screeching sound almost deafens us, and I'm sure half of the screech is poor Homer, attached as he is to the source of the cacophony. Four centuries' worth of dust pours down onto him as well, as cogs previously hidden high in the ceiling trundle down, locking the pendulum into a final, static position.

As the lever I'm pushing also locks into the wall, the blade of the pendulum revolves ninety degrees, its upper edge now spanning the width of the pit – giving the others a means to step across.

"Now we must split up," Crispin orders. "There are four tunnels ahead, seven of us, and only three of them…"

"Ooh – is that Pimm's o'clock?" says my nameless housemate, making me feel thirsty again already. *Twat* – is *she* still here? It's like being trapped in a confined space with a case of bad intestinal gas…

"…They cannot cover all tunnels. I suggest two groups, a three and a four. That way, at least one of them, possibly two, will be on a wild goose chase down an empty tunnel, while we will still outnumber and outwit the remainder."

"Good plan," Luke approves. "Does your… brother know his way around?"

"After his antics earlier tonight, definitely," Crispin nods. "I suggest you and he, partner up with the gentleman and his young lady…" Here he indicates Carvery Slaughter and my housemate Whatserface… "While I will lead Sarah and – Ace, is that right?"

Ace nods, and my heart does the *bossanova*.

"Homer, I suggest we aim for the usual Friday-night meeting-point," says Crispin. "Sarah *Bellummm* – Ace – follow me."

I gulp. Finally – alone with Ace Bumgang! And he's drunk! And there's also a zombie with us, but at least it's not Carvery playing gooseberry…

I try to forget that the zombie in question happens to be the eminently eligible Crispin Dry, who has been so nice to me thus far – and focus all of my thoughts on the possible outcomes I've stored up in my fantasies for this eventuality…

Unfortunately, it's on these occasions that my social skills fail me. Which I don't understand. I can talk endlessly to Mr Wheelie-Bin, at the Body Farm. Obviously it's a bit one-sided, but I would have assumed that the actual practise of talking to a dead guy would be the same as talking to a live one. Only it turns out, I'm apparently wrong…

"So, er – good time at the Summer Ball?" I venture, bobbing along to keep up, with Ace's longer stride.

"Not bad," he says.

And that's it. End of conversation.

My brain works overtime trying to think of the next thing to say, until I'm hearing so much gobbledygook between my own ears, that I wish *I* was a million miles away from my own company as well. Even the creepy chanting of the Frittatas, somewhere behind us, seems to make more sense.

"I have often wondered," Crispin's deep monotone muses, a little way ahead. "Whether my father hid his special clockwork hand in one of these tunnels."

"Are there any more traps down here?" Ace asks.

Why does he sound more articulate when he's talking to someone else? It's not fair…

"There are a few," I hear Crispin say, just as there is an odd sensation of no floor, where I put my foot down in front of me. "But not as big as the last two…"

His voice seems to recede rapidly into the air above, while I begin to realise that I'm falling right into one of those aforementioned *traps*… which contrary to discussion, seems to be exactly my size…

CHAPTER FIFTEEN: GOBBLINGS OF THE LARYNX

I continue to slide unstoppably downwards, like a fat kid on a greasy Helter-Skelter. I even have time to wonder what I might encounter at the bottom. Given the choice of a pit of spikes, a lair of giant monitor lizards, a nest of zombies, or Carvery Slaughter taking a serial-killing detour – I seriously doubt that a *Trevor Baylis* wind-up torch and a set of borrowed silk Paisley pyjamas are going to offer me much in the way of multi-purpose protection.

I dig in my toes, and the heels of my hands into the walls on my descent, attempting to slow down, and ignoring the friction burning that this rewards me with. But there's no purchase, no handholds – all I succeed in doing is loosening bits of rubble, which rattle down around me, making my journey bumpier, and even more ungainly and uncomfortable.

Abruptly, the chute suddenly ends, and I drop into thin air. But before I can fully draw a breath to scream, it's knocked right out of me as I land flat on my back, on a bed of straw. A sickening crack in the posterior of my skull, and warm sticky sensation, sends terror through my veins – as all of my blood supply attempts to escape the point of impact.

Wait a minute… *straw???*

After a second, I put my hand tentatively up to the back of my head. There is no pain. I touch something oozing, slimy… it comes away in my fingers… I almost choke in revulsion. *What have I done to myself…?!*

And then I do scream, when a live chicken lands flapping on my chest, with an irate clucking and gobbling.

Fuck me – it's only the hen-house…

"Aargh…" I gasp, when she has scolded me thoroughly, and moved on in disgust. I push slowly up into a sitting position, tweezing bits of yolk and eggshell out of my hair. "Sorry, chickies…"

I risk a look around the underground cavern, recognising what I think is called 'deep-litter' provision, for keeping hens happy indoors. There is more than enough straw than was required to break my fall, and here and there a hen sitting, giving me a disapproving eye. The occasional clutch of unguarded eggs features in the shadows.

It's as I skim my gaze over these, that I spot a slightly different movement on the straw – a long, narrow, quadruped shape glides silently across, from patch of darkness to patch of darkness. An elongated jaw opens lazily… and an entire mother hen and six eggs vanishes.

Monitor lizard!!

My brain screams until it is blue, but my own larynx has completely closed, in dry-mouthed horror. My arms and legs fight to organise themselves as I scrabble backwards, on all fours.

Progress in this manner is abruptly halted by the rock wall. Petrified, I scan what I can see of this side of the cave, desperately hunting for an escape route…

Then I just about nearly die on the spot, as another many-legged shadow appears over a nest of eggs to my right. But what I think at first is a giant tarantula, stops and hovers over the clutch, before reaching and selecting one discerningly – and in the dim light, I see it is a thin, gray-skinned hand.

Another zombie…!

The hand holding the egg disappears. But a second later, it returns empty – points directly at me, and beckons.

I glance back towards the giant monitor lizard. It is raising its head to taste the air, forked tongue flicking in and out. A hen's feather is stuck to the end of its snout.

Well – that wasn't a difficult decision.

"Are you related to Mr Dry?" I ask of the strange zombie, as I crawl along the new tunnel behind. But it says nothing, merely beckons again.

Too aware of the speed at which the monitor lizard could navigate this low space, I hurry after.

We emerge in another cavern, but this one is definitely not the home of hens. Tree-roots and cobwebs are more the order of the day, and the occasional damp fluttering noise of batwings.

"I don't think I'm meant to be this far down," I ponder, picking my way through the underground flora and fauna, in step with the zombie. "Where does this lead to?"

"My *precioussss…*" the zombie hisses, almost voiceless, it is so old.

I look it up and down, curiously. Hardly anything remains of its clothing. And around one ankle, there hangs a plastic tag, attached with a cable-tie.

"Are you familiar with the Body Farm?" I ask, thoughtfully.

The zombie shoots me a glance, with its one reptilian-green eye, and keeps hobbling onward.

"It's just that I noticed you have a neon pink ankle-tag, which means a *Shallow Grave Study* subject," I continue. "I guess it would be easy for you to get time off to do your own thing, in between those other times, when you're being dug up again for analysis."

The tree-roots get closer together, and we squeeze through the claustrophobic spaces, until we reach what appears to be a natural clearing.

I can hear water rippling, and a pool of moonlight from some chink in the rock high above us, illuminates an underground spring.

The zombie finds a paper boat at the water's edge, and puts the egg inside, before setting it adrift, pushing it so that it wobbles away into the darkness. How very strange…

"Are you here to kiss the frog?" a booming voice greets us, and startled, I immediately wish for dry pyjamas.

"Er, preferably no," I reply to the unseen speaker. "Just looking for the way out."

"Are you sure?" the voice continues. "I have a golden ball…"

"Don't think I want to kiss that either," I remark, resolutely.

A movement on the far side of the water catches my eye, but for some reason I avoid looking too closely to define it, as it approaches the spring to retrieve the floating egg. I have a feeling that several years alone down a well has probably negated the need for clothing.

"There must be something you desire," the deep Shakespearean-actor voice of the third Frittata brother replies. "Otherwise, you would not be here in the wishing-well."

"Really, I just want to find a way back out into the mansion," I say, with conviction – ignoring the thought *'dry pyjamas'*, which tries to make itself heard. "Just been playing a bit of *Hide-and-Seek* with the other Frittatas… oh. I am so sorry…"

The voice roars in rage, and the body-farmed zombie and I both cover our ears.

"That is quite all right," the third Frittata brother says at last, after a moment to compose himself again. I hear the munching of eggshell. "Are you sure there is nothing else you wish for? Seeing as you have come all this way – and survived… so far…"

Something occurs to me, other than damp Paisley-patterned silk nightwear.

"I don't suppose you've seen a clockwork right hand anywhere down here?" I query.

"Ahhhh," the third Frittata brother rumbles.

"My *precioussss*…" the zombie hisses again, nodding vigorously, until I worry that his poor head may drop off.

"You will find it guarded by the third heir to the Dry estate," the bass voice replies, carrying eerily over the water. "But yes – find it, you certainly may – Sarah Bellum."

A cloud moves across the moon, and I can no longer make out the water, or the direction of the speaker. Cold-skinned zombie fingers grasp my own, tugging me to follow again.

"How did he know my name?" I want to know, but the zombie says nothing, leading me away from the tree-roots. "And what third heir? I thought it was just Crispin and Homer?"

At last, the terrain starts to head upwards, becomes less like rough ground, and more even, like broad steps. They narrow progressively, until we are on what is essentially a spiral staircase, like the inside of a church-tower.

After a few minutes of climbing, a studded iron door marks the end of our route. It is unlocked by a nautical-style wheel, and we push it inwards.

It is some sort of storage facility – or laboratory – or study – but far older than Crispin's, in the bunker under the stairs. Instead of a smart garage, armoury, hi-tech computers and sterile refrigerated quarantine sections, this is all yellowing papers and pickled things in jars, under what could be a century of dust.

An ancient, empty leather chair is in front of a desk, where a misty magnifying glass and an old pair of wire spectacles lie abandoned, on an open diary.

I shine my torch onto the handwritten page.

TO CATCH A COMET'S TAIL… it says – and then just a sequence of odd, *Leonardo da Vinci*-style diagrams.

"My *preciousss*," the zombie calls me, and I turn, to see him opening a small white door in the corner, half-hidden behind a pile of old books.

I go to look, and it's the last room I was expecting to see hidden away underground.

It's a baby's nursery.

A wooden painted mobile hangs above a white wooden crib, and a jolly-looking chicken fresco is painted around the walls. There are no photographs.

I know, as I step through the doorway, behind the strange zombie, that I'm entering a shrine.

"*Precioussss…*" moans the zombie, pointing.

I gaze into the crib.

"Yes," I agree, as the beam of torchlight reflects off the surface of the six-litre pickle jar. So peaceful-looking. "Isn't he just?"

CHAPTER SIXTEEN:
NECROMANCING THE BONES

"How did you know this room was even here?" I ask the strange zombie, as it tears its one remaining eye off the sight of the pickled baby in the crib, and starts to fluff pillows and blankets around it, in a proprietary fashion. "I mean, surely Crispin would be down here all the time, looking for clues – if HE knew about it…"

At the name 'Crispin' the zombie moans, sympathetically. I look at him more carefully, in the torchlight.

There does appear to be a family resemblance…

"Do I have the pleasure of guessing correctly that you are Mr. Dry, Senior?" I say at last.

The zombie nods, patting and polishing the jar a little.

"No wonder," I breathe. "But why the Body Farm tag? Is it the equivalent of a summer festival pass, to a zombie? An excuse to lie around in the open air at weekends, meet laid-back girls, catch a few flies – nobody bothering you…?"

The zombie shrugs and nods again, waggling his hands in the universal gesture meaning *'Pretty much, yeah.'*

No wonder they know so much about me already, I realise, blushing fiercely. Eavesdropping on my private one-sided conversations, no doubt, with Mr. Wheelie-Bin under the silver birch tree…

"So who was… is this?" I ask, more gently. The baby's thumb is in its mouth, a forelock of blonde hair waving slowly in the suspension fluid.

The zombie points to the head of the crib, where an engraved brass name plaque becomes obvious.

"Higham Dry," I ponder, and the zombie nods again. "The youngest?"

The Zombie shakes his head, and holds his hand up above his head, as if measuring.

"The eldest?" I whisper, shocked, and am rewarded with another nod. "I'm not surprised that Crispin and Homer felt they failed expectations, then… having a stillborn elder brother who might have fulfilled everything…"

Mr. Dry Senior just shrugs again, and reaches under the blanket. Feeling around for a moment, he produces a pink and white felt rabbit toy, and offers it to me.

"I, er, don't understand…" I falter.

The zombie thrusts the stuffed toy under my nose. It is wearing a red waistcoat, on which is appliquéd a pocket-watch and chain, in golden thread.

"It's the rabbit from *Alice in Wonderland*, yes," I agree. "She fell down a hole – I fell down a hole. I get it…"

"*Noooo*," the zombie replies, and prods the felt rabbit in the middle. The sound of an air-squeaker inside it makes me jump.

"And it squeaks," I add. I'm at a loss. "I don't know what you mean…"

I find myself staring at the toy rabbit's chest, as it is held even closer. The word *SWISS* is embroidered on the white watch-face.

"Is it a clue?" I ask. The zombie's shoulders slump, and he slaps his free hand over his eye in resignation. "Do you want me to take this?"

"*Yessss*," Mr. Dry Senior groans, and shoves it into my own hands. It's surprisingly heavy. "Go *nowww*…"

"Back the same way?" I say in dread, thinking of the naked Frittata brother, with his frog fixation and dubious golden ball in the wishing-well, and the giant monitor lizard in the underground hen-house.

I follow him back out into the study, where he glances sadly back at the nursery before closing the door behind us.

"Up," Mr. Dry Senior says simply, and points to the corner of the wall, above the desk.

A couple of ribbons flutter from a large aluminium air-vent. *Aha…*

I step up onto the desk and start to open it, but he stops me with one hand on the leg of my pyjama-bottoms. I look down to see him closing the leather-bound diary, buckling it shut, and offering it to me as well.

"More clues?" I query, taking it, and tucking it into my waistband.

"*Duhhh…*" The zombie slumps in the chair, and looks defeated, dropping his head into his hands and shaking it slowly.

I think he's deteriorating rapidly. Probably too much time spent outdoors on the Body Farm at the weekends, experiencing alternative forms of decay.

The ventilation shaft is wide and smooth, and the only sound is the echo of my own hands and knees as I crawl along. But I don't trust it. The aluminium throws dark reflections and moving shadows at every turn, and I'm sure that behind me – although I could be imagining it – I hear the scuttling of claws.

What could Mr. Dry want by giving me his stillborn son's toy rabbit, and an old diary full of sketches and drawings? I can only imagine he wants me to pass them on to Crispin – with all his modern technology in the bunker below the stairs, surely he'll be able to decipher it? And maybe find that special hereditary clockwork hand, which will save his home from the clutches of the National Trust…

As I'm thinking this, I suddenly become aware of a smell creeping up on me slowly, along the air-way. The smell of burnt feathers, and rotten eggs. And the mental image of something that stalks chickens on their nests, and devours them whole…

I hear the scaly scrape of a reptile tail against aluminium behind me. Before the echo has even formed, I've never moved so quickly in my life.

I know I don't have a hope in Hell.

Out-crawl a monitor lizard in a low passageway? I might as well try turning around and seeing if I can out-bite it…

But my fear drives me forwards, even knowing that I'm doomed. And around the next corner, my heart jumps vertically up into my throat, and makes a desperate grab for my epiglottis…

A ladder!!

Leading straight up!

Almost crying with relief, I propel myself forward quickly, using the slippery silk of the pyjamas to surf the aluminium floor, and clutch at the rungs of the upward ventilation shaft. No more than six or seven feet up, I feel the violent vibration as a powerful claw twangs the bottom of the ladder, and make the mistake of looking down – into those hungry, poisonous jaws.

God help me… I redouble my efforts to climb, the latticework metal grille at the top a blur as I ascend.

"Help!" I hear a shriek, and then recognise it as my own, while I batter my knuckles and palms of my hands on the underside of the grille. "Let me out! Help me!"

And then I'm punching nothing. Something clamps around my wrist, and I'm dragged bodily out of the vent. I scream again, trying to identify the sensation. Do monitor lizards drag their prey, or bite first? Am I out of the frying pan into a fire?

Then I find myself dangling at eye-level with Carvery Slaughter, and realise that yes – quite possibly I am…

"Why am I always catching you hanging around me at the moment?" he demands.

"Wishful thinking?" I suggest, my voice a mouse's peep.

"Not mine, I think you'll find," he remarks, and deposits me back on my feet, before kicking the grid back over the hole in the floor.

It's a stonework tunnel similar to earlier – I must be back on the level of the secret passageways inside the house. A glance at Carvery does nothing to settle my stomach. Even worse, he seems to be alone.

"Where are the others?" I ask. "And what have you been up to?"

He's covered in blood, for one thing. My hope that it's his own, is quickly dashed.

"Well, Homer won't have to worry about returning that blonde wig to Mrs. Frittata now," Carvery shrugs, and the next thing I note is that he's now in possession of a shotgun. I glance at it nervously, as it rests on his shoulder.

"Why is it that you always pick on the women, and not the men?" I want to know.

"I think that last one was debatable," he grins. "You didn't see her. Nightmare."

He takes a step closer, eyeing me up and down.

"Anyway," he continues. "What are you hiding behind your back? Been collecting a few souvenirs of your own?"

"No!" I cry, holding out my empty hands to show him.

"You're a terrible liar, Sarah," he says. The muzzle of the shotgun is suddenly under my chin. "Turn around and face the wall."

My hands now in the air, petrified, I do as he orders. I let out a whimper, as I feel his own hand go up the back of the pyjama top.

There is an ominous rip. I close my eyes, expecting the worst…

"Hmmm," he says at last. "I put only one hand up there, so why did two come out?"

"What?!" I yell, and try to turn, flinching as the shotgun barrel jabs me in the ear.

The felt rabbit drops on the floor with a last regretful squeak, dissected beyond playroom resuscitation.

Carvery is examining something shiny in the darkness, glinting with polished gemstones.

"This is that clockwork hand thing he was going on about earlier, isn't it?" he says. "What are you doing with it?"

"That was given to me to look after!" I say indignantly. I'm such a dork. It was the actual *hand* that Mr. Dry Senior was entrusting me with! Not the toy at all. "Give it back!"

Carvery looks at it a moment longer, then holds it out.

"Sure," he says, dismissively. "Take it."

Cautiously, I do so.

Then he changes his grip on the gun, and aims it back at my head.

"Now YOU give it back, please," he says, and with a sigh of defeat, I hand it over. "Well done. Remember – never try to negotiate with an armed man, unless you have something bigger up your sleeve."

I wonder if the leather-bound diary counts as something bigger. Knowing my luck, he would find it only mildly less offensive than the contents of my own diary.

But I'm glad it has stayed hidden, in my waistband at the front. Maybe Crispin will still be able to decipher something useful from it.

"Right," Carvery says, as I nod my acquiescence. "Let's go and find the others."

Phew, I think, as I fall into step beside him, pausing only to pick up the remains of Higham Dry's toy rabbit, sentimentally. *I hope that means they're still alive…*

CHAPTER SEVENTEEN: SLIPPED DISCLOSURE

I don't ask how Carvery got separated from the rest of his group, and likewise, he doesn't ask me the same question.

My reason for avoiding curiosity, is he's the one covered in blood, and currently armed with a shotgun. So I just stay silent, as we head deeper into the stone-walled tunnel.

For all I know, we could be the last two left alive in the house… I gulp down my nausea, as I wonder how long would be a respectable amount of time to figure out a way to be the very last one left alive. With sperm-jacking privileges first, obviously…

"Looks like a dead end," he says, eventually. "Oh, no – look, there is something here…"

I shine my torch beam onto the wall. A square sliding panel is set at about waist-height. It's maybe four foot by four, and next to it is an up-down arrow keypad, the type for an elevator.

Carvery levers the panel open, and stale air greets us from the dark, empty shaft. He risks a quick glance inside. I'm sorry to see that his head emerges again, still attached.

"I guess we have to call the dumb waiter," he remarks, letting the panel slide shut, and presses a button. Unseen gears whir into life, and the distant squealing of pulleys announce the approach of the lift.

"Ace seemed to think it was a good party at the University earlier," I venture, trying to make what sounds like normal small-talk, while also fishing for information. "Did he, er, have a lot to drink?"

"Oh, he was buzzing all right," Carvery agrees. "But it's okay, because he told me to skin any women who tried to take advantage. So we both had a pretty good night, in all."

Ah… I didn't realise that sort of social arrangement existed between guys. At least two-thirds of my fantasies, regarding the outcome of cornering Ace Bumgang drunk at some point, immediately shuffle right off the drawing-board.

Damn…

The dumb waiter lift arrives, with an electronic 'ping'.

Carvery and I exchange a look, neither making a move to open the panel first.

"Do you think a monitor lizard might be able to squeeze in there?" I whisper.

"Or a Frittata brother?" he suggests. He hefts the shotgun and points it at the doors. "Or a hungry zombie? You push the button, Sarah."

My breath trapped in my lungs, I reach out with a shaky hand, and do so.

After a pause, and a faint click – the door slides back.

Nothing.

Just a smooth, square, empty box.

"Cool." Carvery lowers the gun. "Right, get in."

"I'm not going first," I argue. "We don't know what's at the top."

"You'd rather stay down here in a dead end on your own?" he asks.

I hear the echo of a hiss in the tunnel behind us, and I blanch, shaking my head.

"Do you hear something moving back there?" I squeak. The familiar scraping sound is followed by a dull metallic clang – *oh, no* – the ventilation shaft…

Carvery sizes up the dumb waiter.

"I reckon we can both fit in," he announces, turns around, and scoots in backwards. He reaches out towards me. "Come on – spoon up."

"You've got to be kidding…"

"Well, take the alternative. A free ride in the digestive tract of a monitor lizard."

The sound of scuttling claws clatters along the dark passageway.

"Maybe if you leave me the gun," I say, willing to take my chances against wildlife, rather than a ride in a small wooden box, with a certified psychopath.

"Fuck that." He leans out and grabs me bodily around the waist, dragging me into the tiny space with him.

Gasping in shock, I have to fold in my arms and legs lotus-style as I'm crushed up against him, my back to his chest. He reaches out once more to punch the button again, and the door slides closed – just as the reptile shape appears out of the gloom, drooling jaws open wide.

Carvery shifts slightly so that I'm trapped between his legs in the tiny lift, which suddenly feels like a coffin, even as it hums into life, grinding slowly upwards. God – I'm in a confined space with Carvery Slaughter – I'm gonna die, I'm gonna die, *I'm gonna die…*

"What the fuck is that in your hair, Sarah?" he breaks the silence first, scattering my preconceptions of what he might be likely to say in this situation.

"Huh?" I swallow. My throat feels like a ball of nerves is trapped in there. "Oh… it's egg. I fell down a hole, into the hen-house."

"That explains the smell too, then," he remarks.

I try not to think about what Carvery smells like. My hormones are staging a mutiny. His mouth is right next to my ear, and his breath tickles.

"Charming," I say instead, fighting thoughts of retaliation, while those gun barrels are still only four inches away from my head as well. "I don't know what my housemate Thingy sees in you."

"Well, she's pretty shallow, so I'm guessing she only sees a wallet, a dick and a Ferrari," he replies, mildly.

"And what do you see in her?" I ask. "A punching bag?"

"Why assume that I'm the one who's violent?" he says. "For all you know, she could be doing it to herself, for the attention. Girls can be a real bitch when they don't get their own way. Or if they just want a new pair of shoes. Chucking themselves down the stairs, and all sorts."

"You don't fool me," I retort, although I feel uneasy. Poor Mr. 'domestic incident' Wheelie-Bin at the Body Farm, with his detached scalp… "She couldn't bite her own thumb off!"

I feel Carvery shrug, behind me.

Damn you, traitorous hormones!

"You never know."

I wonder if he's grinning, while feeding me all these evil ideas, designed to instil self-doubt.

"And what about all of your ex-girlfriends disappearing?" I demand. "Like, under the building foundations where you work?"

"Some women just don't understand the meaning of the words 'restraining order'," he says. "And they're all as kinky as fuck these days. I get home after a hard day's work, and they want to be strung up from the ceiling, flogged, beaten, and tickled with a feather duster for eight hours. What's wrong with you all? Especially when they don't explain in advance that they didn't mean 'strung up' by the neck. Serves them right."

"I don't believe you," I mutter. "I think you're a psycho – who does it for fun."

"Well, why don't you try asking your housemate, Miss Yo-Yo Panties, why she always seems to sustain the *same* injuries, no matter who she's dating?" Carvery suggests. "And then figure out for yourself if she's really that unlucky – or whether she keeps bolt-cutters under her own bed, to snip bits off herself when she's feeling ignored."

The dumb waiter judders, and my stomach lurches in empathy.

"You're lying," I say, after swallowing my stomach contents back down.

"And you're jealous, Sarah," he sighs. "I've read your diary, remember?"

Oh, yes. He would have to remind me about that, while he's got his legs wrapped around me, and a gun next to my head, in a very confined space… I opt to hold my tongue, realising that the moral high ground is a concept that should have been taken into account before I started writing anything down in the first place…

With a final jolt, the dumb waiter stops.

Carvery angles the gun to point outwards, before wiggling the toe of his boot into the gap, to slide the door. Every muscle in my body suddenly feels like a bowstring.

"Don't worry," he says in my ear, and this time I'm sure he's grinning. "There were eight other people in the house to start with. Maybe whatever's on the far side has already eaten by now."

CHAPTER EIGHTEEN: THE COCKERELS OF HERNIA

The door of the dumb waiter slides back, and the first thing I see is a pair of yellow eyes and fangs in a furry gray face, bared and ready for action. But it's only for a split second, because it vanishes into fluffy fragments as Carvery pulls the trigger.

I have to stifle my scream, partly in awareness of the proximity of Carvery's gun which has just half-deafened me – only half, because he has abruptly pulled my head into his chest and covered my ears with his free hand at the same time.

The smoke clears, and it turns out that what I first thought to be a snarling werewolf, is merely a blue fox-fur. It hangs benignly in front of the opening, between a mink coat, and a snow-white fur, of possible endangered-species origin. Both now rather singed beyond elegantly controversial wearability.

"Who puts a dumb waiter in the back of a cloakroom?" Carvery wonders, as he releases his arm-lock from around my head, his self-control in the face of potential danger astounding. "Or a lady's closet? Is it for the dry-cleaning?"

"Maybe an escape route for illicit lovers?" I suggest. "Who would otherwise be caught in the act?"

He gives me a pat on the shoulder. I flinch, automatically, until I realise he's indicating for me to get off his lap.

"That's not a bad idea," he agrees. "Guess you're not as retarded as you look."

I elbow my way off him abruptly, and out of the tiny box.

Noooo, my traitorous hormones protest, denied. I try to ignore them, focusing my thoughts of male companionship on the reassuring memory of Mr. Wheelie-Bin again, and his understanding silence at the Body Farm. My brain can't handle all these animated men at the moment, walking around and talking of their own free will, with their ulterior motives and psychopathic tendencies.

Carvery slides out of the dumb waiter in turn, and nudges the ruined fur coat aside. Beyond the rows of hanging furs, there is indeed the back of a slatted closet door, not unlike the one the zombie Homer N. Dry occupied earlier, dressing up in his mother's clothing.

"Looks like a bedroom," he says, peering through the shotgun-damaged slats. "Come on."

He pushes the door ajar, and we sidle out, warily. Yes – by all appearances, and the smell of lavender beyond the shot powder stink – it's Crispin's mother's suite once more. The familiar pink and white silk is a stark contrast to those dark secret tunnels.

"I know this room," I tell Carvery. "We're up on the second floor."

"Hmmm," he says, noncommittally, and opens a small drawer at random, finding a book inside. "Do zombies usually read *Barbara Cartland?*"

"I couldn't say," I reply. "But I think it was their mother's apartments."

"Is she still around too?" he asks. I shrug, unable to answer that one – dead, undead, or any other way. Carvery replaces the book and seems to case up the rest of the room, at a brief glance. "Well, wherever she is, it looks like she's really into cock."

"Huh?" I'm alarmed. Can men tell so much from a woman's choice of décor? What else can they surmise on purely innocent appearances?

"Cock."

He points.

Ohhh… the pet cockerel is snoozing, one eye half-open watching us, in the middle of the bed. His feathers are all preened, and he looks completely at home.

"That's Crispin's pet!" I say, enormously relieved. "Maybe he can help us find the others… Here, chicky – where's Crispin? Crispin?"

"What are you now, the Cock-Whisperer?" Carvery demands.

"No, look," I say, as the cockerel yawns and stretches, rising up onto his feathered legs. "He understands. There's a good ickle chicky – take us to Prince Crispin…"

"Sarah, you need help," Carvery mutters, as the bird struts regally off the bed, heading for the doors. "Seriously."

"Come on," I urge. "Let's follow him."

"You mean, I follow you," Carvery corrects, shouldering the shotgun again. "While you chase cock."

"If it leads me to Crispin, then I'm better off than just hanging around in his mother's bedroom," I point out.

Carvery looks upwards, thoughtfully.

"You're probably right," he concedes. "Ceiling's too low in here. Nowhere decent to hang you from."

Well – at least that was pretty much what I expected from him.

"I'm following him," I say. "What you decide to do is your problem."

I head after the cockerel as it slips out of the doors to the suite, back out into the second-floor corridor. Behind me, I hear Carvery sigh irritably, and move to follow.

The cockerel jogs along, past the abandoned ironing-board and bits of RC Spitfire, and vaults the tripwire. It glances back as if to check our progress, before continuing across the landing into the opposite wing, ignoring the stairs.

"Don't reckon much on Mrs. Frittata's housekeeping," Carvery remarks, stepping over the ironing board. "Looks like I did the guy a favour."

"Oh, no – that was us, earlier…" I start to say, and he gives me that *You're-so-fucking-weird-I-don't-know-what-to-think* look. "It's a long story. Mind the wire. And watch out for any marbles rolling around on the floor."

"Someone's definitely lost their marbles," he grunts, navigating the tripwire without having to double-check.

We continue in the path of the cockerel, as it hops determinedly along the corridor into the hitherto unexplored wing of this floor. At the far end, it turns right – and bobs its head expectantly at a large, green baize-inlaid door.

"I think he wants us to go in here!" I announce.

"Maybe it's only where they keep the chicken-feed," Carvery chuckles, but still levels the gun barrels, before I try the door. My logic being that a cockerel wouldn't knowingly stroll directly into danger…

The door swings silently inwards, not even an ominous creak. And the cockerel runs in happily, onto deep wool carpet.

"Great," Carvery says. "A completely empty room. Maybe he just wants somewhere new to crap."

"It's not empty," I tell him. "It's a portrait gallery…"

I'm drawn in by the sombre decorum of the dark, silent room. The mahogany walls are hung with dozens of individual portraits, going back how many centuries? But they can't all be of the Dry family, because they've only been here for three generations…

The most recent seem to be nearest the door, and the first is so clearly of Crispin, *ante-mortem*, that I gasp.

So-oooohh Mr. Darcy!

He was as stunning before as he is now, I find myself thinking. Or is that the wrong way around? Just – *stunning*… I could have stared happily into those forget-me-not blue eyes forever, but with a deliberate turn of my heel and a private gulp of embarrassment at my own thoughts, I move on.

Ah. Homer, obviously. In men's attire, but sitting cross-stitching a sampler, beside a large floral arrangement. And as my gaze scans downward – yes – very fetching *Jimmy Choo* stilettos, Homer…

Curious, I go to look at Mr. Dry Senior. He looks academic and serious, both of his eyes intact behind those spectacles – that leather diary tucked under one arm… My hand goes to check it at my waist, unconsciously.

And then Grandfather Dry, evidently as big a fan of poultry as his grandson…

"Ah, I see this one's showing off his cock," Carvery Slaughter interrupts my private artistic musings. "Bigger than the one currently trying to shag the feather cushions on that armchair in the corner."

I avoid looking where he points, all too clearly able to hear the amorous clucking of the cockerel.

"These must be the previous owners further along," I say, curiosity getting the better of me, and hurry onwards. "Oh – no – no, no…"

"What?" Carvery asks, and catches up at his own pace. "Yeah, what about it?"

"Can't you see?" I cry, waving an arm up at the drab gray face in the painting. "The previous owners – they were zombies!"

"The current owners are zombies," Carvery replies, deadpan. "Or had that issue escaped your attention?"

"But they weren't always zombies!" I moan. "You can see – they were normal before. But these older ones – just look at them. The gray skin – and the lifeless eyes!"

"Look like regular old portraits to me," he remarks, licking a finger, and running it down the dull, dingy painted canvas. "Could use a clean-up, perhaps."

"It must be something to do with the house!" I insist. "Maybe there's a curse…"

Carvery's hand covers my mouth, stopping me in my verbal tracks.

"Sshhh," he hisses in emphasis, and jerks his head towards the last painting, on the far wall.

A giant painting. Of a ship. Maybe an early migrant transport, or a slave trader. The figurehead is a snarling totem of a demon, and the sails are blood-red.

Am I imagining it, or is that the creak of timbers in its rigging?

And as the cockerel's ecstasy with its favoured tapestry cushion reaches a crescendo, the surface of the painting *billows*…

CHAPTER NINETEEN:
STARGRAVE

"Is it draughty in here?" I ask, the hope in my voice as steady as a margarine stepladder.

A rumble, like thunder answers me, and the room shakes. The picture-frames reverberate off the walls, in a staccato round of ghostly applause.

The cockerel pauses in his courtship of the soft furnishings, and looks out from behind his current *coussin de jour.*

The giant painting of the ship ripples outward, and then suddenly bulges alarmingly. And then a bright flash of light almost blinds us. Along with the sound of a thunderclap, which at first I mistake for Carvery Slaughter discharging the shotgun again.

"Don't kill me!" I shriek, as the room goes dark and silent once more.

There is a pause.

"You wish," Carvery replies.

A tinkling sound replaces the churning rumble, like the gentlest of wind chimes. And the painting gradually illuminates again – its surface alive, bubbling and criss-crossed with reflections, like translucent mercury.

"It *is* a curse…" I whisper.

"Parlour-trick, more like," says Carvery.

The cockerel hops down from the armchair, his cushion of love forgotten. Instead, he struts up to the undulating surface of the living painting, eerily illuminated from within. He approaches, bobbing his head at the multi-faceted image, making keening and crooning noises.

Not six feet away from him, a white hen abruptly emerges from – no, *through* the painting. Sparkly droplets scatter into the air around her, as she skitters across the floor.

"Another hen-house?" Carvery suggests wryly, as the Casanova cockerel gives chase, circling around us in pursuit. "Looks like this is your department, Sarah."

The avian pair do another circuit of the portrait gallery, and then both dash headlong into the silvery surface of the picture again, sending concentric rings out from their point of impact.

Carvery and I exchange a look.

"Ready to get more egg on your face?" he remarks.

"No," I scoff. "I think we should wait right here."

"Suit yourself." He turns and knocks the cushion off the armchair, before sitting down in its place, drumming his fingers on the stock of the gun. "Let's see what else comes out of that wall next."

The gallery is quiet once more, just the play of light on the walls, from the mysterious mobile surface of the end painting.

Yes – what might come out next…? Chicken? Zombie? *Monitor lizard...?*

But it's a familiar sound, that reaches us first. And not through the wall – from outside, in the corridor.

"Is that what I think it is?" I whisper, frozen still, and straining my ears.

Carvery angles his head slightly.

"Could be," he nods.

"Hi-ho, hi-ho…" I murmur.

"Off to work we go…" Carvery grins. *Oh, God…* "I'm up for a bit of Ben and Jerry."

The chanting draws nearer.

"I think I'll chance the hen-house again," I decide. "Don't think I want to be the only one who brings nothing to the gunfight."

Carvery looks down at himself, with a shrug.

"You brought me," he says. "What else did you want – a wheel-gun?"

I think immediately of the Gatling in the basement. *The armoury!* And those tunnels – maybe there is another way into the bunker…

The cockerel's head pops back out of the painting, looks at each of us, and disappears again.

There is a very definite creak on the floorboards, outside the door.

Carvery gets to his feet, and stands at my shoulder. Both of us facing the approaching danger.

"What am I, your human shield?" I demand.

"Soft landing," he says, checking the gun briefly.

"What?"

"Count to three," he says.

"Why?"

"Two, then."

"What for?"

He shakes his head and clicks his tongue.

"Useless," is all he says, and the butt of the gun catches me right under the chin, flipping me neatly over backwards.

The surface of the painting feels like a tepid outdoor pool – barely any resistance at all. I feel it strike, envelop and transfer me through, all in a flash.

I've barely managed to draw a breath, having landed flat on my back on – not straw this time, but sand – when something lands right on top of me. Hot, hard, and smelling like traitorous hormones kicking in…

"Next time, when I say count, you count," Carvery scolds, elbowing his way back off my body, and getting to his feet. "Right. Where are we?"

I push myself up, more slowly. A dim, golden light filters from a passageway ahead, onto pale yellow stonework. Smooth and architectural – not like the dark dank passages we were in before.

Looking back, for our point of entry, there is nothing but a blank stone wall. No magical painting, no art gallery – and thankfully, no Frittata brothers…

I grip a nearby ledge to pull myself to my feet, and find Carvery already staring at something, right where I had rested my hand.

I jump away.

It's a sarcophagus. The face is painted onto the outside, with glamorous strokes of an *Elizabeth Taylor* retrospective.

Hieroglyphs on the walls swim into focus as I look around.

"I can't handle this," I breathe.

"You were the one who was talking about a curse," Carvery points out. He knocks on the lid. "Anybody home?"

"You're not funny."

"I wasn't being funny. Someone might want to be let out of there."

"Or might be shut in for a reason," I contradict.

A shadow moves in the passageway, and alerted, I cry out.

"Who's there?"

"I didn't say *Knock Knock*," Carvery jokes.

A faint voice replies, fading as if moving away from us.

"Home... home..."

"Homer!" I call. Relief floods through me, incontinently. "Wait!"

Leaving the spooky sarcophagus behind in the chamber, we head out after the pattering zombie. Oh dear. His pink dress is quite the worse for wear, and the crochet shawl merely a shred or two of white cotton.

"Homer, where are the others?" I ask. "And where is this place?"

Although twisting and turning, the passages are still light and sandy. And eventually, open out into a broader, pillared hall.

At the end, the early sunrise is starting to appear, glinting off a river.

"I think I'll get a roof terrace like this one when I renovate my next house," Carvery smirks.

Palm trees wave gently beside us as we step outside. Strange birds soar overhead.

Where the Hell are we?

"Home," says Homer N. Dry, happily.

Oh, no…

CHAPTER TWENTY: DROOL OF THE NILE

The palm trees form an avenue at the bottom of the broad stone steps, leading to the water's edge. My brain is trying not to register the pyramid-shapes on the far bank. It's an optical illusion, I tell myself. Some sort of ultra-modern virtual reality art installation…

Carvery is crouching on the sandy flagstones, testing the groutless joins, with a strange-looking *Swiss Army* kind of tool, full of identically-shaped blades. He squints at the thinnest one critically, as it barely slides in and out of the gap.

"Thinking about how many bodies you could fit under a patio this size?" I observe.

"I think it's fully-booked already," he remarks, straightening up. "Now where's the little gray tranny off to?"

The zombie Homer N. Dry (trailing grubby white crochet and bedraggled locks of blonde Sunday wig) has made it down the steps – only falling on his face twice – and is scampering lopsidedly towards the riverside.

As the sun clears the pyramids on the horizon, the shadows in the water reveal a ship moored. Very similar to the one in the painting, but it looks as though it has had some work done since the original. The demonic totem at the figurehead is still there, and the prow is the same – but instead of the sails, it now features a raised houseboat deck – and a paddle-steamer propulsion system.

"I hope they're expecting him, whoever it is," says Carvery, as Homer lives up to his name, homing in on the vessel. "Or this is going to turn into *Death on the Nile* real fast."

"There they are!" a distant figure shouts, from the same direction. "Carver – Sarah – down here!"

It's Numb-Nuts, my housemate. Waving at us, from the deck of the ship.

Of course, she would still be alive. Seeing as she hasn't spent at least the last hour in the company of girlfriend-batterer-in-denial Carvery Slaughter. A couple of zombies, an immigrant taxi-driver, and a drunk Ace Bumgang wouldn't pose any comparable risk to her safety…

Homer leads the way up the rope-suspended gangplank, and once aboard, I'm cannoned aside by Miss Fuck-Tart launching herself at Carvery, making weird abandoned-stray-cat noises as she burrows into his arms.

"Whatever…" he sighs.

Could he sound as though he could even care less?

"Glad you have made it, Sarah *Bellummm*," says that zombie voice, which makes my spine tingle, and I turn to see Crispin approaching. With a tray of drinks! It seems like hours since that last Gin Sling… "Welcome to my Five a.m. Lounge."

I try to concentrate on downing the drink, keeping my nose in the glass, and not on devouring him with my eyes. And what a sight for sore ones he is…

"It's very impressive," I say at last, replacing the empty glass again. "You have a great home entertainment set-up here."

He waves a hand dismissively.

"Just the basics, just the basics," he moans. He gestures for me to join him on a couch, in the prow of the ship. Wading birds dart in and out of the reeds on the riverbank, and delicate insects skate across the water's surface. "Mother insisted that we drop in regularly, so it was necessary to make visiting arrangements as simple as possible."

"Oh – she's still alive?" I surmise. I swat a mosquito as it lands on my arm, settling into the satin cushions.

"No. Just demanding," he sighs, and turns towards me, leaning in. "I seem to remember that the last time you and I were on a couch together, we had some unfinished business, Sarah *Bellummm…*"

Oh, my…

But before that thought can be followed by any action, a shadow falls across us – and Luke, the Nigerian cab-driver, slumps onto the end of the sofa.

"You know, my ancestors probably built those things," he announces, pointing towards the pyramids.

"There is a certain resemblance, indeed," Crispin agrees. "Perhaps we can introduce you to them later…"

"Home… Gooood…" a familiar zombie-groan interrupts.

Homer emerges from a door to one of the suites in the houseboat section, changed now into *Diana Ross* red sequins and trailing a feather boa, and waddles away to the bar. Carvery and Whatsername have disappeared somewhere else on the ship. I'm wondering how long it will take for bits of her to start floating past.

But also – isn't there someone else, that should be in our group…?

"Ace Bumgang!" I say in recall, far too loudly, as Luke spills his Tequila. "Is he here too?"

"Sure, sure…" Luke brushes himself down. "He's being ill over the starboard."

I get quickly to my feet and hurry to the far side of the boat, overlooking the water. Ace is leaning on the railing, forehead on forearms, groaning as much as any zombie.

In fact I have to check as I approach, that he still looks comparatively alive. A bit pale, perhaps…

"Seasick?" I greet him, timidly.

"Hangover," he replies. "I yacked up in the water just now, and a crocodile ate it."

Crocodiles?

I join him and look over the side of the ship, greeted by the yawn of another giant reptile. A number of them float lazily, treading water in the slow current beside the boat, like bad-tempered logs set adrift.

Well – I guess they give the monitor lizards a bit of healthy competition…

"Did you have any trouble in the tunnels?" I ask. "I lost you guys quite early on, I think."

"Don't remember a whole lot," Ace admits. "Just that it was really dark."

"Makes it more fun that way," Carvery butts in, thumping each of us in the spine, as he appears from behind.

I start at the intrusion, bumped roughly against the railings – and Mr. Dry Senior's leather-bound diary jolts loose from the waistband of my loaned-from-Crispin, silk Paisley pyjamas.

"No!" I gasp.

Before I can make a safety-grab, it slips under the wrought metalwork, tumbles downwards – and lands with a faint slap, in the middle of a crocodile's back.

"What have you dropped?" Carvery wants to know, looking over the side. "Still hiding stuff that might be interesting? Where did you steal that from?"

"It was given to me to look after!" I hiss through gritted teeth, echoing myself from earlier.

"Then I think you ought to be looking after it a bit more carefully, don't you?" he remarks. "Hop over and pick it up."

"I'll never reach that far!"

"We'll just hold you by the ankles – right, Ace?" Carvery looks across at him, and grins. "Won't be the first time today."

The crocodiles shift menacingly in the water, and the leather-bound diary gives a tantalising wobble.

"All right, but not for too long this time," Ace agrees, straightening up. "I'm gunning with all the power of runny custard this morning."

I look from one to the other, with obvious concerns.

"I haven't dropped you yet, have I?" Carvery teases. "Saved your life more than once already."

"That's because he's saving it for later," Ace adds. "You haven't had a ride in the trunk of his car first. You wouldn't want to miss that."

My housemate, Twat-for-Brains, would think this was all so much delightful flirting. Probably how she spends most of her spare time in *Accident and Emergency*, between abusive boyfriends…

"Hurry up, Sarah." Carvery grabs the back of my waistband, and I shriek, scaring myself, as he tilts me over the side. Ace takes hold of the scruff of my collar at the same time, angling my head down towards the water, and I find myself succumbing quickly to the forces of gravity. "Before your borrowed book swims away by itself."

I look down at the spiny scales and jaws of Death, the blood rushing in my ears and pounding in my temples, as I'm lowered gawkily below the railings.

"It's all right, Sarah," Carvery calls out, and gives an evil snigger. "You can see if you're any good at Croc-Whispering, while you're down there."

I gulp.

Keep still – nice crocky…

CHAPTER TWENTY-ONE: REFLEX OF THE JEJUNUM

"I can't quite reach!"

My arms strain downwards, even though I'm aware of the proximity of those crocodile jaws. Reptilian eyes flicker my way, in typical cold-blooded apathetic curiosity, from the others in the water.

I'm just not tall enough.

"Seriously?" Carvery asks from the deck of the ship above me, shifting his grip slightly on my ankle. "Stop being such a pussy. Where's your spunk, Sarah?"

"I'm going to throw up again, right on the back of your head this time," Ace grumbles. His hands around my other ankle definitely have that morning-after-booze clamminess about them, and pressing his admittedly intimidating washboard stomach so hard on the railings is evidently doing him no good either. "If that helps at all."

"I need something to help me reach and grab hold of it with!" The leather-bound diary hovers just out of my grasp, teetering on the knobbly spine of the nearest man-eating leviathan.

"Like what?" Carvery asks.

"Like a…" All I can think of at the moment are the array of Forensics instruments at University. "A… a reticulum – no, speculum… er…"

"God, Sarah – speak English!" Ace groans.

"Forceps?" suggests Carvery. "I think you'll find the others are a bit less on the *grabby* side, and more in the *openy-outy* scheme of things."

I don't want to know how he's so informed about those… But as I stretch my fingers in a completely futile effort, I do have a brainwave.

"The special clockwork hand!" I call up to them. "Pass it down to me!"

"Oh, no," Carvery grins. "Not that old trick."

"Well, have you got anything else?" I challenge. "Come on, it's important. The diary came with it. I don't think one of them has any significance without the other!"

Carvery hesitates, and then reaches into a pocket. The golden bejewelled clockwork hand emerges, and flashes in the early-morning sunlight.

"Aargh," he reacts. "Now I'm blind as well. Damn thing's glowing like a furnace!"

Rubbing his eyes on his sleeve first, he holds it out to me, and I extend one arm back up to my hip, to retrieve it.

He's right. It's dazzling. The cut gemstones set into the back and the knuckle joints seem to be lit up by the sun. I have to turn my head aside, as I use it to try and reach the diary.

"Watch it, Sarah," Ace warns. "I think you might have company coming your way."

I try to look around to identify the danger, and there is a splish-sploshing in the water. I see a brown scaly body roll, as another larger one crawls leisurely across it, making stepping-stones towards me, out of the others of its species.

Looks like somebody thinks I'm being served up for breakfast…

The fingertips of the metal hand just about graze the leather cover of the book.

"I need more time!" I call out, desperately. "Can't you guys distract it?"

"Could give it a warning shot," Carvery says grudgingly, and his free hand appears over the side of the ship again, holding the shotgun. "But I can't see fuck all right now, with that sun-strike I just got. You'll have to tell me where to aim, Ace."

"Depends on what you want to shoot," Ace remarks.

Oh, God… I try another lunge for the book. The crocodile it's sitting on the back of has drifted slightly beyond my reach. I pray for a small wave to wash it nearer to the ship again.

"I could just fire over his head, or in front of his snout," Carvery suggests. "Tell me when I'm about lined up…"

I wonder how many more stupid ways there are that I could be risking my life this morning, other than rescuing an elderly zombie's diary off the back of a crocodile, assisted by a hung-over breaker's yard mechanic, and a serial psychopath who owns a suspect paving and concreting business. Currently blinded and waving a gun around somewhere over my head, while suspending me inverted over the side of a ship…

And what's with this clockwork hand thing? Even in daylight, it's lit up like *Times Square*…

It gives me an idea, and I twist it a little, sending beams of reflected sunlight across the water. One or two idly-onlooking crocodiles flinch.

Ha!

Now, all I need is that next wave to bring the book closer…

"Up a bit…" I hear Ace say to Carvery. "Whoa, wait. Something's coming…"

What??!

"What do you mean, something?" I squeak. I scrabble to reach the diary. *Damn!* Still too far away!

"Another vessel," Ace reports.

A shadow seems to blot out the sun, but the diamonds on the clockwork hand stay bright, so that I have to squint in their glare, still hanging upside-down.

I crane my neck and try to recognise the shape, drifting silently upriver towards us. It's bigger than Crispin's paddle-steamer, and as the sun illuminates it from behind, I can see it has the blood-red sails of the ship in the painting.

"I still can't see," Carvery remarks. "Do you want me to shoot something, or what?"

I look around frantically. The larger croc makes another pass over one of its mates, in my direction. The scattered lights of the clockwork hand have no impact on it.

"Yes, please," I squeal.

"Ahhhh." I suddenly hear the impassive zombie monotone of Crispin's voice, as he appears on our side of the deck. "I see Mother's barge has deigned to join us."

There is a buzz of smaller boats also approaching, and the crocodiles start to disperse, disturbed by the new noises and vibrations through the water.

Not the big croc though. He's still focused on his *Sarah Bellum* kebab, hanging from the side of the paddle-steamer. The fangs bare, ready for snapping shut on the first pizza-delivery-girl-flavoured morsel…

"Crispin!" I call desperately. "Help!"

I feel his cold undead hand grasping me below the knee, and before I get any closer to either Death or the diary, I'm pulled abruptly back up the side of the ship.

"Nooo…" I moan, defeated.

Not even the empty clack of the crocodile's jaws closing on thin air below me is a relief. The three guys deposit me back on deck, and I collapse in a miserable heap.

"Did you get it?" Carvery asks, still rubbing his eyes and blinking.

"No," I cry, all the more distressed as Crispin, the only gentleman of the three, picks me up and dusts me down reassuringly. I try not to be distracted, and shove the sparkling family heirloom under his nose. "Crispin, we found the clockwork hand. But there was a book with it – and it's gone over the side, with the crocodiles, look…"

We all glance downwards.

The leather-bound diary still sits tauntingly on the fat crocodile, drifting now even further away from us on the current.

"We have to get it back!" I say, but I can hear my own uncertainty. "Can't we?"

Crispin takes the clockwork hand and turns it over and over, as bemused by it as I am.

My heart sinks. I thought he'd know what to do about it at once.

As we look across the water again, a small boat orbiting the bigger ship zips by – and a figure reaches out as it passes, snatching the diary from its resting-place on the crocodile.

"Chavs," Ace grunts, shading his eyes beside me. And then leans over the side, and promptly throws up again.

"Oh, *yesss*," Crispin says after a moment, his voice as leaden as the inside of a coffin. "We will most certainly get it back, Sarah *Bellummm*."

CHAPTER TWENTY-TWO: QUIM OF THE DAMNED

One of the small boats, piloted by a weatherbeaten zombie in a loincloth and red leather chaps – I don't ask why, just wonder what Ace Bumgang would look like in them – transports us to the giant barge, when it anchors alongside.

This is where it really does get intimidating, up close – the upper deck is the size of a football field, and I'm sure those sail masts are hundreds of feet high. The blood-red sails attached to them must measure at least an acre each.

The deck succumbs to red-tinted darkness, in their shade.

"Mother's weekend dinghy," Crispin announces, with a vague gesture around the miles and miles of mahogany-coloured timber. "She doesn't get about much these days, but when she does – one could say she 'pushes the boat out' so to speak."

A gigantic flight of stairs leads up to the doors of a pyramid-shaped construction in the centre, and flanked by leather-chapped zombies, we go inside.

The walls are lit by burning torches, which smell faintly of sandalwood and incense, and at the end of the passageway, in the very middle of the pyramid, is a full-height shrine.

In the centre, a very beautiful black onyx statue of a woman stands on a pedestal, in the headdress and typical adornments that Hollywood and history books would have us believe denotes ancient regal status. The decorations feature the usual collection of beetle and bird motifs, modified eye designs and snake heads.

One of the red-chapped zombies strides ahead of us, the leather-bound diary belonging to Mr. Dry Senior in his hands. When he gets to the pedestal, he kneels, and places it reverently on an altar at the foot of the pedestal.

"What is this, *Show and Tell with Mother* day?" Ace asks.

"No," Crispin says, shaking his head, asymmetrically. "I think she always just wanted to know what Father was writing about in that diary, all those years. Maybe hoping to uncover an illicit affair."

"Makes sense," Carvery remarks, nudging me unpleasantly.

I swear – I'm never keeping a diary again…

The zombie returns to stand in front of Crispin, and seems to be expecting something.

Reluctantly, Crispin produces the golden jewelled clockwork hand from inside his jacket, and relinquishes it. The zombie nods, and turns back to face the altar and pedestal.

"One never really knows what to say in these circumstances," Luke whispers in my ear.

"What do you mean?" I ask, of the Nigerian cab-driver.

"Well, when you're in a foreign country, being introduced to someone's parents, the protocols are usually completely different to what you're used to," he remarks. "I mean, are we expected to bow? Or kneel down and touch our foreheads to the ground? Or are we intended to arrive bearing gifts of *Asda* sparkling Chardonnay and copies of *Woman's Weekly?* I remember one young lady in the past whose parents didn't even acknowledge you until you'd delivered a full fish-and-chip supper."

The zombie in the red leather chaps, his back to us, does some minor adjustment to the clockwork hand, and holds it aloft in front of him, pointing it at the statue.

Another zombie swings a hammer at a gong in prompting, vibrating my eardrums just to the point of discomfort, and a brilliant, blinding light shines out of the gemstones on the mysterious ornamental hand, illuminating the statue as if under a disco-ball.

"Is my tie straight?" Crispin asks me, anxiously. I notice that Homer is fluffing the feathers on his ostrich boa self-consciously.

"Ooh, pretty," is all my housemate, Miss Air-Head, comes out with.

Gradually, the black onyx under the beams of light starts to change. Rainbows of colour appear, like in an oil slick on tarmac, and they move in the same way, shimmering over the surface.

"Reminds me," Ace mutters to Carvery. "I need about eight tons' more builder's sand at the breaker's yard."

"No problem," Carvery replies.

The moving rainbows start to split, and the statue moves, as if freed from a waxwork museum.

When the echoes of the gong finally die away, she opens her eyes, and casts an icy green gaze down onto our motley party.

She scans each of us in disdainful silence, as if judging individually. A flicker of fondness appears around her full lips as she espies Homer N. Dry, in his *Diana Ross* sequins.

"This is quite a gathering," she says at last, and accepting a nearby zombie's hand in assistance, she elegantly steps down from the pedestal, descending towards the altar. "Is it my birthday?"

CHAPTER TWENTY-THREE: PRUDE AND PREPUTIUM

The regal vision passes the altar with a cursory glance before approaching us, but I do notice the fleeting look of triumph in those emerald eyes, as she notes the leather-bound diary, waiting in pride of place.

I know what she's thinking.

What did that bastard write about me??

And possibly:

Now we'll find out if all of those sluts were just 'acquaintances'...

Maybe, given the current setting, those strange diagrams that the diary seems to be full of will tell her exactly what she wants to know…

I gaze around at the thousands of hieroglyphs, featuring on every wall and pillar. Under the circumstances, it might be too much to hope that the décor of the pyramid-shrine, aboard the megalith of a barge, is all just a bit of interior-designer *feng shui.*

"Everyone," Crispin begins, while she glides closer, attended by two of the red-leather-chapped zombies. "This is my – and Homer's – dear mother. The Lady Glandula de Bartholine."

"Pray, introduce us, Crispin," she purrs. Her catlike eyes miss nothing, but equally give nothing away, as she takes in our decidedly morning-after appearance. Only Homer has freshly scrubbed up for the occasion. "Don't stand on ceremony on the account of strangers."

Crispin clears his throat, nervously, and gestures along to the far end of the line with a gray-skinned hand.

"Mother, this is Mr. Carvery Slaughter…"

"A powerful one indeed," she muses. "But I would say, a little tainted."

"Ambitious in that direction, certainly," Crispin agrees.

"Understatement," I mutter, thinking of big holes in the ground, dug at the dead of night.

"And what is this?" Lady Glandula asks, her gaze travelling over my housemate, Whatserface. "A pet monkey?"

"Mr. Slaughter's *amour*, Mother," Crispin corrects, a hint of reproach in his tone.

"But it's all made of spare parts!" Lady Glandula scoffs. "A Frankenstein's monkey… and so corrupted in health, one would not know where to put it. Or where to put your what in it. Surely you do not expect me to…"

"*NO*, Mother," Crispin interrupts, raising both hands, in a placating fashion. "It had not even crossed my mind."

Expect her to what? My mind boggles. Not eat Miss Fuckwit's brains, surely? Besides – Lady Glandula doesn't look like your typical zombie. She looks in the peak of health.

Compared to the rest of us, particularly.

"And Mr. Ace Bumgang…" Crispin continues.

Lady Glandula stops a moment, taking in the yummy dark brown eyes, and washboard stomach. I can fully sympathise… even hung over, Ace Bumgang looks like any woman's dream sperm-donor.

"Hmmm," she says at last. "He needs a wash…"

She speaks sidelong to one of her zombie attendants, not taking her eyes off Ace in the meantime.

"Have my bath made ready," she orders. "Lots of rose-petals."

Noooo, my jealousy reflex yells. That was *MY* fantasy… well, one of them, anyway.

Just got to hope she doesn't have a jar of Nutella and a spoon as well…

"Your son, Homer," Crispin adds. "Whom I'm sure you recognise."

"*Hooome*," says Homer, lurching forward, with skinny gray arms outstretched.

"My dear lady, er, boy," the Lady Glandula greets him, permitting a genteel embrace. "I see my old wardrobe is still in vogue."

"Mr. Gaylord Lukan, formerly of Nigeria…"

"Indeed?" she says, and offers her hand. Luke's concerns about introduction protocol seem to evaporate, and relieved, he puts his business card into it.

"Twenty-four hour minicab services, your Ladyship," he beams. "Since 1971."

"Goodness," she says. "A workaholic. I was married to one of those – allegedly. While I was alive."

"And Miss *Bellummm…*" Crispin says, at last.

"Sarah," I amend, and find myself bobbing a curtsey.

"Sarah Bellum…" she ponders, and stops in front of me, her stare calculating, shrivelling any remaining scraps of my self-worth. "You are very scrawny."

"Nervous energy, Ma'am," I excuse myself. My kneecaps are twitching again.

"A fidget, in other words," she surmises. She leans in slightly, and sniffs my neck, exactly as Crispin did last night. "I see… This is the best you could manage, Crispin?"

"I had to order a lot of pizzas, Mother," Crispin says, again a little reproachfully.

"Your theories regarding the identification of virgins leave something to be desired, my son," she remarks. "Unlike your father – who was foolish enough to take a girl's word for it."

"A foolishness that runs in the family, Mother," Crispin nods gloomily. "Hence the perpetuation of the curse."

"I, for one, have no issue there, as I'm sure you can see for yourself," she replies, rather smugly surveying her surroundings. "I do not know why you Dry men even bother with these little mortal beauty contests. I see nothing I wish to trade here."

"Supposing I were not offering a trade," Crispin appeals. "But seeking your approval?"

She turns back sharply to look at him, and her expression is alert and – amused.

"With THAT?" she cries, waving towards me. Laughter bubbles out of her. "And your grandfather's old out-of-date hoodoo-voodoo, hocus-pocus theories? You would seek to cure yourself alone, rather than fulfil the family honour? My boy, you are as selfish as any man."

"The family honour will not be abandoned, Mother," Crispin sighs. "This is – a personal request."

She shakes her head, still chuckling.

"Your ulterior motives shine out of you like a beacon, Crispin." She strides away, calling back over her shoulder. "But make yourselves at home. I so rarely have entertainment. I look forward to the crocodile-feeding later."

She picks up the leather-bound diary as she passes, and disappears somewhere behind the pedestal. As does the zombie in possession of the special clockwork hand, I notice sadly.

We exchange looks, and everyone feels they can safely breathe once more.

"I think that went well," Crispin concludes, with a sigh of defeat.

"*Gooood…*" Homer agrees.

"That's nothing," Carvery remarks. "You should meet MY mother."

"At least she didn't demand fish-and-chips," Luke remarks. "Or a *Woman's Weekly.*"

"What does she mean, needs a wash?" Ace grumbles, looking down at himself. "This is a good day after alcohol, for me…"

"She called me a Frankfurter Minky!" my housemate Fuckwit suddenly explodes, making us all jump.

As for me, I have far too many questions lined up, after that little exchange between Crispin Dry and his mother.

But at the forefront of my mind, is the phrase *'crocodile-feeding'…*

CHAPTER TWENTY-FOUR: THE GRANULATE

"What do we do now?" Luke wants to know. "Are we going to get the treasure back?"

"And the diary?" I add, with more empathy in my voice for poor Mr. Dry Senior than I was expecting. I try not to make eye contact with Carvery Slaughter. "She can't just go around stealing other people's diaries for God knows what diabolical reason…"

Crispin Dry nods, gloomily, while his brother Homer wanders off to dance around a hieroglyph-covered pillar – humming to himself, shedding red sequins and the occasional ostrich-feather.

"I think you may be right, Sarah *Bellummm*," Crispin's zombie monotone agrees. "That clockwork hand allegedly contains other powers, which if unlocked could permanently alter the fabric of the Universe itself. My father was obsessed with trying to analyse the hand's potential, as he believed it could cure the curse of the zombies… but in the wrong… hands, he knew that its potential as a weapon would be exploited."

Homer does a pirouette, and attempts the splits, up against the pillar. It's like watching an X-rated deleted scene from Michael Jackson's *Thriller.*

"So we need a plan," Luke prompts.

"Don't look now, Ace," Carvery remarks. "But I think your bath is ready."

Two zombies – in the token loincloths and red leather chaps – are approaching from the far side of the huge pyramid shrine, both bearing folded towels, and scattering rose-petals.

"Really?" Ace sighs. "That nymphomaniac zombie queen was serious?"

"That's the Dry dude's mother you're talking about!" Luke says, giving him a thump on the arm. "But as I recall – she did mention you needed a wash…"

"Yeah – you've got to take one for the team," Carvery tells him. "Here's your chance to distract her."

"Catch her off-guard," Luke nods in approval. "I like it."

"It is an idea…" Crispin ponders. "All we need to do is recover the golden hand and the diary while she is – preoccupied."

"I have a few rules I like to live by," Ace announces. "Never do a bro's *ho's*, *mo's*, or *pro's*. Especially if they're over four thousand years old. No granny fanny. Or tranny fanny. No offence, Homey."

"*Ouuuuch…*" Homer tries to hang upside-down from the pillar, and collapses head-first, in a heap.

"Come on, fella," Carvery urges. "She's not that dusty. And in the bath, you'll barely notice the squeak. Look at it this way – if you had to choose between her and Sarah, who would you do – if your life depended on it?"

My mouth drops open. *The nerve!* But a small part of my ego wants to know the answer…

Ace shrugs.

"Good point," he concedes. "How long do you guys think you'll need?"

NOT the answer I was hoping for… my shattered ego crawls back under its rock.

The zombies stop in front of us, and indicate for him to join them.

"She may retain the diary close at hand," Crispin warns. "Keep your eyes peeled."

"Crispin, the only thing my eyes are going to stay peeled for, is keeping a look out for if she tries to sneak up on me with any Stone Age whips and dildo shit," Ace tells him. "My job is the distracting. Yours is the snooping around. All right – let's get this horny bitch-demon seen to."

And he heads off with the two zombie attendants, shoving one of them aside, as it tries to shower him with rose-petals.

My ego, peering out from under its rock of shame, sees a narrow margin of opportunity.

"I could follow," I suggest. "And see if I can pick up any clues there, while the rest of you search the surrounding rooms."

"Pervert," Carvery mutters.

I'm as mysterious as mud to him, obviously.

"Excellent idea," Crispin concurs. "We will meet back outside on the main deck of the barge in an hour, should we all become separated."

An hour? The thought burns into my brain, as I scurry after Ace Bumgang and his zombie escorts. What on Earth will he find to distract the Lady Glandula de Bartholine with, for an hour?

The zombies lead Ace down some more steps, by appearances heading deeper into the bowels of the humungous ship, and along a wide pillared hall. Hundreds of candles illuminate it – on every available surface, and hanging from chandeliers in the ceiling.

I try to stay in the shadow of the pillars as I follow, attempting to keep within earshot. But no conversation occurs between Ace and the zombies, *en route*.

At the end of the great hall is a mysterious room divided only from the rest by gauzy silk drapes, and beyond the drapes is the biggest sunken marble bath-tub I've ever seen.

The water ripples invitingly over the edges, featuring more of those red rose-petals. And the scent of roses, citrus and vanilla is heavy in the moist air, rather like having Turkish Delight forced up your nasal cavity until you start to go unconscious…

The zombies hold aside the silk drapes for Ace to pass through, and emboldened by the patches of shade in the folds of the translucent fabric, I creep closer.

The Lady Glandula appears from the far side, swathed only in a strip of similar silk voile, sari-style, also attended by two zombies.

One of whom has in his possession the leather-bound diary – and the other, the clockwork hand.

So it looks as though she doesn't plan to let either out of her sight.

"How good of you to join me, Ace Bumgang," she greets him, in her catlike purr. "Can I offer you a refreshment?"

She gestures towards the bar, flanking the side of the room, where thousands of crystal decanters are displayed, containing a multitude of differently-coloured liquids.

"I'm good, thanks," says Ace. "I already puked a rainbow this morning."

"So I see," she smiles. "I find alcohol such a wonderful disinhibitor of preliminary niceties, don't you?"

And she drops the scrap of silk sari – another of Angelina Jolie's *Lara Croft* impersonators, I note, and scold myself for having enacted such a contrived scene already – and she steps slowly down into the tub. Displaced water gently rolls over the sides and down the shallow lip, like a decadently slow-motion Victoria Falls.

"Mrs. Bartholine, are you trying to seduce me?" Ace asks.

"Is that what you want me to do, Ace Bumgang?" she croons. "Seduce you? I may simply see a man who needs a wash. Join me."

"All right," he grunts. "But only because I know you older birds can't reach your own backs to scrub them…"

And then I nearly scream out loud.

Because a long tentacle whips out of the tub, showering the silk curtain between us with water droplets – and snatches Ace Bumgang off his feet, dragging him bodily into the sunken bath with the zombie monster queen.

"You men always give in so easily," she smiles, as the tip of the tentacle curls lovingly around Ace's ear to tickle it.

I notice in perverse horror and revulsion that the alien appendage is covered in rose-petal-shaped, lip-like suckers, which make kissing noises wherever they touch his wet skin. Both of her arms rest along the edge of the tub at her sides, not touching him at all.

"I'm not going to ask what part of you this is attached to," Ace replies, bracing himself against the marble in turn, as the tentacle tugs him closer. "But you know they do plastic surgery for this sort of thing, if you're interested. Or Carvery Slaughter will do it for free, after you've had a few pints."

I thought they were making that kind of surgery on women illegal in most of the world now? I struggle to keep my thoughts on track. Concentrate! *Focus on the clockwork hand and the diary, Sarah!*

The attendant zombies stand like sentinels at the four corners of the room, motionless, going nowhere.

"Just relax and enjoy yourself, Mr. Bumgang," Lady Glandula continues, in a sing-song tone. The tentacle is making short work of Ace's clothing. I hope some of those flying buttons land close enough to make it into my Ace Bumgang souvenir box. "Technically, I am a widow now – if that helps."

"Yes, and your kids are happily playing upstairs too," Ace agrees, trying to detach a sucker from his left nipple. "I think I'll take that drink now, if you're still offering."

Abruptly, she snaps her fingers at one of the attendant zombies who led us down here, and it turns away to the bar to comply.

I crawl to his former position and hide in a fold of the drapes, hoping for a clearer view… er, of the diary and the golden clockwork hand, of course…

CHAPTER TWENTY-FIVE: PUMP FRICTION

Neither of the zombies in charge of the stolen booty move. They just stand, stock-still, with the golden clockwork hand and the leather-bound diary on their respective red velvet cushions.

The Lady Glandula's own hands, in contrast, seem keen to get in on the undressing-Ace-Bumgang action, as his oil-stained overalls become evidently reluctant to shift below his waist in the bathwater.

"You are a tease, Mr. Bumgang!" she gasps, wrenching ineffectually at his belt.

Perhaps it has shrunk in the wet. My hopes of Ace deliberately saving himself, for a deadly secret crush he's concealing from everyone, soar to my dizzy heights of fantasy. Of course, if he can keep a secret like being *The Stig* on *Top Gear*, he'd definitely be able to disguise where his true love lies…

"And you're cheating," he remarks in response, uncurling the wandering alien tentacle from around his neck. "You have an extra limb sprouting from your… from underwater. Supposing I put this in my mouth and bite it, what happens?"

"Ooohh," she muses, glowing green zombie eyes narrowing, fang-like teeth baring in a smile. "Why don't you try it and see?"

I notice that the zombie guard, relegated to bartender, has apparently finished formulating whatever cocktails are order of the day for bath-side service, as he arranges crystal chalice-style glasses on a silver tray.

Yes… imminent distraction looming… now all I have to do is prioritise my targets…

I find myself wondering, as the potential outcomes for a pro-active strike unroll in my mind, what would Crispin Dry do in this situation? Or Angelina Jolie as *Lara Croft?* Or Gordon

Ramsay… er, maybe not, in that case. Too many theoretical cooks spoil the plot, and all that…

Do I go for the diary, or for the clockwork hand first? An image of Carvery Slaughter crosses my mind, reading my own diary and sniggering, while I was at work – on God knows how many occasions. The thought fuels my indignation…

Stay focused, Sarah!

I try to estimate the pace of the bartender zombie as he approaches the marble bath-tub, while attempting to ignore the distracting sounds of sloshing bathwater, and the slurping of those alien tentacle suction cups, all over the body of Ace Bumgang…

"You will not be disappointed, Mr. Bumgang," Lady Glandula's voice says, oozing over him like treacle. "I have exhausted many armies in my time."

"It's not my armies that are complaining," Ace quips, still keeping himself braced at arm's length, both hands on the marble side of the tub, against the hungry pull of the tentacle trying to draw him in closer.

The zombie attendant places the tray on the edge of the bath, and Lady Glandula de Bartholine, momentarily preoccupied zombie queen, reaches out towards it.

Strike, Sarah, while the iron is hot!

I dive through the silk gauze drapes towards the nearest static zombie guard, and make a frantic, one-chance-only grab at the display cushion in his arms…

A heavy silken tassel at the bottom of the curtain snags on the end of my nose in the headlong plunge, and blinded by fancy knot-work and cord, I force my hands to close anyway, on the estimated location of my target…

A great ripping noise of tortured fabric follows the continuation of my dive onto the fantastically embellished rug – and I roll, shaking my head in an attempt to dislodge the detached tassel, now quite intimate with my right nostril.

In my hands, I have it – I can't quite believe it, but I have it…

I leap upright, helplessly spitting out bits of tassel.

"Nobody move!" I shriek, several octaves higher than normal, due to the nasal blockage, and the effects of a rotational wedgie in the pyjama-bottom department. I brandish the golden clockwork hand between my own, as if it's a genuine *Dirty Harry* .44 Magnum. "Any of you zombie pigs move, and I will eradicate every tentacle-sucking last one of you!"

CHAPTER TWENTY-SIX: DIRTY HARRIDAN

I notice the very briefest flicker of alarm in the zombie queen's iridescent green eyes, before she covers it with a sneer.

But I realise the essential part of a pro-active strike, is to maintain control of the situation…

"I know what you're thinking, Pump," I gulp hurriedly, saying anything that comes into my head. I wave the clockwork bejewelled hand in front of me, in what I hope is a threatening fashion. "You're thinking, does she have a trick shot or just a dive? And do you know what? I can't even remember my name in all this excitement… But considering this is a clockwork Swiss-movement, the most powerful hand in the world, and could blow you clean off…"

Ace Bumgang looks dubious, but I jabber on regardless.

"…You have to ask your selfish quisling: Do I feel lumpy?"

God, this stupid tassel wedged up my nose isn't helping my enunciation either. Shreds of silk drapery and twisted retainer cords from my botched 'surprise entrance' dangle randomly from the ceiling.

"Well?!" I demand, rather too loudly. Hoping to attract the others, if they're within earshot. "Do you? Pump?"

"Sarah, I was just going to dose her with Rohypnol, but you carry on if you think it's helping," Ace remarks, his eyebrows slightly quizzical.

"Perhaps you would like to join us in the tub, Miss Bellum?" Lady Glandula says, slyly. The weird zombie tentacle appendage curls possessively around Ace's neck once more, and tightens perceptibly. "No need to be shy…"

"Let him go," I order, nervously.

Ace doesn't look too bothered yet, fishing in his overall pockets for something.

"…When I know you'd rather be in here, with him?" The zombie queen gives a knowing smile, resting her elbows on the edge of the marble bath-tub. "Why not just indulge your final fantasy – instead of trying to save the world, Sarah?"

I knew it – I knew she'd give something away, without realising…

I act as if taking aim.

"I am a virgin, and I am not afraid to use this!" I shout.

"Really?" Ace warns, still rummaging in his pockets. "You don't know where it's been."

"And it's clockwork." A familiar voice joins us, attached to the familiar body, stepping through the drapes on the far side. "You'll have to keep stopping to wind it up. But I kind of want to see you do that with it anyway."

I've never been so glad to see Carvery Slaughter. Well – edit that. I've NEVER been glad to see Carvery Slaughter. But right at this minute I'm so relieved, I could pee through a dozen mattresses.

"Be a whole lot better than reading your diary, for a start," he continues. He points to me with the butt of the shotgun, and scratches the side of his nose. "Er – you got a little something right here…"

"Fuck it," I say, bravely, and spit out a bit of tassel trying to stick in the corner of my mouth. "You like diaries so much, grab that one belonging to Mr. Dry Senior over there."

"Weirdo," Carvery mutters, but goes ahead and takes it from the other immobile zombie guard.

I don't understand why the guards are not resisting.

Ace finds what he's looking for, and grabs the two drinks off the tray, from the edge of the tub. Something drops from his hand into one of them, and he swirls it quickly.

"Where were we?" he says, nudging the Lady Glandula de Bartholine. "Bottoms up."

"I like my men keen," she purrs, and accepts the crystal chalice.

It's then that the four zombie guards seem to wake up, and become noticeably more menacing. They close in on the sunken bath.

And I realise.

They're here to protect HER – not her property…

"Ace, get out of the tub," Carvery says quietly, reaching into his own pocket.

"In good time, buddy." Ace slowly unwinds the tentacle from around his own neck, as she takes a first sip of her drink, now completely distracted.

The zombies step closer, into the puddles overflowing the sides of the tub, and I look down at the rivulets of rose-petal-peppered water approaching my own feet.

"Back up, Sarah," Carvery warns me.

I see his hand emerging from his pocket – holding the Taser.

Oh, shit…

And then, right in front of me – the gemstones in the clockwork hand start to glow.

"Ace!" I squeak in fright.

"What, you think Carver's never zapped me before?" Ace grumbles, tying a knot in the tentacle, which seems to divert Lady Glandula further in a playful way, for a moment. "It's not only *your* diary he likes to read in his spare time, you know."

"That's not what I'm afraid of right now!" I hiss.

The clockwork hand is acting as if it has a mind of its own. The two middle fingers curl in towards the palm, and the index and pinky extend out straight. The smallest stones along the knuckle joints of the two extended fingers ignite in series, like little blue runway lights.

"Any time you're ready, Ace," Carvery prompts.

"Just getting comfortable, dude."

Ace leans back nonchalantly – and then grabs hold of one of the trailing curtain-cords from the ceiling. Like a gymnast, he hauls himself up out of the water, flipping upside-down, as he swings out of the tub.

Carvery fires the Taser – dead square into the zombie queen's back.

Before she even screams, the clockwork hand has mimicked the Taser current, sending a blue lightning bolt into the same target. But it's doing something strange – the current seems to be moving in reverse, as if the clockwork hand is absorbing power from her – not discharging it…

The Lady Glandula's skin darkens, the tentacle retracts, and that oil-slick on tarmac appearance emerges again. The zombie guards, in contact with the bathwater, do a grotesque double-speed *Thriller* dance, as the electricity courses through them, sending every undead muscle into spasm.

But it doesn't turn them also back into that onyx stone, unlike the queen herself. Once she is cold, dark and solid again, the gemstones dim, and the strange influx of power surging towards me fades, and ceases.

It must be the clockwork hand, I wonder. *Can it give her life, but also reverse it?*

Ace somersaults over the edge of the tub, as Carvery disconnects his own current. The zombie guards look momentarily disoriented.

"Let's bust a move," Ace announces. "Before these guys want to play."

"Come on, Sarah," Carvery nods. "Chop-chop."

Not the best words to hear, coming from him – but I pull myself together, and make to follow.

Before I've gone more than a few steps, Ace Bumgang stops me. He reaches out towards my face – and tugs the tassel abruptly out of my right nostril.

"Ow," I react, as he tosses it over his shoulder into the tub.

"You're welcome," he says, and heads off after Carvery. "Don't dither, Sarah."

I look longingly back at the tassel floating in the tub, with the frozen black onyx zombie queen. But the zombie attendants are starting to recover, and I daren't risk hanging around.

Damn – the one time Ace touches something that was at least temporarily in contact with my own body… and I don't get to keep it for my Ace Bumgang souvenir box!

At least I have the magical clockwork hand… as I hurry after the other two, I start to wonder about these other powers it has, that are so important…

CHAPTER TWENTY-SEVEN: PYGANGLION

"Where are the others?" Ace asks, as we reach the bottom of the steps, heading back up into the giant pyramid shrine aboard the barge.

Carvery shrugs.

"Never touched 'em," he grins.

Uh-oh. I wonder if that means the crocodiles have had an early breakfast…

A figure appears at the top of the stairs, silhouetted against the flickering torchlight. The outline of a regal headdress stops my heart dead in its tracks. My kneecaps file against my body for divorce.

"How the Hell did she do that?" Ace gulps. "Next time, I'm bringing ketamine as well…"

The figure takes two paces towards us, and raises an arm imperiously, to point in our direction. I clutch the mechanical clockwork hand to my chest – but it is dormant, no sign of helpful magical activity coming to our rescue from within it at all…

"*Gooood,*" the distant shape groans.

Then trips over its skirts, and falls flat on its face. A very impressive stair-tumble follows, shedding bangles, headdress, pendants, and unravelled silk.

"Homer!" we all shout, as the now semi-naked gray zombie arrives at our feet.

"Ouuuuuch…"

"Well, we know what he's been up to," Carvery remarks, as we help the bedraggled, undead transvestite Dry brother to his feet. "Found his mother's closet again, by the look of it."

"Do you think we could use this?" Ace suggests, picking up a tail-end of embellished white sari, or toga, or whatever it is.

"Seeing as Homer likes to dress up as his mother already. Could be our ticket out of here."

"*Home!*" cries Homer, and we have to stop him, as he spots the distant bath-tub.

"Risky," Carvery replies, shaking his head. "The guy can't stay upright and facing in one direction all at the same time. But I reckon Sarah could do it."

If my mouth could drop open any further, I'd be obliged to fit it with a manhole cover.

"Cool." Ace holds out the toga and headdress, towards me. "Get your pyjamas off."

Again – *not* the way this fantasy about Ace Bumgang was meant to happen!

"No!" I cry, more in frustration with the way my imaginary love-life seems to be getting bulldozed at the moment, than in response to the request.

Which, under other circumstances, I'd have no problem with at all…

"Come on, Sarah." Carvery waves the shotgun in my general direction, gesturing up and down. "It's not like we haven't seen it all before. Like, when you're asleep. Or sending Ace pictures of it, playing *Draw My Thing* online."

Does this guy stop at nothing??!

"They were good drawings," Ace nods in agreement. "All I had to do was colour them in."

"For the last time, it was a picture of a taco!" I nearly scream at him. "Didn't the clue *'you eat this'* give you any ideas?"

"Yeah," he says. "But not food-related ones. And I guessed the letters C and T, remember?"

"Wasting time, Sarah," Carvery reminds me. "Time in which we might all get eaten, by zombies and crocodiles and stuff."

He's right. The zombies at the far end of the great hall by the marble bath-tub are trying to organise themselves, bumping into one another and attempting to haul the black onyx body of their zombie queen, Lady Glandula, out of the water. They're like honey-bees, prioritising their queen first – luckily for us…

"Okay," I relent at last. "But you guys have to turn around. No peeking."

"NOW you don't want us to look?" Carvery chuckles, as he and Ace, smirking, turn their backs. At least now, they can keep an eye out for danger.

Oh, God, how does this sari-toga thing work? Maybe I could just wrap it around over the pyjamas… but Homer joins in once he sees what I'm doing, flinging the fabric expertly around me, over a shoulder and under and through, pleated here and tucked in there – and in the process, my borrowed pyjamas from Crispin Dry drop discreetly onto the floor.

Phew. No more work for the lawyers of Angelina Jolie and *Lara Croft: Tomb Raider* at the Mutual Film Company today, then…

And now the bangles and headdress… *strange*. The bangles have the same sort of surface engravings and gemstones in as the golden clockwork hand. Maybe it was procured to co-ordinate with the queen's wardrobe, when it was being made in Switzerland?

"You done?" says Carvery Slaughter, and I realise he's been peeking all along. "Let's go. Try to act classy. That means – not like a pizza-delivery girl. Or an alcoholic, sexually-frustrated, closet necrophiliac."

"And Lady Glandula isn't one, I presume?" I retort.

"Good point," Ace agrees. "Just march right up there and ask if anyone wants to see your *Thing*."

"In a classy accent," adds Carvery.

"Just you wait, Carvery Slaughter," I scoff at both of them. "And you, Ace. When we get back – just you wait…"

I turn around, head held high – and with Homer attending carefully to the longer bits of my gown, which would have made Pippa Middleton professionally envious – I start to ascend the grand stairs, back up into the pyramid.

"You know she rolls around naked in the cheese before they put it on your pizza?" I hear Carvery telling Ace, behind me.

…And if I ever find out who invented the idea of keeping a 'secret' diary, I am going to travel back in time and give them a big piece of my mind…

CHAPTER TWENTY-EIGHT: UNDEATH ON THE NILE

The interior of the giant wooden pyramid is quiet, with just the empty pedestal and altar in the centre, and for a moment I take a deep thankful breath.

"I guess we're safe…" I announce, before spotting a movement from a far darkened corner.

Crispin Dry lurches almost into view, and in one terrible split second, I think he's injured.

"Crispin!" I cry out.

He staggers out of the shadows – and then I see what's hindering him. In his arms, is the unmistakeable – if unnameable – body of my housemate, Miss Thingy.

"That's why you should never trust a brain-muncher," Carvery sighs, and is about to level the shotgun at Crispin – when Homer squeaks indignantly, pushing the gun-barrels aside.

Crispin advances on the altar, and we hurry over, as he places her body carefully on its surface.

"What happened, Crispin?" I ask.

"She reached into an urn, and was bitten by one of Mother's pet vipers." Crispin turns over Whatsername's left arm, displaying two ugly blackened circular weals on the inside of her wrist. He looks up at me in despair, and his expression changes as he takes in my new turn-out. "Miss *Bellummm*… you look… you are…"

"Had to change, I know," I explain, blushing fiercely.

Dressing up in his mother's clothing probably not the best thing to do, on an almost-first-date…

"You look… most presentable…" he admits wretchedly, at last. Dragging his gaze back to the body of my housemate, he heaves a dejected sigh. Those broad shoulders in the black wool suit slump, at a loss. "I fear she needs more than an electric shock this time, Mr. Slaughter."

Carvery shrugs.

"I've seen worse," he grunts. "Usually they're fine by the time I get back from work. Waiting for me with their gimp masks, crotchless aprons and feather dusters… it's all just a bit of drama for the attention…"

"I reckon she could actually be dead," Ace remarks. He lifts up Miss Dumb-Ass's other arm, and lets it fall back onto the altar, with a loud *Bonnnk.*

"So are most folk around here," Carvery points out. "No stopping them, though."

"She can be saved," Crispin nods, earnestly. "But we do not have all of the required equipment here. We will have to head for the Six a.m. Lounge."

He pulls a lever on the side of the altar. With a grinding sound, it starts to lower into the floor.

"She will be safe here," he continues. "It was Mother's regeneration casket – while she was alive. Once we have the necessary items to activate it, she will be as good as new."

Am I imagining things – or does Carvery look none too pleased with that idea?

A seamless panel closes over Twat-Face, as she sinks fully below the deck. I wonder if there are air-holes down there, in case she spontaneously recovers. Someone has to pay their share of the rent…

"Who are we missing?" Crispin asks. "Has anyone seen Mr. Lukan?"

"Right here, Mr. Dry!" Luke's voice calls out. He's behind us, in the entranceway to the pyramid. "I think you might all want to come and see this!"

Outside, on the gigantic upper deck of the barge, a strange steady breeze is blowing. And the surface of the river is moving.

Not with crocodiles – but in an oddly geophysical, concentric circular motion.

"I think it's a whirlpool," Luke reports.

We look over the side. Crispin's paddle-steamer, moored on the opposite bank, bobs on its tethers at the edge of the watery disturbance.

"It is not a natural occurrence," says Crispin, grimly.

The rotating phenomenon dips in the centre – and blinks, revealing a huge, reptilian yellow Eye.

"Sarah!" The butt of the shotgun clips the back of my head. Carvery is grimacing, rattling a finger in one ear. "Screaming again, Jeez… control yourself. How many sets of underwear do you get through in a day?"

The Eye starts to rise out of the vortex. Scales… and more of those weird alien tentacles around it too…

"What is it?" I whisper.

"Not what," Crispin murmurs. "More of a who."

Taller than the masts on the giant barge, it towers over the river. The snakelike head curves downward, and swings around, surveying the surroundings. River weed trails from it, and crustaceans tumble from its sides.

"What does it want?" Ace Bumgang asks. "Is this the part where we hand over a convenient virgin sacrifice?"

"Ssshhhh!" I hiss. "This isn't *Fifty New Ways With Virgins* day!"

"Sarah, if you can name fifty new ways with a virgin, and still be a virgin after number one, you're either doing it wrong – or an incredible liar," Carvery remarks.

"They're usually doing it wrong on purpose," Ace tells him. "Because they reckon it doesn't count."

"What?" Carvery scowls. "So you can't change lanes without indicating?"

"It is Atum," Crispin says, sombrely. "It means – there is unfinished business…"

An echoing, bubbling sound comes from deep within the massive serpent's body. Dwarfed alongside, the sides of the barge vibrate, making the timbers creak.

"What kind of business?" Luke asks. He has produced his iPhone, and is trying to take a picture of himself, with the forbidding leviathan towering in the background.

"The business of the fabric of the Universe." Crispin glances meaningfully at the golden clockwork hand, tucked into the belt part of my gown. "If he is disturbed from his waters – it means the world is not yet finished."

"What do we do?" I ask cautiously.

"We try not to get in his way," Crispin confirms.

"Abandon ship?" Luke suggests.

"Yes," Crispin nods. "But in an orderly fashion. Walk, do not run, to the nearest exit."

It feels strange without Miss Fuckwit, as we set off inland away from the monstrous barge, and the even bigger sea-monster.

Could she *really* have been bitten by a viper? I mean, it did look that way, but I can't say I've ever seen an actual snake-bite before – but what if Crispin's not being completely honest?

Could it have been a *zombie*-bite?

Or even – I risk a glance at Carvery Slaughter – a Taser-burn? He definitely didn't look too happy at the thought of her being revived *'as good as new'*…

The serpent-thing, Atum or whatever it is called, is preoccupied with the land around the pyramids, behaving as though something is mislaid – as it scans every surface, nook and cranny, with its huge yellow Eye, on the top of the apparently endless prehensile neck.

"The Six a.m. Lounge will give us a chance to review our situation," Crispin announces, leading the way, in his rolling zombie gait, along another avenue of palm trees. "But the route from here is not the most straightforward…"

"Not more tunnels…" I groan, wearily.

"Not at all." Crispin pauses, and surveys the silent sandstone side-streets. "We merely need to find the travelling carpet-salesman."

"Oh, is that it?" I say. My voice sounds oddly high. *Is this what they call hysteria?*

"Almost," Crispin continues. He seems to sense my unsteadiness, and takes my arm reassuringly, with his cold zombie one. "He also enjoys a good barter, and drives a hard bargain."

Why do I get the feeling that the word 'virgin' is going to be brought up again imminently?

We turn a corner into a pillared square, perhaps an empty market-place.

"This place is dead," Ace remarks. "No offence."

A large sandstone block pitches abruptly into the ground from high above, right in front of us. It's big enough to demonstrate that a direct hit would have made our journey to the Six a.m. Lounge completely unnecessary.

We all look up, and spot the disappointed gray zombie face at the top of a pillar briefly, before it abruptly withdraws.

Suddenly, it seems that every shadow in the square is occupied by other shadows…

"None taken, Mr. Bumgang," Crispin replies. "I think your estimation of the populace here is entirely accurate."

CHAPTER TWENTY-NINE: OCTOPULPY

"Seven of us – a few dozen of them…" Luke muses.

There is an expectant pause. Why is there a certain lack of humorous *Pimm's* reference to follow that remark?

And then it dawns on me…

"Six of us," Carvery corrects him.

"Oh yeah." Luke sighs. "Forgot about your girlfriend. Sorry, man."

Of course. Miss Knob-End, the usual air-headed wit on this occasion, is in a wooden box under the deck of Lady Glandula's gigantic barge. Awaiting any regeneration privileges that might come her way. Or *rigor mortis*. Whichever arrives first.

"No worries," Carvery shrugs. "She acts up like it all the time."

We remain at the apex of the square, or market-place, unwilling to chance another masonry assault from above. The awaiting zombies shift restlessly in the shadows.

"Are these more relatives of yours, Crispin?" Ace Bumgang asks.

"Not mine." Crispin shakes his head, and then glances a little sheepishly over at our Nigerian cab-driver, Luke. "But ancestors of one of our party, most definitely. The original engineers of the pyramids, you could say…"

"You mean slaves?" I gasp. Both Carvery and Ace thump me, on either arm. "Ow…"

"I could try and talk to them," Luke suggests.

Crispin looks even more uncomfortable.

"I think you'll find the, er… *introduction protocols* are a little different to what you may have experienced, Mr. Lukan," he says. "Kneeling down and touching your forehead to the ground might be considered inadvisable, for example – unless you want it cemented there permanently."

"Obvious, in the building trade," Carvery agrees. "Any opportunity for the competition to make off with your tools, when you're not looking."

"Well, what would YOU recommend we do?" I ask him, irritably. "Seeing as you're the expert on the – *stone slab* side of things."

He gives me an assessing glance.

"You're the one dressed as their psychotic zombie queen leader," he points out. "Why don't YOU come up with something?"

I look down at the glittering clockwork hand, tucked safely into the belt of my gown. It merely looks as decorative as the star on a Christmas tree right now. And about as lethal.

"Maybe there's something helpful in that book," I shoot back, indicating Mr. Dry Senior's leather-bound diary, tucked into Carvery's own waistband. "Or would it take you too long to colour all the pictures in first?"

"I've already checked," he says. "No tits in it."

"Or tacos," Ace smirks.

"Friends," Crispin's powerful zombie monotone interrupts, before I can make another riposte. "We are not getting anywhere by arguing amongst ourselves. I suggest we send in a distraction."

As one, we all exchange looks, and turn to look at Homer N. Dry – currently half-disrobed transvestite zombie. Only the ostrich-feather boa remains, from his dressing-up sessions this morning.

"Homer," Crispin announces, solemnly. "I am giving you permission to enact that little fantasy of yours, which Father always prohibited at dinner-parties."

"*Home?*" Homer asks, uncertainly. A look of perverse hope flickers fleetingly across his disturbing gray face.

"Yes." Crispin takes a deep, bracing breath, his own lungs creaking and whistling as he does so. "The one about the ladies of the *Villa Negra* – and the French Foreign Legion…"

Comprehension sinks in. And a broad, manic, evil grin spreads across Homer's face.

The very same chilling grin I first saw of his, on the CCTV footage in Crispin's hi-tech security bunker, last night…

"*Goooood*," Homer approves, rubbing his ragged hands together, and cracking his knuckles.

I peek out tentatively, around a pillar.

"Go on, Sarah." Carvery urges, and I feel the butt of the shotgun nudge me in the spine. "Homer needs an M.C, and you drew the short finger-bone. Don't leave the creepy little zombie dude hanging."

The half-hidden Nigerian slave zombies are still loitering menacingly in the shadows. Homer, preening his leftover ostrich-feathers, is waiting patiently just at my shoulder.

"God, all right!" I grumble, and clear my throat.

I take one cautious pace out into the open, worrying that Carvery appears to have the gun trained on my own head – rather than at any potential attackers.

"I expect you're all wondering why I called this meeting!" I improvise loudly, in my best cut-glass Lady Glandula de Bartholine impression. "Well, er… you've all been very loyal, and very hardworking. Putting up all these huge erections that I demand of you, and stuff. I can't imagine what it must have been like lifting all of this stone, day after day. So, um… I have a little reward for you. A bit of entertainment."

I step aside, sweeping an arm out, in a gesture of introduction.

"Gentlemen, I give you… uh…" My brain frazzles. *Just say anything, Sarah!* "All the way from… a galaxy far, far away… the exotic fjords of… somewhere-or-other… Princess… Homer Rottick!"

"Nice," Carvery mutters.

Homer swirls past me into the empty market square, trailing feather boa, like a rhythmic gymnast. I hear the collective intake of zombie breath, as he pirouettes into the centre of the pavement.

Any minute now, I'm thinking. Any minute now – we're all going to be eaten alive…

"Oooh, I hope they don't notice that…" Luke remarks, right by my ear, sounding equally concerned. "He has a big wang for a dead white fella."

"Must be a family thing," I agree, instantly more worried, as Homer performs a cartwheel.

"That doesn't sound *like a virgin* at all, Sarah," Carvery points out, nastily.

"What?" I snap, wondering why I'm now thinking about Madonna, and elevators. "Why are you hanging around gawking? I thought you had a part in this plan too?"

"Yeah, yeah," Carvery grins. "C'mon, Ace, let's go shift some stuff."

The two of them head off, on their own determined mission.

Crispin has taken out a small pair of opera-glasses, and is scanning the shadows. Some of the strange zombies are starting to move forward slowly into the open, attracted by the bizarre spectacle of burlesque gyrations, performed by Homer N. Dry.

"Any sign of the carpet-salesman?" I ask Crispin, hopefully.

"Not yet," Crispin admits. "I think I will need a better vantage-point. The two of you stay here, and keep an eye on my poor brother. Well – having the time of his life for now, at least…"

While Crispin hurries away also, Luke and I watch the dancing Dry brother, with our own mixture of deep concern and horrified fascination.

I feel like exactly like Rachel did, on *Friends*…

"Oh, God – I can't not look at it…" I quote. My fingers, covering my face, are fighting each other to hide in my mouth.

"They are getting very close," Luke confirms. Homer tickles the end of a zombie's nose with a long feather. "They are going to notice quite soon that he has the wrong qualifications for this sort of lady-dancing."

"Perhaps they've noticed already?" I whisper. "And they aren't bothered?"

On the far side of the square, in the shade of another pillar, I spot Carvery and Ace – levering up a large paving-slab. My heart thumps in sympathy. I crane my neck to try and spot Crispin.

Where on Earth has he got to…??

"Can you see Crispin at all?" I ask Luke.

"Maybe he's scarpered," Luke says grimly, after looking fruitlessly around. "Maybe we were ALL his distraction."

In the middle of the square, Homer continues his grotesque ballet – the strangest, gangliest, deadest Sugar-Plum Zombie Fairy I have ever seen…

"We should take the clockwork hand, and run," Luke suggests. "Give it to me."

"What?" I gasp in shock, as he makes a failed grab for my belt. "No!"

"Crispin has gone!" he insists. "We have to save ourselves!"

"NO!" I shout again, louder than I intended. I stumble backwards, trying to evade his attempts to snatch the precious clockwork hand. "He'll be back! He wouldn't abandon us…"

Suddenly one of the zombies in the market square gives a roar, and we all look around – to see the tallest, thinnest zombie standing over Homer – pointing accusingly.

"Oh, shit…" I mutter.

"Told you," Luke reminds me. "It's just not normal for a white dude to be flaunting THAT about."

Homer twirls coquettishly, trailing ostrich-feather boa – which inexplicably speeds up, until it cracks like a whip…

…And the head of the tallest zombie pops straight off, bounces – and rolls right over to my feet, underneath the long gown belonging to Crispin Dry's mother.

As I snatch up my skirts and leap aside with a scream, I see it give a much more approving grin…

CHAPTER THIRTY:

THE MAGNIFICENT SEPTUM

I don't know whether it's my screaming, or Homer's lethal feather boa snapping around the neck of a second zombie, rendering its future bow-tie wearing rather precarious – but suddenly all Hell breaks loose.

Shotgun rounds fired from behind the upright paving slab where Carvery is hiding immediately take out a few more surprised slave zombies, and running from behind it into the back of the gathering, I see Ace knock down a few more.

Is that an adjustable spanner in his hand?

"Come on!" Luke is still urging me. "Let's go!"

"We have to wait for Crispin!" I hiss.

Why didn't he give us a signal? Or some form of safety code?

Typical man!

Bits of zombie are already flying, peppered with lead shot and shreds of white ostrich-feather. Homer continues to whip and whirl, like Nureyev – minus the tights.

"We have to do something!" I moan. I look down in frustration at the golden clockwork hand. Why isn't it helping us? If only I knew how to make it work!

Ace is dodging from pillar to pillar dealing with the enemy, one unsuspecting undead pyramid-builder at a time. Some of the other zombies have figured out where the gunshots are coming from, and converge on the paving-slab. Bits of them splatter around, as their own front line meets line of fire.

"I'm not waiting here to get my brains eaten by my own ancestors, thank you very much!" Luke announces. "It might be traditional – but it's usually the other way around!"

And he makes one final – and successful – grab for the Dry family heirloom.

"Give that back!" I shout at him. "That was given to me to…"

But he has already gone, kicking up dust, as he runs down another sandy side-street.

"...Fuck!" I shout. Which was not at all how that sentence was meant to end, as it came out of my mouth.

I look back at the others. A huddle of zombies has reached the paving-slab, and Carvery straightens up, kicking it over flat on top of the nearest ones, jumping on top of it with a crunching of distressed bone and skull – giving him a few seconds to re-load.

Homer is holding his own, in the centre of a whirlwind of white feathers.

And Ace... I can't see Ace...

"Sarah!" A hand grabs my shoulder.

All imminent bathroom requirements immediately dispensed with, I try to dislodge my inhaled tongue and turn to see Ace Bumgang behind me. Yes – it's an adjustable spatter in his hand. I mean, *spanner.*

Very spattered, at the moment...

"Where's Luke?" Ace demands.

"He ran off, that way." I wave my arm weakly. "He stole the clockwork hand too..."

"Well – he did say he emigrated to seek his fortune," Ace reminds me. "I guess he's planning on cutting his losses, having worked as a minicab-driver since 1971. Let's find Crispin."

"What about Homer and Carvery?" I ask, allowing Ace to drag me along by the elbow.

At least this is more like one of my Ace Bumgang fantasies... without the added zombie-massacre, maybe...

"Let them finish, they're enjoying themselves," Ace reassures me. "You know Carver's never happy unless he's beaten everyone else's body-count high-score."

I look across into the square as we run behind the pillars. Carvery Slaughter is rapidly disappearing, under a mass of zombies, like bees flocking to subdue an interloping hornet. Every so often a gunshot hole appears in the seething, writhing bundle. I don't hear any screaming.

I wonder if that's a good sign.

Homer is entertaining his last few audience-members – a short fat zombie hopefully holding out a bunch of dead flowers – possibly myopic, considering Homer's 'qualifications' as a seminude exotic dancer… and a couple of even more hopeful-looking zombies, whose posture and own flamboyant air suggest that Homer is eminently qualified, for their concept of this sort of perfomance art.

"There." Ace points upwards.

Crispin is crouched on the top of a fallen pillar, resting at forty-five degrees to the ground, on top of some other dislodged masonry. He is apparently still scanning the area, with his little opera-glasses.

Ace and I scramble up onto the bottom of the sandstone block, and make our way up the incline of the pillar to join him, many feet above the paved market-place.

Goodness – the view from up here is spectacular!

But as I look around, I notice the snakelike river-god, Atum, still looming in the distance over the giant barge and the pyramids, examining its domain, and I gulp. That huge, ominous yellow Eye looks as though it could obliterate the whole continent with one offended glance…

I look down into the square, and am rewarded with a vertiginous lurch in my gut. Homer is still dancing, in a much less threatening manner – evidently delighted to have found his niche market. Carvery is still hidden in a furious ball of zombie rage. A zombie head explodes sharply out of it, making me jump.

Still alive then, I note – only slightly disappointed.

It would be a waste of good DNA if he was torn to pieces…

"Any luck?" Ace asks Crispin.

"We've lost the clockwork hand," I butt in. "Luke ran off with it – the traitor."

"He was probably just scared, Sarah," Ace points out. "I was scared. Look at my hand shaking."

He's such a liar. His own dirty blood-soaked hand is as steady as a rock.

"We were probably just a tad early," Crispin admits, turning to scan another side-street. "The carpet-salesman has an established schedule… aha."

He points into the distance.

"The Oriental gentleman in the coolie hat, with the long whiskers," he says.

"Where?" Ace and I both squint, into the early-morning heat-haze. The streets seem deserted – nothing but shadows and miniature sand-storms, drifting along them.

"We will need a few more minutes," Crispin says. "I hope my brother has enough wind in his sails to stretch out his dance routine a bit longer…"

We all look downwards, to check. Still a good effort from Homer – in the distracting department – being put on below us in the quad. And still a mass of exploding zombies where Carvery Slaughter should be.

"Now – what was that about Mr. Lukan and the clockwork hand?" Crispin asks vaguely, raising his opera-glasses once more…

CHAPTER THIRTY-ONE: THE LIFE OF BRAINS

Fortunately – or possibly unfortunately – something more pressing intervenes on our discussion.

Some of the slave zombies have noticed our position atop the tilted pillar, overlooking the square, and are gradually gathering at the base.

One of them is boosted up onto the uppermost surface by his comrades, and starts to scale the hypotenuse determinedly. Others scrabble to follow.

"Um – I think we have company," I squeak. "And not not the sort you get the best china out for!"

"Carver!" Ace yells.

The boiling sphere of hungry zombies down in the market-place, where Carvery Slaughter's current position can be estimated, seems to rotate slightly, on an unseen axis. A zombie cadaver pops out of it abruptly, and dangles – from the shotgun barrels jammed into its ribcage.

The gun raises, angling upwards, and fires. The zombie corpse shoots across the quad, trailing limbs flapping – and knocks the ascending zombie from its perch, halfway up our pillar.

"Good shot, buddy!" Ace calls out.

The shotgun withdraws into the ball again, and bits of zombie continue exploding out of it.

"Told you he was having fun," Ace tells me – and then disappears, over the edge.

Crispin and I both dive forward at once. Ace is dangling by his fingertips, from the crumbling sandstone.

Another zombie, who had evidently scaled the pillar inverted, like a sloth, is hanging from his ankles. More are now attempting the forty-five degree climb to reach us.

"Crispin, I am so sorry," I gasp, as we each grab hold of one of Ace Bumgang's wrists. I decide to risk the theory of revealing bad news in the face of greater danger. "But Luke has run off with the special clockwork hand…"

"He will not get far, Sarah *Bellummm*," Crispin Dry intones, calmly. "They never do."

"What – it's been taken before?" I ask.

"Still here, you two," Ace chips in, also sounding remarkably cool about things. "Zombie chomping on my trainers, and stuff…"

There is a whiplike crack of air, and the end of Homer's ostrich-feather boa curls around the knees of the suspended zombie. With an expression of horror, it is yanked free.

Homer continues his burlesque dance, while the now detached dangling zombie crashes in a mess of gray splintered bone and sludge, onto the paving. The little fat zombie spectator with the bunch of flowers is now on his knees, in adoration – or perhaps due to his rickets – while the other remaining two more *fey* zombies appear to be taking the critical judgement evaluation standpoint, as they applaud the latest trick in Homer's repertoire.

"It's all right," I say to Ace. "We'll pull you back up…"

He glances past me, over my shoulder, wryly.

"I think I'll stay put, thanks," he replies.

I look up just before the shadow falls across me, and scream in the face of the latest zombie to climb the pillar…

…Just before I'm aware of a sudden rush of air, as a sand-storm blows swiftly down the street, engulfing us – and I feel Crispin grab my shoulders and flip me backwards over the edge as well…

…Falling…

The air is knocked out of me with a thud, as the wind seems to slap me in the face, and suddenly I'm hurtling along at speed – with Ace and Crispin sitting either side of me.

"Ah, just in time," Crispin approves. "Ace – Sarah – may I introduce Justin Time, the carpet-salesman?"

"Justin Time?" we both repeat, dazed.

The Oriental gentleman, as forewarned in the coolie hat and with the long whiskers, looks at us calculatingly over his shoulder. He is also sporting *Biggles*-style aviator goggles, and the traditional white tasselled mohair scarf.

"That is my name," he snaps. "Don't wear it out."

"What happened?" I ask Crispin, wiping the streaming tears from my eyes, caused by wind-speed and sand.

I become aware of the distant view of the market-place wheeling far below us, and the sight of tiny angry gray zombies shaking their fists from the top of the fallen pillar. *What the Hell…??*

We are sitting in a rickshaw!

Mr. Time is perched just in front of us, with a little driving whip and some reins in his hands. And the reins are harnessed to…

…A rug.

The sort you put on the hall floor… an actual *rug*…

Flying!!

More rugs are rolled up at our feet, and strapped to the back. Some of them are wriggling. And not all of them appear to be unoccupied, either.

"Mr. Time," Crispin begins, quite loudly, while I'm sure I can hear pleas for mercy emerging from some of the carpet-bundles. "We need to get to the Six a.m. Lounge. But would you be so kind as to pick up the rest of our party on the way?"

"That will cost extra," Mr. Time snaps again.

"I can offer you – two days off."

"Hah!" Mr. Time leans the rickshaw. It's as if he wants to scare us. "Twenty! In August!"

Ace is brushing bits of zombie finger off his *Caterpillar* hi-tops, before resting his feet up on one of the struggling sausages of rolled-up carpet.

"I can perhaps stretch to a long weekend in September?" Crispin ponders.

I look over the side as we circle the square again, and squeal as a zombie skull hurtles skywards past us, its eye-sockets full of white ostrich-feather.

"You insult me, Mr. Dry!" Justin Time froths, slapping the reins crossly on the back of the flying carpet. It bucks, bouncing us in our seats. "Twenty days! If you are lucky, maybe I even clean your dirty rugs too!"

"God, just give him his days off!" I appeal. A zombie arm arcs slowly over us, tumbling gently, and I suddenly find myself the surprise recipient of a dead floral bouquet.

"We have to do this," Crispin whispers. "It is traditional to exchange the barter and the insults, so that he will feel better about it when he wins."

He clears his throat.

"A week, Mr. Time!" he proposes. "Late July! And a long weekend in September!"

"Not listening, Mr. Dry!" our pilot shouts. "La-la-la! I want August!"

They continue their obligatory negotiations, while my mind spins, and my stomach – well, I've never flown before, put it that way.

"Thanks," Ace remarks, trying to inch further away from me in the seat. "I think you actually found a clean bit of my overalls that I missed yacking on myself, earlier."

"Sorry." I use a tail of Lady Glandula's borrowed robes to wipe my mouth.

A loud bang comes from the side of our carriage, and a ragged hole appears right beside him.

"Ow!" Ace flinches, and snatches his elbow off the sill of the rickshaw. Blood trickles from a large nick in his arm. "All right Crispin, hurry up. Carvery just shot me."

"Twenty days in August, Mr. Dry!" shrieks our driver, not budging one iota.

"A fortnight in August!" Crispin relents.

Justin looks back at us, a glint of triumph in his smile.

"And a virgin!" he amends.

Oh, God… I seem to recall seeing that one coming…

But then an even bigger elephant in the room suddenly raises its ugly head – quite literally…

"Look out, Mr. Time…" Crispin points.

The pilot turns abruptly, and veers to avoid the gigantic yellow Eye of the river-god, Atum. I slide sharply along the seat, sandwiched between Ace and Crispin. Ace grunts resentfully, as his shotgun-pellet wound smacks hard into the side of the rickshaw.

"Out of my way!" Mr. Time rants, waving his arm ineffectually at the looming sea-monster. "Stupid great snake! Like you own the place!"

"Technically…" Crispin begins, but then catches both of our eyes, and appears to think better of it.

The frightening rumble emanates again from the endless scaly column, and the prehensile neck curls around to follow our path, as Justin Time disciplines his wayward rug to hightail it back in the direction of the square. There is a bump, as we just clip the tip of the tallest mast on Lady Glandula's barge, in passing.

"We will discuss the terms *en route*," Crispin continues, smoothly.

I don't get it – is that him agreeing to the price, or not yet?

"…But first, my brother…?" he reminds the pilot.

"You Dry people, you all the same…" Mr. Time grumbles and raves, half to himself. Nonetheless, the rug swoops obediently into the quad.

Crispin leans out over the side as we barely kiss the air above the ground, and locks arms with his brother, just as Homer strikes a dramatic pose in his final flourish…

…And as we climb again steeply over the far side, the transvestite dancing zombie securely flying skywards with us – the ball of fighting zombies erupts, and a protruding hand grabs the very end of the trailing feather boa…

Carvery Slaughter ejects from the writhing mass, still in possession of the shotgun – which is handy as he blows the head off one last determined zombie, trying to grab hold of his foot as he is lifted free.

"Excellent," Crispin announces, and the remainder of our group soar into the sky, away from the riverside and the frustrated slave zombies. "We will catch up with Mr. Lukan later. But for now – the Six a.m. Lounge, please, Justin Time…"

CHAPTER THIRTY-TWO: BIG TROUBLE IN RECEPTACULUM CHYLI

Homer and Carvery haul themselves up the sides of the flying rickshaw to perch on the back of our passenger seat, on top of those other lashed-down, struggling rolled-up rugs. A few of them give indignant grunts or squeaks, as the two plonk themselves down heartily.

I immediately flinch, as Carvery's knees clamp around my shoulders.

"No seatbelts," he excuses himself. "Maybe I should hold onto your hair as well."

I try to make myself as small and inaccessible as I can, on the padded leather bench.

"Did you get bitten?" I ask, although it's not the first thing on my mind. *Damn my traitorous hormones again…!*

"Nope."

And he spits out what turns out to be a ragged gray ear, right onto my lap.

"I can imagine why not," I mutter, trying to shake off the piece of discarded zombie.

Any undead saliva meeting Carvery Slaughter would only make his bloodstream cleaner, for one thing…

Homer – our transvestite exotic zombie dancer – is looking very pleased with himself, fluffing up his remaining ostrich-feathers once more.

I feel as though some sort of artistic award or tribute is due for his life-saving performance just now, and hand him the bouquet of dead flowers, which had found me as we flew over the square. He is unashamedly thrilled, simpering dreadfully and fanning his own face with his free hand, as if overcome with emotion.

Bless him…

We pass through early-morning ribbons of cloud, the harnessed flying carpet skilfully directed by our strange pilot, Mr.

Justin Time. He is quietly focused on his task, but at one point raises an arm and waves.

Stretching my neck to see over the side, past Ace Bumgang, I just catch a glimpse of another flying shape in the distance, heading back the way we came – but I can't make out what it is.

Ace suddenly turns in his seat, and punches Carvery on the quadricep.

"That's for shooting me," he says, still nursing the nick in his arm, licking the blood off.

"I was aiming for Sarah," Carvery grins. "Sorry, dude."

"We are almost there," Crispin interrupts, his creaking zombie voice a balm to my suppressed anger, as usual. "The Six a.m. Lounge is often quite busy, and some of its denizens and regular clientele are the private sort, who may be suspicious of strangers. We must proceed with caution."

My heart sinks. So it doesn't sound like we're back at Crispin's brownsign mansion yet…

As we dip below the clouds, the sun disappears, and we find ourselves skimming over darkened, rain-soaked streets. Not the dry dusty sandstone of the Five a.m. Lounge – and less architecturally magnificent, consisting of a higgledy-piggledy of corrugated iron shacks, strange tenements, rainbow-illuminated storefronts, and many small temples of differing size and denomination. Ordinary rickshaws bob along the muddy cobbles, and every street seems to feature rows of bunting-festooned market-stalls, right on the doorsteps of the regular shops, businesses and houses. People just seem to exist right on top of one another here…

Scrawny dogs and tiny children with pot-bellies wander around loose, unattended. As I stare in horror, I notice a small boy with his mongrel terrier tethered on a piece of string, both happily pooping in the gutter.

It's like something off *Rough Guides Uncut*…

"That is our destination." Crispin points, and on a hill overlooking the bizarre town, stretching from horizon to horizon on either side, a huge stone fort appears out of the low-lying, gunmetal-gray clouds. Every arrow-slot is illuminated, and the distant flying dots of other airborne vessels arrive and depart from its roof, in a stream of early-morning industriousness.

"Remember what I said about caution," Crispin re-iterates, as we dip over the walls of the fort. "There are people here who would suck out your soul, and rape it in front of you."

"Cool," says Carvery. "Get to put my feet up and watch for once."

"Yeah," Ace agrees, grudgingly. "Wouldn't be the first time I got sperm-jacked in my sleep."

"It'd be all right for Sarah." Carvery scruffs my long hair, which immediately tries to stand perpendicular, in shock. "She doesn't have a soul. They'd be poking around hopelessly lost in there for ever. Like chucking a toothpick down the Thames."

"I imagine it's somewhat like finding out some weirdo has whacked off while reading my diary!" I bristle, meaningfully.

"Sarah, it'd be like wanking on my Nan's shopping list," Carvery sighs, shaking his head. "Even my taxation accounts are sexier than your diary."

The rickshaw comes to a bumpy halt on an illuminated runway, on the roof of the fort. We seem to be in a queue of similar arrivals. Helmeted guards are moving along the flanks, speaking to drivers, and scratching notes on slate tablets.

"Identification?" the approaching guard says to Justin Time, peering at us out of the corner of his faceplate.

"Tell your mother, she needs to move her stuff out of my brother's caravan!" says Justin.

Er – not the way I was ever taught to speak to men in uniform. We all listen, in deathly silence.

"What have you brought today?" the official continues benignly, apparently immune to our pilot's Tourette's Syndrome.

We all let out our trapped breath.

"I want the bounty on these rugs," snaps Justin, slapping one of the rolls of carpet behind him, which squeals for pity. "The ones that those slave boys were stealing to impress rich girls with. I have a dozen of them to return."

"And your passengers?" the guard continues. "Identification?"

"You don't need to see their identification," Justin Time scoffs. "These aren't the virgins you're looking for."

My heart seems to contract to the size of a hazelnut, in fear. *Not again…*

"Ah – Mr. Dry!" the guard suddenly exclaims, and pushes up his faceplate, greeting Crispin with a much less intimidating smile. "I did not see you there… are these people all with you?"

Before Crispin can reply, a crack of thunder explodes overhead, followed by a prong of forked lightning. It strikes down a cluster of guards, scattering them like ten-pins.

"Uh-oh," Mr. Time gulps. He reaches out and prods our own gawping guard, with his little rug-driving whip. "Hurry up, Dumb-Ass! Let us through – I am a businessman, you know!"

A second fork of lightning grounds itself on the roof of the fort, and remains there, sizzling and sending up sparks from the stonework.

The dark cloud above swirls around its vertical axis, in the same way the river had swirled earlier before revealing Atum the sea-god, in the Five a.m. Lounge…

But this time, no gigantic leviathan appears.

Instead, three bat-like shapes descend, like ragged firemen sliding down a station pole. They land with thunderclaps onto the roof, and fold their gauntleted arms, faces half-hidden behind chain-mail and coolie hats.

At least a third larger than the average man here, they tower menacingly as they stand beside the lightning fork, which reflects off their armour in flashes of ultramarine light.

"Who are they?" I hiss.

"Bounty hunters," Crispin whispers back.

The middle one takes one pace forward, his head turning slowly – until his sight rests on our little flying rickshaw.

"Justin Time…" the tall bounty hunter rumbles, in a voice like the quaking of continents. "*Thief…*"

And the three newcomers all raise their arms, to point at our equally quaking driver.

I know immediately where I've seen those twinkly glinting blue lights before…

FUCK...

…They *ALL* have clockwork hands…

CHAPTER THIRTY-THREE: THE MEN WHO STARE AT GLUTES

"What do we do now, Crispin?" I ask, my voice by now only marginally less hysterical than the *Sinclair C-5* concept.

"We disembark," Crispin announces. "Quite rapidly…"

None of us need to be told twice. In fact, I think being told the once was pushing it.

We scramble out of the rickshaw hurriedly, over the restrained and thrashing rugs – while in the true spirit of battle, our pilot Mr. Time reaches for the sky, and surrenders.

"*Parlez!*" he cries, lapsing into the language of longevity.

"Crispin," I pant, as we scurry away, along the battlements of the enormous fort. "Those bounty hunters – they all have…"

"Yes, clockwork hands," he agrees. "I know."

"But they are…" I look down at my own hands, flexing them. "Attached!"

"That does not mean they have more power than the original," he replies. "Although they might outnumber it…"

We follow his lead to a grand archway set into the rooftop gatehouse, barricaded by more guards, and a portcullis. I'm expecting more hard negotiations – but our approach is punctuated by a shout, from high above.

"Crispin!" hails the high-pitched, crackly-as-old-wallpaper voice. "And *Ho-o-o-merrr*… What do I owe this pleasure?"

"Yes, yes," Crispin calls out to the unseen speaker, sheepishly, as we draw to a halt. "Hello – Grandpappy…"

"Grand-*what?*" Ace asks, as Carvery snorts.

"My father's father," Crispin coughs. "Higham Dry Senior."

Higham Dry! Is this who the stillborn Dry sibling in the pickle jar was named after?

A wisp of cloud above the battlements moves, and we spot a pigtailed, white-haired ancient old man, in black and emerald green dragon-embroidered robes, leaning over the parapet squinting at us.

"What-what-what?!" Higham Dry Senior repeats, taking in our group. "So many guests! Is it my birthday?"

"Why do I get the feeling that you're not well-known for remembering family birthdays, Crispin?" Carvery smirks.

"You interrupt my experiments!" Higham Dry cackles. "But I be right down…"

He ducks down and disappears momentarily, and reappears again with a fat hen in one hand, and a cannonball in the other.

"Now – which one will hit the ground first?" he announces, and we leap aside – as the cannonball and chicken both sail over the brickwork.

It's a close one. Mainly because the hen is chained to the cannonball, by one leg.

"Stupid chicken," says Crispin's grandfather, shaking his head sadly. "If she learn to fly faster, then maybe she beat cannonball. Okey-dokey – here I come…"

And he steps off the ledge. My reward for screaming, is another cuff around the ear from Carvery, and a wince from Ace Bumgang, who is still clutching his bleeding arm.

But Higham Dry Senior merely drifts gently to the ground, his robes inflated around him like a *Disney*-esque parachute.

And looks mightily pleased with himself too – I can see where Homer gets his self-confidence from…

"You see any Jedi Master do that?" he asks, sniggering. "Maybe – but I don't watch all of the series. *Sooooo…* you like my experiment? Chicken wasn't always fixed to cannonball, but too many chickens just fly away. Did you know they can fly? Who knew, right? But one day, I will find a chicken who can move faster than a cannonball. Then that be really fast food, no? Come downstairs. We make chicken soup."

"Your grandfather…" Ace begins quietly, as the portcullis raises for us. "Is he a zombie too, or just really old?"

"Oh, he passed away many years ago." Crispin taps himself on the sternum. "It's all clockwork in there. Have you ever seen *Sucker Punch*? Kind of like the soldiers in that movie. Only harder to kill." He sighs. "It's not like Mother hasn't tried…"

"Oh, you been to see the Lady Glandula de Bartholine?" Higham Dry Senior's hearing evidently hasn't deteriorated a jot. He leads the way down some stone stairs, illuminated by candle-lit wrought-iron chandeliers. "Blood-sucking harlot. How is she these days?"

"Much the same, Grandpappy," Crispin admits.

"Yay," Ace seconds him, sorely.

"Slept her way out of the primordial ooze, she did." Higham Dry Senior's carved bone walking-stick clatters along the stone floor ahead of us, at quite a respectable pace. "Jumping from body to body like a secretary at staff Christmas party. She still hanging onto the last one? It run out of entropy quite soon, I think."

"Spending most of her time dormant, yes," Crispin confirms.

"I thought it very quiet around here lately. Nice and peaceful." Higham Dry nods. "But when she find a new one she likes, you wait. It be all boiling oil and crocodiles and embalming people alive again."

We find ourselves in a vast galley kitchen, designed evidently to serve the mountainous fort. You could have fitted Silverstone race track in it quite comfortably.

I glance at Ace to see if I can gauge his attitude regarding the subject of indoor drag-racing possibly crossing his thoughts, but his *I-am-not-The-Stig* poker-face is as inscrutable as ever.

I imagine what other secrets those dreamy brown eyes might also be hiding, and sigh…

…A billy goat trots past us along the longest granite worktop I have ever seen, breaking wind happily, while chefs with cleavers try to catch up with it.

"Oh, what a shame, goat escape from bath-tub again," Higham Dry Senior sympathises. "We have a new chef from foreign place, I don't know where – I think maybe Basildon? Chef *Reggae Reggae*. He promise us recipe for goat curry. We been trying to marinade this goat in Guinness for three weeks already, but it drink it all every time, then run away. So we stuck with chicken soup for now. And the barracks very upset, all Guinness gone, they trying to make their own in the laundry. Not good. They blow it up nearly every day, trying to figure out secret ingredient. But as a result, we now know how to make napalm, so something good come of it."

"How do you catch the goat?" I ask.

"We wait for it to fall asleep with big hangover, then just follow smell," Higham Dry Senior shrugs. "Simple… All of you, come with me. You all look very peaky. Need chicken soup."

I realise, as the cooking smells in the cavernous kitchen envelop us, that I haven't eaten since Crispin's strangely erotic food game, when I arrived at his mansion last night – and my stomach rumbles disturbingly. Yes. Food would certainly be welcome…

"I'm full," says Carvery, picking his teeth, and finding what appears to be a fingernail, extracting it thoughtfully. It gives me an unpleasant lurch in my own gut. "Zombie *Nando's*."

"Don't know if I'm up for eating anything yet," Ace grumbles. "Not since Sarah puked on me as well."

"Everyone feel better after soup," Higham Dry assures us, and hands the failed speed-chicken and cannonball to one of the chefs. "Oooh, look who joining us for breakfast… just in time too! We go to dining-room…"

I look around to see the miserable flying rickshaw pilot, Justin Time, being hustled in by the three scarily larger-than-life, faceless bounty hunters. Higham Dry Senior gestures for them to follow as well.

The dining-room, a short walk from the kitchen, is another vast room, its vaulted ceiling supported by many pillars. Twin candle-sconces on every pillar give the impression of each having glowing eyes, watching all proceedings in this particular room.

Higham Dry hobbles rapidly to a throne-like chair at the head table, and two guards mysteriously appear at his sides. It is evident by the change in atmosphere that we don't have permission to sit yet.

So we hover nervously, while Justin Time is deposited in a prostrate heap, sobbing, on the carpet-runner in front of him.

"He was stealing those flying rugs himself, as you suspected, Lord," the first bounty hunter rumbles, in his unearthly deep voice. "And holding them to ransom."

"Ooohh," Higham Dry smiles, nodding his elderly glee and rubbing his hands together, which crack like a bag of walnuts under a lump-hammer. "You very naughty boy, Mr. Time! What I do with you, eh?"

"Be merciful, Lord!" Justin Time cries, his mouth full of thankfully less sapient carpet. "I was testing our security measures – an example of where improvements might be needed…"

"Hmmm, where have I heard that before…?" Higham Dry Senior ponders. "What was that film with the also very naughty children… Oh yes, *Mission Without Permission!* I don't fall for your weak excuses this time, Mr. Justin Time. I think maybe I show YOU an example, of my Jedi mind powers…"

"No…" Justin Time pleads. "Not that… anything but the mind tricks, Lord…"

"You!" Higham Dry Senior points suddenly, with a tremulously wizened forefinger. "Yes, you, the *Calvin Klein* poster-boy, with the shotgun. You are under my spell, you hear me?"

Carvery looks over his shoulder, just in case there is another gunman in the room, and then shrugs.

Higham Dry points to the biggest guard, on his left.

"Kill this man."

Carvery shrugs again, and blows the guard's head off.

"Ooh." Higham Dry rattles the finger in his ear. "That was loud!"

"Doesn't prove anything." Ace, Crispin and I all state the obvious.

"And you!" The old man points at Homer. "You, now, are under my spell… Now dance! Like a *sexy* concubine!"

Homer shrugs in turn, and pirouettes away around the pillars, shedding his last ostrich-feathers – giving it his all.

"Oh, God," Ace mutters. "This is going to be a really long morning…"

CHAPTER THIRTY-FOUR: THE LOST BONES

"Now you!" Higham Dry Senior's shaking finger of doom finds me, pointing in an almost accusatory manner. "You are in my power… your mind is bending to my will…"

I don't feel any different. But then, I wasn't exactly expecting to. Mostly just curious – at what he might find to instruct that I would cheerfully have done anyway, like Carvery Slaughter and Homer just demonstrated…

"Mercy!" the prisoner Justin Time pleads into the carpet, ignored.

Apparently he is the only one falling for this little sideshow.

The elderly robed man gestures at Ace Bumgang, standing next to me.

"Kiss him!" he snaps, a glint in his eye. "Like you mean it!"

Ooohh – any excuse!

But as I turn to look at Ace and catch *HIS* eye, it's evident that someone in the room has bigger mental powers than the Dry brothers' zombie grandfather.

I can almost hear Ace's voice in my head…

Sarah, you so much as try it, and you're going home in a padded envelope…

I gulp, wondering what the punishment is for rebelling against supposed Jedi mind tricks. Either the old man's, or Ace Bumgang's.

But as I procrastinate over what I would rather die doing, we are interrupted by breakfast arriving.

"Ahhhh, you all get off lightly this morning!" the old man cries appreciatively, smacking his lips as the servers file into the dining hall, with silver tureens and platters. "Just in time – sit. And the rest of you. We eat first. Then play more mind games."

We all move cautiously towards the long table, and Justin Time peels himself tentatively off the floor. The only ones who move confidently are the three outsized bounty hunters, who settle themselves into the three largest chairs, and take out their own chopsticks.

Even Higham Dry Senior's remaining guard is included, although he pauses before seating himself to tie a bib onto the old man first.

It has a picture of a white rabbit in a waistcoat on it. *Now why does that remind me of something...?*

"Chicken soup!" Higham Dry Senior approves, lifting the lid of his own tureen. "Mmmmm… and plenty of extras. Everybody must eat. Good for your *braaiiins*."

Two of the servers heave the body of the dead guard onto their shoulders.

"Tell him when he wake up that he only get his usual rest break allowance!" says Higham Dry. "I am not running a hotel for layabouts here!"

The two servers nod, and carry the body out between them.

The soup does smell appetizing. I examine mine first for any bits of chicken anatomy that can't be identified. Or ones which I'd rather not.

The enthusiastic slurping of the bounty hunters behind their chain-mail veils indicates that it's safe to start, so we pick up our spoons in turn.

"Maggots!" the old man suddenly shrieks, and I drop my own spoon in fright.

The others take no notice. He is prodding something yellow on his side-plate, and a server hurries over to his side.

"What sort of cheese is this?" Higham Dry demands, poking at it.

"Goat's cheese, Lord," the server informs him, obsequiously lowering his eyes, in a half-bow as he speaks.

"I told you before, you cannot make cheese out of billy-goat!" the old man rants. "And not even one maggot! It taste of nothing, I tell you! Bring me the blue cheese. With the holes in. The one that hums when you blow on it."

"Yes, Lord." The server removes the offending plate, and scurries away.

We continue eating, although I check to make sure my soup has no active swimmers in it. Even Carvery and Ace, who claimed not be hungry, are tempted enough by the aromas to taste their food.

Crispin and Homer both have their heads down, eating as heartily as the bounty hunters and the wayward rickshaw pilot, who is eating and sobbing at the same time. I wonder what that means the elderly man has in store to follow…

"I see you enjoying your noodles, my boys," Higham Dry beams, nodding his approval at the two younger Dry zombies. "Gobble up so fast, too. You must all have the worms, no?"

"Just very hungry, Grandpappy," Crispin replies, while Homer pats his own naked gray belly in agreement.

"Something to drink!" shouts Higham Dry. "Bring the special brew!"

"I can't face Special Brew this early," Ace remarks, as more servers rush to comply. "I downed enough dirty pints last night."

A huge tea urn is wheeled in, steaming, and many small cups are quickly arranged.

"This stuff very good," Higham Dry tells us. "Make men of you! Put hair on your palms."

The bounty hunters exchange glances, and I swear I can sense their evil grins, behind that chain-mail covering their faces.

The cups of hot brown translucent liquid are distributed, and I look at mine with concern. But it seems benign, and has only a faint scent of cinnamon.

Higham Dry raises his tiny cup in salute.

"Everyone drink!" he says. The bounty hunters put down their chopsticks, and do likewise. "Later, we go up on the roof again. More flying experiments. We see if Mr. Time has enough hot air in him to float unaided now…"

CHAPTER THIRTY-FIVE: INDEFINABLE BONES & THE TEMPLES OF GLOOM

Reluctantly, I pick up the tiny bone-china cup along with the others, and prompted by Higham Dry Senior, we all drink.

It's not bad. Rather like Chai tea, with some sort of fermented kick. I hiccup, and immediately start to feel light-headed. Wow – this is better than a Sloe Gin Sling! The men around the table exchange more knowing looks at the taste, and grin at each other.

Maybe it's moonshine. Perhaps they're spiking it with whatever the soldiers are supposedly trying to brew in the laundry, having lost their Guinness rations – to a Caribbean chef from Basildon, and an alcoholic goat…

"How do you plan to get the clockwork hand back?" I ask of Crispin between mouthfuls, who is seated to my left. "Luke could be anywhere, back amongst those pyramids. Or could have been eaten already."

Crispin dabs his mouth with a linen napkin.

"I imagine that as a treasure-seeker, he will be most interested in its worth, rather than its powers," he tells me. "So it would make sense to anticipate that he will take it somewhere that its basic mineral value can be estimated. In which case there are few such places he will find any direct route to, from the Five a.m. Lounge."

"But what if he's interested in its powers?" I press him. "What is the worst case scenario?"

"If the worst case scenario arises," says Crispin, "I would suggest we enjoy our last meal, and look forward to the next instalment of my grandfather's flying experiments."

"Does this have anything to do with the giant river-god?" I ask. "What was its name?"

"Atum," Crispin murmurs, in an even more hushed voice. "Everything has Atumic significance, yes."

"You said it had been taken before?" I remind him. "What happened?"

He gestures with his spoon, in the direction of the bounty hunters.

"Those clockwork hands worn by our breakfast companions," he begins. "…Were based on the original, made under the Dry family's supervision. There were only ever intended to be four, in total. And the three you see here have remained intact on their wearers since the day they were wrought. On a number of occasions in the past, however – the original has been… misplaced. Sometimes only down the back of the couch, or left in coat pockets in strange cloakrooms. But in a few cases – stolen."

"Stolen?" I repeat, horrified.

How could they be so careless, with such a precious family heirloom?

"Yes – by grave-robbers, or amoral museum curators – the occasional power-crazed super-villain," Crispin whispers. "Even an entire cult, once or twice. Fortunately none of them were able to unlock its full potential, before it was recovered."

"But if it's so important – what's it doing just knocking around loose on your estate?" I demand. "Surely it should be locked away for safekeeping – in a bank-vault, or some sort of anonymous high-security storage facility…"

"Ahhh – but that is the first place they would look, Sarah *Bellummm*," he murmurs. "Turning up with their safecrackers and cat-burglar skills, and whatnot."

"So what do we do?" I ask, again. "Do we have any way of tracking its movements?"

Crispin looks uncomfortable.

"It was lost for a great deal of the time, Sarah," he admits. "Electronically tagging it would have been a foresight indeed, if the technology were available the last time it was seen."

"That reminds me." Carvery Slaughter puts his foot up on the table, hikes up the leg of his jeans revealing a cuff around his ankle, and scratches around it. "You're welcome to this one. This is probably giving the Old Bill a proper headache right now."

"We will catch up with Mr. Lukan," Crispin reassures me, as Carvery puts his foot back down again, and continues eating. No-one seems to have taken offence – but then, Carvery is the only one who has a gun at the table with him. "No-one has succeeded in getting away with it before."

"But there's always a first time!" I snap, my voice rising above the gentle tinkling of bowls and cutlery.

"Ooohh!" Higham Dry Senior's eyes sparkle, and I shrink in embarrassment. "You looking for your first time? You have to give an old man more notice… it take a while to get this bad boy warmed up." He looks down at his robes, below the table. "I have to get the special key to wind him and everything…"

"I must apologise for Sarah *Bellummm*, Grandpappy," Crispin says. "She is exhausted already after all the running around this morning."

"Shame! But you perk up quickly with proper breakfast inside you. You have a sweet tooth, maybe? I get the staff to bring dessert early." He snaps his palest gray, almost white zombie fingers at one of the servers by the tea urn. "Bring the chilled monk brains! Young lady here need energy, for her first time on Mister Whizz."

"Monkey brains?" Ace repeats, slowly, as the server bows and heads back to the kitchen.

"No, not monkey brains!" Higham Dry's face scrunches up in disgust. "Filthy things." He taps his own temple meaningfully. "Monk brains. Nice and clean, no naughty thoughts allowed. Make you feel like super-hero, mmmm?"

"Maybe we could cut dessert and go straight to the flying experiments?" I suggest, weakly.

Higham Dry Senior's eyes widen, like emerging quail's eggs.

"You so keen!" he approves. "But we finish eating first. Then have a little tour of fort."

I wonder if it's going to be anything like the tour of Crispin's mansion earlier… and then all my thoughts are scattered, as a large silver platter is placed in the centre of the table.

"Oohh," says the old man. "We have the whole choir today!"

Chilled monk brains – served *à la tete*…

CHAPTER THIRTY-SIX: CROUCHING TIBIA, HIDDEN DUODENUM

I'm horrified to see both Carvery Slaughter and Ace Bumgang pick up spoons, along with the zombies and the overgrown bounty hunters.

"What?" Carvery asks, meeting my eye over his serving cranium of chilled monk's gray matter. "I already ate my way through half a dozen deadbeats trying to munch on me earlier."

Good point… I switch my gaze to Ace, trying to appeal to what must be his very well-hidden inner gentle nature. Maybe he's under Higham Dry Senior's mind-spell after all…

"I've definitely eaten worse things, for a bet," Ace grunts, spoonful of monastic brains already in hand. "Not to mention – even those pizzas you deliver sometimes, Sarah."

"Gross, man," Carvery scoffs, his mouth full. "I told you what she does with the cheese, didn't I?"

"Yeah," Ace shrugs.

"But – I didn't tell you what she does with the pepperoni…"

"I'm full," I announce, suddenly finding myself on my feet. "And, er – I'd like to use the little girl's room…"

"This look like a spa to you?" Higham Dry asks, his eyes rounder than ever. "This is a fort! Built for fighting men. Not for wussy ladies. No little girl's room here. Unless you count cupboard under stairs. I should maybe check it again – last time I look, goat asleep in there."

I sink miserably back down into my seat, and try not to watch, as the others finish up their breakfast.

"Everybody done?" Higham Dry asks, and is answered with a series of belches. "Good! We go for tour of fort. Oh dear. Mr. Time, help an old man up. Him old leggy gone to sleep again. Sit down too long."

The sniffling rickshaw pilot dries his mouth on his napkin, and his eyes manfully on his sleeve, and hurries around the table to take the elderly zombie's arm on one side, while the guard takes the other, lifting him out of his chair between them. His legs appear to be locked in a sitting position, drawn almost up to his chest.

"What am I supposed to do like this – levitate? Like Maharishi on mushrooms?" Higham Dry Senior squawks. "Sort it out down there!"

Justin Time and the guard exchange a look over the old man's braided white head, and then shake him up and down vigorously, like a salt-cellar.

"Ung-*nung-nung-nung-nung-nung*…" Higham Dry jabbers, and suddenly his legs shoot out straight, with a pop of cartilage. "Ooohhh… *ahhh*… That was fun! Do it again!"

"We don't want your legs to drop off altogether, Grandpappy," Crispin chides, gently. "Not like the last time you visited the Five a.m. Lounge."

"No, quite right. Very lucky, crocodiles too fat to swim away with them fast enough," Higham Dry agrees, allowing his aides to set him down onto his feet. "Now, we go on tour! Follow the crazy old fool, everybody."

"Here is barracks!" Higham Dry announces proudly, as the giant studded oak doors swing aside with a groan. "Pooh! Smell like sleeping-bag farts, no? Many soldiers bunk up in here."

I can well believe it. The many parallel avenues of bunkbeds, four high, disappear to vanishing point in the far distance.

As we step inside, those occupants who are currently off-duty leap to attention – from bunks, floor, and even slop-out bucket…

"Hello, hello," Higham Dry Senior waves regally and proprietorially, before strolling in, one hand behind his back, in typical hierarchical-visitor fashion. "At ease, soldiers. You!"

His finger whips out from behind his back and points suddenly, at one of the men evidently caught half-asleep.

"Is it *Dress-Down Friday*?"

"Not any more, Lord!" the terrified soldier squeaks. "But I believe yesterday was Friday…"

"So – you sleep in your party frock, hmmmm?" The old man scans the unfortunate soldier up and down, taking in the floral hair adornments, and sequinned tube dress – not unlike Homer's from earlier on, only blue.

"There was a birthday," says the soldier, wretchedly. "I was the entertainment…"

"Ohhhh… like in *It Ain't Half Hot, Mum*, hmmm?" Higham Dry nods, sagely. "Very clever, very clever. You improvise, good work. You invite me next time, yes?"

"Yes, Lord!"

"And you…" Crispin's grandfather turns to another soldier, whose blankets heaped on the bunk behind him suddenly contort violently, and sneeze. "Did I mention that we do not have a *Bring Your Children To Work Day*, not even once in the whole calendar?"

"Yes, Lord," says the second soldier, grimly.

"Daddy," his blanket solemnly joins in. "I need you to wipe my bogey."

There is a deathly pause.

"What is 'bogey'?" Higham Dry's brow furrows, turning to Crispin.

"Booger, Grandpappy."

"Oh, thank goodness." The old man's face brightens. "We have enough people camping out here without finding bogeymen under the beds as well. Issue this soldier with clean handkerchiefs. And some colouring-books, for his non-existent children. Homer! That dress is not in your size. Put the poor man down. We move on – leave our hard-working boys in peace, no?"

"This is laundry," says Higham Dry. "You must all be very careful in here. Never know what come out of it."

The reinforced black iron door slides open, and a giant ball of pink steam unrolls from within. He sniffs, suspiciously.

"Smell all rosy, like lady flowers," he muses, wrinkling his nose. "Usually, smell of napalm and sweaty jock strap in this room. Occasionally, smell of goat, chewing on socks. Many sock darning needed. What you call this, naughty boys?! Why it smell all lovely for a change?"

A handful of white-aproned, shirtless muscular attendants rush out of the steam, line up and bow in front of us.

"Laundry day, Lord!" the middle one cries.

"You not trying to make Guinness today?" Higham Dry demands.

"Only if it turns out that the secret ingredient is Lotus Blossom fabric softener, Lord!"

"I am very confused, my man-shorts never smell like Lotus Blossom." Higham Dry shakes his head. "What are my soldiers going to do, prancing around smelling of lady flowers?"

"There was a mix-up, Lord," the attendant grovels. "Our usual Sea Breeze softener was delivered to Madam Dingdong's *Bring Your Own Towel Sauna and Spa*, and the Lotus Blossom was given to us in turn."

"I cannot have my soldiers smelling girly, you go to Madam Dingdong and you rectify immediately," says the old man. "And bring back my favourite towel while you there."

"Yes, Lord." The attendant bows again, and scurries out of the laundry.

"What a shame, no luck on Guinness brewing yet," Higham Dry sighs, as he leads the way back out. "But never mind. We go up on roof. Get away from girly smell."

The walls of the fort are sheer – as is the mountainside. We are so high up, that clouds below us obscure the ground.

However many miles down THAT is…

"Now, Mr. Time," the ancient zombie Higham Dry announces. "We discuss your flying carpet kleptomania."

Two of the bounty hunters seize Justin Time's arms, and hoist him onto the battlements.

"I hope you study art of flying very closely," Higham Dry chortles.

"Lord, have mercy!" the rickshaw pilot sobs. "I only meant to help… I am very fond of my own little aerobatic rug…"

"Well, we see if he come and save you now," Higham Dry says cheerily. "Maybe he more loyal than his owner, hmmm? You hope."

"Is this necessary?" I plea of Crispin. "Look at him – those are real tears coming out of his nose and everything…"

"Oh, is the young lady volunteering to join Mr. Time?" the old man interrupts, and I suddenly find my elbows grasped by the third bounty hunter, and my feet deposited on the edge. "It a long way down. You be at Seven a.m. Lounge before you reach the bottom."

I try to look over my shoulder to see if anyone is coming to my rescue.

"It's true, Sarah *Bellummm*," Crispin says, unexpectedly. "Just look for the exit to the Seven a.m. Lounge on the way down, and we will meet up with you there. I have a feeling the boys are keen to continue the tour as far as Madam Dingdong's first."

"What?" I cry, as Ace and Carvery both nod their agreement. "You're ditching me to go to some – *Bring Your Own Towel Sauna*?"

"Plenty of towels here for everyone to take along," Higham Dry nods. "But I need witness to report if Justin Time able to fly unaided now. So you go with him. Crispin and Homer and the boys catch up with you later. Bye-bye!"

And with a shove – both Justin Time and I pitch over the edge.

As I tumble, I just catch a glimpse of their faces over the brickwork, before the view is swallowed up by the zombie-gray mist.

"You're not screaming," I say, to Justin Time's rictus of horror nearby.

He seems to wake up, and scowls.

"I was waiting for you," he says, annoyed. "Ladies first."

Oh. Of course…

AaaaaaaaAAA*AAAAAHHHHHHHHHHHHHH*…

CHAPTER THIRTY-SEVEN: THE MALPIGHIAN'S NEPHRITIS

Instead of joining in the screaming as we plummet – presumably – to our inevitable deaths, down the endless mountainside, Justin Time takes out a hip flask and unscrews the lid, for a large swig.

I don't know whether I run out of breath, or the frustration with his lack of physical panic gets to me first.

"We're going to die!" I shout, hoping for a reaction.

"A purely existential assumption," he shrugs, the air passing by at speed causing his driving-cape to billow, from the slight movement of his shoulders. He takes another slug from the silver flask.

"But – I don't want to die!"

"Then don't," he grumbles, and mutters, although I still hear him. "Stupid girl…"

So frustrating! The things you have to put up with, when you no longer have a Carvery Slaughter handy, with a gun…

Mr. Time puts away his flask, smacks his lips a few times, and then lets out a strange, piercing, eerie whistling sound. It echoes off the rocks and along the miles and miles of valleys, obscured by mist.

"What was that for?" I ask.

"Thought that was the noise we supposed to make," he says, surprised. "Before 'splat!' You never watch *Roadrunner?* Higham Dry Senior, he love that cartoon. He throw people off roof all the time, having *Who-Make-The-Best-Wheeeeeeeeeee-Splatttt-Noise* competitions. Very funny."

And he sighs, reminiscently.

Damn. I thought he was summoning his magic flying rickshaw, or something helpful like that…

"I suppose we should try for the Seven a.m. Lounge, then?" I hint. "How do we find it?"

"Oh, you can't miss it. It got big neon sign and an arrow, saying *'Seven a.m. Lounge'*. And you just dive right in."

"Really?" I strain my eyes hopefully, through the all-encompassing gray mists.

"Yes." Justin Time nods. His long whiskers trail vertically upwards, in the rushing air. "Right next to sign pointing straight down that say *'Certain Death'*. Make sure you not aim for that one, if you struggle with concept of existentialist existence."

I spend the next few minutes desperately scanning the obstinately unoccupied air all around me, for any hint of neon illumination.

"Are we nearly there yet?" I demand at last, my patience having been tested to snapping point.

"I was thinking it should have been two, maybe three minutes ago," Mr. Time remarks. "Oh well. Perhaps there is a power cut. Or someone pull wrong switch when going to toilet. It happen two, three, sometimes five hundred times a day…"

"What?!"

"Big fort," Justin Time mutters, as if I'm an overly-critical, nagging Great-Auntie. He reaches for his flask again resignedly. "Lots of soldiers use same toilet."

"But… but… b…" I realise I'm now doing that thing called 'blustering'. Or is it 'bumbling'? No… I'm sure one of them means 'lost for words' while the other means 'couldn't find their own arse even if their head was up it'…

At times, I feel as though I need a word for myself that means both at once…

"Oh, no," Justin Time chirps. "There it is…"

And his boot certainly does find my arse – a head of any description up it at the time, or not. I somersault through the air, and only have a split second to glimpse the glowing green and blue flickering glass tubes spelling out 'Seven a.m. Lounge' before I tumble into the circle of pitch blackness beneath.

I get an even briefer glimpse of the other red sign, pointing down the way we were previously heading – but all I see of it is the word 'Death' before I am sucked into an apparent vacuum of darkness.

"Justin!" I shout. My words are whipped away, and do not seem to travel with any great volume at all. I can neither see, hear… nor smell the rickshaw-less pilot.

Did he make it through? Is he behind me, somewhere in this black Hell-hole?

Or is he drinking his last minutes into oblivion… no doubt before making a record-breaking *'splattt'?*

And then I have the most terrifying thought… the Seven a.m. Lounge – *what if this is it?!*

Just more tunnels! Sucking one along twists and turns indefinitely, like being inside the innards of a gluttonous vacuum cleaner! *Supposing this leads nowhere?!* Following this invisible giant intestine for ever, around any corner of which could be the final giant acid-bath of a stomach…

How long before I pray aloud for the end, and the sweet mercy of total digestion?

The tears are milked from my very tear-ducts by the controlled and continuous drop in directional air pressure, and my ears pop their own wax like corks from Cristal.

It will be my fingernails next, I find myself thinking. Then eyeballs… then the hair from my follicles… like a slow-motion, deep-space piece of human jetsam…

"Crispin!" I cry out my last words, I believe – sucked right from my mouth, making no sound at all. "Help me, Crispin Dry! You're my only hope…"

Relentlessly, the walls of the tunnel whoosh by, unseen…

My feet strike something solid, and gravity suddenly reasserts itself, jolting me awake from the semi-coma where consciousness had been drawn out of my body in turn. I am upright, in darkness still – and the surface I am standing on feels wobbly and unstable.

My arms flail instinctively, scrabbling at the air around me for purchase. Nothing – until the very tips of my fingers, and typically blunt, chewed nails just graze the unmistakable feel of brickwork. But as I snatch my chafed fingertips back from the bite of baked clay and mortar, the surface I am standing on lurches – as does my stomach.

"Where am I?" I cry out, feeling the bubbling hysteria already gathering lubrication at the back of my throat and nasal cavity. But at least my voice has returned! "Ace! Carvery! Crispin Dry! Justin Time! Over here!"

"Oooh," I hear a strange, clipped English voice nearby. "Sounds like there's a fish-and-chip cart hiding down this alleyway…"

Not the first thing I was expecting to hear, by a long straw…

"Fish and chips!?" I repeat, stunned.

"See – told you!" says the voice, now drawing nearer. I think I can make out the faint glow of a bobbing torch or lamp approaching, and through what I can only describe as a pea-souper of smog, the yellowish light flickers faintly off the tall narrow brick walls flanking me on either side. "Bloody interlopers!"

"Let's get a closer look at the competition," a nastier voice remarks. It sounds like it comes with sharp edges and blunt instruments attached. And possibly, industrial-sized deep-fat fryers…

I look down, in a panic, as my eyes adjust slowly to the gloom. I'm about six feet off the ground, standing on…

…Standing on…

The back of the rickshaw!

…*Yes!!!*

And the rug is still harnessed, undulating idly at the front – as if taking a light snooze.

Fear propels me into action. I reach down and snatch up the long leather reins. My left hand finds the driving-whip, stashed in a holster down the side.

Without waiting to seat myself traditionally down below, I whirl the whip wildly around my head, and flick it down violently, hoping to alert the flying carpet.

It does more than that.

The whip cracks like a gunshot in the narrow dank alleyway, and the carpet rears up. The rickshaw tilts in turn – and if it wasn't for my hand on the reins, my now prone position would be on the pavement. Not still on the top, with my toes frantically gripping the canopy.

"Look out!" shouts the first voice. "It's an invasion – from the Six a.m. Lounge!"

"Let's leggit!" yells the other. "We'll need reinforcements!"

"Forward, er – Oh Great Flying Carpet!" I order, in my most imperious voice. Trying to sound a little bit like I imagine the zombie Lord Higham Dry Senior would chivvy one of these along, or scary zombie queen the Lady Glandula de Bartholine.

The rickshaw rights itself, and I do indeed find myself moving forward. And at what a pace!

We leave the alleyway up on one wheel, and through the smog find I am hurtling through a street-market. It is dark, like night, but the darkness seems to be a factor of the heaviness of the sooty fog, and not of the time of day.

Stallholders scream and scatter upon espying the flying carpet charging their way, including butchers, flower-sellers, ironmongers – where *IS* this place?!

After decimating a hundred yards of market-stalls, it occurs to me that the rug can do more…

"Up, Great Flying Carpet!" I command, sticking with the theory that flattery will get me everywhere…

And it does…

We – or rather, I, and the carpet-propelled flying rickshaw – clip the tops of the last few stalls, and soar over the rooftops.

In the paler gray fog above the streets, I make out narrow byways, a strange domed cathedral, a clock tower – and a great river…

It can't be…

LONDON???

"Down, Oh Great Flying…" I whisper, and the carpet dips towards those iconic banks, and the promenade.

"Hrrrrmmmph?" a strange voice pipes up. "Oh, *nooooo*. We here already?"

A smaller rug below me on the rickshaw moves aside, and a decidedly-smelling-of-moonshine Justin Time pops his head out, empty hip-flask in hand.

"How did YOU get here?" I ask, amazed.

"Well, obliviously…" He waves an arm in a drunken, all-encompassing-in-every-context-of-the-word gesture. "I whistled for the flying run, and he come rugging, innit?"

And he burps, worthy of any foghorn.

I'm so flabbergasted, staring down at him from my perch standing atop the rickshaw's canopy, that I completely forget that we are still barrelling along apace.

Or to look out for the crossbar of the street-lamp, as it cracks into my sternum like a poleaxe…

CHAPTER THIRTY-EIGHT: SHALLOW GRAVY

The reins are jerked clean out of my hand, as the collision with the street lamp catapults me from the roof of the rickshaw, sending me flying backwards with no control whatsoever. The only thing I keep hold of is the driving whip, and as I arc heels over head, pulled inescapably down by the force of gravity, my arms fly up to protect myself against the eventual impact.

It is softer than I expected – warm, crunchy, squishy – and briefly, also screaming.

Makes a change from hearing my own scream, I have to say…

But as I recover, and attempt to get up, I'm aware that some terrible incident has occurred…

"Justin!" I hiss, desperately. The rickshaw has stopped, evidently due to loss of whipping and steering. "Justin! Come here, quickly!"

The inebriated former rickshaw pilot rolls out of the passenger-seat of the cab, and tries to rearrange his legs. I don't think the word 'quickly' is currently in his vocabulary.

Looking back down at the issue on the ground, I notice that the grotesque twitching has already stopped, and a sizeable puddle has also formed. But my conscience kicks in anyway, although even I'm aware that it's arrived too late to the party.

"Um, Miss?" I croak, stepping aside as the dark puddle heads towards my own feet. "Are you all right, Miss?"

I wonder if maybe I should try to work the driving-whip free, or whether I should leave it *in situ*. Or does that only count if the victim is still breathing? Damn, I can't remember…

…And worse, I think I can hear footsteps approaching… are those shapes, forming in the smog ahead of me?

"Justin!" I squeak, looking over my shoulder again, at the rickshaw pilot rolling around in the dirt. "Hurry up!"

And then yell in terror, as a hand clamps around my elbow.

"Oh, dear, Sarah *Bellummm…*"

"Crispin!" I cry out, in relief. My underpants don't even want to know about it.

"Nice one, Sarah," the much more unwelcome Carvery Slaughter joins in, leaning over to have a look. "You've made a Streetwalker Kebab."

"Shutup, shutup!" I panic. "It was an accident, I fell off the roof of the rickshaw."

"So this should have been you, splatted on the ground?" Carvery asks, disappointed. "What a shame. And I would have missed it, too. Oh, well – better luck next time."

"Where are Ace and Homer?" I ask, ignoring him.

"Ace is having the stress of meeting Lady Glandula earlier massaged out of him at Madam Dingdong's," Crispin replies, and my heart sinks that little bit further. "Where Homer is also currently indulging in a make-over session. They will catch up with us soon. Ah. I see that Justin Time has also fallen off the wagon."

"You mean rickshaw?" I venture.

"No, I mean he is drinking again, Sarah *Bellummm*." Crispin lets out a zombie sigh – a cross between a hiss, and a death-rattle. "Well, hopefully he will have sobered up enough by the time his services are next required. Or when Grandpappy catches up with him, to find out the results of his flying experiment. Do you have anything interesting to report in that department?"

"Crispin," I say, patiently. "There is a dead woman on the ground, with our driver's whip stuck in her…"

Carvery yanks it free. A stream of blood droplets arcs anaemically into the air between us, like an apologetic low-rent fountain.

"…A dead woman on the ground," I amend, meaningfully.

"*Yesss*," Crispin acknowledges, at last. "We should move her somewhere more respectable…"

"How about into the river?" Carvery suggests.

"An excellent idea, Mr. Slaughter," Crispin agrees. "But currently the police in the Seven a.m. Lounge are very keen on dredging the river regularly to fill their tea kitty, rather like looking for spare change down the back of a sofa. We will take her somewhere indoors, where passers-by will be less likely to stumble across her, tripping and hurting themselves."

Crispin and Carvery hoist the poor woman between them, and carry her to the rickshaw, where they make a wrapping around her from the smaller rug, which Justin Time had been using as a blanket. Hopefully that means it does not have any special powers – although the power of divine resuscitation would certainly have come in handy.

Justin is currently snoring into the cobbles. Carvery wipes the driving-whip on his own jeans, and tucks it underneath the snoozing rickshaw pilot.

"There are many small boarding-houses and derelict buildings near here," says Crispin, as they hoist the body between them again. "This way."

We hurry along the narrow alleyways, away from the riverbanks. Passing bawdy calls from windows, and ragged, solitary market-stalls and sellers of less definable wares. It seems like the least maintained part of the Seven a.m. Lounge.

"Here," says Crispin, and we go through a low doorway with only half a door and one hinge attached to its remnants, finding ourselves in a filthy abandoned hovel.

Only a small square table and a bunk with one dirty linen left on it occupy the space. A rat's nest is in one corner, and mice run out from under the sheet, as Crispin and Carvery deposit the body upon the bunk. Crispin tugs the rug free like a magician with a tablecloth, so that the body rolls face-up.

I try not to heave.

"Thank you for helping," I say, timidly – my conscience vaguely aware that the poor lady's state is still my fault.

"Not at all." Crispin passes the rug to Carvery, and seems to size up the body with his eyes, while his stomach rumbles loudly. "It seems a pity to let the spare parts go to rot and waste. Do you have any sharp instruments on you, Mr. Slaughter?"

"Only always," Carvery shrugs, and shoves the rug into my arms, while he starts going through his pockets.

"What?!" I explode, for possibly the hundredth time already, since last night. "You're not going to… to… harvest her organs??! For your stupid zombie cure experiments??"

"Not exactly," says Crispin. "They may also be necessary to revive your housemate. Miss… er… Whatever Her Name Is."

Ohhhhh… I'd forgotten all about Whatserface. Currently entombed on Lady Glandula's barge, suffering from a fatal snake-bite/zombie mauling/possible Taser burn…

"Well, I'm not going to stay and watch," I say, repulsed. "I'll be back at the rickshaw checking up on Justin."

"You'd rather be back with a questionably drunk witness, and where the murder weapon is, than hanging around with your two most reliable alibis?" Carvery asks, handing Crispin what looks like a *Swiss Army* knife. "Sure – enjoy your stay in the Seven a.m. Lounge, Sarah."

I so hate it when Carvery is right… Instead I hover uncomfortably in the doorway, keeping a look-out. Trying to ignore the squelchy sounds, and the men bemoaning the fact that Ace is not here – who has many cargo pockets on his overalls, which could be made use of for transportation.

"Are you nearly done?" I call, nervously. "I think I hear company coming…"

"Stall them, Sarah *Bellummm*," Crispin orders. I hear a rip. "We need to fashion a carrier-bag out of this poor woman's apron…"

I stiffen as the footfalls draw nearer, and hope that I block the part of the doorway that the remains of the door doesn't.

"Hello, young lady," says a voice. "Business slow today, is it?"

I look at the two swarthy gentlemen in horror. Both in black, wearing dusty bowler-hats, I can't tell if they are tramps, businessmen, undertakers, or police officers…

"I'm guarding this room," I hear myself say, defensively, and a feeling of greater horror overtakes me, as I realise what my mouth is trying to persuade my brain is a good idea. "There's been a terrible murder. We're waiting for the police to bring reinforcements."

"The police, you say?" One of the men takes out a notepad and pencil. "What sort of murder? Nice and gwizzly? Fwont page nooze?"

"Fwont… er, front page? I should think so," I nod, getting my head around his fascinating impediment smoothly. I tap the side of my nose. "They say it was, erm… the work of – *The Whipper.*"

Oh, my God. I can't believe I just said that out loud.

"*The Whipper*, eh?" He scribbles frantically on his pad. "And what has the dweadful *Whipper* done here today?"

"A poor defenceless woman," I tell him. "Eviscerated in her bed…"

"Eviscerwated?" He sucks in his breath between his teeth. "Oh my. Woger, I think we may need the photogwapher – huwwy back to the pub, wake him up, and don't let the other hacks know we're onto a biggy…"

"But Ted – what if they won't let him leave without paying his slate? They only listen to you…"

"You know I can't cawwy the gweat fat oaf and his equipment on my own, Woger…"

"I'll be here," I assure them, as they both look at me like hungry puppy-dogs. "You can both run and fetch him, and I'll make sure no-one else gets first look…"

"You, my girl, are a diamond," says Ted. "One more thing – this *Whipper* – does he have a first name? Weginald? Wichard?"

"I'm sure it's not my place to hijack the real name of *The Whipper*," I say, shaking my head, as Woger – I mean Roger – drags him away.

"*Jack* is weally the name of *The Whipper*, you say?" he calls out, disappearing into the smog.

"No, er…" I begin, weakly, but they have gone – shouting about keeping something a secret. *Damn it…*

"Have they gone?" Carvery asks, jabbing me between the shoulder-blades. "Let's go. By the sound of it, those two couldn't keep a secret if they put it where the sun doesn't shine."

"Good work, Sarah *Bellummm*," Crispin says, much more approvingly, emerging behind him with a large, handmade, bloodied linen bag. "But I think Mr. Slaughter has a point. The residents of the Seven a.m. Lounge are rather more curious than cautious, and the whiff of gossip will have them out like a pack of hounds…"

“It’s them!” a distant voice suddenly hails, echoing along the alleyways. “The invasion has started – from the Six a.m. Lounge!”

“Ah,” Crispin continues. “It sounds like my brother Homer and Ace Bumgang have caught up with us. No doubt smelling distinctly of Madam Dingdong’s *Bring Your Own Towel Sauna And Spa* Eau de Toilette.”

CHAPTER THIRTY-NINE: THE LEG OF EXTRANEOUS GENITO-URINARY MEDICINE

Almost immediately, we are inspired to run. The sound of stampeding feet seems to come from all directions in the maze of alleyways, accompanied by the angry shouting of the Seven a.m. Lounge denizens – which sounds exactly as though it comes complete with cleavers, butcher's knives, pitchforks and flaming torches attached.

"Ruddy Six a.m. Loungers!" I hear a cry, too close for comfort. "Sneaking up on us – with your fancy flying hearth-rugs, and hocus-pocus!"

"I don't suppose you want to try out your Lady Glandula impression on them, do you, Sarah?" Carvery asks me as we pause for breath in the shadow of a doorway, with a nasty grin. "Seeing as you've still got her dress on. That'd put the heebie-jeebies up them all right."

"You may not have noticed, but I'm lacking a certain limb to complete the job description of *Quim of the Damned*," I retort. "I'm a bit short in the alien tentacle department."

"I'm sure there's a piece of gizzard left over from that woman you just skewered that we could stick up your nightdress," he suggests. "I bet no-one here has seen the real thing. You could get away with it."

But I'm distracted from answering by another immediate fact.

"Where has Crispin gone?" I demand, looking around.

But as I look back again – Carvery has also vanished. Into the smog, the shadows, thin air – I have no idea…

Oh, God. Do I stay put? *Do I run??*

"There's one of 'em!" a voice cries, and I see torchlight at the end of the alleyway.

I take my chances, and run. Blindly. Anywhere.

Hoping that any turn I take doesn't lead to a…

…Dead end…

I feel as though the endless brick-wall alleys are turning into those dreaded tunnels, back in the Three a.m. Lounge – or was that the Four a.m. Lounge? What bloodthirsty maneaters could turn up here? Monitor lizards? Crocodiles? More of Crispin and Homer's eccentric zombie ancestors?

The winding routes make me dizzy, and the crossways bring tears to my eyes. Which way? *Which way?* I run onwards, hoping to find my way at least to the river, where maybe I could reach the safety of the rickshaw and flying carpet…

Trying to stay one step ahead of the noise of angry residents, I double-back after one left turn and hurry back the way I came, only to realise – too late – that I can hear running feet also approaching the same junction.

I try to double my speed, hoping to bisect the crossway before anyone else reaches it…

…And collide with a mass of tanned muscle, smelling of Sea Breeze fabric softener, and Lotus Blossom massage oil…

"It's me," says Ace, taking his hand off my mouth. He obviously knows my scream reflex too well by now. "Where is everyone else?"

"I don't know, Ace," I sob. "We got separated…"

I try to fling myself into his arms, tragic-heroine style – but he steps aside too quickly, so that I merely deflect clumsily off the wall.

"They'll be around somewhere," he shrugs. "Come on."

So I'm resigned to stumbling along hurriedly in his path, hiking up my skirts gracelessly. God… Why is it never like the movies? Why hasn't he swept me off my feet and carried me to safety?

How much more obvious do I have to be??!

A sound like a gunshot startles me from my thoughts of romantically fickle injustice, and the rickshaw pulls up abruptly at the next junction, the flying rug rearing up like a stallion, pawing the air.

"Quickly, Sarah *Bellummm*," Crispin calls out from the driving-seat. "We will have to meet the others at the water's edge. The turning tide means that our transport to the Eight a.m. Lounge will not delay much longer."

"Can't we take the flying rickshaw to get there?" I ask, as Ace and I scramble in on either side.

"The rickshaw will not leave its driver behind in such a state as Mr. Time currently is," Crispin explains. "I am afraid Mr. Time has already found his bed to sober up in at one of the Seven a.m. Lounge's delightful constabularies. So we will take the optional transportation route – which hopefully will put us back on the path of Mr. Lukan, and the stolen clockwork hand. Now – hold on tight, please…"

And the rug strikes out again at the crack of the whip, jerking us into forward motion once more, as two legions of Seven a.m. Lounge residents converge on our spot from both directions.

Looking behind, I see them charging in pursuit, throwing half-bricks and other missiles. And from above – I'm fairly certain that they are on the rooftops as well…

"What about the other two?" Ace asks. "I think Homer stopped to try and buy a hat."

Crispin mutters something that is probably a curse against cross-dressing.

"…Father would never forgive me if I left the little painted trollop behind," he grumbles at last. "He knows his own way about… probably the safest of us on his own here, he is so popular amongst the seamstresses… Hang on. I know where he will most likely be found."

And we turn hard right, out of the labyrinth of alleyways into wider roads, dodging horse-drawn cabs, and startling pedestrians.

Oh no – this looks like the way back to the market-place…

"It's all right, so long as they think we're still back there around the houses," Ace points out. "Whoa, watch out for the flower-seller… never mind. She looked old anyway…"

"There's Carvery!" I cry. "Over there – fighting with that Geisha-girl…"

"THAT is no girl," Crispin remarks, grimly.

I look again.

Ohhhh… And it doesn't look like they're fighting, on second glance. To be honest, it looks as though the Geisha-girl is refusing to leave a shop by hanging onto the doorway for dear life, in spite of Carvery tugging on the other arm…

"Homer!" I hear Carvery yelling. "It's not even your colour! Let go of the stupid hat and let's go!"

Homer, who has evidently just had 'the full works' at Madam Dingdong's, is indeed painted, primped and preened beyond recognition. The white face powder. The rose-red cupid's bow of a mouth. The black hairpiece, complete with ornaments. The fabulously decorated kimono…

"*Gooood…*" Homer protests.

He scrabbles at the doorway of the hat-shop, as Carvery makes a heroic effort, and hoists the skinny transvestite zombie over his shoulder – in exactly the way I so wished Ace had done with me – before running towards us in the rickshaw.

"Go!" Carvery yells, dumping Homer on the floor at our feet, and jumping in.

"Well done, Mr. Slaughter," Crispin says, and I sense his relief – at having the difficult job of corralling Homer done for him, so efficiently.

The rug twitches into life again, and this time we soar over the market-stalls, taking a different route towards the river.

"Ace, buddy," Carvery greets him. "You smell like a cheerleader's gym locker."

"Dude," Ace frowns at him. "You just gave a fireman's lift to a zombie drag queen."

"Meaning?" Carvery raises an eyebrow.

"Meaning, you smell like a cheerleader's armpit." Ace dodges as Carvery aims an elbow at his head, meaning I get it in the ear instead.

"Ow!" I yell indignantly.

"Please, do not fight amongst yourselves," Crispin urges, trying to concentrate on steering the flying rug. "We are nearly there…"

And not a moment too soon. Already we can hear the angry mob closing in, and deliberately-aimed roof-tiles bounce off the canopy of the rickshaw.

"Can't we go higher?" I ask.

"Our transport is rather more low-profile this time, Sarah *Bellummm*," says Crispin, and I spot a glint of streetlamp reflected off the river in the distance, as we near the water's edge. "And like I said – it will not wait around, due to the tide."

A great creaking and groaning sound reaches our ears, and the end of the road where it stops at the riverbank suddenly darkens, eclipsed by the rising of a strange monolith from the river itself. Water cascades from its sides, and for one terrible moment I believe that the river-god Atum has arrived, to decimate the city with its omnipotent Eye of doom…

But instead of scales, the shape is covered in riveted metal plates. As we approach, a drawbridge lowers from it, onto the pier alongside.

"That is our transport to the Eight a.m. Lounge," Crispin announces. "The Colossal U-Boat – *The Great Nematode*."

CHAPTER FORTY:
THE HUNT FOR RECTAL OEDEMA

I can well believe the need for a high tide. Goodness – the upper surface of the boat as it emerges from the depths stretches the length of the docks as far as I can make out, in either direction. Even with the smog drifting a few feet overhead, it is still quite a distance.

"That's a sub?" Ace gasps. "Holy shit."

"Don't," Carvery grunts. "Reminds me of something Miss Fuckwit greeted me with after work once, suggesting we should try out. Luckily there were no batteries in the house, or I'd have had to fake a slipped disc again. The amount of total crap she keeps hidden in her wardrobes… just the stuff she thinks is needed to set the mood now is like playing *Ann Summers Buckaroo*."

"Sciatica," Ace nods. "That's a good one. Good excuse to lie on the beanbag chair with a beer playing *Metal Gear Solid* all night, and tell 'em to go play with their toys on their own."

"I can fake *Metal Gear Solid* too," Carvery grins. "Just leave it on demo and lock the door to the den, while I read a bit of *Dean Koontz* and get some sleep for once."

"I'm stealing that idea, dude," Ace tells him.

A thud on the roof of the rickshaw interrupts, but Carvery simply puts the muzzle of the shotgun to the canopy and pulls the trigger. There is an unearthly shriek, and the body of a Seven a.m. Lounge zombie crashes onto the cobbled dock behind us, as we head onwards along the pier.

"Women," Carvery sighs. "Way more trouble than zombies."

"Not if you treat them the same," Ace points out. "Oh, wait… you DO treat them the same."

A figure appears on the gangplank from inside the enormous submarine, as we finally pull up and tumble out of the rickshaw.

"This is our u-boat's captain," Crispin introduces us. "Rima Glottidis – Captain of *The Great Nematode*."

The man, who looks strangely exotic for a Naval officer, bows very formally. He is dressed more as a nobleman of the desert than a member of the military, and sports a well-groomed beard.

"Just the five of you today, Mr. Dry?" Captain Rima Glottidis asks of Crispin, in a clipped baritone. "I must have been mistaken – I was expecting seven."

"It has been a night of many surprises, Captain Rima," Crispin confirms. "I will fill you in *en route*."

"Then let us not delay." Captain Rima steps back, and gestures inside. "Time and tide waits for no man."

The interior of the u-boat is brightly-lit and carpeted, not how preconceptions of sound-stage constructed movie-sets of submarines have been ingrained in me. It's more like being in the inside-cabin section of a very swish ocean-liner.

The drawbridge closes behind us, and Captain Rima picks up a white courtesy telephone receiver from the wall just beside it, as massive wheels and bolts seal us within.

"Make ready to depart," he orders simply, and replaces the handset. "And now – this way. The guest quarters you will find pleasing, I hope."

I would have found them more pleasing if I didn't find myself alone… some nautical nonsense about underwater gender segregation. My new fantasy of being away at sea, in some romantic clincher with either Ace Bumgang or Crispin Dry, cannot resolve itself to the four uninterrupted blank walls facing me. It would have been so perfect – locked in a u-boat, God knows how many leagues under the sea – no escape for either of them… er, I mean *us*…

The suite is comfortable – more than comfortable. The white walls have gold accents to match the gold fittings in the bathroom, and dark blue wool carpets, and the only sound is the faintest distant humming of the submarine's propulsion system. There is not even the sensation of movement to detract from how inviting the crisp linens on the bed look, and how long it feels since I last slept… or rather snoozed, back in the hospital emergency room last night… but I resist.

No. *No going to bed alone*, I scold myself. Not when Ace or Crispin might only be the thickness of a wall away…

But it is the uncertainty of what the adjoining rooms might contain that prevent me experimenting with any tapping on those walls, *Morse-code* style. Maybe some unknown zombie naval officers, or even prisoners, are my neighbours for the journey. Or worse – I could find myself on the end of a Carvery Slaughter sleep-deprivation shotgun solution, or hours of helping Homer N. Dry attempt repairs to his new Geisha wig…

Worst of all – when I try the door – I am locked in.

Reluctantly, I eventually curl up in the cool sheets. With no idea where we are going – or at least, what the Eight a.m. Lounge has in store.

A brisk staccato rapping noise on the cabin door rouses me, and I am instantly alert.

"Are you awake, Sarah *Bellummm*?" Crispin's unmistakeable zombie drawl hails me from the far side.

Yes! I check myself hurriedly in the mirror, and instantly regret it.

I do indeed still look exactly like a scrawny pizza-delivery girl, who has fallen into a hen-house, crawled through rank underground tunnels, stumbled across desert sands, toppled off the roof of a giant Oriental fort, and accidentally stabbed a middle-aged Victorian streetwalker.

I try to wipe the scabby blood from my face with a corner of Lady Glandula's robes, which are not so much worse for wear as fully ravaged. I attempt to tweak them into a more alluring position, but only succeed in finding a mess of more blood, and dried vomit. Oh yes. A scrawny pizza-delivery girl who has also been repeatedly sick…

I cut my losses and give up on my turn-out. Maybe accessibility will trump appearance.

"I am awake, Crispin!" I reply loudly. "What is it?"

The door opens, and I am ashamed. He has made some attempt at personal grooming of his own, having brushed the dust and grime off his fine black suit, and his gray zombie countenance is far cleaner than my own.

"I was just going to freshen up," I add, alarmed, and scurry into the *en-suite*, slamming the door.

"Oh, good, Miss *Bellummm*," he coughs. "You will find clean apparel in the airing cupboard. Captain Rima Glottidis has requested our attendance in the Mission Hall."

"Mission Hall?" I repeat, splashing water onto my face and arms. Urgh. Not so much cleaning it off as moving it around…

"We need to discuss plans to retrieve the clockwork hand, Sarah *Bellummm*," he explains. "As you were so keen to pursue the matter, I thought…"

"Oh – yes, yes – of course!" I cry. I chase the soap around the basin ineffectually. "I will be right out!"

And I dunk my whole head into the warm water, hoping for the best.

I am finally presentable for the first time since last night. Now wearing a u-boat issue tailored navy-blue trouser uniform with gilt buttons, and my slowly-drying hair scraped back into a bun secured by bobby-pins borrowed from Homer's own wig, we follow Crispin through the bowels of *The Great Nematode*.

Halfway, we meet up with Ace and Carvery, who have also both been issued clean uniforms. My dormant DNA-seeking hormones spring to attention like internal hunting-dogs. *Damn them…* I am also irked by the fact that their uniforms seem to be higher-ranking than my own plain blue one…

Homer N. Dry is the only one of us who has not required a clean-up, having only recently had the full attention of all the skills at Madam Dingdong's disposal.

"You look like a singing telegram," Ace greets me.

"You look like a strip-a-gram," I snap back.

"You wish," Carvery chuckles. Who still looks like a lady-killer, in all senses of the word.

We find ourselves in a long conference room. A porcelain tea-set is on the far end of the table being attended to by a servant, and Captain Rima beckons us to join him.

"My suggestion is that we take the Northern approach to the Eight a.m. Lounge," he begins, and an illuminated spherical 3-D map appears in the centre of the room. I can make neither head nor tail of it, except for the virtual shapes of swimming whales and giant squid glowing within, and what might be shipwrecks flickering at the lower peripheral edge. "We will moor at the subterranean docks, and you can make an undetected entrance in the most convenient manner for your destination."

"Where are we going, exactly?" I ask.

"The Eight a.m. Lounge, Dumb-Ass," Carvery reminds me.

"I was hoping for more detail," I mumble.

"The detail only becomes apparent on our arrival, Sarah *Bellummm*," Crispin says. "Time does not work in the same way between the Lounges. All that is certain is the time of day on our arrival. Everything else is fractal."

"We are making good progress," Captain Rima assures us. "Tea?"

We all concede our thirst, and sit down to the dainty cups and saucers.

"Finger?" the Captain asks me directly, and I feel my eyes widen in horror – before daring to look down at the plate of crumbly sugared shortcake.

"Thank you," I barely whisper.

"Have you considered what the risks might be, should your fugitive Mr. Lukan unlock the powers of the clockwork hand?" rumbles Captain Rima, as he takes the seat at the head of the table.

"It is of no consequence," Crispin says dismissively. "Atum would not allow it."

"But the wrath of Atum would have far greater consequence," the Captain points out.

Crispin shrugs.

"Here today," he muses, and finishes his biscuit. "Gone tomorrow."

"*Gooood*," Homer nods, sipping his tea, with his own little finger crooked upwards.

The rest of us sit in bemused silence. My mind is racing. Are they talking about Atum the giant river-god? I daren't ask what the wrath of the colossal sea-serpent would entail…

There is a slight judder, tinkling the china on the tea-tray, and the distant hum of the propulsion system becomes a faint jarring vibration.

Captain Rima exchanges a look with Crispin, and beckons to his servant. The servant picks up a second tray upon which is a white courtesy phone, and brings it to his side.

The Captain picks up the receiver.

"Status report," he orders, and listens. "I see."

He replaces the handset, and gets to his feet.

"I am afraid I must leave you and attend to the bridge," he says, and clicks his heels smartly. "There is a minor issue to address. Please make yourselves at home."

And he strides out.

"What does he mean, a minor issue?" I ask. A second judder clatters a silver spoon out of the sugar-bowl.

"Well, as he is attending to it personally," Crispin ponders. "It sounds like it could be sabotage. Would anyone care for a digestive? Chocolate Hob-Nob?"

CHAPTER FORTY-ONE: CREMASTER TIED

"Shouldn't we do something?" I ask. "Isn't there – an emergency in progress? An evacuation procedure, or battle stations alert?"

"Sarah," Ace says carefully. "We're in a submarine."

"Mr. Bumgang is correct," Crispin agrees. "And the best thing to do under the circumstances is to remain calm. If it would take your mind off things, we can always move to the Games Room."

"I wonder what it would be like to play darts underwater," Carvery remarks. "Probably got to be really sure you're aiming for the dartboard and not the walls…"

I don't understand these guys. Surely the worst case scenario on a u-boat has to be sabotage?

"I really would be more comfortable knowing what is going on," I announce. "Can't we go with Captain Rima to the bridge?"

But Crispin merely gets to his feet and offers me his arm.

"Shall we, Sarah *Bellummm*?" he says. "The Captain will alert us if there is anything we need to know."

Oh, when he puts it like that, of course… I jump to my feet and latch on, like a friendly limpet-mine.

"Forget it," Ace grunts, as the optimistic Geisha Homer N. Dry sidles up to him, on his block-soled slippers.

Homer takes a speculative look at Carvery Slaughter in turn – but it seems, from that one frosty exchanged glance, that even zombies have an instinctive sense of self-preservation. So the gray Geisha is resigned to trooping along unescorted, as usual.

We head down some further stairs, and find ourselves at the foredeck of the u-boat. In a vast leisure-room, where some off-duty officers – as quirky and exotic-looking as our Captain – are partaking of a quiet drink, and a game of dominoes. A panoramic glass window reveals what on first glance look like stars… but they move, changing shape and colour, or ripple and fluoresce, and I realise they are alive, the deep-sea denizens of wherever-we-are…

I go to stare out at the inky depths, while Ace and Carvery head for the Air-Hockey table, and Homer homes in on the spotlit karaoke stage.

"What do you think, Sarah *Bellummm*?" Crispin Dry asks me, appearing at my side.

"Breathtaking," I admit, wondering how thick the glass is – now that Ace seems intent on sending the hockey puck off the table, with a bet on how many drinking-glasses he can smash within a minute. "And you have all of this on your doorstep – virtually…"

"Oh, there is nothing virtual about it, Miss *Bellummm*," Crispin replies. "It is all part of the family's hereditary munitions trading routes. The highest bidders can afford to tear holes in the seat of the pants of time and space – if it means getting their hands on the best technology before the competition does."

"So now you're no longer in the weapons industry, you just use these access routes and locations as your… your…" I forage for a word. One that means *'showing off your substitute manhood to impress women.'*

"My *droit de seigneur*, Miss *Bellummm*?" he suggests.

"I don't know what you mean by *Dry to Say Nyah*, but it certainly looks like a big show-off *Nyah-Nyah-Nyanah-Nyah* to me, when you put it that way," I remark.

"How kind of you to notice," he says, with that devastating half-smile of his.

But before I can think of a smart reply (to be truthful, that could have taken me the best part of a week) Homer's karaoke rendition of *Gooood Vibrations* is suddenly interrupted by a low pulsing siren, and the disco lights are switched off, to be replaced by an all-encompassing red-blue phasing alert.

"All hands to the bridge," Captain Rima's voice announces over the tannoy. "That is all."

The off-duty officers jump to their feet, and hurry over to what I had previously thought was a dance-pole, to the left of the stage. One at a time, they grasp it and slide downwards, disappearing below the floor.

"Let's go!" says Carvery, and he and Ace follow suit.

"We should attend too," says Crispin, as Homer waddles quickly after Ace and Carvery. Can't say I blame him… "Just do as I do."

I watch him grip the pole, hand over hand, and slide below deck. Once the coast seems clear, I reach out and try to cling on likewise, sloth-like.

"Too tight, Sarah *Bellummm*," Crispin's voice rises to my ears. "Loosen your grip."

I do as bidden – and the floor of the deck below smacks into my coccyx like a demolition ball.

"Well done," Crispin greets me, and hauls me upright, as I wonder if I'll ever walk again. I've lost all sensation below the ribcage, but as he sets me on my feet, issues of *Instant Pain* are filed from multiple complainants around my anatomy. "This is the bridge."

Officers are attending to various consoles and 3-D displays, showing not only the earlier underwater 'maps' but also the layout of the u-boat. Sections of the diagnostics flash alarmingly, or are lit up red, in ways that remind me of Crispin's home security bunker back at the mansion – when he was looking for the security breach.

"We have intercepted a partial distress call," Captain Rima Glottidis announces, directing Crispin to look at a readout on a console. "We have a location and the first five codewords. However, these codewords in another sequence also form a scrambled declaration of war. So without the rest of the message, we cannot act in a fully-informed response."

"And the sabotage?" asks Crispin.

"We have hull breaches in a number of our flotation tanks," Captain Rima continues. "But no arms signatures. I believe the breaches may be parasitic."

"It is spawning season," Crispin agrees, in a pondering tone. "We are not within Atum's consecrated waters, I hope?"

"Our charts say no," the Captain assures him. "But – Atum himself could easily mislead us, if he so wanted…"

"Of course," Crispin nods. I sense the tension in the air, taut like the elastic in a pair of control-top pantyhose on a Hull school dinner-lady, never mind the hull of the u-boat.

"So what's the plan?" Ace asks. "Go and check out this place where the partial distress call came from?"

"That is our first priority, indeed," says Captain Rima. "Because our response would be to launch recovery vehicles, in that instance. But in the alternative declaration of war, by whichever Lounge initiated it – our obligation is to launch a pre-emptive strike. Have you upset anyone, on your journey so far this morning?"

We all exchange dubious glances.

"I think Madam Dingdong might be missing a few knick-knacks," says Carvery quietly, jerking a thumb meaningfully at Homer N. Dry, who is currently preoccupied with alternative entertainment uses for the pole we have just entered the bridge by.

The rest of us mumble agreement, keen to delegate any responsibility for an 'upset' thus far.

"I suggest that the engineers focus on the hull breach," says Crispin. "Mr. Slaughter and Mr. Bumgang – your expertise there would be appreciated."

"Dude, I can fill a six-foot-by-six hole faster than you can blink," Carvery remarks.

"You won't even *see* the welding-marks on any cut-and-shut of mine," Ace chips in.

"Excellent," Captain Rima booms. "Officer Lyra will show you down."

A small dark gentleman appears next to Captain Rima and bows smartly, and the two guys follow him out of the bridge. My stomach lurches in panic.

Whatever happens down there – I hope at least their DNA makes it back intact…

"Who is analysing the distress call?" Crispin continues.

"I am handling it myself." Captain Rima moves aside, so that we can see the console more clearly. But I don't recognise anything about the hieroglyphs on the screen – except…

"I've seen these drawings before!" I cry out.

"But my dear, that is impossible," says the Captain, patiently. "This is top-secret code."

"In the diary – your father's diary, Crispin!" I insist. "I'm sure of it! The one that was in the room with the clockwork hand…"

"Where is this 'diary'?" Captain Rima frowns, looking from me to Crispin, and back again.

I rack my brains.

"I think Carvery had it last," I say. "In his pocket. Yes!"

Captain Rima beckons to another officer.

"Go after Lyra, and see if either of the men in his team have Mr. Dry Senior's diary on them," he orders. "And check their quarters also, for the same. There may be other codeword sequences listed in it, relevant to this transmission."

"Sir – yes, Sir!" The officer hurries away.

"Sir!" Another officer, by one of the 3-D spherical maps, calls for his attention. "Unidentified bogey dead ahead, Sir!"

The Captain and Crispin move swiftly to look, and I dart after them.

A massive blob shape appears glowing in the projection field, and as we watch, begins to uncoil, into an even larger, seemingly endless helix.

"It is the parasitic saboteur I feared," Captain Rima says. "The *Great Abyss Tapeworm*."

"Are you sure?" I ask. "It looks like Atum… from what I recall, I mean… God help us."

"I think I have the experience required to recognise monsters of the deep, Miss Bellum," says Captain Rima, curtly.

"And if it is Atum, then we are indeed at war," Crispin points out. "Not even God will help us, in that case."

"Bogey closing, Sir!" a voice hails the Captain again. "Standing by for orders to attack, Sir!"

The helix of the beast in the virtual map continues to unwind and extend, gradually filling the field of the 3-D projection, like an unravelling ball of yarn in a basket.

"We will shortly be surrounded," Crispin notes aloud. "You had better be sure, Captain Rima."

"Stand by!" shouts the Captain, but I notice a single bead of sweat emerging onto his forehead from his turban, as he studies the map. My heart contracts in terror.

He's waiting for something… which means he's not sure…

CHAPTER FORTY-TWO: 20,000 LEGS UNDER THE SEA

"Target acquired, Sir!" comes the shout again from the crew, on the bridge of the Colossal U-Boat, *The Great Nematode*. "Orders, Sir!"

Captain Rima Glottidis puts his eyes to the dual magnifying scope beside the 3-D underwater map. The unravelling beast of a sea-parasite, whose territory we have crossed into, now spans the spherical projection.

The Captain twists dials and turns knobs. I worry that there will be nothing left of *The Great Nematode* before he makes a decision, as further vibrations jar the giant hull.

"We must ensure that your subterranean route to the Eight a.m. Lounge is not blocked," he murmurs, tapping commands into the touch screen controls.

I reach for Crispin Dry's hand, for reassurance, and feel his cold zombie fingers curl through my own.

"Ready the Chthonic Sonar!" Captain Rima suddenly barks, and crew-members spurt into action. He raises his head and looks towards us with a steely gaze, no sign of uncertainty in his features at all. "It will not destroy – but it will disperse. And in the event of Atum's presence, it will not register to him as an act of aggression."

"I respect your decision, Captain Rima," Crispin concurs with a nod.

"You may find yourselves having to confront any remaining hostiles face-to-face," the Captain warns, and Crispin merely concedes again with another subtle nod of understanding.

What? *Face-to-face?* What does he mean?

"Sonar ready, Captain!" hails the crewman manning the weapons console, turning a key beside a large green button. The u-boat rocks and lurches, like an overweight pigeon landing on a rotating washing-line.

“Maximum power!” orders the Captain. “One pulse!”

“Aye, Sir!”

The crewman strikes the green button.

I suddenly know how a dog-whistle feels. It’s as though a high-speed tornado has just shot through all of my bones.

The unravelling Abyss Tapeworm on the projection reacts, contracting once, and then cracking like a whip. *The Great Nematode* tilts dangerously, foredeck-down. We, and the crew, have to brace ourselves at the consoles.

“Again!” shouts Rima. “Second pulse!”

“Aye, Sir!”

Again, the terrible sense of disruptive distortion rips through me. The parasite contracts again, like a coiled spring of intent…

“Fire again!” the Captain roars.

A third pulse of the Chthonic Sonar is discharged, and it feels as though all sorts of bodily fluids are following suit. For one terrible second, the Abyss Tapeworm remains coiled to respond…

…And then spontaneously breaks apart. *The Great Nematode* slowly rights itself, as the segments of the parasite drift gently outwards across the 3-D map, on the current.

“Bogey neutralized, Sir!” the confirmation report finally reaches our ravaged ears.

“Received,” Captain Rima replies, curtly. He turns to Crispin. “Some of those pouches will be mature. You will have to exercise great caution on the next stage of your journey.”

“Understood, Captain.” Crispin turns back to the communications console. “And the transmission you intercepted?”

“I think it best if we lie low on the edge of the Deep Ocean Trench until it can be fully de-coded,” says the Captain. “Which means you can reconnoitre with us if so required, after the Eight a.m. Lounge.”

“Do not delay your mission on our account, Captain,” Crispin tells him.

“It is a privilege, Mr. Dry.” Captain Rima’s smart nod of acknowledgement is almost a bow. He glances at the diagnostics of the u-boat. “It seems that our hull breaches are almost fully repaired. Allow me to escort you to the air-lock.”

As we turn to leave the bridge, beckoning to Homer to detach himself from the crewman's pole and join us, the officer who had been sent after Mr. Dry Senior's diary returns.

"No luck, Sir," the officer apologises. "Mr. Slaughter, the guest in question, believes the diary may have been left behind in the Six a.m. Lounge – at Madam Dingdong's *Bring Your Own Towel Sauna And Spa*."

Oh, no…

We meet up again with Carvery Slaughter and Ace Bumgang as we reach the airlock, where a range of diving-suits and equipment is stored, ready for use.

"You have patched up the hull of *The Great Nematode* well, as I understand," says the Captain. "Your hard work is appreciated, men."

"Nobody wants uninvited eggs laid in his premises," Carvery remarks, giving me a nasty wink. "Just because some big old hermaphrodite worm thinks it looks like a good incubator."

"If women ever figure out how to do that, we are fucked," Ace agrees. "Talk about woman's inhumanity to man."

Damn – there goes most of the other half of my future fantasy plans, regarding Ace and the accessibility of his DNA…

"You will be able to make it to the subterranean level of the Eight a.m. Lounge from here on foot," the Captain continues, gesturing at the display of underwater gear. "And here I must leave you all, and return to my duties. There is the small matter of arrangements to recover Mr. Dry Senior's diary, from the Six a.m. Lounge. Officer Lyra will assist you."

On *FOOT??!*

Captain Rima Glottidis does not elucidate further, merely clicks his heels with a nod, and departs.

I feel as though I'm in a daze, trying to take in the concept, even though the deep-sea space-suits with their fishbowl-shaped helmets are self-explanatory.

"We've got to cross the sea-bed?" I ask, weakly. "In – just those things…?"

"*The Great Nematode* is too large to dock closer," Crispin explains, as Officer Lyra unhooks a diving-suit and holds it out, ready for him to step into. "And there are many residents in the Eight a.m. Lounge who would not approve of it surfacing in their vicinity. Different ocean-bound regulations apply here. We cannot afford too many perceived declarations of war in just the one morning, you understand."

I note Ace and Carvery grinning at each other knowingly, as they shrug on the huge protective suits over their Naval uniforms. Carvery still has Mrs. Frittata's shotgun, which is sealed up in a special additional watertight holster, and strapped to his leg. Homer is hiking up his Geisha kimono quite cheerfully, and tucking it into his undergarments to fit inside.

Officer Lyra holds out a slightly smaller diving-suit for me obligingly, and with great trepidation and dread, I step inside.

It's not so much wearing the suit, as being encased in it. It is stifling and claustrophobic, like being zipped up and buckled inside a watertight sleeping-bag. Only after the helmet is clipped into place and the hiss of the heavy oxygen-canister starts, initiating a draft of cool air which circulates around me in the suit, do I feel any relief from the sweltering incarceration of it.

"This way," Crispin's voice prompts, and I realise there is a two-way radio built in also. "We will undergo pressure compensation in the airlock."

Officer Lyra presses a sequence of buttons on the wall, and spins a wheel to open a vault-like door, and we file into the bare metal cell. Lyra salutes our departure, and closes the door again behind us.

"What now?" I ask, as we shuffle around.

Crispin indicates for us all to grab hold of a strap from the ceiling, like being in a subway car.

"They flood the airlock," he says.

A light starts to flash overhead, and valves open all around the walls, at ankle-height. Suddenly water gushes through, swirling and rising rapidly.

"Your suits will compensate for the pressure automatically," he continues, and I'm aware of my own suit apparently inflating, while the water-level in the airlock advances above my knees.

Even though I'm dry inside, it doesn't feel normal for a human being.

"Now I know how the little plastic dude in the fish-tank always feels," Ace comments, the water now up to his chest, and already over my shoulders.

"You've certainly achieved his exact look," I reply, before the foaming water bubbles up past my face, momentarily obscuring everything.

Once it is above my head, I can see. I'm surprised how much everything looks the same underwater – just – slower.

When the tank is full, the light stops flashing, and turns green.

"We can still communicate," Crispin reminds us, after a short silence.

It is followed by the very definite sound of radio-transmitted flatulence. Nobody owns up to it, although we all exchange suspicious glances, to see who might be suffering the side-effect of extra gas in their air-supply.

Fortunately, the outer doors slide open.

"Before we leave," Crispin adds. "You may now arm yourselves."

He opens a previously unnoticed cabinet just inside the outer doors, which is revealed to be full of harpoon guns.

"Cool," Ace remarks.

"Is that all?" groans Carvery, but takes one anyway. "What are we doing now – *Colossal Squid* acupuncture?"

"There will still be *Great Abyss Tapeworm* eggs adrift in the water," Crispin reminds us, as we step out onto the gangplank. "Some may be mature, and looking for a host. Plus the usual sharks, giant octopus, maybe even *Colossal Squid* indeed, Mr. Slaughter…"

…Not to mention Carvery Slaughter now armed with a harpoon, I think to myself, and try to make sure I don't have my back to him, at least…

I take a first look at our surroundings. The u-boat, *The Great Nematode*, towers over us like an entire mobile underwater precinct. Beyond it is a bottomless blackness, which must be the Deep Ocean Trench. And we are standing on what is essentially a shelf on the edge of that trench, a rocky, sandy, weed-and-crustacean coated outpost of sea-floor.

We must be just close enough to the surface to benefit from a little natural blue-tinged light from above, although our visibility in all directions is probably less than sixty or seventy feet.

"There!" Crispin points, and we all turn. A large white shape floats innocently on the current – resembling a huge, plastic, supermarket carrier-bag – until something indefinable wriggles within. "It may look benign now, but if that larva is ready to hatch, it will start to eat its way through the hull of any vessel passing through."

The egg drifts out of range, into the darkness of the trench, where it abruptly vanishes.

"Of course, some will be eaten by larger predators first," he concedes.

I feel as though I've just had to swallow a stone. I hope none of those 'larger predators' like to pop out of the Deep Ocean Trench for a stroll…

We proceed slowly away in the opposite direction across the sea-bed, only the resistance of the water pressure around us our main hindrance. Shoals of small fish dart by, and the occasional lobster flaps between the rocks – but nothing menacing seems to occupy these particular waters – so far.

"Something just ran over my foot," Ace says, behind me. "There's another…"

The sand beside me erupts, and a six-foot-long, many-segmented exoskeletal insect scurries in front of me. I scream, without thinking.

"Great, now I'm deaf, from electronic audiofeedback," Carvery says. "One more scream out of you, Sarah, and the only way you'll be getting out of here is as a dolphin-friendly, harpooned tinned twat."

"We are close to our destination," Crispin announces, as another multi-limbed critter hurries past, and disappears under the sand once more. "These are the juveniles of the *Burrowing Sea-Centipede*. The tunnels of the adult Centipede should be in the cliffs ahead."

Sure enough, a craggy pale limestone wall gradually appears through the waters in front of us, peppered with caves, and sprinkled with self-anchoring sea-creatures, many of which could be mistaken for plants.

"How big are these adult Sea-Centipedes?" Ace wants to know, saving me the trouble of asking for myself.

"We must aim for the largest tunnel," Crispin announces. "It leads to the subterranean docking platform. But do not worry. The Centipede that burrowed this original tunnel is long dead."

"Not that it makes any difference around here," Carvery chuckles. "I'd quite like to see a Zombie Centipede…"

I can't say I agree with him – as we approach the underwater cliff-face, and an almost perfectly circular cavern, fifty feet in diameter, looms above us…

CHAPTER FORTY-THREE: SPLAT

"We will have to climb a little way," Crispin points out, over the two-way radio. "But it is not treacherous."

Hmmm – not exactly what I was thinking… The opening of the giant tunnel in the underwater cliff-face is still a good thirty or so feet above the floor of the ocean shelf we are currently occupying, in our deep-sea diving-suits. And as we draw closer, I see more of those juvenile Burrowing Sea Centipedes popping disturbingly in and out of the vertical surface of the limestone.

It's rather like watching a demon-possessed Hornby train-set.

"After you," I say warily, to Ace Bumgang.

I don't like the idea of either him or Carvery Slaughter bringing up my rear at the moment. Not while they're armed with harpoon guns, particularly.

So I hang back, until even the zombie transvestite Homer N. Dry is in front of me, his Geisha wig now slightly lopsided inside his diving helmet. I watch carefully where he places his hands and feet in the limestone wall, observing the safest potential route upwards.

The water provides a little buoyancy, even though the diving boots are weighted, for ease and stability of traversing the sea-bed.

"Watch out for the Cannibal Corals," Crispin's voice warns. "They are more territorial than you might think."

I snatch my left hand away from a pit in the surface, as a young Centipede head emerges from it, scattering limestone sand into the ocean current. It pauses, before heading out across the surface of the wall, on its many articulated legs.

It passes over the living branches and folds of a Coral outcrop, which instantly reacts, extruding some whitish tripe-like fleshy mantle from within, attacking and enveloping the intruder. Within seconds, the struggling seven-foot-long Sea Centipede has been stripped of all living tissue, leaving behind a fragile shell of exoskeleton.

Within a few more brief seconds, the segments of remaining shell are washed apart by the current, adrift on the tide.

A giant Brittlestar or Basket Starfish picks its way carefully over the wall's surface in the meantime, ominously, like a passing tumbleweed.

I can almost hear the Mexican *bandito* flutes…

Crispin and Carvery have reached the summit, and turn to assist Ace next. As I look up, the great shadow of a Manta Ray emerges from the tunnel over their heads, soaring above us silently, like a stealth bomber.

All of my internal organs scrunch into a messy knot, until the long whip of its deadly tail finally curls out of range and vanishes, in the direction of the Deep Ocean Trench.

One at a time, Ace and Homer also complete the climb, and disappear over the top into the giant tunnel.

"Did you see that?" I hear Carvery say, over the radio. "Something moved back there…"

"Stay vigilant," Crispin's voice advises. "Wait… yes. Do not make any sudden moves…"

I freeze in my ascent. Does that order even include me?

What's going on up there?!

For the next few moments, I hear nothing. My brain goes slowly and horribly numb.

What are they doing?

Are they still alive??!

I decide I will have to risk a peek, or stay clinging to the underwater limestone cliffs for ever. Determinedly, I reach up with my right hand, for another hand-hold. And then another, levering myself upward in the heavy boots…

A Sea Centipede bursts out of the rock at eye-level, and I swallow my scream, wary of pissing off Carvery Slaughter any more than I already have – if he's still around to act on it, that is.

But that's not the worst of it…

The juvenile insect seems as startled as I am, and lunges. With the sound of hailstones against a windowpane, dozens of armoured legs stampede around my diving helmet, treating me to a close-up view of the long pale undercarriage of the creature, and its almost mechanically-moving segments as they wrap around and around…

It drags me off-balance, away from the limestone cliff, and I lurch backwards towards the sea-floor once more, scrabbling to try and grab the wriggling beast as it runs all over me in a territorial frenzy.

And then just as quickly, it is torn away. By what, I can't see – and I'm still falling.

Until something closes on my upper arms from behind, like steel pincers, halting my sinking progress through the waters. *What on Earth…?*

My journey suddenly reverses, and at an alarming speed, I shoot upwards again.

…Right to the top of the wall I was climbing, and the entrance to the tunnel. Where I'm deposited gently onto my feet once more.

In the distance, I can see the others moving around by the flashlights set into their headgear, in the darkness ahead. *But what just…?*

The pincer-sensation is released, and I manage to turn around, trying to ready my harpoon gun. Just as I raise it level, it is abruptly snatched from my grip.

I gasp in shock.

For I'm gazing into the green eyes of the most beautiful man I've ever seen – who has no diving-gear, no shirt on – just a snake tattoo, and a bit of strategically-placed seaweed – and my harpoon gun, in his right hand.

He blows a kissing salute on the two forefingers of his other hand, and grins – and then is gone, with the powerful flick of a muscular silver tail – which nearly sends me over backwards again.

"Watch out for the Humungous Rock Scorpions," I hear Crispin saying, as I wonder if there's anything else new left to see in the world now. My mind is reeling. "They respond well to a show of strength – our harpoons may need to be deployed here."

Well… if that isn't just bloody typical…

CHAPTER FORTY-FOUR: THE UVULA STRIKES BACK

"What took you so long?" Ace asks, when I catch up with the others.

The underwater cavern could be described as 'forbidding' – only it's more than forbidding. It's the full *Trespassers Will Be Prosecuted* notice, *Jesus-is-Watching-You* sign, and restraining order.

That's how *forbidding* it is.

I can already sense my brain-stem drafting out its Diminished Responsibility plea for the condition that this diving-suit will be returned in.

"I slipped," I explain, knowing that I'm not even in the neighbourhood of the truth, let alone close to it. "And, er – I dropped my harpoon gun…"

An explosion in the water between us causes similar in my trousers, as the weapon being discussed – in this case, Crispin Dry's harpoon gun – fires at something behind me. I turn to face a giant, yawning, vicelike claw, lined with exoskeletal barbs.

It freezes in its apparently ready stance to snap around my neck, and then abruptly withdraws into a cloud of sand and bubbles.

"Rock Scorpion," says Crispin, over the radio. "We must keep moving."

Heading deeper into the tunnel, we climb over a jagged outcrop of white limestone stalagmites. I look upwards, half expecting to see similar stalactites overhead… but the cave is so vast, the ceiling is hidden in darkness, and drifting ocean silt.

"Are you sure the Sea Centipede who dug this tunnel is dead?" Carvery Slaughter asks, voicing something I was wondering about myself.

"Fairly certain," Crispin replies. "She was not too bothered about us clambering over her teeth just now, so if we survive the journey all the way along the alimentary canal to the other end, I think we can safely assume that 'dead' is her current state."

"Really?" Carvery points his harpoon at the nearest wall, and fires. It goes fairly deep, sending up dark shards of old rotted carcass into the almost stagnant seawater. "Guess so."

"What's an alimentary canal?" Ace asks. "Do we have to get on another barge? Because the last one kind of did me enough damage for today."

"Nah, you don't need a barge on an alimentary canal," Carvery tells him. "It's a misnomer. Not so much like a real canal – more like a flume."

"What, one you ride on a rubber ring?" says Ace.

"If we spot one on the way, you're welcome to it," I mutter under my breath, but forget that they can hear me over the radio.

"I wouldn't try it, if I were you," Carvery replies to Ace, ignoring me. "It's over-rated."

"I'll let you ride shotgun," Ace suggests.

Carvery seems to ponder.

"Not my cup of tea," he says at last. "And anyway – judging by the size of this mother, it'd be like throwing a couple of Tic-Tacs down a well."

We continue to pick our way carefully through the darkness, the only illumination being from the lights built into our own diving helmets.

Another Humungous Rock Scorpion lunges out into our path, and this time I get a better view as it swings for Homer. The segmented carapace is black with yellow underneath, spotted like a leopard, and those giant claws are highlighted with angry red *Go-Faster* stripes. It reminds me of an old Formula One, *John Player Special*-sponsored *Decepticon Transformer.*

Ace's harpoon flies into its side, and sticks in the join between head armour and thorax. It immediately turns back, scrabbling to try and dislodge the piercing, and forgetting about Homer N. Dry – who minces onward happily.

How can he still walk like that underwater, in that dirty great diving-suit? It must be the added buoyancy… I feel as though as I'm doing a *Pingu* impression, myself…

"See that light ahead?" Crispin announces, and we all strain to see anything through the murk. "The exit is about another hundred yards or so, and we will find ourselves at the bottom of the subterranean dock, for the Eight a.m. Lounge."

It sounds hopeful, and we put in a renewed effort. I'm relieved to see Carvery and Ace re-cocking their harpoon guns, just in case.

I wonder about that mysterious creature who rescued me back on the cliff-face, stealing my own harpoon gun in exchange. What would a man with a fishtail want with a harpoon gun? Surely if there were any danger to him underwater, he could just turn his tail into legs and run away up the beach somewhere?

Or maybe they don't do that in this reality… perhaps *Disney* made it up…

"Watch it," Ace's voice interrupts my thoughts. "I just stepped in something squishy."

I look down, the beams of my head-lights sparkling off the sand and dirt swirling up from the sediment. The floor has taken on a bobbled appearance under the muck, like a huge puff-patchwork quilt.

"It was one of these blobby things," Ace continues, kicking his foot into another. It breaks open, like a deflating balloon, and releases inky black liquid and greenish slime into the water. "Maybe the giant centipede had a big peptic ulcer problem."

"I hope so," Carvery remarks. "Because otherwise it looks like we've taken a wrong turn at the buffet car, and found where they're hiding the caviare."

CHAPTER FORTY-FIVE: ILIUM RESURRECTION

"Eggs," Crispin confirms. "But not Sea Centipede eggs. These are laid by another parasite – one that needs underwater carrion to incubate its clutch. The small amount of heat given off during decay accelerates the development process."

"What are they from?" Ace asks, prodding another, with the toe of his boot.

"Hermit Squidmorphs," says Crispin. "They go through a series of parasitic stages before becoming fully mature and independent."

"Let me guess," Carvery suggests. "The next stage after the eggs is the vampire face-hugging phase, yes?"

"No," Crispin looks a little offended, through his diving helmet. "Squidmorphs are not facially-orientated in the slightest. Quite the opposite, in fact."

"Alien anal probing?" Carvery remarks.

The radio silence between us all becomes distinctly more unpleasant.

"I think we should keep moving," I announce, my voice higher than Salvador Dali on LSD.

Ace and Carvery are both looking at the floor with concern now.

"Good idea," Ace murmurs. "Don't think I want to meet a vampire butt-hugger either."

We try not to jostle one another in expressions of blind panic as we continue through the gut of the giant centipede carcass. A few more eggs get stepped on in the shambolic rush, releasing their premature black squid ink into the water.

"Are there likely to be any more of those Rock Scorpions down here?" Carvery's voice comes across the radio again, as it seems to get inexplicably darker. Damn this ink – it doesn't seem to disperse at all…

"Er, no," Crispin replies, from up ahead. "They will not enter the nursery when hatching is due. Hermit Squidmorphs are not fussy about the species of host they occupy."

Holy Mother… I saw the armour-plated shells on those scorpions! Even Homer, in front of me, seems to double the pace of his mincing strut, into an underwater scurrying.

Thankfully, the knee-high eggs start to thin out from what I can see of the ground underfoot, and we start to climb a little as the terrain slopes upward.

"What?" Carvery wants to know, and I stumble into Homer's back. "Why are we stopping?"

There is a pause. I glance behind us, my own insides fluttering with adrenal abuse.

"Underwater landslide," I hear Crispin say, grimly. "Our exit is blocked."

I push past Homer, determined to see for myself.

A wall of rubble marks the end of our path. Jagged segments of centipede armour are either side, allowing only a narrow current of water and silt to drift through.

"Let's have a look," says Carvery. "I've demolished almost as many walls as I've had to put up."

I wonder how much of that involved the interment of his ex-girlfriends?

He assesses the slurry of mixed shapes and sizes of rock, before apparently picking a few at random and pulling them free. Dust clouds billow into the seawater, but the rest of the rock-face holds.

"That's as many as we can safely move," he says, at last. "It's like *Jenga*. Pull the wrong stone out, and the whole shebang comes down."

"Man, we still won't fit through there," Ace tells him, patting the surface. "It's like a cat-door."

"How far are we from the surface, Crispin?" asks Carvery.

Crispin considers.

"Fifty feet – perhaps sixty," he says eventually. "At a slight upward angle, through these rocks and out the other side. We will find a stone platform just beyond, with a steel ladder embedded into the rock, leading up to it."

"Reckon we could make it without suits?" Carvery suggests.

"What?!" I gasp.

Take off our breathing apparatus? Is he *crazy?*

"It is possible…" Crispin ponders. "But during hatching, the Squidmorph eggs release acid into the water as well as ink. We will have to work fast."

"Cool." Carvery seems decided on the matter. Since when was he in charge? "Homer – you're the thinnest of us. You go first."

"*Ho-ooo-ome?*" Homer asks, doubtfully.

"It's quite all right, Homer," Crispin reassures his zombie brother. "Mr. Slaughter is thinking clearly. Nice deep breaths first. Like Bette Midler, before a Vegas show."

"*Goooood,*" Homer agrees, and we all hear his lungs creaking and whistling like a frog on a night out with the lads, as he dutifully exercises his diaphragm before reaching for the clasps on his suit.

"Fuck," Ace curses. "Forgot about the kimono."

Homer is still dressed as *Madam Butterfly* underneath the diving-suit. Between them, Carvery and Ace quickly pull apart the bulkiest parts of the sash, bow and bustle.

Finally down to a scrap of embroidery, Homer makes for the opening in the rocks, and darts through, with a kick of his heels.

God – not much of a gap there…

"You're next in size, Sarah," Carvery says, turning to me. "Deep breaths now."

"Why is it in order of size?" I demand, feeling panic rising up my gullet like a victory flag.

"Smallest go first, less likelihood of dislodging any more rocks on the way through," he reasons, with perfect logic. "Come on. Less talk. More deep breaths."

I do as instructed, filling my last lungfuls of air from the gas-tanks. Blessed gas-tanks – how I will miss you…

"While we're still young, Sarah," Carvery prompts.

"Yeah – I think I just saw one of those eggs wriggle," Ace chips in. "I think something else's young might be joining us quite soon."

"Aim for the ladder directly ahead as you exit the rock-slide, Sarah," Crispin tells me. "When you feel the rungs in front of you, head straight upwards – do not hesitate."

"No chance of me hesitating," I say, and I mean it. "Don't worry about that."

I reach for my clasps. One – two – three on the front of the diving-suit. One – two on either side of the diving helmet. I brace myself – and I am free…

The cold water gurgles instantly into my suit, and slaps me about the face. *Aargh!* It's gross… I dread to think what living or dead particles are finding their way into my eyes and ears and nose already…

Even more gross is feeling Carvery and Ace both shove me towards the opening in the rocks, and the grating of my Naval uniform gold-gilt buttons from the *Great Nematode* u-boat, as they scrape along the surface. With one last glimpse of Crispin out of the corner of my eye, I am fully inserted into the hole…

I have a little elbow-room, and can kick my feet to propel myself forward – but the channel through the rock-slide is longer than I thought. I squirm my way along, my throat burning as I struggle to keep what air I have in my lungs.

And yes! I can see a blue-tinged light at the far end! That must be what Crispin was referring to earlier – we *are* near the surface, at last. I push forward, dog-paddling my way through the tunnel.

My eyes must be suffering from the dirt in here. It's getting cloudy…

…But then I see the cloudiness billow, and the opening at the other end of the tunnel turns briefly black…

Oh my God – parasitic alien butt-hugger squid eggs…

They must be on *BOTH* sides of the rock-slide!

I can't go backwards in this channel. For all I know, one of the others is already behind me – and back there – no escape. Just a mile of Giant Sea Centipede alimentary tract, leading out onto the Deep Ocean Trench, populated by recently-armed Fish-Man. And me with no diving-suit on…

I shut my eyes tight – and various other orifices that I can think of – and swim forward. As fast as I can…

Something hits my nose, and I almost forget myself by opening my mouth to scream. The taste of rank seawater and battery acid rushes in. My hands shoot up to meet my face protectively – and snag on a rigid metal bar.

The ladder!

Do not hesitate, Crispin's voice echoes in my mind.

I kick my way up the underwater ladder, my fingers finding more rungs as I try to increase my ascending speed. Surely this is more than sixty feet from where I started?

Just as it seems my bursting lungs are about to tear their way out of my chest, the water breaks over my head – and my brain sloshes painfully at the unexpected loss of buoyancy.

"*Gooooood*," Homer's voice greets me, grabbing my arm.

"Homer!" I cry in gratitude.

As manfully as he's possibly ever done, the skinny gray zombie hauls me up onto the strange, livid green stone of the subterranean platform. We are still underground – but high overhead, daylight filters down from the top of a tower-like stairwell.

We've done it – we're here. I've never been so glad to see the sky as I am now…

I'm barely taking my first full breath, dragging myself onto the cool and welcome flat surface – when something closes around my left ankle – still overhanging the edge – like a bear-trap.

"Owwww!" I yell, and try to snatch my leg in towards me – but whatever has me caught in its embrace is firmly anchored.

And it *tugs*…

I look down in utter dread, in time to see a third coil of red speckled tentacle loop around and up, aiming for better grip below my knee. My foot is already obscured by some horrible, barbed, knobbly, eight-fingered, arachnid claw…

And *boy* – do I scream! Maybe because Carvery Slaughter is nowhere near – I really let one rip.

"Geddoff!" I shriek. "*Off!* AAAAAAARRRRGHHH!"

Bless Homer – he bravely goes for the tentacle lashed around my shin, and bites and bites it. It squirts black ink over his head, and I promptly vomit in turn.

It tugs again abruptly, and I shoot backwards, suddenly back in the water up to my waist. Homer grabs my hand, as I scrabble for any purchase on the stone ledge.

"Please help me," I beg, already knowing that Homer is losing the battle, with all of the undead power in his pathetic, weedy, cross-dressing physique. "I don't want an alien butt-plug…"

Another lash of the horrible tentacle suddenly whips around my neck, and its barbed little hooks bite into my flesh like burning needles of red-hot ice. It makes the suckers on Lady Glandula's weird appendage in the Five a.m. Lounge seem almost an attractive prospect in comparison…

"Homer…" I sob.

I see the despair in his black eyes, as I recede helplessly back into the deadly water. I feel it lapping at my ears, the smell of battery-acid already corroding the hairs on the inside of my nostrils…

Suddenly I feel my trapped leg jerk abruptly, and a mouthful of the vile seawater makes its way down my throat – before I realise that my neck is now free once more.

Homer gives a heave, and I progress forward slightly, like a *Tug o'War* rope. Oh God – please let me live… I'll never lick another pizza box again…

Another strange tearing sensation underwater, and my leg is also free.

Homer heaves again, and I slither the rest of the way back onto the stone platform. *Thank God – thank God…*

"Thank you…" I blubber, not sure how much of the damp on my face is tears, sea-gunk or snot by now. "Oh, thank you…"

…And Carvery Slaughter bursts out of the water, hopping up onto the platform from the topmost rung of the ladder with ease.

"Carvery!" I gasp.

"Shotgun works underwater," he remarks, brandishing the remains of the tattered waterproof holster. "At least, while it was inside this. That was one ugly calamari, Sarah."

Ace appears right behind him – minus his jacket and shirt.

Oh, boy… I've gone from *All Systems Panic Stations* to *All Hormones Conception Stations* in four seconds flat.

"Tight squeeze," he says, by way of explanation. He shakes the water from his spiky dark hair, like a *Davidoff* model. I'm glad I'm still sitting on the ground, as I don't think my legs could stand the moral challenge of such a display. "I don't envy Crispin, trying to squirm his way through those rocks."

"Did you see any more of those squid eggs hatching down there?" I ask Carvery, nervously.

"Too dark." Carvery tips seawater out of the shotgun barrels. "Too much squid ink."

We all look down at the swirling surface of the water, and wait.

And wait…

CHAPTER FORTY-SIX: GNASHER NAIL TREASURE

"Anyone fancy going back in to see if he's all right?" Ace asks eventually.

We all stare hard into the darkening water. I dread to think how many vampire squid eggs have hatched by now, to create so much inky blackness down there.

"Maybe he needs a bit of guidance," Carvery suggests. "Who's got a light?"

A small part of my mostly-useless brain leaps to attention.

"Yes – yes, I have!" I fish the *Trevor Baylis* clockwork keyring torch out of my pocket, and wind it quickly. The light flashes randomly and intermittently, evidently a little damaged by the seawater, but I hold it close to the surface anyway – hoping that the blinking brilliance will penetrate the contaminated depths. I pray that he can see it… "Come on, Crispin…"

"*Ho-oooo-ome*," groans Homer, unhappily.

A scream escapes me, as a single hand bursts forth from the water, clamping firmly around my wrist.

"Pull him out!" shouts Ace. "Attaboy, Crispin…"

Between us, we haul the zombie entrepreneur Crispin Dry out onto the subterranean platform. To my secret disapointment, still fully-clothed, although his fine black suit is showing signs of wear-and-tear from squeezing through the underwater rock-slide.

"Welcome back, dude," Carvery greets him. "You look like you just escaped from New Jersey."

"Are you okay?" I ask. "Oh, no – you're hurt…"

Crispin sits up and thumps himself in the chest. Water gushes out from a fresh gash in his neck, and from unseen ribcage compromises under his shirt.

"I will be fine, Sarah *Bellummm*," he says, he voice croaky and bubbling. "Let us continue. We must catch up with Mr.

Lukan, and hope that he is still in possession of the golden clockwork hand."

Hope that he is still in *possession* of it? But I'm too concerned with Crispin's welfare to demand any further exposition right now. We help him to his feet, and I notice Ace and Carvery immediately checking out his rear view.

"Er, Crispin – that's a pretty big rip in the ass of your pants," Carvery remarks. "Didn't feel anything gnashing on your own alimentary canal while you were down there?"

"Yeah, are you sure you don't have any Squidmorph hitch-hikers in those trousers with you?" Ace queries, speculatively. "Feeling bloated at all? Any strange cravings?"

"The only desire I feel at present is for the light of day," says Crispin. "If you look upwards, you will see our route to the Eight a.m. Lounge from here."

We all look up at the rickety stairwell, the steps ascending around the walls in a spiral.

"Stairs," Ace nods. "Cool. Doesn't look too risky."

"They are over three thousand years old," says Crispin proudly, and you can sense the relief in the group dissipating slightly. "This used to be a freshwater well, until the Sea Centipedes burrowed through it from the Deep Ocean Trench. There is still an ancient rope-and-bucket system you might be able to make out, about halfway up."

"No time like the present," Carvery mutters grimly, and leads the way to the foot of the stairs.

Ace follows, and I hurry to catch up. My torchlight beam clicks on, evidently having dried out by now – and I shine it onto the mossy stone slab of the first step.

"Doesn't look too bad," I echo Ace, tentatively.

And promptly slip on the slimy green coating, cracking myself on the knee. *Owww…*

"Mind the weed," says Carvery. "Bit slippy."

"Thanks," I grumble, and pick my way more carefully upwards.

There is no handrail – only a knotted, mouldy old rope slung through rusted iron hooks at waist-height around the wall as we climb. I reach for it only when footholds are uncertain, as it seems equally hazardous, and not likely to bear the weight of much more than a death-sliding mouse.

"What happens if someone comes down the other way?" I ask, all too aware of how narrow our worn path is, at frighteningly frequent intervals.

"The usual protocol is a *Fight to the Death*," Crispin replies, from the rear. "But at certain points there is space enough for a polite nod, and sometimes a handshake."

"What about creepy-crawlies?" Carvery enquires from up ahead. "Do they get right-of-way?"

"Not many animals use the stairs," says Crispin, reassuringly. "There are certain times of day while the bats are roosting that it can become – unpleasant."

I look up. For the first time, I see hundreds of furry bodies huddled together, suspended on the underside of the stone steps as they coil around the walls.

Ewww – no wonder so much moss and slime grows on these slabs…

…And a piercing screech nearly deafens me, as a great flapping shape swoops down, claws extended – and snatches two handfuls of the drowsy bats from their inverted perch…

"The Bat-Eater Owls do have unspoken right-of-way, though," Crispin admits.

A second owl slams into Ace's shoulder. He swipes at it, managing to keep his footing, and it is deflected straight into my face.

"Do I look like a bat?" I cry, as its hooklike claws scrabble in my hair, its inwardly-curved beak pecking at my scalp.

"I believe that's a *yes*," Carvery replies.

I grab for the unsafe rope to stay upright, my other hand waving ineffectually at my lively new headdress. The rope is as slippery as the steps. Useless… but I seize it anyway, badly grazing my already-chewed nail-beds against the harsh rock wall.

"You could try looking like a Pinstriped Leatherback Viper, Sarah *Bellummm*," Crispin suggests, and sounds like he's being serious. "They are the next up in the food chain to the Bat-Eater Owls."

"What do they sound like?" I ask, still trying to dislodge the hungry owl. "Do they hiss?"

"I suppose so, *yessss…*"

"Sssssssss!" I hiss loudly, flapping at the bird. "Sssssss! Ssssssssss!!"

"*Hhhhhhuuuuuussssssssssssssssssss…*" A much longer and louder hissing noise interrupts my feeble efforts, and the owl disengages instantly, backing off with a squawk.

"Thanks, Homer," I gasp, glancing behind me – but Homer is shaking his head silently.

He points at my hand, still around the safety guide-rope.

I feel it twist and writhe, under my grip.

Hhhhhhuuuuuussssssssssssssssss…

"Aaarrrghhh!" I yell, snatching my hand away – and take one unwise step backwards. Onto poor Homer's foot.

"Homer!"

I grab for his arm as he topples over the edge of the stairs, but only succeed in detaching his last scrap of embroidered silk kimono.

And Homer is gone – into the darkness of the stairwell.

"NO!" I shout.

"Nice fumble, Sarah," Carvery snaps.

HHHHHHUUUUUUUSSSSSSSSSSSS… The dreaded viper-sound is even closer, and is followed by an even worse one…

…The grating of loose stonework underfoot…

CHAPTER FORTY-SEVEN: BEETLEJUGULAR

"Homer!" I sob. "Oh, no – Homer…"

I feel Crispin's hands on my shoulders from behind, and am convinced that I'm about to join his brother at the bottom of the stairwell.

"Homer has survived far worse, Miss *Bellummm*," Crispin's grating zombie monotone says reassuringly – and most unexpectedly. "Do not waste your concentration. We must still make it out of here ourselves…"

"Big snake," Carvery's voice warns, from higher up on the steps. "Twelve o'clock."

"I thought it was only Eight o'clock?" I ask.

"Dead ahead, Dumb-Ass," he calls out, sarkily.

Hhhhhhhuuuuuuuussssssssssss… The sinister hissing takes on an evil undercurrent, and a swishing noise close to my head sounds like a whip being coiled, preparing to strike…

"Shoot it!" Ace Bumgang tells him.

"Gun's still too wet." Carvery shakes it, then changes his grip to hold it by the barrels, and swings it outwards sharply. It connects with something, with a dull smack that sounds like a cricket bat hitting an old leather punch-bag. "Think I just broke one of its teeth, though."

"Quickly!" Crispin urges. "While it is disorientated!"

We duck under the coils of the giant snake and hurry upwards. But as I scramble to keep up with Ace, I hear a muffled thud and a scrape behind me.

"Crispin!" I shout over my shoulder – just in time to see him swing out into the yawning chasm of the stairwell, suspended by one ankle in a loop of snake-tail.

"Keep going, Sarah *Bellummm*!" he orders – and is dropped into the darkness, after his brother.

"Nooooo…!" I cry out.

Carvery and Ace are already far ahead, almost a complete circuit of the stairwell above me. Only a few more storeys, and they'll reach the top… I try to increase my own effort.

And trip…

I stamp my foot forward to regain my balance, and the stone slab slides smoothly and horrifyingly free of the rock wall, pitching down into the black hole below.

And my balance goes with it…

Flailing helplessly in thin air, I find myself falling – yet again!

Great, I think. Pizza girl about to make giant pizza-topping splat, on top of double-decker zombie pizza-base…

…Or worse, I realise – remembering the hatching Squidmorphs in the water below. If my buttocks could clench any tighter, I'd probably turn inside-out.

It would save THEM the trouble altogether…

Then the air leaves my body abruptly – at both ends – as I hit something wooden and precarious.

"What the…" I gasp.

"*Gooooood*," a familiar voice greets me.

The bucket – for the well!

"This is a bucket?" I say in amazement, sitting up. "How much water were these people using?!"

Homer glances back at me. He is leaning over the side, reaching down for something.

"As Homer says, good of you to join us, Sarah *Bellummmm*," Crispin's voice echoes around the dark walls. "Perhaps you could help him pull me up, and we will see about getting the ratchet system working again."

I crawl quickly forward, and lean over the edge. I grab Crispin's other arm, and we haul him safely inside the giant bucket with us.

"Thank you," he says, giving me a pat on the shoulder, and heads straight for the lever and linkage in the centre. "Let us hope we catch up with the others quickly. Leatherback Vipers have very bad tempers once aroused. Keep a look out in case either of them decide to join us as well."

He frees the lever and winds a handle, and gradually we start to ascend up the creaking rope.

"Is it always this hard to get to the Eight a.m. Lounge?" I ask him.

"Oh, there are other ways," he replies, dismissively. "But it is rush hour, you understand. I never take the busiest routes."

"You mean all this time we could have been sitting in some nice quiet traffic jam, instead of risking our lives down here?" I demand, shocked.

"I didn't say they were safer routes," Crispin says, mildly. "Just alternatives. If you accept the job of secretary, I will introduce you to all of the alternatives – eventually…"

My mouth gapes like a hippo's yawn.

"You're offering me a job?" I can barely say the words aloud. "But – it wasn't me that was looking for a job…"

"Not you, Miss *Bellummm*?" Crispin looks genuinely surprised.

"No." I shake my head. "It was my housemate – you know – Miss Numbskull? Thinks black-and-blue is the new black? Currently a corpse under your mother's decking? She sent me to the interview in her place. I was supposed to slip you her credentials afterwards – but I forgot…"

The great squeaking and groaning bucket carries us further upward.

"You did seem very distracted, Sarah *Bellummm*," he reminds me, thoughtfully.

"Yes," I agree, only thoughtlessly, in my case. "I mean, er – well, I was rather…"

There is a snapping noise just overhead, and Crispin pushes me abruptly to the floor. The bucket rocks violently, and I just see the snake's aggressive tail entangling in our suspension ropes, whipping wildly through the air.

"It is trying to upset us," Crispin remarks.

"It's more than just upsetting me!" I say indignantly.

"I meant the bucket, Sarah *Bellummm*," he says.

Why is he always so calm and patient about everything?! It's enough to make a girl scream… well – I suppose, technically he is dead. That, combined with any disposition of his OTHER than inert, would make most people scream.

I sigh, as the bucket shakes us around, like unfortunate beach cockles.

"How do you usually get past one of these Leatherback snakes, then?" I relent. Hoping there's a simple answer.

"*Welllll*," he begins slowly, "they are partial to a vir…"

"Oh, God…" I groan. "Really? The old 'virgin' chestnut again?"

"*Noooo*, Sarah *Bellummmm*," Crispin says, aghast. "They are partial to a virtuoso singing performance. Ahem. Homer – do the honours, if you *pleeease…*"

Grinning in his usual too-disturbing fashion, Homer clears his throat and clings determinedly to the ropes, striking an operatic pose.

Right before a falling rock bounces off his head – and he keels over like a mining canary…

CHAPTER FORTY-EIGHT: HAIRY PALATE & THE CHAMBER OF SECRETIONS

"Heads up, dudes!" Ace's voice calls from high above. "Look sharp!"

Another rock pitches down, and scores the giant viper's flank. Our bucket tilts nauseatingly.

I squint up at the top of the stairwell. As I guessed, Ace and Carvery Slaughter have reached the summit – and are bombarding the reptile with stony missiles.

"Pinstriped Leatherback Vipers enjoy singing, not stoning!" I yell up at them. "You're just making things worse!"

Poor Homer N. Dry is out for the count. A dribble of blackened blood trickles from his angular gray cranium.

"Do we look like a boy band to you?" Carvery scoffs. I have to bite my tongue on that one. Girlfriend-battering psychopath Carvery Slaughter, and dodgy breaker's yard mechanic Ace Bumgang together look like any girl's poster-boy dream duo. "You want to play snake-charmer, you go ahead and sing to it!"

I gulp and look towards the viper's angry face as it curls its body around the rickety bucket. One tooth broken already by the stock of Carvery's shotgun, its eyes remind me of *Kaa* from *The Jungle Book* – swirling pools of deadly hypnotic venom, in a head the size of an inflatable dinghy. Long whiskers trail from the corners of its mouth, as in the renderings of Oriental dragons.

Not as big as the river-god Atum, by a long shot – but could easily pass for his evil gamete…

Oh, God – the only singer I can impersonate is a *Singer* sewing-machine!

I clear my throat, merely succeeding in nearly choking on the lump of rising bile at the back of my tongue – and open my mouth…

But instead of my usual *Enter Sandman* opener I usually attempt alone on *Nintendo Wii X-Factor*, an ethereal crooning sound echoes around the bucket. It envelops me like a tangible jade mist, joined by a tinkling of the most delicate bells.

What the Hell? Am I channelling *Enya*?

The snake pauses in its constriction manoeuvres around the woodwork containing us, and tilts its head, questing the air.

The choral vocals soar up the underground stairwell.

"It's beautiful…" I hear myself breathe, drawn to lean over the edge of the rim, straining to hear more. I feel as though I want the whole song to climb up inside me, possess me…

Crispin's hand closes around my arm.

"It is the hatching Squidmorphs, Sarah *Bellummm*," he says, gravely. "Do not let their call seduce you."

Ooohhhh… I recoil from the edge slowly. Climb up and possess me, indeed! But surely, something so magnificent could not be produced by something so vile?

One of the choral voices breaks off abruptly, with a piercing, piteous scream. The viper shakes its head as if dislodging water, or slowly awaking from a trance.

I'm sure I just heard the *swisshhh-thuddd* of a harpoon gun, far below…

Crispin tugs on the pulley arrangement, and our carrier jolts swiftly skywards again, overtaking the head of the snake, as it moves groggily to tighten its coils around the bucket.

Swisshhhh-thuddd!

Another horrific scream punctuates the singing rising up from the inky black water. And with a deep, indignant hiss, the Pinstriped Leatherback Viper darts after us in pursuit.

"What's that?!" I shout, as we jar to an unexpected halt. "Why have we stopped?"

"Something is stuck in the ropes, Sarah *Bellummmm*," Crispin reports. "It looks like…"

"Snake fang," Carvery calls out, and drops another rock, missing the dodging and weaving viper. "My bad. Sorry about that."

Crispin reaches up and works it free. Good Lord – it's longer than his arm…

Released once more, the ratchet system grinds and cranks us further up the rope.

Only a few more storeys to go… A formation of five Bat-Eater Owls barrels past, picking off prey from the underside of the stone steps – and turning, flies straight into the gape of the one-toothed snake.

Swallowed whole!

"Screw this," I hear Ace muttering overhead, and see him unhitching his own harpoon gun and fiddling around with the tip. "Carver – give me a spark."

Carvery takes out his Taser. What are they doing?

Three more owls circle around us, and as the largest swoops under the stonework and emerges again with claws full of bat, there is a *twanggg* from above. A bright streak blazes down from the sky, and Ace's harpoon, ignited, neatly pierces the owl's outstretched wing.

"Ohh!" I gasp in empathy. "It's hurt!"

"Yeah, I hope so," Ace says, grimly.

The owl shrieks, flapping on the end of the harpoon and wire tether, its wings starting to smoulder. Its momentum carries it in a continuation of a wide arc, straight towards the awaiting maw of the giant viper…

And just as its prehistoric jaws close – Carvery stabs the Taser into the extended cable.

A lightning bolt courses down the wire, directly into the locked mandible. The viper freezes in midair, suddenly ramrod straight – and smoke pours from those acidic eyes.

"Stop it!" I shout. The stench is terrible.

Crispin snatches up the broken snake-fang, and swings it like a cutlass. The tether breaks free – and gently, the Leatherback Viper falls down, down – down into the darkness of the underground Squidmorph nest.

"Well?" Ace asks, as he and Carvery seize the ropes and help to guide the bucket up over the edge. "Did you want our help or not?"

"You didn't have to do it in quite such a nasty way!" I snap, scrambling out of the wooden contraption.

And then I'm completely overwhelmed by the sensation of dry ground underfoot. Oh – blessed sand. And rocks! How glorious do those sun-baked stones look?

“Thank you, gentlemen,” Crispin says, much more courteously, as he lifts his brother Homer out of the bucket. “No, Mr. Slaughter, I do not think my brother requires electro-convulsive resuscitation just yet. Perhaps just a cool shady spot in which to recover. I think it best if we take him straight to the Spice Market, where he can be treated with a milder form of tonic.”

“I’ll take a large Gin in mine,” I burble, having found the friendliest-looking rock I can, and hugging it to my cheek, like a long-lost relative. Terra Firma… Mmmmmm…

“Something was attacking the Squidmorphs,” Carvery observes. “Didn’t you hear them hollering after the singing? That snake would have had you for an entrée.”

“Maybe something was protecting us from the Squidmorphs, in case we fell,” I say, haughtily, stroking my new pet rock. “Did that occur to you?”

“Then why didn’t it start sooner?” he wants to know. “Like while we were down there when they were hatching, and trying to get into all of our pants?”

“Sarah,” Ace says slowly. “Why are you nuzzling that stone?”

“I’m just glad to be alive,” I remark, and toss it aside dismissively. A dull thunk, and a groan from Homer behind me cause a moment’s temporary embarrassment. “But anywho – what’s this Spice Market? Are really in the Eight a.m Lounge at last, Crispin?”

We survey the landscape. Another desert, with just few scrubby bushes, and some distant mountains against the clouds of a storm on the horizon… but as a heat-haze shifts, and the dust blows aside – a dazzling array of bright colours appears, thrown across the russet sand like a patchwork quilt. Tents of all shapes and sizes – hundreds of them, as far as the eye can see – and as my own eyes adjust, the equally russet domes, walls and minarets of a permanent settlement amongst them – almost invisible by their camouflage.

“We are here,” Crispin confirms. “Welcome to the Eight a.m. Lounge – and here is also the most likely place we shall find Mr. Lukan has absconded to – with the golden clockwork hand.”

Oh, my word – however shall we find him in this? It’ll be like looking for a needle in a haystack…

A shape starts to emerge from the middle distance, appearing out of the reflective air distortion of a mirage like something from *Star Trek*. It splits into several shapes as it approaches, wobbling and lurching in a very familiar fashion.

"Our transport has arrived," says Crispin, approvingly. "Try not to look them directly in the teeth."

"No worries," Ace grunts. "Same applies when meeting Carver's mum."

"Your mum's teeth are still in a cup in my bathroom, Ace," Carvery quips.

"Where's the rest of her?" I ask, automatically.

"You should know – you've been sitting on her face," Carvery replies, just as quickly. "While you've been eating your sandwiches under the silver birch tree, at the Body Farm."

CHAPTER FORTY-NINE: LOBULES OF AREOLA

The approaching silhouettes jog towards us, as fast and steadily as horses, and yet with all the co-ordination of string-puppets. Their joints seem to bend in all directions at once, their feet clomp heavily in the desert dust like suet puddings being thrown against a wall, and their noses point towards the sky with all of the arrogance (and smell) of the *Great Unwashed.*

Crispin looks on fondly. I suppose with their wobbly hanging necks and lofty attitude, the camels do have a little in common with his pet cockerel and brood, back at the mansion.

"Mr. Dry!" a voice hails, from the leading beast. "What a pleasure that you bring company to see us on this fine day!"

As he draws closer, I can make out a tall figure in black robes from head to foot, with barely his eyebrows visible inside the turban and headscarf. In fact he even has dark glasses on over that. A long curved scimitar is in his belt, and a large semi-automatic rifle is strapped to his shoulder.

"My cousin," Crispin says. "Asum al Dj'eBraah."

"But my friends call me Sandy!" the man booms. The camel sags, all knees and hips at the same time, and its legs concertina beneath it, allowing the robed individual to leap off energetically. "I see you penetrated the Well of Our Souls to get here. Are the Squidmorphs hatching?"

"Very much so," Crispin nods, scratching the hole in the seat of his trousers.

"Our souls were very nearly penetrated as well," Ace agrees.

Asum al Dj'eBraah leans over the edge, cupping his ear, with a critical expression.

"Yes," he says, straightening up. "They sing for their salvation! But by the sound of it, no luck today. They will be dead larval vulture pickings by noon."

Vultures?! Eewww – are there no cute fluffy animals anymore? Or are those elusive lovable critters just a *Facebook* fantasy? Everything here, unless it's a chicken, seems to be a slavering bloodthirsty monster…

"Cool," says Carvery Slaughter, the biggest sentient bloodthirsty monster on the current page of events. "I'd like to see that."

"I think you may enjoy the Noonday Lounge in that case, Mr. Slaughter," Crispin acknowledges. "But that is four hours away. Let us enjoy what the Eight a.m. Lounge has to offer first."

Asum – or Sandy – peels off his Ray-Bans and unwinds his headscarf, greeting us with a wide, toothsome grin. He is a handsome, aquiline man with brooding dark eyes, no doubt a legacy of Rudolph Valentino's creation. The kind of model male that women hate to love, and men love to hate.

Didn't they call him 'Vaselino'? I'm sure I read that on *Wiki*…

"It is quite a circus you have been missing so far this morning, Crispin!" he announces, and seems to end every statement with an exclamation point. "We have seen robbery, trespassing and worse. The Surgeons of Justice are looking forward to collecting some hands today!"

"Hands?" I whisper, in enquiry.

"The hands of thieves," Crispin returns quietly. "Not the clockwork variety. But be careful. Where there are thieves, there are also my grandfather Higham Dry Senior's men, collecting bounty. It can create conflicts of interest between the Lounges. My grandfather wanting complete subjects for his flying experiments. The court-appointed Surgeons wanting their dues first, in guilty body-parts. This is why the bounty hunters are all a hand short already. The Surgeons of Justice insisted on a demonstration of goodwill, to collaborate with inter-Lounge criminal proceedings. A thief must be proved to have stolen from my grandfather first, to be extradited intact."

"What about Mr. Lukan?" I ask. "Who has he stolen from, technically?"

"Technically?" Crispin repeats, pondering. "Well, technically – YOU, Miss *Bellummmm*. Seeing as you were looking after the golden clockwork hand at the time."

Me?! I gulp. What sort of punishments lie in wait for a criminal taking Dry property from a pizza-delivery girl? Or possibly, even – from a just-employed secretary to one of the Dry family? God – my housemate Miss Fuck-Nuts is going to be pissed over that one, if she ever wakes up… she'll accuse me of trying to steal Carvery Slaughter from her next…

"All right, Sarah," Carvery interrupts my thoughts, immediately putting psychotropic pictures in my mind of his consent to the concept. "Let's see you wrap your legs around this great big hairy thing."

"Hmmm?" I look over at him, nonplussed, to see him patting the neck of a large white camel – which appears to be chewing tobacco, drooling yellow slime. "Oh – well, it can't be worse than riding a *Pizza Heaven* scooter…"

Oh, but it is. Clambering aboard, I lurch into the air on what feels like a drunken *Bucking Bronco*.

Thank God I've already been sick…

"Well done!" shouts Sandy. Homer is hoisted across his pommel, thrown under a blanket to shade his mottled gray wizened skin from the baking sun. "We will head straight for refreshments, in the Spice Market!"

I glance warily over at Crispin, adjusting himself in the saddle of his mount. Worrying that perhaps he looks a bit too uncomfortable. I notice Ace and Carvery nodding at one another also, in a meaningful fashion.

"And then we will visit the tailors!" Sandy continues, prodding his ride into forward motion. "Get you some new breeches made up, Crispin!"

"With an elasticated maternity panel?" Ace suggests, nastily. "Feel any kicking and squirming yet, Crispin old buddy?"

"If he starts looking at little knitted squidling-rompers in the market, I'm out of here," Carvery concurs.

…Maybe Carvery Slaughter wouldn't be such a great candidate to sperm-jack, I find myself thinking, unwittingly. My mind wanders further down this precarious footpath of fantasy. You'd expect even the most unwilling of DNA-donors to have a heart, at the end of the day. But perhaps it's not the case… Ace sounds like he'd be more sympathetic, though… he might be the sort to pick up where a less responsible man left off…

My camel stumbles, and I pitch forward onto its neck. It continues onwards regardless, as I slip round to cling underneath, terrified of tangling with those bulletproof knobbly knees.

"Sarah, stop showing off," Ace remarks. "You look like a sloth."

"Down!" I try to command the camel, hanging on grimly. "Stop! Lie down!"

Eventually, the beast seems to get the idea – or I just wear out its patience – and it stoops slowly to the ground again, with a flatulent groan. I scrabble to get back on board, before it can change its mind.

Now – what was I thinking about? I squint to focus on my travel-companions' receding backs, as they vanish into the shimmering heat-haze. Oh, *yes* – who would I rather be left holding the Squidmorph-baby by…?

Well, to be honest, being abandoned by any of them would be considered a win. It would suggest at least some sort of interaction had occurred previously.

Which is a hundred percent more than I've racked up in my life so far…

My camel is in no hurry to catch up. I try a lethargic bounce up and down on the blankets, and a kick of my heels.

"Yah!" I shout, because that's what they say in the movies. Hoping it means *'Go Faster, Stupid!'*

But my ride just sighs, and breaks wind again morosely.

"God, no wonder nothing grows around here," I grumble. "I think I'll name you *'Captain Farty-Pants'*…"

"Sarah's got a squidling!" I hear Ace shouting, up ahead. "I can hear her talking to it, and thinking of baby-names!"

"I was talking to the camel!" I shout back. "How do you make it go faster?"

"You impersonate the roar of a Maneless Camel-Eating Lion!" calls out Crispin's cousin, over his shoulder. "And then they run, like the desert storm winds!"

"What?" I cry – but am immediately drowned out by an Earth-shattering rumble directly behind me. It vibrates my toes, knocks my knees, dislocates both my hips, cracks my spine like a whip, and pops my ears, like two bullfrogs belching.

"Yes!" Crispin shouts, as I feel my animal go rigid with fright. I have the presence of mind to grab hold of the fur on the back of its neck, with both hands. "Just like that, Sarah *Bellummm*!"

"Good to know!" I reply in passing, as I overtake them all like a hirsute missile – hanging on for dear life.

Wow. Sandy wasn't joking. These creatures certainly can move, when they want to…

CHAPTER FIFTY:
SECTS AND THE CITADEL, TOO

My mount gallops determinedly through the heat-haze and dust devils, and gradually slows as the reassuring rainbow array of tents becomes clearer. The voices of stallholders and market-traders can be heard carrying over the barren sands.

But its only a precursor of the backdrop. What I thought was the main encampment, are merely the early birds, the eager beavers awaiting visitors to what I realise is a whole city inside the terracotta walls beyond. I can see plumes of fragrant smoke, hear the call of exotic captive wildlife, and the chanting of early-morning prayers from the minarets within. The scent of sandalwood and frankincense wafts by, on the arid desert air.

Maneless Camel-Eating Lions forgotten, I am entranced as my beast's stride shortens to a less uncomfortable lope. Everything shines or gleams or sparkles. It's like finding a multifaceted crystal prism boutique, in an oasis of coloured silks, in the middle of a nomad's land.

The traders are as wrapped up against the sun's glare as Crispin's cousin, Asum 'Sandy' al Dj'eBraah. I can't tell through their robes whether any of them are zombies… although my stomach's reaction is telling me that someone is most definitely selling *Fried Spiced Brains on a Stick* somewhere close by. Hmmm – what was the last thing I ate…?

"Something smells good!" Sandy's voice interrupts my thoughts, catching up. "No wonder the lions are lurking. Possibly a banquet later!"

"For the lions?" I ask, dubiously – but he just grins.

"We shall see!" he says, jovially. "Whenever a great rumour circulates here, we plan for the best possible outcome. A celebration. No one can gossip on an empty stomach. Or revel. And if the gods declare war, no-one can fight or die well on an empty stomach either!"

"What gods?" I enquire. "Have you seen the great river-god Atum too?"

"Atum? He is whitebait, compared to some of the demons I have seen!" Sandy chuckles. The others trot up behind him. "But they are not our concern today. Thieves are our concern! And catching them is always a cause for celebration! Also, for the lions. There are always leftovers, after the Surgeons of Justice have had their piece."

"Are we going to stick around long enough to see that?" Carvery cuts in. "Because I don't want to miss all the cool stuff. We had hardly any time at all in *Madam Dingdong's Bring Your Own Towel Sauna and Spa* earlier."

"And I'm sobering up," Ace warns. "I'm actually starting to feel like I could use a coffee right now. That's not good. I'll be walking straight next."

Aha – that explains *his* Ace-is-in-charge episode, just recently. I get a little involuntary tremble of excitement. Ooh. Ace *sober.* That's something I hadn't considered as a possibility before, in any of my fantasies… imagine what his lap-times as *The Stig* would be like on *Top Gear*, driving under the influence of only coffee and sobriety?

"Well, you men have had no fun yet at all, I can see!" Sandy agrees, as my thoughts spin dizzily. "But first, we will see to Homer. My strangest cousin is not himself after a swim among the Squidmorph eggs, it seems."

"I'm glad you noticed that too," Crispin remarks. "Perhaps he could be examined for parasites while recovering."

Oh… we exchange glances. Of course – Homer isn't wearing any trousers to display telltale holes. If a squidling had taken a fancy to his pants-wearing area as its potential incubator-host, it wouldn't even have had to nudge him first to get his attention… it'd only have had to lean in his general direction…

So we head off between the tents, with their mind-boggling display of wares – everything from carpets to pots and pans, jewellery and footwear, to confectionery and hot food.

I'm sure I smell the familiar barbecue scent of the chicken wings I ate at Crispin's last night, causing a blush to steal across my face.

God, I could eat *him* alive. Or dead. I'm not fussy.

I wonder if it's possible to sperm-jack a zombie? Maybe so… and if he's still keen on that *sleeping-with-a-virgin-cure* idea later on, I might actually get something out of the deal…

Particularly if that crazy witch-doctoring notion about a 'cure' actually works.

Although it would of course contravene all of my Forensic Anthropology dissertation research. And might get me thrown out of the *Germaine Greer Readers' Society* at Cramps University.

Gosh, having interesting sectarian morals instead of a rabid sex-life is such a burden! Just think, if I'd only got drunk on Fresher's week instead of working at *Pizza Heaven* to pay my half of the rent, I could now be knocked up, knocked about, and nailed under the floorboards, just like my floozy housemate Miss Thing – whatever her name is. Exciting, experienced, and dead to the world. A notch on any number of sports jocks' baseball bats. Just a notch, of course, not a name. And possibly some deadly splinters.

But it looks like any opportunity of mine to play fast and loose with zombie anatomy, risky though that may be, is a long way off yet. Particularly with Ace and Carvery still hanging around, knocking ideas into my libido like a *Newton's Cradle* of live machismo. Gaahh. Damn them.

I need a King Solomon to slice me in two, so there's enough to go around. Or maybe three, with room for the zombie experiments as well…

As if reading my mind, Sandy draws his scimitar, approaching the high wooden gateway of the citadel.

"Stay close behind me," he warns. "These predators will separate the old and the weak, and before you know it, you will buy much furniture, and more camels than your armies can handle!"

"I'm not lifting anything with more than two legs," Carvery remarks.

"Two legs or less," Ace adds, meaningfully.

"Dude, you did one with three earlier," Carvery reminds him. "Lady Glandula de Bathtub."

"That was no leg," says Ace. "That was a big alien sucker tentacle."

"Maybe it was a squidling up her," muses Carvery. "You did a zombie queen with one up the spout already."

"Nothing new about that," Ace shrugs. "Your mum, for example."

"No, the Squidmorph tentacles were different," I interrupt, before I can stop myself. "They've got hooks, not suckers…"

They both stare at me.

"I'm watching you, Sarah Bellum," Carvery says, sharply. "If you so much as fart a tiny tentacle, or burp black ink, you're going home in a tin pail."

We stick close together, aware of the eyes of all stallholders and storekeepers on us as we navigate our way through the baked-clay streets. It feels like vultures are watching our passage, waiting for one of us to fall back, or take a wrong turn…

"Here," Sandy announces, leaping from his camel, outside an arch in the narrow passageway. It is curtained by an ornate rug. He taps the tip of his scimitar lightly on a bell attached to the outside wall. "We will see if the Doctor is in."

Momentarily, the rug is tweaked aside, and a pair of shrewd black eyes assesses us from inside a clean white linen yashmak.

"Amiira!" Sandy bows. "Is our brother the Doctor at home? Poor Homer has had a nasty turn, in the Well of Our Souls."

The lady in white nods and steps back, gesturing for him to enter. He beckons to Ace and Carvery, who help to lift Homer down off the camel, and carry him inside.

I'm left outside the surgery with Crispin, holding the camels.

"How do you like it so far, Miss *Bellummm*?" he asks presently, after fidgeting for a while, and clearing his throat.

"What?" I ask, obtusely. "The Eight a.m. Lounge? Um – it's very hot…"

The Naval uniform I'm still dressed in feels as though it's been felted onto me, in the heat after the depths of the well.

"I meant more…" He pauses and scratches his head. "The thought of being my new secretary."

"Oh – that…" I recall our half-finished conversation awkwardly. "I think my housemate Whatserface really had her heart set on the job, to be honest. I'm quite happy delivering pizzas for a living."

"Really?" he asks, surprised.

"Why?" I snap. "What's weird about that?"

He shrugs.

"Everything?" he suggests, helplessly.

How could I expect him to understand… the freedom. The open road. The looks on customers' faces, when their food arrives… especially Ace's, when I've been waiting for him outside *Bumgang & Sons' Breaker's Yard* unannounced, with a Chinese Meat Feast and Garlicky Dough Balls… the exhilaration of chasing him down the road when he leaves by the other gate!

"You wouldn't understand, Crispin," I sigh. "You're rich. And privileged…"

"And dead?" he suggests.

"No!" I cry, horrified by his dejected expression. "No, no! Some of the best people I know of are dead. At the Body Farm. Mr. Wheelie-Bin, for example – such a good listener…"

"I see." Crispin sounds a little colder, and his back goes stiffer, as he stares at me.

"But not such a good talker," I finish, wretchedly.

But the damage is done. Crispin says no more to me, as we wait with the camels outside the surgery. Not even when Carvery's camel decides to sit down heavily on my foot, parping all the way, like a bean-fed brass section.

Damn. Damn, damn, damn…

CHAPTER FIFTY-ONE: CASABLADDER

Presently, Sandy emerges from the surgery, and his face is as grave as a four-by-eight hole in the ground.

"Homer has had quite a booboo on the old noggin!" he announces. "My brother A'Bandaiid is doing his best, but he needs stronger medicine, to reduce the risk of water-on-the-brain. I will have to go to the Caruncula, in the Spice Market. Miss Bellum – you will do me the honour of accompanying me there!"

"I will?" I ask, nonplussed.

"Your companions Mr. Bumgang and Mr. Slaughter will guard the camels, and my fine cousin Crispin will stay with his brother," Sandy explains. "It may be necessary – Crispin has been researching a cure, you know," he adds, confidentially.

Yes – that I most certainly know…

I look at Crispin, who turns his face away from me, and stalks inside the surgery without a word.

My heart sinks, bootwards. Still not talking to me, then… only the welcome emergence of Ace and Carvery in turn halts my dejectedly blood-pumping organ on its descent.

"You heard the gossip in the surgery?" Sandy asks them, and they nod. "Good men. Keep those eyes peeled! Come, Miss Bellum!"

Oh – the gossip…

"What is happening here?" I ask, scampering to keep up with Asum al Dj'eBraah – I mean, Sandy's longer stride. "You haven't told me what this gossip is – only something about thieves…"

"Treason, Miss Bellum!" Sandy hisses, in a stage whisper. He takes an impossibly unpredictable route through the dusty labyrinth of streets, as if following an inner compass, twisting and turning until I feel like a *Whirling Dervish*. "But we cannot talk here. The walls have earwigs, as you say!"

I nod. I've seen enough wildlife already today not to doubt that in the slightest. Any 'earwigs' being casually (or mistakenly) referred to, most probably occupy that context with maximum presence and ferocity.

"The Caruncula is a safe meeting-place," he continues. "Here, people from all over come to buy and barter goods, in exchange for a quiet corner and a bar tab."

We cross a square to a white pillared façade, above which – out-of-place, it seems – is a neon sign, reading *Casabladder.*

Sandy points at the signwriting. "My brother, the owner, also calls it *The Wee House*. From the Scots, you understand. Be careful, though! Mercenaries visit, and sometimes have scores to settle."

We go through the arched doorway. The layout is open-plan, the bar in the centre and potted plants all around, with a pianist and woodwind players on a podium to our right. But what could easily be an elegant corner of *The Ritz* or *Savoy Hotel* is rendered seedy by the buzz of the eclectic clientele – arguing, bartering, dealing and partaking in every corner.

"I am sick of diamonds!" I hear a rotund man grumble, as he tosses something bright and shiny back across the table at his unfortunate zombie companion – who looks starved, wearing only rags with his lopsided turban. "Everybody brings diamonds. Nothing but cheap mistress-magnets. Show me something new…"

Distracted by the impromptu sideshow, I walk straight into a wall of scented linen robes.

"Of all the elbow-joints in all of the dive bars in the world, you have to walk into mine?" a voice exclaims.

"Sarah Bellum," Sandy says, catching my arm as the man turns, drawing himself up to an impressive six foot six height, examining the damage done to his robe by the spilled Champagne. "This is my brother, the owner of *Casabladder.* May I present to you B'Dah B'Dim al Dj'eBraah – but the customers know him as Cottoneye Joe."

B'Dah B'Dim – or Cottoneye Joe – looks down at me, his eyes glittering like polished granite.

"So this is Sarah *Bellummm*," he rumbles, and I feel it right down to my curling toes. He beckons to the bartender. "A Sloe Gin Sling for the lady! And another bottle of Champagne."

"My brother, we need medicine," Sandy tells him – although a Sloe Gin Sling is more like something I've definitely felt was missing in the last three hours. "Homer has had an accident in the Well of Our Souls."

"That Well of Our Souls is a liability," grunts Cottoneye Joe. He nods to an armed attendant, who hurries away. "Remind me again why we do not dynamite it?"

"Someone did, remember?" Sandy hisses, in a low voice. "And someone else was not pleased!"

I wonder if that was what caused the underwater rock-fall we had to negotiate our way through… and who might not be pleased…? But before I can expand on those thoughts, the largest, frostiest, most delicious-looking Sloe Gin Sling is placed on the bar in front of me.

Oh, my – never mind the Well of Our Souls, I'd walk across broken glass, hot coals and any number of even hotter corpses to get to one of those…

"Miss *Bellummm*," Cottoneye Joe says courteously, passing it into my eager hands. He gives Sandy a filled Champagne glass, before raising his own, in salute. "To my many guests."

"Here is looking at your kids!" Sandy toasts me effervescently, before drinking.

"Er…" I cough slightly, my mouth desert-dry – but a gulp from the Gin Sling is wonderful. "Thank you."

"Play something special for my brothers!" Cottoneye Joe hails the band. "Play *'Sign O'The Times'*…"

Strange choice, I think, as the band strikes up anew, with the eponymous hit by sex-thimble *Prince*. Rather melancholy… but the clientele seem to indulge their host, and merely nod and smile benevolently at him, raising glasses in turn, or adopting distantly introspective expressions of empathy.

How very curious…

Cottoneye Joe's attendant returns, with a case. He opens it upon the bar. Sandy and his taller brother inspect the contents.

I peer over Sandy's shoulder. It contains many small brown glass bottles and vials.

"Gizzard of Vulture?" Cottoneye Joe suggests. "Sweetbreads of Mongoose?"

"Something a little stronger, I fear!" Sandy concedes. "It is the water on the brain we need to divert. And a tonic for the kidneys, perhaps…"

"Hmmm." Cottoneye Joe's deep rumble curls my toes again, and I knock back another huge slug of Gin Sling to try and unwind. "A dose of Tree-Frog Venom? Mixed with Tongue of Vampire Bat, perhaps…?"

They are discussing medicines, I guess. The drink seems to be bypassing my brain and heading straight for my lower limbs, and I find myself sinking into a seat at a small table.

My thoughts return reluctantly to Crispin, waiting for the medicines with Homer at the surgery. *Damn.* How did I upset him? I mentioned Mr. Wheelie-Bin at the Body Farm, that was all – and he acted as though he was jealous! All we were doing was discussing his job offer to me – and he thought I was turning it down on the grounds of his being dead – and I tried to give him a compliment… He took it completely the wrong way…

The band plays on.

Some say a man ain't happy truly, until a man truly dies, oh why?

But if he believes he has so much to offer – how can he be threatened by the thought of my talking to a rapidly-liquefying cadaver in a plastic wheelie-bin? Crispin can't have any real insecurities, surely?

I let out a morose sigh, and a shadow falls across my table.

"Sarah Bellum," a stranger's voice jolts me from my musings. "I was just here hoping to see your boss."

"My boss?" I repeat. "It's too late to see my boss. *Pizza Heaven* doesn't re-open until noon."

The voice chuckles, and its owner seats himself opposite, uninvited. I can't tell if he is a zombie or otherwise. What I can see of his face through his turban and headdress is badly scarred, and the skin of his hands has a green tinge, mottled with purple papillomas.

"You don't fool me, Miss Bellum," he warns. "I know you are here with Crispin Dry. If you give me what he owes, perhaps I will forget the fact."

What? I'm horrified. *Crispin has unpaid debts?!*

"I'm afraid I don't know what you're talking about," I say, as coolly as I can muster. I wish Sandy or Cottoneye Joe would turn and see my little predicament. Even more, I wish Ace and Carvery were here, instead of camel-herding. They love any excuse for a bar-brawl. "I'm a delivery-girl for *Pizza Heaven*, and I have no idea what or who you're referring to."

"Don't play games with me, Miss Bellum," the stranger continues. "You are a secretary for Crispin Dry at Dry Goods Inc, and a traitor. More fast-food delivery boys and girls have disappeared before you than you can possibly imagine…"

A traitor?? What the Hell?

"The more you try to convince me, Mister Scary Weird Green Guy," I tell him, trying to raise my voice a little to attract attention, "the more your words will slip straight over my head."

Finally – Sandy turns and sees the stranger sitting across from me, and reacts. And what a reaction!

With a roar of rage, Sandy draws his scimitar – and with a dull thud, the stranger's head bounces off the table – and rolls onto the floor…

A terrible silence unfurls across the bar.

"Nothing to see here," Cottoneye Joe announces, and waves to the band to continue playing. He claps his hands to signal the staff. "Clean-up at table seven!"

CHAPTER FIFTY-TWO: DIURETIC 13

I drain my Sloe Gin Sling quickly, as Sandy hurries to my side.

"Are you all right, Miss Bellum?" he asks.

"I think I just need some fresh air," I say, rising unsteadily from my seat. "Who was that?"

"No-one of interest," he assures me. "There are other parasites here besides the Squidmorphs! We will take a turn around the fountain in the courtyard. The scent of the lilies and wisteria will revive you."

He gallantly offers me his arm. We head through the bustling bar and out through the far side, into the glorious dappled sunshine of a shady walled garden within the buildings. A bubbling fountain in the centre cools the air, and the rainbow array of flowers are a soothing contrast to the harsh hubbub indoors.

I try to take deep breaths as we walk around this little oasis, before my brain is overwhelmed with further adjectives.

"This is quite normal for the Caruncula *Casabladder*, Miss Bellum," Sandy reassures me, as I rest on the tiled edge of the fountain. The decoratively cool mosaic design is a relief through the seat of my all-too-thermal Naval uniform. "You must not take anything personally. But it is safe to talk here. It is one of the few places where it is safe to talk."

For some reason I don't feel like talking right now. I've just seen a man decapitated for sitting down at a table with me, and calling me a traitor. I'm more wary of further offending any other law-abiding citizens of the Eight a.m. Lounge, after that little display.

"You did mention treason," I say at last, cautiously. "What constitutes treason here, exactly?"

"Attempting to broker or sell sacred hereditary objects, either whole or in constituent parts," Sandy replies. "Sleeping with one's mistress within the Palace walls, or courting a new one in his Lordship's apartments. Procuring a beast for carnal knowledge. Watering-down of lamp-oil or medicinal spirits. Entering the *Temple of the Moon* on a Tuesday morning after 09:20 hours wearing a blue feather – Homer has had some narrow escapes there, I can tell you. Public preaching of sacrilegious texts, or unconfirmed UFO sightings. Many things, Miss Bellum. There is a six-hundred page moral addendum in the *Library of Scrolls* here if you would care to look – but it can only be accessed on a Thursday between 10:04 and 16:17 hours without committing…"

"Treason?" I guess, and he nods.

"Wise indeed. I can tell you are a woman who respects cultural differences!" he approves. "And what is your own personal heathen faith, if you will permit me to ask?"

"I would not dream of offending you by mentioning it aloud," I reply, politely.

He grins broadly, revealing several gold molars.

"Clever girl." He gestures around the courtyard. "We like to consider this a free society, in our decadent little Eight a.m. Lounge *pied à terre*, away from the rest of the civilized world – but you would be amazed how careful folk are. More than anywhere else. To do business in such a confined and limiting space, you will find good manners are learned quickly."

He sighs. "Life here functions very well. But there are others who are envious, who would wish to tax and regulate such a successful independent enclave. Introduce their hypermarket monopoly culture, and fast-food chains. Their modern places of mass consumer worship. Destroying the solitary businessman. Destroying the soul's own unique journey through life – and the afterlife."

"I can see why defending the Lounge is so important," I venture.

"You will have noticed similar tendencies elsewhere also!" he agrees, in his usual enthusiastic way. "Arming themselves to the teeth, ready for any invasion from either side, yes? Practising their skills and manoeuvres, maybe?"

A small part of my hindbrain kicks me in the upper lobes. Perhaps what he means, is: *HAVE you noticed similar tendencies elsewhere?*

Is he fishing for tactical information on the sly…?

"I wouldn't be qualified to answer," I reply at last, honestly. "I saw a lot of laundry being done, and some failed attempts to brew Guinness. But that's about it."

"Hmmm," he muses. "Yes… where Guinness is involved, a plentiful supply of clean laundry is certainly necessary. I do not think you have anything to concern yourself about there, Miss Bellum."

I'm already concerned… in a tactic of my own, I try changing the subject.

"Will Cottoneye Joe – I mean, your brother B'Dah B'Dim – will he have the right medicines for Homer?" I query.

"The best tonics known to mankind are right here in the Caruncula *Casabladder*," Sandy confirms, proudly. "We will soon have that curious brain and those wayward kidneys of my cousin's functioning properly again."

A sudden supersonic roar overhead makes me jump, and three triangular flat shadows streak above the courtyard. Across the walled city, a *Doppler* of automatic rifle-fire follows them, joined by a chorus of indignant shouting.

"What was that?" I ask, half-deafened by the noise.

"Those are aerial spies from the Nine a.m. Lounge," Sandy tells me. "Every day, they fly past, hoping to find us swallowed up by the desert, so that they may move in and expand their territory. Fools. They look forward to the day they believe that the taxmen and regulators will flatten our haven of peaceful business, and turn it into some ghastly modern theme park of glass and cement. They are too narrow-minded to see that without the Eight a.m. Lounge, there is no Nine a.m."

He reaches inside a fold of his robes. I gulp.

Am I about to be sacrificed also?

But instead of the dagger I am expecting, he produces a tiny handmade notebook – almost an exact miniature replica of Mr. Dry Senior's diary!

He turns it reverently in his fingers. It is only about an inch tall.

"You will take this micro-text to the Nine a.m. Lounge," he states. It does not sound like a request. "There, you will give it to our contact in the Dry family empire. He will know what to do."

Oh, my God – I'm being press-ganged into becoming a spy!

"But…" I begin, as he embeds the small leather-bound book into my hand and closes my fingers around it. "Who? How will I tell?"

Before Sandy can speak again, there is a crash in the wisteria behind him, as something falls heavily from the roof. We both turn to view the damage.

A dusty shape groans, and tries to stand upright.

I'd recognise that brown *Christian Audigier* hooded jacket with the gold skull motif on anywhere…

"Luke!" I shout, as Sandy's scimitar finds his sword-hand again, prepared to strike.

Our Nigerian taxi-driver – and *thief*, Mr. Lukan – leaps free of the shrubbery, eyes widening wildly. From a standing jump, he avoids the sweep of Sandy al Dj'eBraah's blade, flying onto the uppermost rim of the stone fountain.

"Sarah!" he cries out to me, running around the narrow circumference to evade the slashing thrusts, kicking up diamond-like droplets of water from the shallow marble bowl. "It's not what you think!"

"You stole the clockwork hand!" I shout back at him. "That was given to me to look after!"

"You don't understand!" he yells, on his second or third lap of the fountain. "It doesn't belong…"

He is interrupted by a second flying shadow. From the terracotta tiled roof of *Casabladder*, a glistening flash of bare-torsoed wiry muscle and dark Naval uniform trousers leaps, coiled like a spring, and lands with a menacing splash – right in the marble alongside.

My heart implodes. Oh boy – Ace Bumgang *sober*…

"Cough it up, dude," Ace says, without any attempt at preliminary Machiavellian wordplay.

Luke curses, and jumps in the opposite direction, desperately. Fear propels him to the far side of the roof, where he barely grabs the guttering before scrambling upward the rest of the way, and disappearing across the protesting clay tiles.

"Ace!" I cry. He glances down at me briefly, muscles twitching and ready, like an Adonis on Aspartame. My heart is using my uvula as a trapeze! I try to swallow it back down. "Ace – who's looking after the camels?"

Nice, Sarah Bellum, says my self-esteem – putting my ego into a headlock and drop-kicking it into my large intestine. *Show him where your priorities lie, why don't you?*

"Carvery and Amiira," he replies, flatly. He shrugs to flex his shoulders, and clicks his neck. "Stay there, I'm going after Luke."

And he jumps clear across the square to the other rooftop, landing with both feet on the tiles before running after the taxi-driver, in pursuit.

"They must be stopped!" Sandy gasps as they depart, sheathing his sword. "It is forbidden. There will be uproar! The hounds will be unleashed!"

"Let me guess," I say, once my heart has recovered from Ace's energetic display. I wave my hand in the direction he has just taken. "Treason?"

"Yes! You have a keen mind, Sarah Bellum!" Sandy claps me on the shoulder, almost knocking me over. "But not by Mr. Bumgang…"

"I meant Luke – for stealing the clockwork hand!" I interrupt, trying to explain.

"No, no, Miss Bellum!" Sandy is almost frothing at the beard. "Our sister Amiira has been left alone with the camels – and Mr. Slaughter! No chaperone! It is forbidden!"

"Really?" I exclaim, but he is already ahead of me. I hurry after him, back into the bar.

Ooohh – I wonder which bits of Carvery they'll cut off first?? I hope we're not too late to see that…

CHAPTER FIFTY-THREE: CARUNCULA ROYALE

We dash past the customers of Casabladder, who deign to turn their icy stares of apathy at us, as we hurtle through without caution.

"My brother!" Cottoneye Joe bellows, and Sandy skids abruptly to a stop, while I cannon into his back, like a Newton's twat. "Your medicine. For our cousin."

He holds out a green glass bottle with a cork stopper, held in place with an intricately-twisted gold filigree wire.

Sandy accepts it, with a deep bow. I find myself sagging in the same manner automatically in self-preservation, still determined not to offend anyone if I can help it.

"Thank you, B'Dah B'Dim!" Sandy shouts at his own sandals, before tucking the bottle inside his belt and snapping upright again, in a way that would have put most men's hamstrings on the *At-Risk* register. "Come, Miss Bellum!"

Remarkably, nothing is disturbed in our wake, as we rush back outside into the streets of the citadel comprising the Eight a.m. Lounge.

"What will happen to Carvery and Amiira?" I gasp, struggling to keep pace.

"That is up to the Surgeons of Justice!" Sandy calls over his shoulder. "Let us hope the officials are having a good day!"

We pound along the narrow alleyways, getting busier now with traders and hagglers. Somehow, Sandy keeps his robes clear of the stalls and passers-by in the headlong rush.

Two shadows fly overhead again, and I recognise Ace still in pursuit of Luke, across the rooftops.

"Stop, you stringy chav!" Ace's voice is heard yelling. It is followed by the sound of gunshots, which almost stops my exhausted heart in its tracks.

"Why are they shooting?" I cry.

"They are easily excited, Miss Bellum!" Sandy tells me. "They all want to be part of the chase and the capture! A running thief is vermin here – open season is declared!"

"Sounds more like '*Open Fire!*'" I retort, and am rewarded with a volley of further shots.

I try to keep my eyes on Ace as he runs along the ridge-poles and gutters, after our errant taxi-driver. They clatter over the clay tiles, and slither over laundry laid out on the baking terracotta to dry, in the morning sun. More than once they cross the alleyway, leaping from aerial flight-path to flight-path, as Luke attempts to shake off his pursuer.

"If you didn't nick it…" Ace hollers. "Why are you running?"

"Only dead men stand still!" Luke cries over his shoulder, and is almost proven right on the spot, as a brick chimney beside him is shot to pieces.

He clutches his hands to his head, cursing, and dashes wildly away again.

Ace runs straight through the wreckage of the chimney, kicking the rubble aside, and disappears after him, out of sight from the ground below.

"Hurry, Miss Bellum!" Sandy urges me.

I realise that I've been staring into space at the spot where Ace was a second before, and pull myself together once more. Oh, yes. What will happen to Carvery? I hope they have some special torture policy here prior to cutting bits off him… or just a little room somewhere with a broken deckchair and some manacles… maybe do a few choice things to him with a knotty rope and some hot water…

What's it called, the torture thing they do, with the board? Wakeboarding? Surfboarding? Maybe I made it up…

We reach the alleyway outside the surgery, and at first I only see the huddle of camels.

"Amiira!" Sandy roars. "Where are you? Make it known that you are chaperoned, my white desert lily!"

Carvery steps out from behind the largest camel, frowning.

"What's with all the yelling?" he grumbles.

"Ace said you were here alone with Amiira," I pant, catching up.

"Should have known he'd go and drop me in it," Carvery scoffs. "He won the toss over who got to chase Luke when we recognised him, and left me here on my own. For all I know, Amiira's still inside, with Crispin and Homer and A'Bandaiid."

Sandy hurries inside. But as for me, I've never felt so disappointed. The tears are pricking at my eyelashes before I can stop them.

"What?" Carvery asks, suddenly grinning. "You look like you've lost a dollar and found a dead donkey."

"But… but…" I blab, the exhaustion and adrenaline too much for me all at once. "I only wanted to see them do the cheese-board thing before they cut anything off…"

"Why are you obsessing over what you're missing out on in the world of cheese?" he wants to know. "If you're that hungry, I'm sure there are some spare parts from the Seven a.m. Lounge that Crispin might let you nibble on. He could probably spare you a kidney."

One of the camels groans, in almost a human fashion. Carvery slaps it on the many layers of blankets sharply, and it stops.

"No, I'm not hungry," I sigh, and slump against the wall dejectedly. Damn. No entertaining torture for Carvery Slaughter yet. I'd have loved to see him get cheese-boarded, I acknowledge shamefully.

Yes. Tie him to a large Blue Stilton and force a well-matured Stinking Bishop up his nose until his brains explode out of his ears…

"Sarah," Carvery says, in that warning voice that suggests he knows exactly what I'm thinking. "You're drooling again."

"Sorry." I wipe my chin absently.

"Are you sure you haven't had a stroke?"

Sandy emerges again, looking concerned.

"She has gone off alone, it appears," he announces, and scratches his brow in agitation. "She must have sneaked out when you noticed the thief, Mr. Slaughter! My brother B'Dah B'Dim will cut off her allowance if she keeps gallivanting about like this!"

"That sounds painful," I empathise, quickly. "How is Homer? Will we know if the medicine works soon?"

"He is not himself at all, Miss Bellum!" Sandy shakes his head sadly. "I fear that knock on the head may have affected him permanently!"

He whirls and goes back into the surgery, and I gulp. Poor Homer… and poor Crispin! How is he coping? But I daren't go inside to find out. I have a feeling I'm still not going to be in his good books.

A crash overhead and a plummeting flowerpot indicates the passing of Luke once more, and his silhouette sails across the passage outside the surgery, disturbing the camels. It is followed by a skidding noise, and suddenly a stream of tiles flies after him, spinning one by one through the air, as if fired from a clay-pigeon trap.

"Wanker!" shouts Ace, skimming a sixth or seventh terracotta tile.

A distant yelp from Luke answers him, as one of the missiles evidently strikes its target. The yelp is succeeded by a loud crash, and looking up, I see Ace crouch, just before he clears the alleyway with another single leap, heading in the direction of the commotion.

Shouting erupts, and someone calls for a net.

"Sounds like they got him," Carvery remarks, and gives the camel a sharp dig with his elbow, as it groans again in a pained manner. "I really hope we're not missing all the grisly stuff."

"Quite," I agree, still thinking about Carvery getting cheese-boarded.

So unfair… even a little cottage cheese in the armpits, or some cold *Dairylea*, right in the ear-canal… I'd pay to see that…

CHAPTER FIFTY-FOUR: SORE

My thoughts are scattered though, as Crispin Dry suddenly stalks out of the surgery doorway, his gray zombie countenance as dark as any thunderstorm. My inexperienced libido immediately starts cooking me from the inside-out, making my already too-hot, sticky Naval uniform feel like an *Uncle Ben's Rice* Boil-in-the-Bag in the desert heat.

Damn these hormones!

I bet he's still in a stupid mood with me as well, over that mention of Mr. Wheelie-Bin…

"They have the errant Mr. Lukan, Mr. Slaughter?" he asks Carvery coldly, sparing me not a glance.

"Looks that way," Carvery replies. "Are they going to torture him? Do we get to watch?"

"Better," Crispin concurs, with a nod.

Sandy emerges beside him, and claps his hands loudly, in a rhythmic sequence. He announces something to the city at large in a foreign tongue I don't understand, although I'm sure the name *Amiira* is mentioned, and possibly the word *'infidels'* – although I wouldn't want to offend anyone even by thinking such a thing around here…

My heart leaps sideways, as I most definitely hear the words *'Ace Bumgang'* and *'The Stig'* uttered in the same sentence – and I'm sure it isn't my imagination furnishing my ears with the roar of response by nearby gossips and traders.

"What was that about?" I ask, timidly.

Crispin finally rewards me, with the stony flicker of one jet-black eye.

"The morning *News* summary," he replies, shortly. "It is the responsibility of whomever the grapevine determines shall broadcast it."

I'm suddenly aware of a great horde of people, all in a strange shade of pale blue or green approaching us. There is great excitement, and shouting of orders and instructions, and we are quickly relieved of the camel reins and hustled forward at the crest of the crowd, as it rolls along the dusty street. Sandy disappears briefly back inside the surgery with a number of others, and Homer N. Dry is borne out on a stretcher, carried above the heads of many.

Poor Homer – his withered gray skin is almost white! Like the ash, coating a slow-burning cinder…

"Where are we going now?" I cry, hurrying ahead to avoid being trampled.

"To the trial," Crispin says, his tone still as flat and as brusque as before. He so doesn't want to talk to me right now! "At the Tank."

The Tank? What new horror is this?

The new horror is soon illustrated, as the crowd herds us to a square, filled with people, all jeering and braying and barking further orders to one another. At the centre is a deep square pit, under glass strong enough for a man to stand on.

The pit is lined with ceramic tiles, and contains nothing but a sink and lavatory, and an old metal bunk, each item against a separate wall. Iron rings are screwed into the fourth wall, and from these rings is suspended the miserable figure of our taxi-driver, Luke, fully chained.

Ace is standing thoughtfully at the edge of the Tank, waiting for us.

"This is a trial?" I ask. "It looks more like he's already been imprisoned…"

"And that is his trial, Miss Bellum!" Sandy announces, as we gather alongside Ace. His words struggle to find any foothold between my ears when I notice the beads of sweat glinting on Ace's bare torso, and promptly all thoughts of zombie infatuation are drop-kicked out of the ballpark by both of my ovaries at once.

"A witch-hunter trial," Ace remarks. "If he escapes, he's guilty. If he dies, he was innocent. That sort of thing."

"You mean there's no such thing as luck?" I demand. "Or a fair hearing?"

"Just a demonstration of either his reliance on heathen magic, or his defiance in death," Crispin agrees by my left ear, unexpectedly. My thoughts of Ace Bumgang run and hide, in an equally guilt-ridden fashion. "But there is more to it, Sarah *Bellummm…*"

I notice that Homer is being lowered into a shaft beside the pit, and shortly a steel vault door opens beside the sink in the underground cell. Homer's stretcher is placed onto the rigid metal bunk, and the bearers leer at Luke, before departing again.

I notice Luke's eyes rolling in terror, and searching the audience above, seeking out our gaze in an appeal for mercy.

"The Surgeons are hoping that my cousin Homer will awaken with an appetite!" Sandy nods in approval. "Another challenge for our prisoner's foreign wizarding skills!"

The crowd certainly approve as well, applauding as Homer stirs lethargically.

"Did Luke have the clockwork hand on him?" I ask Ace, who shakes his head.

"He says it's somewhere safe, but won't say where," Ace replies. "So I think they're hoping this will scare it out of him."

"If he's put it up there, that shouldn't take too long," Carvery agrees. "Especially if they gave him *Ex-Lax* first."

"But they'd torture him anyway, from what I gather," Ace continues. "Whether he's got it on him or not."

I tear myself away from the spectacle and go to the shaft beside the Tank, where the stretcher-bearers have just emerged. A hand-cranked metal elevator is the only means of accessing the underground cell, and the operator grins toothlessly at me.

"Hoping for a closer look, Sarah *Bellummm?*" Crispin's voice says beside me again, and I jump. I turn to see him looking past me into the elevator shaft, his manner still quite cold and distant. "I'm sure it could be arranged…"

And suddenly I see nothing but the inside of a hessian sack, smelling strongly of chemicals…

The light is murky and greenish as I open my eyes groggily, the chemical smell now mixed with a dank mildewy scent, and a suffocating, stagnant silence – compared to the racket of the citadel. But as I look up, I can still see the dozens of bearded and excited faces looking down through the thick, mould-spotted glass.

"Must be soundproofed," I mumble aloud, and my words echo back to my ears painfully, from the stained ceramic tiles.

Oh, God – I'm in the Tank as well!

My right arm is chained to the pipes under the sink. To my left, Homer is still unconscious on the bunk. To the other side, Luke is upright, chained to the rings affixed to the wall.

The opposite wall is in shadow, as the sun is not yet high enough to illuminate it.

"What happened?" I ask, woozily.

"My guess is, someone wants to know if you're the kind of girl to harbour more than one lover," Luke croaks, and to my great offence I realise he's laughing at the idea, even through his pain. "That if Homer wakes up hungry and decides on a little *Sarah Bellum* appetizer, any sign of my heathen magic being used to save your life will condemn you as a scarlet woman."

"Ah," I say, gloomily. "So if I die I'm innocent, if I live I'm guilty, yes?"

"Yup," Luke grins. "And I don't have any magic, so it was nice knowing you."

Homer's stomach gurgles, on cue, and he mutters something in his sleep.

It sounds like *Goooood…*

"Where's the clockwork hand?" I demand, grasping for the one thing I know that does have special powers, which I've come across recently.

"In a safe place," Luke replies, suddenly brittle.

"Because if it's where Carvery thinks it is, now would be a good time to start thinking about prune juice."

"What?"

"Well, at least we might have a chance," I snap. "They are intending to leave us here to die, you realise? Because if we don't die, we're guilty of something – which means more torture and possibly death will follow."

Homer's stomach rumbles again, and I glance nervously at it.

"And it might be more than just a zombie with a breakfast appetite in here with us," I continue. I try to define the horrible mixture of smells in our subterranean prison, wondering if one of the contributing aromas might resemble seawater mixed with battery acid. "There might be a zombie-harboured Squidmorph as well…"

"A squat what?" Luke demands.

"A kind of sea-parasite," I explain. "It hides up your bottom like an alien space-probe when you skinny-dip, and eventually grows to the size of a battleship. So if you have anything useful hidden up *your* bottom to fight one of those with, make like a supermodel, and flush out that colon!"

Luke looks from me to Homer in horror, and then rattles his chains.

"Let me out!" he screams. "I'm trapped in here with a zombie and a girl obsessed with probing my ass!"

But before I can protest, I notice that the sunlight is starting to reach the far wall, where the lavatory is installed. And as the light quality in the shadows changes, I spot another familiar shape.

"What are *YOU* doing in here?" I gasp, astonished.

Carvery looks up from the little tiny leather-bound book in his hands.

Oh, shit – the micro-diary that I was given, to look after!

But how did he…?

"Well," he says, uncrossing and re-crossing his legs from where they rest up on the chainsaw, at his feet. "Just in case Homer fails to hatch a squidling, or to wake up at all, the Surgeons decided I was the next best thing to a wildcard against you two."

I stare at him, open-mouthed. He finally looks up from his – typically *stolen* – reading matter.

"I volunteered," he grins.

CHAPTER FIFTY-FIVE: FERMAT'S WOMB

"It's a trick," Luke gasps, before I can open my mouth to protest. "They still want the information on the clockwork hand. He's here to deal with Homer – or any alien squid-monster that pops out – if it looks like there's any chance I can tell them what they want first."

Carvery just grins.

"One possibility," he agrees. "What do you think, Sarah?"

I pull ineffectually on the chain securing my arm behind the dirty sink.

"I think you'd jump at any chance to be the only armed man in a room with two restrained prisoners and an unconscious zombie," I reply. "It'd give you the opportunity to live up to your name, *Carvery Slaughter.*"

"Could be, could be," he nods, turning the page of the tiny diary. "Could be all of the above. Where did you get this copy of Mr. Dry Senior's diary?"

"That was given to me to look after!" I hiss through gritted teeth, half-truthfully this time. "And you shouldn't be reading it – as usual…"

"It's all in code anyway," he shrugs. "Code and little drawings. Like he was playing *Draw My Thing* online. On his own, in a little notebook. Or *Hangman*. Anyway, you missed one. I might be down here to defend Homer, in case you two manage to get loose."

"Still sounds like a win-win for Carvery," I grouch.

"Well, unless you've got anything on either of you that beats a chainsaw, it's not exactly an evenly weighted contest, is it?" Carvery sighs, and sounds almost bored. "They could have let me down here unarmed and I'd still have the upper hand, no pun intended. I think they gave me the chainsaw just because they like a bit of theatrics. Plus it deters any onlookers considering a bit of treason after breakfast."

Luke starts to twitch. It's slight at first, but gradually becomes more spastic and uncontrolled. I wonder if he's being bitten.

"Are you okay?" I gulp, wondering about the size of fleas or body-lice that might be encountered down here.

"Maybe he got the *Ex-Lax* treatment after all," Carvery remarks. "You might want to turn your head away, in that case. And maybe tuck your feet in."

"Let me out!" is all Luke screams. "It's not what you think!"

"Maybe he's got a Squidmorph too," Carvery suggests. "Keep your legs crossed, Sarah. It might look for somewhere new to hide after getting flushed out prematurely…"

"Why are we chained up anyway?" I ask suddenly, as something occurs to me. "In a completely inaccessible underground room, beneath a glass floor in the public square above, with everyone watching? Surely there'd be no need to chain us up – unless it's *'torture by withholding use of nearby toilet'…*"

Carvery looks down between his own legs at the offending piece of bathroom furniture, which he is currently employing as occasional seating in our stinking, subterranean tiled cell.

"Maybe there's a way out, is what I'm saying," I continue. "Maybe they've had people escape before."

"Maybe it's fear of whatever imaginary magic they think Luke himself is withholding," Carvery replies, nodding towards the spasmodic Mr. Lukan. "He doesn't look too happy now. I can picture them placing bets on something exploding out of him fairly shortly, laxative or no laxative."

The worrying silence seems a bit more hollow for a moment, and I'm sure a sense a distant rumble. Like an earthquake.

"Did you feel that?" I ask. "I'm sure the Earth just moved."

"Sarah, I'm nowhere near you," Carvery grumbles. "Control yourself, for God's sake."

Before a retort comes to mind, there is another judder, closer this time. It has a mechanical edge to it.

And then a horrible fingernail-on-slate noise – and Homer's metal bunk scrapes two inches inwards, into the room.

"That wall just moved!" I exclaim.

The scraping sound is still echoing away as Carvery gets to his feet, crosses the cell, and crouches to inspect the floor under the steel bed.

"There are scratch marks here," he reports, after a moment's dark silence. I can see his eyes follow the direction of the scoring, across the width of the room. "It looks like it's been moved before…"

"It's their Joker," Luke pants, rejoining the conversation from his current delirium. "Or their ace – whatever you want to call it. If the zombie fails – or the squid-monster – or the psychopath in the room – the room itself is the final device…"

"Ah," Carvery muses. "And there was I, thinking that being stuck in a room with a hormone-riddled idiot necrophiliac was going to be the definition of Hell. And what an incredible smell you've discovered down here, Sarah? I can see that not improving, over the next hour or so…"

The distant rumble vibrates along the plumbing again.

"We have to do something!" I cry, trying to suppress some very real hysteria now creeping up on me. "And God – what's wrong with him??"

Luke is shaking again, and suddenly lets out a stifled scream – this time with no words.

Carvery clicks his tongue disapprovingly.

"That's what happens when you don't breathe through the contractions, dude," he warns. "Take your time, and let the suspect chocolate-flavoured medicine do the hard work for you…"

"I think he's really sick!" I interrupt, but a new scraping sound joins in – this time a metallic, hurried skittering noise over the tiles. "Oh, no – what's that now?!"

"Where?" Carvery asks, reaching for the chainsaw.

"Something's running around on the floor…" I begin, and the noise increases in volume.

And then I scream in turn – as something hard and unyielding snaps around my ankle like a clamp!

"It's got me! It's got me!" I shriek, kicking out at first, not brave enough to reach down with my free hand – not wanting to risk losing that as well.

"Great!" Carvery enthuses, cheerfully. "Which bit of you do you want cut off?"

But it doesn't feel like a Squidmorph tentacle. Not this time. Homer is still supine on the metal bunk. Luke is shuddering on the end of his manacles, his violent spasms now reduced to a trembling shiver, as if from non-existent cold.

The *Thing* seems to latch itself shut around my right leg.

"I can't see what it is," I moan.

"Pull your trouser-leg up, Dumb-Ass," Carvery says, leaning down to look – chainsaw at the ready.

Shaking in fear, I tweak the sweat-drenched fabric up a little. And something glitters…

"Cover it up," Carvery snaps. "Quick. Before they see it."

"Why?" I squeal, dropping the hem from my fingertips at once. "What is it?"

"Well, it's not an electronic tag," he grins, tapping his own ankle in indication and winking. "Looks like Luke was hiding the clockwork hand on him all along."

"Like I said," Luke manages to whisper. "It doesn't belong – to anyone. It chooses you."

What? *What does he mean?*

"It's chosen *you*, Sarah," he adds, rolling his bloodshot eyes towards me.

"Maybe it knows you were meant to be looking after it." Carvery squints up at the glass ceiling. "I wonder if Crispin guessed that too, and threw you in here for that reason?"

"I was planted in here?" I conclude, shocked. "To get the clockwork hand back?"

The metal bunk scrapes further inwards on the tiled floor, with another mechanical groan. Homer stirs flatulently and mutters again, in his convalescent slumber.

There is a sudden whiff of battery acid in the fetid air…

"I don't think they're going to let us off that easily," Carvery grins.

CHAPTER FIFTY-SIX: PARANODULE

"Cut us free," Luke suggests.

For a moment, I actually wonder if there's a Squidmorph concealing itself in my own lower intestine. Everything below the waist threatens to explosively migrate, as Carvery looks from the chainsaw in his hand to my arm restrained at the back of the sink, speculatively.

"I think I might be able to amputate your arm at the ear," he agrees.

"Er, let's not rush things," I squeak, hurriedly. *Why isn't the clockwork hand helping us?!* Stupid thing, running and hiding up my trouser-leg like that… "What plan do we have?"

Carvery sighs, bored once more, and goes back to sit on the edge of the lavatory

"If you cut us down, we might be able to brace that moving wall between us," Luke continues, nodding towards the metal bunk and the unconscious zombie Homer N. Dry, against the – presently static – deadly tiled wall, opposite him.

"I don't know if that's a good idea," I worry, squinting up at the dank glass ceiling, where the dwellers of the Eight a.m. Lounge are still watching our predicament from the town square above. I'm sure I see some cash exchanging hands, and as I seek out and find Ace Bumgang looking down on us from overhead as well, I notice something else. "I have a feeling any cutting that happens down here as an escape plan, is going to be replayed out there too. They've got Ace at sword-point!"

Carvery and Luke look up to confirm. Yes – Ace's hands are now bound roughly with rope. He's a prisoner as much as we are, and as his captors see us looking, they make threatening motions with various knives and cutlasses towards him.

"So?" Carvery grunts. "Less dead weight for us."

The plumbing gurgles again, and this time seems to come from the toilet.

"God – flush, man!" Luke groans.

"Wasn't me." Carvery raises his feet and swings his legs. "Maybe this wall moves also…"

But instead of a grinding of invisible cogs and the traversing of deadly chamber-ware menacingly into the room, there is another gurgle, and a splosh. A fountain of acrid water spurts out of the bowl between Carvery's legs, and bubbles across the slimy floor.

"Eeeww!" Carvery jumps up. "They have some crack cowboy plumbing in here." He hisses as he tries to brush the water from his trousers. "Ow…"

"What?" Luke asks.

"I think they've overdone the *Toilet Duck*." Carvery wipes his hand on the wall. "It's burning through to my skin."

Alarmed, I look at the pool of water trickling over the tiles, as it creeps towards me.

It's black. It smells of battery acid. And it's *fizzing*…

"The plumbing in here must lead to to the Well of Our Souls," I whisper. "Carvery – that's not *Toilet Duck*. It's Squidmorph ink!"

"What do we do?" Luke moans, rattling his chains hopelessly.

"Whatever you do," I begin, "don't let it…"

A massive tentacle whips out of the bowl, showering the interior of the cell with burning droplets – and whips straight around Carvery's ankle, turning him upside down and shaking him.

"Don't let it what?" he jokes, as his head is bounced repeatedly off the disgusting floor. "Ow… ow… ow…"

"Don't let it…"

"…GET HOLD OF THE CHAINSAW!" Luke shrieks for me.

The chainsaw, on cue, flies out of Carvery's hand as he is pounded deliberately against the wall, and spins wildly across the tiles. It hits the corner closest to Luke, and with a squeal he snatches both feet up off the floor, grateful at least for now that he is suspended higher up the wall on his manacles.

"Oh, no you don't," Carvery snaps, as the tentacle drops him unceremoniously and flails around instead to find the escaped weapon. He leaps back onto the hooked appendage, trying to hinder its attempt to arm itself further. "Bad calamari!"

"Luke!" I shout. "The chainsaw – see if you can slide it over here…"

"You're crazy!" Luke squeaks.

I reach out encouragingly with my free hand.

"If I can get loose, we can beat it," I say, beckoning. "Just nudge it over this way. And, er, try not to switch it on. Or this escape attempt will be over very quickly…"

Luke nods, and with one eye on the ongoing battle between Carvery and the tentacle, stretches out carefully with one foot.

"Yes!" I urge, patting the floor in front of me. "Over here…"

Luke times his soccer touch perfectly. The perfect speed, the perfect curve, the perfect amount of spin…

…And the tentacle, with a whip-crack, detaches Carvery violently, sending him flying backwards onto the bunk on top of the unconscious Homer, and barrels towards me like an express train…

My hand closes around empty air – as inexplicably, the chainsaw rears up above my head. With a flick of its hooks, the giant tentacle switches on the whirring blade, with a roar…

I close my eyes.

The second roar echoes around the cell, and I'm suddenly swamped in a coating of tepid, sticky, oozing, suffocating slime.

Oh, God – I'm like the bad magician's glamorous assistant. Sawn in half… drowning in my own entrails!

"Aaargh!"

But surely I shouldn't be able to cry out? Or to still feel that stabbing in my ankle, from the tenacious golden clockwork hand, hiding up my trouser-leg?

I open one eye, tentatively. Just in time to see Carvery walking over to flush the toilet.

The last remnants of scaly, blubbery skin vanish down the pan. Carvery turns back to look at me, and I see Mrs. Frittata's shotgun in his other hand.

"Gun must have dried out properly," he remarks. "Just in time."

"You had the gun on you all along?" I exclaim, shaking now more with rage than with fear and revulsion. "Where were you hiding it?"

"Down my pants," he scoffs. "Right behind my knob."

"Well, that's reassuring," I snap. "Knowing that you can conceal an offensive weapon behind the one you already have."

Even while retaliating, I'm aware of consciously trying not to picture the implied scale of the aforementioned deadly Carvery Slaughter attachment… *Stupid traitorous hormones!!*

We all look up. Some more cash is grudgingly exchanging owners above us in the street, but Ace is still upright. Thank God…

Homer's bed grinds another three inches inwards, across the floor.

"I don't understand," I whimper. "We've got the diary – we've got the clockwork hand. What are they waiting for? Why are they torturing us?"

"I think they're still waiting for the heathen magic," Carvery reminds us. "Sure you don't have any voodoo on you, Luke? They've even provided you with a half-dead zombie to start you off."

"They're crazy!" Luke yelps. "You're all crazy…"

I start to get pins-and-needles in my ankle, at the location of the clockwork hand. And as the wall inches closer inwards again, evidently working now over shorter consecutive periods – like the road-markings approaching the end of a freeway – the tingling starts to heat up. It feels as though a candle has been lit under my foot.

"I don't know about you," I mutter, "but something hoodoo is happening down here…"

The tiles on the floor around me start to click rhythmically, and seem to slide against one another like a picture-puzzle. The walls bulge, organically this time.

"Dude," Carvery remarks. "There's a weird light shining out of the toilet…"

Before he finishes speaking, the room *revolves* ninety degrees.

The light gets brighter, gradually outshining the daylight from above. The onlookers in the citadel square overhead back away, covering their eyes.

"Fuck!" Carvery suddenly exclaims, still looking into the toilet-bowl, like a lightweight freshman on his first *Rag Week* night out. "It blinked!"

Luke's shaking stops. As he breathes out calmly and the light in his own eyes changes, it is apparent that perhaps he does have a little knowledge of the occult…

"It's a scrying bowl," he states quietly. "It's Atum. He's keeping his Eye on us. And on the clockwork hand – and on the little book."

"From the toilet?" I can't stop myself from scoffing. "If he's the most all-powerful god of all creation, surely he'd find somewhere better to watch us from?"

"Careful what you wish for, Sarah Bellum," Luke warns.

And the entire floor suddenly drops away, beneath us…

CHAPTER FIFTY-SEVEN: MEDIASTINUM IMPOSSIBLE

Several things seem to happen at once. Luke and I both scream, but due to our manacles attaching us to the walls, go nowhere other than to dangle from our chains, while the tiled floor rapidly recedes downward. Carvery drops the chainsaw, favouring to retain the gun in his other hand, and grabs the edge of the toilet bowl to halt his fall, and the metal bunk upon which Homer is still unconscious merely tilts a little, apparently bolted to the tiled surface as well.

"If that's the Well of Our Souls down there…" Carvery begins.

"Don't remind me," I say through gritted teeth, twirling on the end of my one restrained arm. "What are they up to now?"

I look up. There seems to be a commotion in the square.

"I don't think that little incident was our captors' fault," Luke replies. "They're not happy either…"

To my concern, I see Ace Bumgang being prodded around sharply with sword-points on the glass ceiling above our heads. He skips out of the way, and glancing down at us past his feet, stamps a few times on the glass.

"Look away," Carvery says, hitching up the shotgun again. "Time for that escape attempt…"

I close my eyes just before he fires, picking up the hint just in time. Chips of glass spray down onto our heads, and a huge crack shoots widthways in turn. Ace does a back-flip from a standing jump, and as he lands, feet together, on the spot above the metal bunk, the great fracture feathers outward abruptly, and he punches through.

His *Caterpillar* work boots just miss the zombie Homer's face, scraping his gray ears on either side, as he lands astride him.

Two unwary bystanders from the citadel square plummet by, in the centre of the room – shrieking piteously and scrabbling the air for non-existent handholds.

They seem to continue falling for a very long time…

I gulp.

"What now?" I ask. Other angry city-dwellers are waving their swords at us from the perimeter of the bottomless room above. "Do we have a plan? Are we going up or down?"

"I think the only way we'll be going up is as dog meat paste," Ace remarks, and Luke yelps as a cutlass-point nicks his knuckles, still clamped in their restraints. "They think you've got voodoo, Luke. Now would be a good time for the old hocus-pocus, if you've got any."

"Do I look like *Mister Dynamo* to you?" Luke splutters.

"Well, you are wearing a hoody," Carvery points out.

"And you played Old Harry with the security guards at the University campus all right," I say, encouragingly. "Do it again."

"That's just a load of old tricks and nonsense," Luke sighs. "Nothing beats the use of good old-fashioned force."

Unexpectedly, the mechanical grinding groan echoes around us again – and Homer's bunk, still attached to the wall with no floor, crawls inwards once more.

"What the fuck?" I cry. "We're STILL getting crushed in this stupid crazy room?"

"Best it'll do now is scrape us off the walls," Carvery agrees. "Except Luke, of course. He's facing it, so he's definitely getting squished. Unless his secret magic wand that he's not telling us about works in his favour, of course."

"Man, if my magic wand could stop that wall, my wife would never have kicked me out of the house forty years ago," Luke grumbles. "I would be President of Nigeria now, not a taxi-driver for drunk medical students."

"Oh, God," I sob. "Where's a Flying Carpet when you need one…?"

Of course!

I try to remember. What had Justin Time done to summon the flying rickshaw?

"Sarah," Carvery warns, as I whistle a few bars experimentally. "This is no time to play *Name That Tune*."

"I disagree," Ace counters. "Let me guess… is it *Don't Fear The Reaper?*"

As the bunk carrying Homer and Ace approaches a few more inches inwards, with an unsteady wobble, all I can do is hope that I was right.

But didn't it take a while to respond? Like, the distance between two Lounges… with another lump in my throat, I recall there was another apparently bottomless fall involved back then as well…

"Where's Crispin?" I ask Ace. "What have they done with him?"

"I wouldn't worry," says Ace, wryly. "From what I could tell, all this was his idea."

"What?"

"Do you remember that spy movie? The re-make, with that short celebrity cult guy with all the sunglasses and teeth. Hanging around in rooms where they don't have security cameras installed. The opening scene. I think it's what they call a *Mole Op*. Weeding out the bad guys from your own team."

"What?!" I repeat. "He can't think that! Haven't we all been trying to help…?"

The three guys exchange looks.

"Well, forgive me for saying, but Luke's a Nigerian jewel thief compensating for the fact he can't satisfy a woman long enough to keep a roof over his head," Ace continues. "And Carvery has been leaving big dents in anything female crossing our path since we started. Madam Dingdong didn't need a tip after we went to her *Sauna And Spa*, put it that way. And I basically humiliated the zombie guy's mother. Apparently it's rude not to give a four thousand-year-old zombie queen a seeing-to when she's asked nicely, and I should have spiked my own drink and taken one for the team instead of the other way around. Who knew, right?"

I can't believe it. I must be desensitized from living around all these psychopaths and abusers.

"All sounds perfectly normal to me," I grumble at the wall, which I'm currently facing on the end of my wrist-chain, at the back of the sink.

"Yeah, zombies have morals and ethics, what a bummer that turned out to be." Out of the corner of my eye, Ace sits sideways across Homer's stomach and swings his feet over the precipice, evidently unconcerned about about potential squid hatchlings.

"And you – well, you summoned Atum, so of course they're going to be pissed at that."

"Atum?" I exclaim, nose still to greasy ceramic tile. "I had nothing to do with that great mythical monster turning up!"

"They don't see it that way. What they see is a male-DNA-motivated obsessive female virgin, who works with dead bodies. According to them, that makes you a necromancer."

"Necrophiliac," Carvery corrects him. "Nothing romantic about it, buddy."

"And Atum – well, basically, he's… er…"

"The spirit of the first gamete," Luke interjects, in sombre tones. "I warned you, Sarah Bellum – be careful what you wish for."

"Great." Carvery is nodding, as red-faced, I rotate on the end of my chain to face into the shrinking room once more. "First, I thought it was bad enough being trapped in a room with a hormone-riddled idiot necrophiliac. Now it turns out, it's a hormone-riddled, sperm-jacking idiot necrophiliac, who's haunted by the gigantic vengeful manifestation of the first ever spermatozoa."

"Yeah," Ace says, sourly. "That's the last time I knock one out to internet snuff porn."

"I told, you, Ace – that stuff'll give you nightmares," Carvery tells him. "Sometimes while you're awake. Making you do stuff that you'll want to deny later."

"If you want to know what denial is, it's a big river that you should be floating down, in a large padlocked packing-case," I snap at him.

"Oh, I'm just as pissed off as you are," he remarks. "I'm hanging by one arm from a toilet in an underground torture-chamber, on the basis of some speculation by superstitious zombies, and the failure of a taxi-driver with persistent erectile dysfunction to come up with a miracle."

"That's what *she* said," Ace and Luke both agree at once.

I heave a sigh.

"Well," I begin, annoyed that I'm twisting back around again to face the wall, "we do have what they want. We've got the clockwork hand – even though it's not doing much other than scratching my ankle at the moment. We've got a copy of Mr. Dry Senior's diary. Do you think they'd let us fall to our deaths?"

We all look up at the threat from above. *Hmmm*. It does appear that most of the prodding with swords and shouting is for appearances' sake.

Luke tests his chains, which squeak against their metal rings in the wall.

"Carvery Slaughter," he says at last. "How good is your aim, with that shotgun?"

Oh. *Shit*…

CHAPTER FIFTY-EIGHT: GURNEY TO THE CENTER OF THE EARTH

"Ace," Carvery says. "See if you can kick one end of that bed away from the wall, so it swings out into the room. We need something to break our fall."

"Good thinking, Batman," Ace grunts, and grabbing the foot-rail of the metal bunk, kicks it away from the bracket attaching it to the slimy tiles.

With a groan, the bunk lurches slowly inwards over the bottomless drop. Homer, still unconscious, doesn't even stir, as Ace tries to keep his weight balanced across the barely-there mattress at his feet.

"Think you can reach, Luke?" he asks.

Luke raises his own feet from the far wall, and tries to stretch forward towards the foot of the creaking metal bed.

"Now when we *NEED* that wall to bloody move…" he grumbles.

Ace leans out and just manages to grab his ankles.

"Now?" Carvery queries.

"Yup, we're good," Ace confirms.

I jump out of my skin, as with his free hand, Carvery fires the shotgun at the wall above Luke's wrists. The tiles shatter, and the restraining cuffs break away, pitching Luke upside-down, suspended now by his legs from the edge of the precarious bunk.

Ace grabs his belt and hauls him aboard. Rocking the bed back and forth slightly, they grab Carvery's arm from where he is still hanging from the toilet-bowl, and soon he is on top of the bed hanging over thin air as well.

"You next, Sarah," Ace tells me, as they rock the now dangerously-overloaded bunk towards the sink, to which I am still attached. "Stick your legs out. And maybe better cover your face."

With a gulp, I note Carvery reloading the shotgun, while Luke and Ace each grab hold of one of my ankles.

"Any last requests?" Carvery enquires.

"You wouldn't be able to pronounce it," I snap. "Needless to say it involves evisceration and disembowelling."

"Don't flatter yourself," he replies. "As if my tongue could reach from here anyway."

I just remember to cover my reddening face as he fires over my head. My arm is freed from the pipework with a sickening bang, and I lurch backwards over the hole where the floor used to be. I'm sure they allow me to dangle there longer than necessary, before pulling me back up.

A commotion is going on above us in the citadel square overlooking our cell, and together we look up to see Crispin's disapproving gray face joining the audience of angry, frustrated onlookers. They had backed off, as Carvery fired the shots.

"He's not happy," Ace observes. "Must be your fault, Sarah."

I'm perfectly aware that it is. I gulp, but I'm not going to discuss it with them.

"What now?" I ask instead.

"All the way to the bottom, I reckon," Carvery remarks. "Don't think we want to go back up there."

As we watch, something appears in Crispin's hands, which he starts unravelling slowly.

Oh. My. God.

It's a *noose*.

"I agree," I say at once. "Get us out of here."

Carvery grins, and fires the gun at the last bracket holding the bed to the vertical surface. The tiles splinter, and the bed sags a little more.

Right on cue, we hear the grinding of the mechanical press in the wall starting up again – no doubt to start with the squishing action once more…

"Give us a boot, Ace," Carvery prompts.

Ace nods, and kicks us away from the deadly wall.

There is a split second of inactivity – and then a horrible, pitching, metal-shearing, scraping squeal of breakage…

The torrid air blasts past my ears as we fall, accelerating, into the void. The daylight overhead shrinks rapidly to a blessed dot.

I struggle to get Crispin's expression out of my mind, as he unwound that rope…

"Where does this hole lead to?" I ask aloud.

Jagged rocks are barely visible in the darkness, and I pull the *Trevor Baylis* torch out of my sleeve and crank it up to try and see anything. I get a small fright, as the first thing it illuminates, briefly, are the faces of the two townsfolk who fell earlier – watching us fly past curiously from handholds they had evidently grabbed in the fall.

Just as fast, they are gone – and we are still falling.

"All the way," Luke says, grimly.

The chasm widens, from the width of the cell we formerly occupied, to a vast cavernous space – from cathedral-sized, to football field, to infinity… and inexplicably illuminated, with glowing blue, green and lilac patches on the surface of the rocks.

"Must be some sort of fungus," Ace muses.

"Yeah – a radioactive one," Carvery adds wryly. "An old mine, maybe?"

"What was that?!" Luke yelps. We all look at him. He points into the darkness. "Something flapped past us – right there!"

We strain our eyes into the gloom. The rushing of stagnant air through the steel bedstead whistles and hoots eerily, making it hard to pick out any other ambient noises.

"You're imagining things," Ace grunts. "Too much hoodoo on the brain. There's nothing down here…"

A thump on the head-rail of the metal bunk interrupts him, and a shadow blots out the glow from the infected stalactites.

"Zombie!" Luke squeaks.

But it's not – oh, no, it's not… it has the gray leathery skin, the xylophone-like ribcage and warty knees… but no zombie has that giant scissor beak – with *TEETH* – or those membranous wings, which would out-span the rotor blades of a *Chinook* helicopter…

"Carver," Ace whispers. "It's your Mum. I'd recognise those bingo wings anywhere."

Carvery merely clips the back of Ace's head with the shotgun butt.

"It's a Pterodactyl!" I gasp. "What's it doing down here? How could it survive for so long?"

And then we're all nearly thrown off the bed, as with a deafening scream of metal, we hit an unseen railroad track, and proceed to slide onward. Only the braking provided by the beast's outstretched wings stops us all from being catapulted to our deaths.

"The dinosaurs never died out," Luke tells me. "They just – moved downstairs…"

The massive beak stretches in a yawn, and the giant bird-lizard assesses each of us, with a blinking yellow-orange eye.

"What do you suppose it eats?" Carvery ponders, and I can see him weighing up the option of shooting it pre-emptively, as opposed to waiting to see what it will do first. At the moment, our only balance on the narrow track is provided by its sail-like skin membranes.

Homer sits up, slowly, rubbing the back of his bald gray head.

He must have been jolted awake by our landing. As he focuses gradually, the Pterodactyl lets out a long, low, guttural clicking sound – like something from Ridley Scott's *Aliens*…

Homer turns his head, to look up at the towering monster perched on the head-rail of our mobile gurney.

"Do you know what it wants, Homer?" I ask, hopefully.

My heart sinks, as I see the withered zombie's shoulders hunch nervously. He tries to inch backwards towards us, huddled at the foot of the metal bunk.

"*Braiiiinssss*," he croaks at last.

And the great monster winks at us…

CHAPTER FIFTY-NINE: A TOWN CALLED PANCREAS (PANCRÉAS AU VILLAGE)

"Homer!" I exclaim. "You said 'brains'!"

"He's a zombie, Numb-Nuts," Ace tells me. "Of course he says *braiiinsss*."

"Not Homer – he only says 'home' and 'good' usually," I point out. "Maybe that bump on the head has fixed him…"

"I'm less concerned with his vocabulary, than his answer to 'What does the Pterodactyl want?' being *'braiiinsss'*," Carvery cuts in.

We all look at the giant perching bird-lizard on the head of the metal gurney, as we squeal precariously onwards down the underground tracks.

"It's how they survived for so long," Luke mumbles.

"You mean, how they failed to die out," Carvery replies. "Zombie dinos. That's all we need."

My bladder contracts to the size of a pea at his words.

And yes, I do mean *'pea'*. Not the alternative spelling, or meaning. I wonder how long it's been since I last went. And if I can hold it this time.

"You mean, there could be others?" I whisper.

"You know, on this tin bedstead, we look just as though we could be in a dino-sized take-out carton," Ace pipes up cheerfully. "Chef's Special Noodles."

"Don't you mean Brain's Special Faggots?" I say sourly, and get a clip around the ear.

"Chicken Balls in Cowardy Custard?" Luke suggests.

"We'll be Crispy Sitting Duck in a minute," says Carvery.

"*Spaaare Riiibs*," Homer agrees, and pokes me in the right mammary, with a bony gray knuckle.

"You are improving, Homer," Ace observes. "Although I don't think there's much going spare on Sarah."

"You wish," I mutter, aping Carvery Slaughter's most typical comeback – only not loud enough to be heard, of course.

"When we've all stopped discussing Tit Wings and Brain Crackers, it might be an idea to figure out what to do about not becoming a buffet," Carvery reminds us. "Like she says, how many of those things are likely to be out there? And if we shortchange this one, will it piss them all off?"

An eerie hooting and cawing echoes around us, in the darkness.

"Okay," Carvery continues. "There are lots more of them. That answers that question."

"This is all my fault!" I bawl at last, unable to stop myself.

"No, really?" Ace snaps sarkily.

"Really!" I blub into my sleeve. "Crispin was trying to make me a job offer to be his new secretary, and I mentioned someone – well, a corpse – at the Body Farm, and it made him cross. And it was me that knocked Homer out as well, earlier. I'm so sorry. And now we're hurtling into the middle of the Earth on a gurney to be eaten by zombie Pterodactyls, and it's all my fault!"

"This is happening because you turned down a job?" Ace says, incredulous. "Wow. How big does your head feel on a normal day, Sarah?"

"Not nearly as big as yours, when you figure out it's only because she'd rather stalk you with a pizza," Carvery remarks. "I'm going to shoot this bird in a minute just because I'm bored, you realise…"

There is a sudden *whoosh*, and another thud in the middle of the bunk, between us and the monster.

Only a brief impression of a tattered black suit and a rope tell us anything…

"Crispin!" I gasp, raising the *Trevor Baylis* torch, to confirm who has unexpectedly dropped in.

He turns, and his black eyes seem to flash.

"We will need this," he says, tonelessly – and extends the rope, with the noose at the end.

With a flick of his wrist, he lassos the unwary Pterodactyl.

"What are you doing?" Luke shrieks. "Are you crazy?"

"There is an alternative, if you prefer." Crispin nods behind us, in the direction we are heading.

We look.

Funny. Molten lava does appear exactly the same as Hollywood would have us believe…

…And every ledge on the way down seems to be lined with teeth…

"Is that a…" Carvery begins.

"Zombisaurus Rex," Ace grins, as we fly past, its ash-white jaws closing just short on the burnt air in our wake. The torchlight shines right through its battle-scarred ribcage, its heart a pulsating blackened mess, dribbling clotted opaque slime.

Oh my God… it's like wishing you'd never peeked into the back of the ambulance… and those jaws alone could contain a whole dormitory, never mind one lonely narrow metal bunk…

"Pull up the corners of the blanket," Crispin orders, taking charge once more. "It should be able to hold us all."

We scoot to the middle and bunch up the corners, like a hastily-grabbed picnic cloth in the rain. Standing in the centre, Crispin secures the end of the rope around the scrunched-up hem, so that we are enclosed in a tight, sweaty bundle – a hobo's worldly possessions.

"Mr. Slaughter," Crispin says, after checking the tension in the knots. "Please fire a shot to alarm the beast. But not to hit it."

"There's a lot of it not to hit," Carvery grumbles, but manages to lean out of a fold in the blanket anyway, to check his lack of aim. Ace and Luke each grab hold of one of his legs to weight him down, and Carvery hollers, his voice slightly muffled. "Tell Sarah if she goes near my ass, she'll lose her teeth!"

"Yeah, I heard that about your ass!" I shout back, and clap a hand over my own mouth, horrified.

Did I say that out loud?!

Being below sea-level must be having a serious effect on my self-control…

But fortunately for me, everyone seems to have other concerns right now…

"Here we go," Crispin announces, grimly.

The gun roars.

And with a shriek, the Pterodactyl protests, and apparently flaps free of the head-rail.

We all crack heads as we collide in the bottom of the blanket, and I taste Pirelli-flavoured vulcanised rubber as Carvery's heel catches me in the mouth.

I remember thinking, *Ahhh – so that's what he meant about teeth…*

But then the ominous sound of tearing from below, and a squeak of terror from Luke indicates something else…

"We're caught on a spring!" Ace calls out.

"Mr. Slaughter!" Crispin shouts. "Shoot us free of the bunk!"

"Watch it!" yells Luke. "My ass is hanging half out of that hole already!"

"Better clench then, buddy!" Carvery's voice warns.

There is a second resounding boom from outside. The Pterodactyl screams indignantly at the noise. And a sudden sensation of weightlessness, as we are catapulted into the air…

CHAPTER SIXTY:
JURASSIC PRICK

"Where will it take us?" Luke demands, now trying to hold the small rip in the blanket together, having extricated his buttocks from it. We are swinging rather dangerously around in the bundle suspended from the Pterodactyl's neck, and I'm currently hoping that Carvery's trigger-happy shotgun has a safety catch on it.

"Not to its nest, I hope?" Ace adds.

"Most likely it will only try to dislodge us," Crispin replies. "Possibly by finding a nice flat rock to pound us against."

"Well, of course," says Carvery. "If it's going to eat our brains, it'll want to get us out of the wrapper first."

"*Braaaiiiiiiinsss*," Homer agrees, mournfully.

Luke suddenly yelps.

"Hey, who's got their tongue in my ear?" he hollers.

"Sarah…" Ace warns.

"It's not me!" I say indignantly.

"Hard to tell in this tangle," Carvery grumbles. "There's at least two dicks poking into *my* lug-hole."

"They're not mine either," I snap.

"I think Homer's appetite may be returning," Crispin ponders. "He has been a zombie a while longer than me – and his deterioration will be more advanced. I will need to get him back to the house for further treatment."

"You're talking about more organ transplants?" I ask.

"Yes," he says. "And there are certain psychotropic drugs which will subdue his natural appetites."

"Un-natural, you mean," Luke replies, and there is a shove somewhere in our collected mess of limbs. "Homer! I am not a popsicle!"

"Who's trying to feel up my leg?" Carvery adds. "Someone's groping around my electronic tag."

I recall the golden clockwork hand currently clamped around my own ankle, and try to tuck my legs underneath me, making them inaccessible.

There might still be a potential thief among us…

But that thought subsequently reminds me – Mr Dry Senior's micro-diary!

The little tiny leather-bound copy that Sandy al Dj'eBraah gave me, to take to the Nine a.m. Lounge! Carvery has it in his pocket!

Hmmm. In all the dimness, elbowing and confusion, this might be my only chance of recovery.

Surreptitiously, I test each of the limbs around me. Old frayed denim – that must be Luke's knee, up by my left ear. Down between my legs… *aargh!* My probing fingertip goes straight through old desiccated skin, like ancient baking parchment. Some portion of Homer, although I dare not guess what, and I withdraw hurriedly. Against my right shoulder, the familiar heavy wool cloth, which at least three of us are wearing, in the form of our borrowed Naval uniform trousers – *only* the trousers, in Ace's case.

Idly, I poke a little higher, knowing that if I find shirtless abdominal muscle, these aren't the trousers I'm looking for. Every part of me tingles at the thought of actually sneaking a touch of his bare skin… but I control my trembling excitement and try to focus on the mission at hand.

A little higher…

It's only a jolt of the blanket, but I'm almost disappointed, as I feel the scratch of a jacket hem against my knuckle. But my heart leaps with renewed vigour, as I realise that I have identified the wearer. Carvery.

Target acquired, I tell myself. A deadly target, but the right target. Now – just to pick that pocket.

Strike like a cobra, my subconscious guides me. I picture my hand as the head of a serpent, penetrating without sound or detection… yes. It's almost as if I've done this sort of thing before…

"Sarah *Bellummm*," Crispin's low, manly voice interrupts my concentration. "Thank you for checking again, but I can assure you it has still not dropped off."

"Oh." I withdraw my hand abruptly, as if burned. I just find the nerve to add in a small voice: "Good."

No wonder it felt so familiar! I had forgotten all about our encounter in the Cramps University Hospital elevator. And his black wool suit – not much difference in texture to the Naval uniforms.

"But, if you have concerns, you may undertake a more thorough examination in private later," he adds, closer to my ear.

Ohhh, *my…*

Before I can respond, there is a tearing noise from the corners of the blanket overhead.

"Quickly, Mr. Lukan!" Crispin commands. "What does our exit look like?"

There is a scuffling, as Luke checks the hole in the bottom of the blanket.

"Nothing!" he reports. "No – wait… it can't be…"

"What is it?" Ace demands.

"There's a… a rickshaw flying beneath us!" Luke gasps. "Being towed by a dirty old rug!"

YES! It worked!

I summoned the rickshaw!

"That's what we must aim for!" says Crispin. "Everyone hold on!"

"To what?" Carvery states the obvious.

Crispin cuts the rope from the Pterodactyl's neck. After a split second of inertia, the whole bundle of us plummets.

Our fall is broken by rolled-up rugs on the back of the rickshaw, some of which yelp piteously. We arrange ourselves as quickly as possible, with only a small complaint from Luke, who has not encountered the flying machine before.

"Little help back here, folks?" he suggests.

We find him hanging grimly by one arm from the back, and Carvery and Ace haul him aboard. Above us, the Pterodactyl squawks as it soars away, disappearing into a distant cave high in a rock wall.

For the first time we get a clear look at our surroundings. There is light still, from the strange fluorescent fungi, by which purple-tinged plants flourish, and the glint of water flows down endless precipices.

I draw my breath sharply, as I spot a herd of beasts on a distant hillside. They jog along on their two turkey-like legs, balanced by elongated reptilian tails and small bony-crested heads.

"It's a whole new world!" I gasp, leaning out over the side of the flying rickshaw, to get a better look.

"An old world, Sarah *Bellummm*," Crispin corrects, almost sadly.

"Evicted from the surface by the arrival of humans," Luke agrees. "They would not have survived at all, were it not for the zombie curse…"

"Not a curse," Crispin counters, his stiff-upper-lip tone returning abruptly. "A disease. An illness. The reason they were interred. One which I am working to cure."

"You'd bring all these monsters back to life?" Luke says, incredulous. "Back to the surface?"

"If a cure is found, it most certainly should not be selective," says Crispin, philanthropically. "Leaving anything undead and untreated would only preserve the opportunity for another catastrophic outbreak in the future."

"Like smallpox," I nod.

"Exactly." His confirmation brings a little warmth to my heart. "No-one and nothing will be discriminated against having treatment – for any reason."

Gosh. He's better than Bob Geldof. He really does just want to save the world…

"Well," Ace remarks. "At least the *Creationists* will be happy."

"Let's hope they've also got the secret as to how we co-exist with all these ugly dino-fuckers," Carvery remarks.

"Who do you think gave the dinosaurs the zombie curse in the first place?" Luke mutters darkly.

We watch as the creatures scatter, foreshadowing the arrival of a much larger hunting carnivore, causing them to stampede.

"Is this the Nine a.m. Lounge?" I query, still worrying about the diary in Carvery's pocket, and who and where my unknown contact might be.

"No, Miss *Bellummm*," Crispin reassures me. "This is merely a byway. A subterranean route." He clicks his tongue a number of times at the rug, which deftly changes direction. "There are many junctions here in the cliffs between the Lounges, rather like Bank

Underground Station in London. But I must warn you about our most direct route from here…"

"What?" I ask, immediately feeling an imminent need to cross my legs, to prevent the inevitable.

"It is through the Five Thousand Mile Cave," he says, as we hurtle towards a large, dark aperture in the cliffs. "Home of the Five Billion Vampire Bats."

CHAPTER SIXTY-ONE: DEATH FACE

The cliff-face approaches with terrifying speed, and our flying rug seems to gird itself for further acceleration, as the gap closes.

"Well, that's only a million vampire bats per mile," says Carvery. "In *Chiroptera* terms, for that size of cave, it's practically deserted."

I'm stunned. Carvery can do division – without a calculator? And did he just use the species terminology of the bat family?

"Don't you mean *Desmoda Rotunda?*" Ace queries. "I read online that they roost with up to nine other species of bat. That's potentially ten million *Chiropterae* per mile over all, with only one in ten being a blood-sucker."

My mouth is open at this point, which in less than a minute, might be inadvisable.

"Ace – you can read?" I repeat, disbelieving. "In *Latin?!*"

"Remind me of this conversation, if I ever agree to join these two for a dudes' night out on the town," Luke says aside to me. "That kind of careless talk can close a woman's legs, before she's even had so much as a sniff of the Rohypnol."

"There is room for speculation about the exact number of vampires in the cave," Crispin concedes. "Considering particularly that it is pitch black in there."

And with that, the pitch black engulfs us, like a giant, stinking shroud of tar. My mouth, still agog, snaps shut just in time.

The air vibrates with the flutter of membranous wings, in every direction. As one, we all dive under the tattered blanket, which had previously held us captive.

"Can't this thing go any faster?" Luke demands.

"You are joking, I hope?" I say, the sour wind stripping tears from my eyes, like a cheese-grater against my face. "How long until we reach the Nine a.m. Lounge, Crispin?"

There is a distinctly surprised silence.

"Nine a.m., Sarah *Bellummm*," he replies. "Of course."

Of course. Stupid stupid girl…

The rolled-up rugs beneath us press deeper into my spine with the gravitational forces, as the lead rug pulling our flying rickshaw cranks up another gear.

But that implies that we're going over five thousand miles an hour… assuming he means, Nine a.m. today…

Something bounces off my knee, and I hear Homer squawk indignantly.

"Did you feel that?" I hiss, desperately. "They're dive-bombing us!"

"*Yesss*," Crispin agrees. "Stay under cover…"

The squawk is echoed, deeper and hollowly, somewhere behind us – and repeated twice more.

"They aren't the only ones," Ace points out. "Sarah – pass me the torch."

I hand over the *Trevor Baylis*, and Ace points it briefly into our slipstream.

"Here they come," he reports.

"What?" Luke asks. "The bats?"

"Nope." Ace passes the torch to Carvery, who takes a look in turn. "Three zombie Pterodactyls on our six. Big ones."

"*Braaaiiiiinnnssss*," Homer moans, clamping both hands over his frayed ears.

"They're not going to get your brains, Homer," Carvery says calmly, putting the torch between his teeth and re-loading the shotgun again. "If they're fast enough to catch up, they're fast enough for target practice."

I risk a look over the seat-rail, and see the formation of three giant winged pursuers, against the dim light of the distant cave entrance behind us.

The view is suddenly blocked by a frenzy of fluttering, and an evil, snub-nosed snout with beady eyes appears over the railing. Before I can even gasp, a needle-lined yawn lunges directly for my face…

"Fuck off," Carvery grunts, and with a crunchy squeak, the hungry critter disintegrates messily under the butt of the shotgun. "She's ugly enough already, without a vampire bat beard."

"Thank you," I remember to say, after what seems like quite a few moments of waiting for the shock to wear off.

"Don't mention it," he remarks, turning the gun around to point the muzzle outwards, over the back of the seat. "I mean it. If you ever mention it to anyone, I'll kill you. And Miss Fuck-Tart, your housemate."

Oh yes. Why do I keep forgetting about her?

Idly, I wonder if she's starting to smell, and if anyone back on the Great Barge in the Five a.m. Lounge has noticed…

The leading Pterodactyl opens its beak in another yammering, jabbering caw – and then belches flame.

The blast of heat almost cooks my tongue onto the roof of my already terror-dried mouth. In the afterglow, frazzled bats shower from the air, trailing smoke, like dud fireworks dropping out of the sky.

"My God, they're armed," Luke whispers.

"And fully operational," Crispin acknowledges. "Their teeth have turned to flint after so many centuries undead – and they make a spark by agitating them, which ignites the methane created by the bats in the cave. It protects them from the blood-sucking, burns off excess gas before it can reach critical underground levels, forms a light-source for them to hunt by, cooks their prey, and also de-louses them in the process. It's really quite fascinating."

A second Pterodactyl clacks its jaws a few times, and sears the cave wall with another billow of incendiary fumigation.

"Remind me never to go out on the pull with him either," Luke adds.

"Maybe they fancy a bit of fast food?" Ace suggests, as a third flame almost passes right in front of us, covering our blanket with lumps of squeaking, furry charcoal.

"Burger van's closed," says Carvery, and takes a shot at the nearest Pterodactyl, to the left.

A gaping hole appears in one wing, and it pinwheels out of control, bouncing off the walls and disappearing under an avalanche of peckish, bloodthirsty bats.

Meanwhile, another flaming belch from the middle pursuer lightly singes one of our rolled-up rugs on the back of the rickshaw, which promptly starts crying.

"I'm pretty sure floor coverings shouldn't soil themselves," Ace comments, and tries to switch places with me. "Sarah, you can have the wet patch."

I hear the sobbing emerging more loudly as I shuffle reluctantly along the bench. I try a conciliatory pat or two.

"There, there," I murmur, meaninglessly.

How do you reassure a captive flying carpet?

Another fireball explodes overhead. A flaming bat plummets from the roof, straight through the hole in the middle of our blanket. Homer screams.

"Why do I smell Crispy Chicken Balls?" asks Luke.

"It's just Homer, saving himself the trouble of going for the full operation," says Ace, and crawls downward to try and beat out any remaining flames. "Pass the wet rug, I'll see if I can damp it down."

Gratefully, I roll the sodden carpet towards the foot of the rickshaw, which hisses as it traverses the groaning Homer.

Carvery fires again, but the Pterodactyls are learning, and take evasive manoeuvres.

"*Braaaiiiinnnssss*," Homer pleads. "*Sarah Braaaiiinnnsss... Goooood...*"

"I think Homer wants to eat your brains, Sarah," Ace reports back.

"Don't see why not," says Carvery. "It won't exactly spoil his dinner later."

"I think my brother means, you should use your brains, Sarah *Bellummm*," Crispin says, quietly. "Trust your feelings..."

Use my brains? I boggle, momentarily. All my feelings are currently telling me, is I'm starting to recall that I was rather violently air-sick on this rickshaw earlier... and the similar self-control by the captive rugs isn't helping...

"Heads up, Carvery!" Luke shouts.

Carvery swings the shotgun like a club, slamming an enormous bat into the wall, and to the voracious mercy of its own kind.

"You have to watch the bats, Sarah *Bellummm*," Crispin guides me. "They are a hive. They work as a unit, if you observe..."

I strain my eyes into the darkness ahead of us. There seems to be a swirling ahead, a gyroscopic sensation in the air – a corruption of the horizon… a tilting…

My eyes adjust to the vortex of skin and fur awaiting us, deeper into the cave.

"Oh my God," I breathe. "They're going to try and flip us over…"

It's a whirlpool of wings and teeth, creating a deadly torsional slipstream. And as I stare in horror – under the blanket, something runs straight up my leg.

"Baaa…" I begin to scream, but it is already skittering past my chest, and to my utter shock, clamps over my mouth.

My second thought is even worse than *'Bat'*.

Squidmorph!

But there is no battery-acid odour, no larval tentacle looping around my neck… and as my mind frantically tries to reconnect with the petrified paralysis in my limbs, I see the glinting, and recognise the scrape of warm metal against my lips and teeth.

The clockwork hand!

I peel it away from my face and stare at it, while Carvery drops back down onto the bench to re-load.

"These are the last of my cartridges," he says.

I barely hear him, my thoughts racing.

How did I make this thing work before? I remember getting angry – something about a curtain tassel…

…Yes!!

"I am a virgin!" I shout, gripping the clockwork device in both hands, like a *.44 Magnum*.

"You're going to die a virgin," Carvery nods sagely, still slotting in cartridges.

I let his words go over my head, and sit up. More bravely, I try to raise myself higher, up on my knees. I point the golden clockwork hand into the deadly darkness ahead of us, at the danger as yet unseen by the others…

"I am a virgin!" I yell, more deliberately. "And I am not afraid to use this!"

"God, Sarah – get a room," Ace groans, still somewhere further down. "No, Homer, I'm not going to look after it for you. You get your own pockets…"

Why won't it activate?

"Come on!" I urge. "What do you want from me?"

"Have faith, Sarah *Bellummm*," Crispin says, soothingly.

The vicious vortex of conspiring, co-operative *Chiropterae* gets closer – closer...

A shriek from one of the last two Pterodactyls behind me freezes my blood, and I feel its intake of breath at the nape of my neck, hear the clicking of its flinty teeth as starts to summon a spark...

...And suddenly everything seems to slow down. We are still hurtling along the tunnel, still surrounded by whirling bloodthirsty bats – but my mind is now at the eye of the storm, seeing everything, thinking clearly...

...I drop back on my haunches, and raise the clockwork hand high above my head.

The fireball erupts, and every gemstone on the clockwork hand lights up, again akin to a disco-ball. Instead of turning into a flying rickshaw barbecue, the flames shrink as rapidly as they exploded, sucked into the unknown potential of the clockwork device.

Carvery shoots the startled Pterodactyl, and it takes a direct hit to the sternum, barrelling into its remaining wingman, sending them both crashing into the depths of the cave.

I point the clockwork hand in front of us, hoping now for a miracle.

"Go ahead," Crispin whispers. "Make my day."

"Ummm..." I murmur.

The pinky and index finger of the clockwork hand uncurl, and pause, as if awaiting instructions.

It can't possibly be that obvious...

I clear my throat. The stones in the clockwork hand are glowing malevolently red, like illuminated rubies. The roar of the circling bats is almost deafening.

The rickshaw starts to tilt and struggles to right itself, rendered lopsided by the suction of the angular updraft.

"Fire?" I suggest, timidly.

And then it seems that the world explodes, as everything at the end of my arms flashes a blinding, brilliant white...

CHAPTER SIXTY-TWO: MENOPAUSE IN BLACK

The darkness after the flash is even darker, outlined in red and green, imprinted with the pattern of the blood vessels in my own eyeballs. The air is still rushing past, our flying rickshaw now soaring unimpeded, as straight as an arrow. And the clockwork hand is dull and lifeless, its power absorbed from the Pterodactyl flames completely spent. The only new sensation is a strange tickling, as if the air is full of downy-soft feathers, or warm snowflakes.

There is a mechanical whir beside me, and I recognise the sound of the *Trevor Baylis* torch being wound up, before the beam clicks on again.

"Great shot, Fuckwit," says Carvery, grudgingly. "That was one genocide in a million."

The torchlight bounces back off hundreds of thousands of little white skeletons, scattered over our blanket on the rickshaw, and hanging as if at roost from the ceiling of the cave. Carvery holds out a hand to catch a tiny bat skull as it drifts by. It is perfect in every detail, clean and as dry as – well, dry as a bone.

Carvery blows on it, and it vanishes into a powder.

Halloween snowflakes, indeed…

We exchange a look, and he gestures at the golden clockwork hand still gripped in my own, with the barrel of the shotgun, still in his.

"I'm saving one cartridge," he says. "So if you ever point that thing at me, just remember that I'll blow your fucking head off."

"She'd probably enjoy that," Ace Bumgang replies. "It'd be the first time anyone's blown anything of hers."

Carvery nods wryly, and hands me my torch back. It's still warm from his hand, and I get a guilty thrill, recalling that Ace handled it briefly as well.

I wonder how much viable DNA I could recover, from either of them touching it? I wish I had an evidence bag, or a surgical swab on me…

"Not far now," Crispin's deep voice intones. "Remember – the clockwork hand's power can be renewed – always."

"I think I see the light," Luke confirms.

We stare into the distance, the endless reams of skeletons now starting to thin out a little. Ace clambers back up from the foot of the rickshaw for a better view, brushing white bone dust off his distractingly muscular arms and bare chest.

Oh – what I wouldn't do for some of that DNA…

"You missed a bit," Carvery says. "Looks like you've done whizz."

Ace checks the crotch of his Naval uniform trousers, bemused.

"Not that kind of whizz." Carvery points at his nose. "You got a *Go-Faster* speed stripe right there."

Ace's brow unfurrows in comprehension, and he rubs his face with the back of his arm.

"If I did snort this stuff," he says, between wipes, "would I turn into a vampire?"

"You could try, Mr. Bumgang," Crispin ponders, mildly. "I am sure, after the blast, all traces of rabies and other diseases will have been eradicated."

Ace shrugs, looks at the remaining white residue on his hands, and tests it out on his tongue.

"What's it like?" Carvery asks.

"Bit like a fart in an old people's home." Ace rubs a finger around his teeth, into his gums. "Menthol and *Werther's*, with a hint of coffee and dead thing."

"Sounds like the secret ingredient for brewing Guinness, that they might be missing in the Six a.m. Lounge," Carvery remarks.

"What, old people?" I repeat.

"We'll just tell them to substitute menthol, *Werther's*, coffee and dead thing," Carvery reassures me. "Although knowing Crispin's Grandpappy, most likely they're already using dead thing, of one species or another."

"And old people," Ace agrees, dusting the last of the powder from his hands. "Speaking of old people and dead things,

Homer's not doing too well down there, Crispin. He keeps trying to pull bits of himself off. And not for fun."

Crispin immediately crouches down by his brother's side, to check his current state.

"He still needs medical attention," he announces, grimly. "We must hope that the Nine a.m. Lounge residents are amenable today…"

"Nine a.m. Lounge?" a strange, muffled voice cries out in alarm.

"Who said that?" Luke demands.

"I can't go to the Nine a.m. Lounge!" The almost-familiar voice sounds as though it is shouting through… layers and layers of wet carpet…

"Ah, Justin Time," Crispin greets the stowaway. "What treason have you committed now?"

The disgraced roll of carpet thrashes around in the footwell of the rickshaw, and bursts open, to reveal the whiskered, runaway, bounty hunters' most-wanted rickshaw pilot, Mr. Justin Time.

"You left me in the Seven a.m. Lounge!" he practically broils. I'm not sure he's even close to sober either. "Do you know what they did to me, in their cold stinky little gaol cell?"

"I'm sure you will elucidate us anyway," Crispin encourages, concentrating on his brother's position, and seeing that he is comfortable.

My heart seems to heave a sigh of empathy. Oh, if only Crispin hadn't been so keen on the idea of me taking up his job offer… he really is the nicest corpse any woman could wish for…

…If she wasn't also being constantly distracted by the thought of arrogantly good-looking live male genetics, I remind myself, as Ace wipes his hands clean on my sleeve.

"Don't," Carvery mutters. "You'll only get your hands dirtier. You don't know where she's been."

"They gave me *A Nice Cup of Tea*," Justin Time fumes. "And asked if they could contact my wife for me! If my wife ever finds out where I am, I am a dead man! No offence, Mr. Dry… But we are not talking about an unreasonable woman here! We are talking about a homicidal maniac! Have you ever been married to a homicidal maniac?"

The men all shake their heads. Both Carvery and Ace pointedly step away from me, as if denying any such detailed association.

"No," says Carvery. "But we've met Crispin's mother."

"Yup," Ace grimaces.

"I've been married, but not to a homicidal maniac," Luke says, gloomily. "To a sex maniac." He sighs. "Just not when I was around, sadly."

"You see?" Justin splutters. "That's the sort of woman I would be a happy man to be married to! But what do I get? I get the Medusa, the Furie, the Siren, the witch-beast from Hell… and the pasty desk clerk with the badly-made suit at the gaol, is sitting there offering to send a singing telegram to tell her where I am, and that I am quite well enough for her to collect! Hah! To collect my bones and suck out my soul and flay my skin into a sail for her Ship of Doom!"

"Are you sure that you and Crispin aren't related in some way?" Ace says, quizzically. "Does she ever turn herself into stone at all? Or keep pet zombies – in red leather pants with no ass to them?"

"I wish!" Justin Time rages.

"I bet they offered you Marriage Guidance as well, bro," Luke sympathises. "The elders at my village told me I'd have to sacrifice a white cock to satisfy my old lady. I told them she was getting plenty of that already, from what I'd heard… And not the sort I could afford to sacrifice and get away with."

"Unfortunately, Mr. Time, we are most definitely heading for the Nine a.m. Lounge," Crispin tells him. "But perhaps you could remain under cover until we have disembarked."

"This is costing you, Mr. Dry!" Justin snaps. "I want Christmas and New Year off!"

"But you don't celebrate Christmas and New Year, Mr. Time," Crispin points out.

"No, but my girlfriend in New York, it a very big thing for her," the rickshaw pilot wheedles. "She puts on this little frilly *negligence* with all tinsel and flashing lights in, and a strawberry liquorice rope instead of a…"

"I'm actually starting to like him," Carvery grins.

"Yeah, me too," says Ace.

Suddenly, the darkness fades to misty gray. I switch the flashlight off. Instead of bare rock and desiccated skeletal matter, evidence of creepers and other greenery indicates that we are nearing more hospitable depths.

We all shade our eyes, at the first flash of daylight…

The flying carpet decelerates as we burst through the foliage, disturbing unseen birds and animals, revealed by the noise of their cries and squalling.

"Stupid rug!" Justin Time dives to grapple with the harness, reining in its enthusiasm for the outside world. "Not above the jungle canopy! This is a war zone!"

"A war zone, Crispin?" I repeat, aghast.

I recall those two strange planes that had flown low over the Eight a.m. Lounge, and what Sandy had told me.

Damn! I need that diary, out of Carvery's pocket…

"You'd barely notice," Crispin shrugs, but I recognise his look of discomfort. "Most of the folk here just go about their usual business…"

A whistling in the air is punctuated by a rapid succession of thuds, and our rug and blanket bristle with acquired arrows, in a passable porcupine impersonation.

"Dude, your trousers are on fire," Ace tells Carvery.

"Quick!" I say, leaping at any opportunity to rummage in those pockets. "Take them off…"

Carvery looks down at the burning arrow sticking out of the steel-lined toecap of his boot, at an apologetic angle.

"Why do I get the flaming arrow?" Carvery wants to know, twisting it free and tossing it over the side of the rickshaw, in flagrant disregard for the local ecology.

"…Their usual business being, shall we say, a gung-ho approach to home security," Crispin finishes. "Mr. Time! We need somewhere safe to land! My brother will not last much longer in the air!"

All of us hunker down as more arrows arc overhead, and I crawl downward, to be with Crispin at Homer's side.

"What is it?" I ask in a low voice. "Should he be that colour?"

Homer's deteriorated skin seems to be uniformly weeping a strange, purplish sweat or mucus, accompanied by a smell not unlike a blocked drain. His consumptive belly is distended, as if inflated by a surgical pump.

"No bump to the head has caused this," Crispin tells me, to my private relief. "We need to be near salt water. Mr. Time! Take us to the shoreline!"

"Ohhhh, no!" Justin Time shakes his head and purses his lips. "I'm not going near any open sea! Straight into the jaws of Death for me, that is!"

"What would you rather risk?" Crispin asks him. "A possible chance encounter with your wife? Or a very definite encounter with an adolescent Squidmorph, in need of immediate liquid sustenance?"

I try not to recoil in horror, knowing what Homer means to his brother.

All that time, it wasn't my own hysteria for once, bringing up thoughts of the dread larval sea-parasite – here it is, festering in the most obvious incubator it could find…

We break cover from the jungle, and the sunlight is too painful at first to reveal our new surroundings.

But as the rickshaw churns up bleached white sand and driftwood, and the salt spray from the surf smacks me in the face like a dissatisfied pizza-delivery customer, I can make a rough guess.

I'm not prepared for the view, as my eyes adjust to the glare.

"Whoa," Luke gasps.

It is a picture-postcard tropical beach – deserted, almost pristine. Sprouting coconuts are washed up on the damp sand. Emerald-green islands of all shapes and sizes stand like sentinels in the sapphire-blue sea.

Only a forest-fire burning cheerfully perhaps a mile to our right, pumping the perfectly still blue skies full of black smoke, spoils the scenery.

"Hmmm," Ace remarks. "Smells like Guinness napalm to me."

"Do not wander far," Crispin warns, as Luke, Ace and Carvery disembark to explore, and Justin fusses over the rug, plucking out arrows. "These are indeed times of hostility between the Lounges. Nine a.m. is of particular umbrage to many."

I ignore the others, and help Crispin to lift Homer into a more level position.

"What do we do?" I ask. "What does he need?"

"Nothing, Sarah *Bellummm*," Crispin says, taking his brother's hand and patting it. "We just have to ensure that the first thing the young squidling sees is the ocean – and that we do not get in its way…"

Homer's belly starts to squirm and rumble in an unearthly fashion. As I look down, a trickle of black ink appears down his bony thigh, followed by a whiff of battery acid.

"How long does it…" I begin.

There is the sound of a champagne cork popping, and a glistening white streak across the sand.

Far out to sea, a thunderclap records the breaking of the sound barrier – only then followed by the waterspout of an entry-point, on the horizon.

Homer's belly subsides, like a deflating *Whoopee* cushion.

"…Wow," I say, because there doesn't seem to be anything else suitable.

And then, because Crispin is there, I move to officially check the state of Homer, the patient.

"Careful, Sarah *Bellummm*," Crispin warns. "Sometimes there is…"

An insurmountable force throws me backwards off the rickshaw, and I land flat on my own back, in the very edge of the surf.

Warm slime seems to envelop me, and I blink it away to stare directly into the flat iridescent eyes, and anemone-like pink tentacles, of a newborn Squidmorph parasite.

"A twin," Crispin calls out, unnecessarily.

I gulp, as the parasite arches its spine, revealing a scorpion-like tail.

"Hello," I say, wondering where this ranks in Famous Last Words.

It freezes mid-poise and stares back, then blinks obliquely.

"Hello," it says, quite clearly. "Mother."

And shoots from my hands, like a bar of soap in a gym shower.

"I'm not your mother!" I yell.

Only the distant thunderclap answers me.

Great, I think. That's going to take some explaining, when it comes looking for me in sixteen years' time…

*CHAPTER SIXTY-THREE: M*A*S*H*E*D*

"Justin Time!" a voice hails, and then, rather predictably I feel: "Traitor!"

"Who have you upset now, Justin?" I ask, struggling to my feet, brushing sand and alien squid-goo from my clothing.

"Bah, it is only my cousin," Justin grumbles. "Everyone, meet Seymour Time. Seymour, meet everyone. There, introductions made."

The wiry dark individual, in the combat trousers and red bandana, armed with a crossbow, sidles out of the tree-line at the top of the beach, eyeing us with the sort of suspicion reserved for religious doorstep salesmen.

"Your wife has been asking after you, cousin!" the newcomer greets our coolie-hatted rickshaw pilot. "She has tortured at least six good men to death already."

"She is here?" Justin's voice becomes a desperate squeak.

"Not now, she got bored, went fishing," Seymour shrugs, and shoulders his crossbow. "Ah, Mr. Dry. A privilege to see you, sir."

"Mr. Seymour Time," Crispin acknowledges, straightening up. "Can you take us to the medical facility? My brother Homer needs attention. He has just delivered a pair of bouncing baby Squidmorphs."

"You're telling me," I groan, having just performed service as *'the bouncee'* – still trying to clean slime from my ears.

"Good man! That would kill a lesser person. Yes, you must come to the field hospital. That blanket will make a stretcher."

"Of course." Crispin arranges Homer on the old blanket. "Sarah, call the others, to assist."

Reluctantly, I shade my eyes to seek out Ace, Carvery and Luke, who have wandered further down the beach to look at the blaze going on in the forest.

"Hey!" I yell. "We're moving on!"

We trudge along the barely-there footpath through the jungle, the sad ravaged gray sack of skin and bone that is Homer suspended in the blanket between Crispin, Carvery, Ace and Luke. Seymour leads the way, and I follow behind with Justin Time, who is decidedly jumpy, and flinches at every waving leaf.

We emerge from the trees into an open encampment of khaki tents, some haphazardly marked with blood-red crosses. Men wearing a mixture of combat fatigues and Hawaiian shirts are occupied with moving crates of supplies, transporting patients from one tent to another, or playing croquet on the small air-strip.

"Good thing you didn't choose to land here," Seymour remarks. "The Colonel hates it when you mess up his game."

"He'd have been even worse off, trying to catch a hatching Squidmorph," says Justin wryly.

Seymour shouts in foreign, I don't know what, and a few others hurry over and guide us to the largest temporary shelter.

As our eyes adjust to the gloom, lamps are switched on, and Homer is lifted and transferred onto a polished steel gurney – far cleaner and more hygienic than the one we just left in the Eight a.m. Lounge.

"Poor guy, he looks like the world dropped out of his bottom," says Seymour. There is a flurry of activity, as people are lathering up their hands and being tugged into scrubs left and right. "We will need more than one donor, it appears."

"I have organs here." Crispin produces the linen bag from inside his jacket, containing the spare pieces of unfortunate Victorian streetwalker.

I blush horribly, from the inside-out. Seymour opens the bag, and sniffs the contents.

"These are lady-parts," he observes.

"They were intended for another patient," says Crispin. "But they are all we have to offer."

"I don't think Homer will complain," Ace points out, while Carvery seems to be taking far too much interest in the array of surgical saws on the nearby trolley.

"Proceed," Seymour shrugs, handing over the bag to a nurse, before turning to look me up and down. "You – Miss *Hot-Limps*. You are not sterile enough for this environment. Go to the outdoor shower and wash that squid ejaculate off. Take some clean scrubs with you."

I've seen enough spontaneous surgery already, after my housemate's revival back at the University, and the streetwalker's impromptu dissection. I'm not sure I want to watch zombie quacks perform a sex-change on top of that.

I'd rather be back on the Body Farm, waiting for things to rot in peace. Not watching them get recycled and bounding around ghoulishly afterwards. Privately, I wonder how much of Crispin is original, and if he's hiding something physiologically hijacked of his own up his sleeve – or anywhere else on his person…

"Now," I hear Seymour saying, as I turn to head back outside. "Clean this V.I.P. patient up. Someone find the *XY* to *XX* re-plumbing diagram…"

"Ah," Luke joins in, evidently fascinated, in his own cultural way. "I can see clearly now the brains have gone…"

I head back out into the sunshine with my armful of folded clean outerwear, just missing a golf-ball as it zips past my nose.

They seem rather playful for a warring tribe, here in the Nine a.m. Lounge. To my right, a one-legged man in a wheelchair is drinking something out of a cut-off Wellington boot. To my left, two soldiers sit playing dominoes, a wireless playing Barry White's *'My Everything'* crackling between them.

The shower is a *Heath-Robinson*-esque contraption under a large rainwater-collection barrel, shielded only from the world by a curtain rail. A rickety wash-stand proudly features a sliver of enthusiastically worn-down soap, a completely flattened long-handled scrubbing brush, and a bloodstained wire-wool pad.

I gulp. Some quite possibly psychotic ablutions have been performed here.

I step onto the non-slip rubber mat on the bare earth, and turn on the creaking tap. Jungle-tepid, gray-tinted water sputters from the colander overhead. I'm not sure it has the power to move any of this rapidly-thickening sludge from my person, but I pull the curtain around, and strip off the heavy Naval uniform anyway. The stupid clockwork hand, now dormant again, is currently clamped around my wrist, inextricable, like an OTT piece of Gothic bling.

I make the most of the remaining soap. Although I think I'm only making the hard brown bar of goodness knows what cleaner, rather than it cleaning me. I can see why the wire-wool pad is here… but I use the matted scrubbing brush instead, vainly trying to achieve the slightest squeak of cleanliness against my own skin. At least the soap smell is surgical enough under the grime… maybe sandalwood, or pine.

Perhaps smelling like a tree helps a soldier to hide in the forest…?

"It looks like Homer will recover, Sarah *Bellummmm*," that devastating familiar voice interrupts my thoughts.

"Er, really?" I rub the feeble suds from my eyes to see Crispin standing in the shower cubicle with me, fully-clothed and apparently unaware of the half-hearted cascade of dirty water. But he looks so downcast, I try not to make an issue of the fact. "That is good news…"

"I am not sure that having ovaries and a uterus will benefit him," Crispin sighs. "It is enough that he goes around dressed in Mother's clothes, without asking if they make him look fat and getting depressed on a monthly basis as well."

"Mmmm," I agree, vaguely. *Damn!* Why didn't I pick up a towel beforehand? I try to make myself as small and modest as possible behind the long-handled scrubbing brush. "Have you, erm, yourself, ever had any – transplants?"

"What?" His head raises from his introspective gloom. "No, Sarah *Bellummm*. I have only been dead a fortnight. Nothing has fallen off – or fallen out – yet. But Homer has put himself through the wars. This is at least his third alimentary tract replacement. He did himself terrible damage when I first found him in the shed, surviving on broken beer-bottles and hedgehogs."

"Oh, dear." I try not to picture Crispin reduced to such monosyllabic unsophistication, forgetting his mansion and vending machine empire, chomping on rats and fast-food wrappers at the bottom of some alleyway garbage skip. I shudder, wondering how long such a deterioration took to set in.

"We will have to find other bodily replacements for your housemate, Miss, Er… back on Mother's barge in the Five a.m. Lounge," Crispin adds, apologetically.

"Oh yes, her… umm…" I nod quickly. One of these days her name will just pop into my mind, I reassure myself. "Can she still be revived?"

"The ambient spells aboard the Great Barge will keep her suspended for a little while, by proxy," he tells me. "Mr. Slaughter and Mr. Lukan have gone to rummage in the medical waste bins for any identifiable rejects which could be utilised. Although I think Mr. Lukan is convinced the entrails of a goat could be substituted, and Mr. Slaughter does not seem to be enthusiastic at all."

"What about Ace?" I ask, recklessly, perhaps rebelling against the intrusion onto my *al fresco* toilette.

"He has been asked to look at a problem with one of the ambulance trucks, since his suggestion that human organs could be substituted with a 50cc water-cooled two-stroke engine," Crispin sighs. "It is a good thing my Grandfather, Higham Dry Senior, is not within earshot. He's always on the look-out for alternative technology to clockwork organ replacements. He would shanghai Mr. Bumgang away to one of his surgical sweat-shops in an instant…"

I have no time to respond, as the end of his sentence is drowned out by the low whir of a siren, getting louder and higher, like the whine of a giant hornet.

"Air-raid!" someone shouts. "Incoming rickshaws, twelve o'clock!"

"Quickly, Sarah *Bellummm*!" Crispin grabs my hand and tries to pull me out of the cubicle. "To the shelters!"

"But…" I make a desperate grab for the clean scrubs, clutching them to me defensively as I am hustled out into the open. "I'm not rinsed off yet!"

Arrows and spears are already thudding into the ground, as we race for the half-submerged corrugated-iron Nissen hut entrance. I am shoved unceremoniously inside, where the pitch darkness makes it impossible to see anything, at first.

The drumming of arrowheads onto the iron roof, under its thin covering of earth, is almost deafening, while I attempt to pull on the cotton scrubs. It's only when I find myself lacking a head-hole that I realise I must have put my legs down the sleeves, and have to start over.

A loudspeaker somewhere outside joins the sound of the siren.

"Camp update: Mr. Crispin Dry and his naked lady-friend, *Hot-Limps*, have made it to the air-raid shelter in twenty-two seconds," the announcer says, cheerfully. "No more bets please, and the initial figures say we have only one winner in this morning's race, not including the sweepstakes… And now, some music. Another track from the walnuts of love, Mick Jagger and the *Rolling Stones* – this one goes out to all of you with wives and girlfriends – let's hope they never find out about each other, so we can all enjoy a little more of that *Brown Sugar*…"

CHAPTER SIXTY-FOUR: GOOD MOANING, VERAMONTANUM

"Is that Justin Time on the speakers?" I ask the darkness, glad that no-one can see me, while I continue to struggle with putting on the clean scrubs.

"In the Nine a.m. Lounge, he is known as D.J. *Hammer Time*," Crispin confides, with a sigh. "I am sure that most of the hostilities between the Lounges would be quickly resolved, if he did not find it all so personally lucrative."

"Let us imagine what sort of conversation Crispin Dry was having with Miss *Hot-Limps*, before they were so rudely interrupted!" the undercover disc jockey announces, over the tannoy. "'Oh Crispin, does this shower cubicle make me look fat?' 'Hot-Limps, you have no fear of any degrading sexist judgements from me. I am only interested in your *braiiinsss…*'"

I turn quietly scarlet in the darkness of the air-raid shelter, while bawdy laughter from the field hospital staff follows Mr. Time's squeaky impersonations.

"Sometimes he goes too far," Crispin adds grimly.

"Sir, Mr. Dry, sir!" an abrupt voice joins us, and from its general direction, I guess the owner is standing to attention under the low steel roof. "Would you like to file an official complaint, sir!"

"Not really necessary, Corporal Punishment," Crispin replies. "Sarah *Bellummmm*, this is my first cousin once removed – Corporal Abandon Punishment."

"What an unusual name," I venture, attempting to get an arm through a sleeve before any motion towards hand-shaking is made.

"Full name Abandon Hope All Ye Who Enter Here Punishment, Miss Bellum!" says the hitherto unseen relative. "Adopted by the Dry family in Malawi, Miss Bellum! Where they hope I will some day be President, Miss Bellum!"

"Corporal Punishment was an orphan, raised by a witch-doctor who unfortunately contracted fatal intestinal worms from eating roadkill sacrifice soup," Crispin explains. "My cousin, Beneficience Vassally Dry, took little Abandon under her wing, and put him through the proper schools, church and… military service."

"What do you hope to gain from your service here, Abandon?" I ask politely, feeling rather like a consort, being given a tour of the local people.

"Perhaps a nice clerical job, Miss Bellum!" says Corporal Punishment.

"Abandon is very keen on filing things, Miss *Bellummmm*," Crispin says. "Complaints, stocktaking reports, daily menus, track requests for the radio station, death certificates… occasionally without checking the remains of the deceased first…"

"Sometimes they get up in the night and run away, Miss Bellum!" Corporal Punishment agrees.

"But you have other talents, don't you, Corporal?" Crispin continues. "Enemy codes and transmissions, for example?"

"Just a hobby, Mr. Dry, sir!" announces the Corporal, modestly. "I would really like to work in a library one day, sir!"

Oohhh – I wonder if this workaholic jobsworthy imp is the contact Sandy was hinting about? Who would be able to make sense of Crispin's father's diary? I've most certainly never heard of a rescued Third World orphan discussing their librarian aspirations before… Usually, they want to be doctors, astronauts or lawyers – or sometimes pop stars, or supermodels.

Even future Presidents. Not gray little clerks whose job it is to point at a sign reading 'Sshhhh!' every ten minutes…

Before I can venture another enquiry to establish whether this is my contact, the siren sounds again, this time in reverse, winding down in tone and volume.

"It is the all-clear," Crispin says, patting my knee in the darkness reassuringly. Thankfully, I've managed to get a trouser-leg on by this time. "We can head back to surgery and check on Homer and the others."

The sunlight is dazzling back in the open air of the field hospital, and I can see a number of gunned-down, shattered Six a.m. Lounge rickshaws on the ground, their pilots hanging from trees, or in a few cases being dragging pleading and crying towards the tent marked ORGAN DONORS.

"What a pity," Crispin notes sadly. "If Homer could have waited half an hour longer for surgery, he might have had transplants of the right gender available to him."

"Um – what gender would that be, Crispin?" I query.

"Excellent point, Sarah *Bellummm*." Crispin's grim face relaxes a little, and he looks at me kindly. "Errr… You have your scrubs on back-to-front…"

"Never mind," I reply swiftly, loathe to strip off and rearrange everything again so soon.

"Shall I serve Mr. Time with a formal complaint, Mr. Dry?!" Corporal Punishment's eager voice joins in.

I turn to look at the ambitious adoptee of the Dry family, and gulp. As black as onyx – only a double-take confirms he is not made of such – with eyes as white as Mother-of-Pearl. A carved bone that suspiciously resembles a letter-opener is through his nasal septum, and human vertebrae are inserted into the expanded piercing holes in his earlobes.

He salutes at my visual assessment, doffing his camouflage peaked cap gallantly.

Crispin hesitates, and the tannoy crackles again.

"As usual, the Nine a.m. Lounge-Lizards pillage and plunder from every Lounger that passes through!" Justin, a.k.a. D.J. *Hammer Time* announces, from wherever he is concealing himself in the encampment. "On the Specials menu today, the officers will be eating rickshaw pilot liver, with some forearms, and a nice kidney. Followed by *castrati* of goat, if they can catch the bugger and stop it drinking all the medical alcohol. With any luck, after the interlopers have been battered to death, boiled alive, breaded and fried, there might be enough left for Crispin and Miss *Hot-Limps* to collect in a small carry-out bag, to resuscitate their friend currently lying dead in the Five a.m. Lounge – so long as she doesn't mind waking up as a billy goat. Baa-aa-aahhh…"

"*Yessss*," Crispin sighs. "Bring him to the General's office. In one piece, Corporal Punishment."

"Yes sir, Mr. Dry, sir!" Abandon Punishment barks, saluting stiffly, his glee skilfully under control – and then he turns and scampers away, crab-like, elbows and knees flapping like a voodoo cockerel.

"Perhaps I ought to go with him?" I volunteer, spotting an open window of opportunity for my investigation. "To make sure his interpretation of 'one piece' doesn't mean 'a piece of'?"

"Good idea," Crispin nods, still in that asymmetric wonky fashion that so weakens my popliteal regions. "We will meet at the General's office – in the silver static caravan."

I waste no time, recover the power of my hamstrings, and hurry after the Corporal.

"Mr. Punishment – wait for me!"

I catch up only by the laws of physics and geography, as Corporal Punishment moves at great speed, but in a randomly zig-zagging fashion – meaning I merely need to travel in a straight line, hopefully of the right direction, that he will eventually bisect.

We collide fortuitously beside what could be either a gunner's bunker, or a golf bunker…

"My apologies, Miss Bellum!" Corporal Punishment cries.

"Not at all, Punishment…" I pick myself up and spit out as much sand as I can. "I thought I would provide support if Justin – I mean, Mr. *Hammer Time* – offers up any resistance."

Corporal Punishment looks me up and down several times, as if wondering where on my person I am storing the physical power and propensity for such services, then beams a toothsome grin at me regardless.

"I am very grateful, Miss Bellum!" he says graciously. "This way!"

I skip to keep up, although by his galloping route, we could be heading anywhere.

"I'm very impressed by your range of extra-curricular interests," I announce, as we circle the flagpole twice.

"Thank you, Miss Bellum!"

"Are you familiar with hieroglyphs at all? Pictogram writing?"

And I almost cannon into his beanpole spine, as he stops dead, staring beatifically into space.

For a moment, I wonder if I've said some magic word that is pre-programmed to put him into a trance.

"The flow of images," he breathes, for once, his voice now a reverent whisper. "The energy… the life in every line… and yet so refined – so elegantly restrained…"

"Oh…" This sounds positive!

But before my lips can form the start of another question, the radio tannoy seems to clear its electronic throat once more.

"And now we have some guests on our little field hospital radio show!" Justin squawks, evidently enjoying his freedom of speech from behind the safety of his microphone, in its unknown location. "I'd like you all to welcome Mr. Gaylord Lukan from Nigeria, and Mr. Carvery Slaughter from… from… *Your Mother's Back Porch*, or so I'm told. Both of whom have some interesting experiences with organ-donors that I'm sure they'd like to share – right after this next song. Ben E. King with *Stand By Me*. But please leave the lights on… a healthy man could wake up minus his wallet and watch, and you don't know how hard it is to get a good ticker around here. Never mind how good it is to get hard…"

My mouth is now an ampersand of repulsion, instead of a query of hopefulness.

"He's a shock jock!" I gasp.

"That is not the least of it, Miss Bellum!" Corporal Punishment concurs, with dubious grammatical accuracy. "We must hurry, before he gets carried away and announces a game of *Musical Autopsy*!"

"What?!" I demand, dashing haphazardly after him.

"Anyone not holding an organ when the music stops is out, Miss Bellum!"

Unlike Corporal Punishment's sense of direction, I can see exactly where this is going…

CHAPTER SIXTY-FIVE:
DAD'S ARMLESS

The Malawian Corporal Abandon Hope All Ye Who Enter Here Punishment eventually co-ordinates his motile efforts in the direction of a rainbow-emblazoned *Winnebago* amongst the khaki tents, which looks very out-of-place in the Nine a.m. Lounge military field hospital.

A large satellite dish and a cluster of tannoy speakers perch on the roof. In the grubby window is a battered cardboard notice, upon which is scrawled (in red ink? *Blood??*) the words:

PANIC STATIONS – 911-999FM.

"I have here a poem dedicated to Mr. Dry and Miss Hot-Limps!" Justin Time's voice announces from within. "Ahem… *'There was a young lady from Buckingham'* …Oh no. This cannot be right. I am reliably informed by Mr. Slaughter that Miss Hot-Limps is still a virgin…"

A strange man in safari shorts, with a tea-towel tied around his head against the jungle sunshine, sits outside smoking a pipe. Another red sign hangs around his neck.

ON AIR.

"Looks like he's on more than just air," I speculate. "More than gas and air, even…"

Corporal Punishment ignores the warning sign, and raps smartly on the *Winnebago's* side door.

"Open up!" he barks. "In the name of the General!"

The music inside lowers slightly.

"What name would that be?" the voice queries, after a pause. "General Ignorance? General Incompetence? Or just General Sense of Purposelessness?"

Corporal Punishment draws himself up to his full – and extremely intimidating, primeval warrior-like – height.

"General Sunny-Jim!" Punishment snaps. "Full name as you are well aware Mr. Time, General You Are Going Home In The Back Of An Ambulance Sunny-Jim!"

After another pause, the door in the mobile home cracks open, revealing the familiar face and coolie hat.

"General Sunny-Jim is on visiting duty?" Justin Time whispers, and gulps. "From the Six a.m. Lounge?"

"We are honoured to welcome all of our military ambassadors!" Punishment concurs. "Today, we are playing host to General Sunny-Jim, Captain Intraveinous Mainlining and Lance-Corporal Layabout Pikey from the Elevensies Lounge, and General Lissima Domina from the…"

Justin blanches so white, he almost illuminates the darkened doorway with his anaemic glow.

"…Lissima Domina…" he echoes, hoarsely. "Cutthroat Liss? Mrs. Reaper? The old lady?! The ball and chain??! The millwheel around my neck at the bottom of *Davy Jones' Locker?!!*"

"Yes," confirms Punishment. "Your wife is visiting in her official capacity today, Mr. Time!"

"This I have got to see," Luke chips in, appearing behind the errant rickshaw pilot, alongside Carvery Slaughter. "What are we waiting for? Let's go!"

"What? What is going on out there?" a woman's voice calls from inside the trailer.

"Nothing, erm, Mother!" says Justin, hurriedly. "My mother is here. She is not well. I am looking after her, you see…"

"Justin…" moans another woman's voice. "I'm bored. Come back inside…"

"Your mothers both sound in good health to me!" announces Corporal Punishment. "Perhaps Mr. Slaughter could stay and entertain them for you?"

Carvery shrugs amenably, and cracks his knuckles.

"You might want to check that they have their *Wills* written and in order first," I suggest. "Just in case, Justin Time."

The rickshaw pilot procrastinates in the doorway, apparently loathe to either leave, or to leave Carvery in charge of his harem of potential mothers/possible radio show fans.

"Okay, okay – I come to stupid General's office!" he snaps at last. "We will see if I am ripe for the reaping yet! Er – Mother –

you stay in bed. Both of you. No catching colds while I am out. Or touching anything, without me."

He hustles Luke and Carvery outside, and emerges into the blistering sunshine. But before he can close the door, Carvery's foot is somehow caught in it.

"Forgot something," he says – kicks the door back open again, disappears inside – and locks it.

"Damn!" I yell out loud, before Justin even has the chance. His mouth sags, in formation of whatever expletive had sprung to mind.

"Yes," he agrees, subdued. "What she said."

But of course, I'm not thinking of the wellbeing of Justin Time's female company. I'm thinking of that little diary in Carvery's trouser pocket, and how I'm supposed to get Corporal Punishment to decipher it so that I can understand the supposedly important power of this stupid golden clockwork hand…

"From what I understand, he won't be long," Luke reassures us, unexpectedly. "Let's go. I want to meet your famous wife, Justin! See if she's really as bad as you make out. I swear, no-one has beaten mine yet. I wish they would. Even Carvery said he would have to charge me for it."

Between them, Luke and Punishment manhandle the sobbing rickshaw pilot/rogue disc jockey away from the *Winnebago*, as the music in the mobile home is cranked back up to full volume. It starts to rock erratically, on its hard-standing of paving slabs laid on the scrubby jungle floor.

Damn, damn, *damn!*

I hurry after the three anyway, and as I catch up with their longer stride, something thumps me in the spine.

"Hey, where are we going?" Ace Bumgang greets me.

My heart and bladder fight to switch back to their rightful places again.

What part of his body did he just touch me with? I'll be re-living that one in my mind at night for months…

"We are going to meet Justin Time's wife!" says Luke, cheerfully.

I guess he's happy to meet anyone's wife other than his own.

"Cool," Ace remarks. "Hey, I found out what was wrong with the ambulance. They were trying to make their own moonshine gasoline, and got the mix wrong."

"How wrong?" Carvery asks, suddenly catching up.

Luke was right. That was suspiciously fast… Maybe he keeps a stopwatch on him, and is trying to beat his own personal best.

Perhaps hanging out with *The Stig* too much has made him competitive…

"Well, I reckon they've accidentally cracked the secret recipe for Guinness." Ace pulls a pint glass from his trouser-pocket, two-thirds full of a black liquid topped with creamy white foam, and holds it out. "Siphoned from the reserve tank just now."

Carvery accepts the glass, and sniffs it before taking a sip.

"Yup," he remarks. "That's definitely not napalm. I smell a future peace treaty brewing."

"Peace treaty?" Justin Time splutters. "Noooo! No money in making peace treaty! They just not succeed in making cheap gasoline yet! You know the story – the man, who say: 'I not fail seven thousand times. I discover seven thousand ways not to succeed.'"

"Well, in the Six a.m. Lounge they're failing to make Guinness, while here in the Nine a.m. Lounge they're failing to make rocket fuel," Ace remarks.

"Yeah," Carvery agrees. "How much money do you think that sort of information is worth? Properly worded, of course?"

"How much money do you think the information that a certain rickshaw-flying trans-Lounge operator is hiding that information is worth?" Ace grins.

"An arm and a leg?" Carvery suggests.

"And a head and a foot and two testicles and a man's proportional representation!" Justin shouts. "It is not Guinness, I tell you! It is just bad combustion engineering chemistry, by amateur scientists and part-time amputee surgeons!"

"Well, I've heard it called worse," Ace shrugs.

"In my experience, Mr. Time, if it looks like an elephant, smells like an elephant, and has a poacher's head stamped underfoot like an elephant, it is an elephant!" announces Corporal Punishment, wisely. "Come to the Okavango Delta in flood season, and I challenge you to deny the existence of elephant, when it is staring you in the back of your screaming head!"

"Anyway, anyway," Justin Time recovers himself. "They give up on chemistry already. So no more failed jet fuel and they throw all evidence away, hah! Tomorrow, they convert all ambulances to gas power!"

"Good, they can run on your hot air, Mr. Time!" Punishment approves.

"Seems to be a popular opinion of you, Justin," I remark, recalling damply the moment that Higham Dry Senior decided to test our ability to fly unaided, from the top of the mountain fortress.

"Shame they don't have a way of running on Sarah's nervous bladder as well," says Carvery. "They'd be unstoppable."

"And what was stopping *you* just now?" I bristle.

"Just checking to see if Justin Time's mothers had any organs on them that they didn't need," he replies. "Still looking for replacements for Fuck-Tits back on the giant barge, now that Crispin has used the ones you skewered earlier to save Homer."

"Oh." I look at his hands, to check for bloodstains. Well – up to the elbows, could be normal for him on any given day. "Any luck?"

He shakes his head.

"Nah. They'd had that thing done already, where it's all been snipped and turned inside-out, and stuffed with silicone."

I boggle.

"Mummified?" I gasp.

"A lot of effort to pass as anyone's mother, definitely," he nods, agreeing with me for once. "That's why as a guy, in some cases you can only be certain once you've cut them open."

"They do like it up them, Miss Bellum!" Corporal Punishment confirms, tapping his bayonet. "Right up the fuzzy-wuzzy…"

"First zombies, now mummies…" I groan. "I dread to think now what's happening to… um… to your girlfr… Miss… er… Thingummyjig…"

"To be fair, Sarah, I don't think they like being called *'Mummies'*," Ace informs me. "I think they prefer *'Ladies'*."

"No worries." Carvery looks unconcerned. "The state we last saw Bruiser in, I doubt anyone could tell either way what she started out as."

"A Frankenminky," I agree gloomily, echoing Crispin's own mother's opinion, and both the boys nod. "Oh – the General's office. Is this it?"

A long silver *Airstream* is stationed in the shade, on the outskirts of the camp. As we approach, Justin Time visibly shrinks in direct proportion to its proximity, accompanied by the increasing volume of his knocking kneecaps.

"*Gooood* of you to join us," says that devastatingly deep voice, and Crispin steps ominously out of the shadow of an overhanging Strangler Fig. "Would you be so kind as to step this way?"

My own knees sympathise with Justin's. Gosh – I keep forgetting how manly he is… I mean, *was*…

"Permission to squeak, Sir!" says Justin, jabbering now through his chattering teeth. Crispin glowers at him darkly, before deigning to nod. "Thank you, Sir! Er… eeee-EEEEEE-HHHK!".

CHAPTER SIXTY-SIX: FULL METACARPAL JACKET

The door of the *Airstream* opens with a creak, hinting at inefficient home-made *WD-40* oiling the hinges. There is an accompanying whiff, akin to stale ale.

"Enter," summons a low voice.

Justin Time, now a skin bag of mostly knocking knees and chattering teeth, is hauled in front of the great oak desk within, between Luke and Corporal Punishment.

Four strangers sit at the desk. An imposing Oriental General with a monocle and clipboard. A rotund, ginger-whiskered Captain tucking into a pot of tea and a large cream bun. A young and skinny Lance-Corporal in a knitted scarf and mittens, arms folded sulkily, as if he wishes he was elsewhere…

…And an exquisitely beautiful Afro-Oriental female officer in khaki fatigues, who rises to her feet slowly. While at the same time Justin drops completely to the floor and prostrates himself, as if he is hoping it will part and swallow him whole…

She speaks only one word, and with it, the fate of all in the room is apparently clear.

"Tea?" she says, politely.

"Not a drop of it, you loathsome spawn of Hell!" Justin shouts, slightly muffled by the rather nice Persian carpet.

"Three sugars, please," Luke beams.

"Black," says Carvery.

"White, no sugar," says Ace. "You're sweet enough to keep me going."

She smiles and nods, and turns to the large, gleaming chrome vending machine. Another one of Crispin's high-end refreshment models, no doubt…

"Corporal Punishment?" she asks, over her shoulder.

"I'm a giver, not a receiver." Carvery shakes his head.

"Hot water only if you please, General Domina, Ma'am," Corporal Punishment acknowledges gratefully.

"Not much fun you can have with that," Carvery tells him. "Maybe inflict a few minor scalds and blisters… You need to get out more."

"Miss Bellum?"

I jump as she addresses me. I'm still wondering how to get that little diary out of Carvery's pocket without him noticing.

"Um," I reply, wondering if my bladder can handle any more liquids today, or whether I should just wait for the next Sloe Gin Sling to cross my path, which would be preferable. "I could perhaps just nibble a sugar-lump…"

She nods, and proffers the bowl.

An immaculate set of tiny vintage engraved silver sugar-tongs perch on top of the sparkling white and brown cubes.

"Thank you," I murmur, helping myself to a lump. The tongs spring back and forth between my fingertips, suggestively. "Do you mind? I just want to admire these for a moment…"

"Justin Time," the monocled General Sunny-Jim interrupts, fortunately distracting everyone from my budding plan. "You have been brought before us to face the outstanding charges of flying carpet theft, distribution of counterfeit *One Thousand Yard Stare Masters Degree* certificates, and absconding without leave. And also charges of defamatory statements about our patron broadcast by you on *Panic Stations FM*, abusing your position on the field hospital radio. Do you have anything to say in your defence?"

"Yes," Justin tells the carpet.

"Silence, when you are addressing the General!" bellows the ginger Captain. A glacé cherry vibrates, stuck in his moustache.

"As I thought," the General continues, turning the page on his clipboard, while Lissima Domina serves the tea. "Insolence and insubordinance as well. Do you deny the charges?"

Justin chews the carpet, but says nothing.

"The General asked you a question, Mr. Time!" roars the Captain, rattling the teacups.

The spotty Lance-Corporal stuffs the ends of his woolly scarf into his ears, and pouts.

"I…" Justin peeps.

"SILENCE!"

"Prisoner's non-co-operation duly noted." The General writes neatly onto his pad. "It appears we have reached an impasse. The options for your admonition facing us include collective forfeit, whereby the entire barracks is punished for your misdemeanours and you are thrown upon their mercy…"

"Hear, hear," bumbles the Captain, slurping some of his tea from the saucer, having swirled it around to cool it down.

"Or you are handed over to General Lissima Domina for detention at sea and automatic loss of all flying privileges, for an indefinite period until your behaviour can be seen to be fully reformed…"

The carpet barely muffles a gulp. Back in her seat, General Domina merely smiles coyly at the mention of her name.

"…Unless our patron, Mr. Crispin Dry, has alternative suggestions of merit?"

A hopeful eyebrow is raised from the cut pile underfoot.

But Crispin's expression is as gray and stony as it has ever been. Even my heart sinks on Justin's behalf.

"I have complete faith in the military justice system, Sunny-Jim," Crispin replies, curtly. "Although I suspect that a woman's touch is often more effective than wire-wool and soap."

Where have I recently seen wire-wool and soap? I look down at my back-to-front field hospital scrubs, unable to place them already in my memory…

But the sight of the little silver sugar-tongs in my hand triggers something…

The coded diary! In Carvery's pocket!

Now – if only I can recall which pocket he has it in… because I'm sure there's also probably still something in one of the pockets that I wouldn't want to be poking at with anything metallic…

"Give me the wire-wool and soap!" Justin's voice rises from the floor. "Mercy!"

"How dare you address superiors with suggestions for your method of torture!" The Captain is puce. "Lance-Corporal Pikey, I order you to throw your beaker of weak lemonade over the prisoner at once!"

The still-sulky Layabout Pikey picks up his brimming plastic cup, and tosses it across the desk, where it rebounds off the back of Justin's ear with a satisfying bonk and a splosh.

"Now what am I going to dunk my pink wafers in, Uncle?" Pikey demands under his breath.

"I tend to agree with Mr. Dry," General Sunny-Jim muses, poring over his notes. "So if you will wait a moment while we thrash out the finer details… I'm sorry. Detail the finer thrashings."

And he beckons to Crispin Dry and General Lissima to peruse his clipboard.

Now, I'm thinking, sidling closer to Carvery. Now, now, *now…*

"Don't you have some information to negotiate with, Justin?" Ace mutters meaningfully.

"Mmph?" says the fluff on the carpet.

"Yeah," Carvery grunts, winking at Ace. "Something to do with the Six a.m. Lounge withholding their chemical capabilities, wasn't it? Or was it the Nine a.m. Lounge withholding their brewery capabilities? I'm sure one of them might offer you asylum."

"That is what he is afraid of, Mr. Slaughter!" Corporal Punishment agrees. "The asylum is generally agreed to be worse than the confining to the solitary, with the wire-wool and the soap!"

Now… now… *now or never!*

"Sarah…" a warning voice interrupts my thoughts. "You are going to need considerably bigger forceps than those, if you are going where I think you're going with them."

I drop the little silver sugar-tongs with a gulp, and kick them swiftly under the desk.

"What forceps?" I ask.

Damn it all, already!

Carvery's amber gaze is as deadly as usual.

"One cartridge, remember?" He taps the stock of Mrs. Frittata's shotgun.

"Permission to speak!" Justin shouts into the carpet.

"Silence!" The glacé cherry is fired abruptly from the Captain's whiskers, whereupon it sticks neatly to Corporal Punishment's khaki lapel.

But Justin leaps upright, and lunges for the shotgun.

…And I swear Carvery just grins and hands it to him…

"Say hello to my widdle friend!" shouts Justin.

"Hello, Widdle," obliges Lance-Corporal Pikey, through a mouthful of pink wafer.

Carvery and Ace both look at me automatically, and to the floor beneath my feet.

"Not even a puddle big enough to paddle in," Ace remarks. "She must be sobering up."

"I will be leaving now!" says Justin, waving the shotgun and backing towards the door. "And you will not be following me!"

There is a series of mechanical clicks, as both Generals, Captain Mainlining and Lance-Corporal Pikey all draw their weapons from beneath the desk. The Captain's bayonet neatly impales an iced cinnamon roll, as he levels it above the tea service.

The skewered pastry oozes sugar syrup menacingly onto the French polish.

"That might be inadvisable, Mr. Time," says Crispin, straightening up. "As you can see, it appears you have only brought one cartridge to a bunfight."

Justin lets out a yell, and raises his weapon, trying to pick a target as he jerks it back and forth.

"Fuck's sake." Carvery reaches into his pockets and fumbles around. "Where is it… here, hold this…"

…And he drops the little leather-bound diary right into my astonished hand.

"Dude," Ace says. "I'm sure I read somewhere that you shouldn't Taser an armed man."

"It's not for him." Carvery finds his Taser. "He's just stepped off the carpet onto the floorboards. We need a bigger widdle puddle…"

"Corporal Punishment!" I gasp, and throw the tiny book. "The pictograms – catch!"

The Taser contacts stab into my throat, like the bite of a soulless vampire…

…Every muscle in my body spasms, and the last cocktail I drank leaves via the emergency exit.

The gemstones in the clockwork hand clamped around my wrist immediately light up, and everything else slows down…

I see Justin looking down at the puddle seeping under his feet, and losing his footing on the polished floor… I see Ace diving in to give him a rugby-tackle followed by a wedgie, and Luke reaching out to grab the shotgun barrels and point them harmlessly towards the ceiling as he disarms the rickshaw pilot…

…And Corporal Punishment's long-fingered ebony-black hand closes in mid-air around the little diary, which he opens curiously…

I am still on my feet – *how?*

The stones on the clockwork hand glitter like disco-lights, and with a flash of pins-and-needles I feel the Taser charge rushing down my arm towards it, followed by a blissful numbness. But it still won't let go, hugging my carpals like a bulletproof jacket.

"Guys," I say, feeling light-headed as I watch Ace and the shrieking Justin wrestling on the floor. "Why are you playing in my wee-wee?"

The door to the *Airstream* bursts open, and a figure is outlined against the daylight to be greeted by the impromptu floorshow.

"*Gooood*," the newcomer approves.

"That's more like it, Homer," Luke greets him. "You look like a great big weight has been lifted off your lap…"

"Ah, it appears I now have a sister," says Crispin, as Homer steps inside, over Justin's kicking legs.

"An ugly sister," Lance-Corporal Pikey notes.

"…I told you it didn't seem right swinging around on a dead white fella," Luke adds.

"It did upstage the *dead white fella* part," Carvery muses.

"Really, Mr. Dry," Captain Mainlining remarks, lowering his rifle and retrieving the sticky bun from his bayonet. "A woman shouldn't be running around the camp like that. Put some clean clothes on him, somebody."

"What?" I ask vaguely, my head still up in the clouds. I look down at myself. "It's only pee…"

Lance-Corporal Pikey reluctantly parts with his woolly scarf and mittens, which Homer accepts graciously.

"I find this plan of action to be satisfactory," Crispin announces, checking the clipboard again. "Do you, General Lissima?"

"Quite satisfactory, Mr. Dry." She re-holsters her firearm.

"I don't know what's bothering you, man," Luke tells Justin, as he returns the shotgun to Carvery with the final cartridge still intact, and picks up his cup of three-sugared tea once more. "Your wife seems like a perfectly reasonable lady. I told you she couldn't be worse than mine."

Homer is managing to fashion a sarong out of the woolly scarf, and has put the mittens proudly onto his knobbly gray feet.

In the meantime, I notice Corporal Punishment turning the pages of the little replica of Mr. Dry Senior's diary, his lips moving silently as he reads…

…YES! He understands it!!

"Mr. Time," General Sunny-Jim announces, standing up along with the others. "You will accompany General Lissima Domina to the docks, to begin your detention immediately."

"Never!" cries the mutinous rickshaw pilot, as Ace jerks him to his feet, holding him by the elbows to face the officers.

There is a whip-crack, and a giant, familiar-looking, sucker-covered tentacle lashes out across the desk and coils around the gibbering Justin Time's neck.

"He's the same whenever we have to go home," Cutthroat Liss smiles, while giving her husband an intimate squeeze.

Luke's teacup drops onto the floor, and his eyes pop.

"Hey, Justin," says Ace. "If it's any consolation, I know what you're going through. I think I've had her sister."

CHAPTER SIXTY-SEVEN: APOPHYSIS NOW

"Hah!" General Cutthroat Liss smiles, baring some extremely pointed teeth, while she bounces Justin Time up and down by the neck, like a yo-yo on the end of her alien tentacle appendage. "Where is your New York pet *Playbunny Boy* now, Justin? She too busy twirling her tassels to come to your rescue?"

"*Hooooome?*" Homer pricks up his post-operatively trans-gender ears behind his yashmak of striped woolly scarf.

"Her name is Cynthia, and she is not a Boy!" spits Justin, turning rapidly purple. "Of that I am almost certain! Fifty-fifty!"

"Perhaps we should go and visit her in the Ten a.m. Lounge now, hmmm?" Cutthroat suggests. "See if we can determine her qualifications once and for all?"

"We are heading for the Ten a.m. Lounge," Crispin joins in. "Can we impose on you for a military escort through the Friendly Fire zone, General Domina?"

"Of course, Mr. Dry." Cutthroat Liss grins even more broadly. "You are always welcome on my little skiff."

"Hey," Ace hisses at Carvery. "Maybe these tentacle chicks have something against dry land."

"Was that 'Dry' with a capital D?" Carvery mutters.

"General Sunny-Jim," Crispin turns to the visiting officers, who salute. "It has been a pleasure. Give Higham Dry Senior my regards. Captain Mainlining – Lance-Corporal Pikey – I will see you presently, in the Elevensies Lounge."

"The kettle is always on, Mr. Dry!" barks the Captain. "Come, Pikey. Before you catch a chill."

"It's the jungle, Uncle," Lance-Corporal Layabout Pikey groans, slouching out of the static caravan after him. "I could strip right down to my long-johns, and not even catch a lukewarm…"

We follow them outside into what is indeed the beating tropical sunshine, and watch as the two Elevensies delegates march not-quite synchronously towards a small armoured helicopter in the middle of the field hospital site, and get in, still grumbling to one another. The awaiting soldiers flanking it salute stiffly.

Instead of an impressive engine turning over, or the rotor-blades even starting up, it is merely lifted up on long poles by the soldiers on the ground either side, and carried off into the jungle.

"I can see that moonshine fuel idea getting increasingly lucrative," Ace observes.

"You will like the Elevensies Lounge, Sarah *Bellummm*," Crispin says beside me. "They are extremely cultured when you get to know them."

"Everyone I have met so far today is cultured, Crispin," I reply. "Some of them from cultures I thought were completely extinct."

I leave his surprised side, and run ahead a little to catch up with the loping warrior gait of Corporal Abandon Hope All Ye Who Enter Here Punishment, whose nose is still buried in the tiny leather-bound diary of hieroglyphs. His stride is now mysteriously managing to maintain a straight line, as if under a magic spell.

"You can read it, Corporal Punishment?" I pant, bobbing to keep up, like a cork in a bath-tub. "It makes sense to you?"

"It is very interesting, Miss Bellum!" he announces. "They are the Missing Incantations!"

"Incantations? What incantations?"

"Numbers sixteen, eighteen and nineteen, Miss Bellum!" He turns a page, still not looking where he is going, but walking confidently ahead nonetheless. "Numbers forty-eight and forty-nine! Numbers fifty-one and fifty-two! Number sixty! Number…"

"Numbers?" I ask, nonplussed.

"For going out into the day! For seeing in the dark! For not falling upon the icicle of frozen poop! For not succumbing to the spell of the Sirens! For hearing the word of Atum! For…"

"Icicle of frozen poop?!" I squeak, looking all around at the sweltering jungle in horror, before a vague concept of thermal dynamics reassures me that this is not an immediate threat. "Atum… did you just say Atum? Massive river-snake thing, big scary Eye, barnacles?"

"Oh, Atum is *soooo* over-rated," General Lissima calls back over her shoulder, as she lovingly drags her husband, the unfortunate Justin Time, through the mud and undergrowth, occasionally slapping him against a tree. "Always turning up when things are half-done like a desperate theatre critic, saying *'It's not finished, wah wah wah'*. Of course not, stupid great snake. You just show up too early, before Big Reveal."

"There is a Cult of Atum in the Ten a.m. Lounge, Sarah *Bellummm*," Crispin says. "Organised by a renegade General. He has been predicting terrible things about the Lounges and their stability."

"He has also been trying to make Jack Daniels by distilling his own wee-wee, Miss Bellum!" Corporal Punishment adds earnestly.

"The horror…" I murmur. "He must be losing his mind…"

"Yes, Miss Bellum! Everyone knows Jack Daniels is not made from human wee-wee!"

"Er…" Something prevents me from asking the obvious, probably a sudden concern that I may have imbibed a Jack Daniels Sling or two in the past, when the Sloe Gin had run out.

I look back along our path, to where Luke, Carvery and Ace are trailing behind, sharing the last of the pint glass of failed ambulance fuel/potential Guinness substitute. Fortunately, they don't seem to be paying attention to the conversation. And Homer is skipping along between all of us, having already made himself a grass skirt to go with his woolly scarf and mitten-slippers.

Or should that be 'her?' I can't get my head around it. Perhaps if they'd given him a shave and a make-over too…

"Ah, here we are, my beloved," says General Lissima, as we reach a riverbank and a wooden jetty.

"May you rot at the bottom of the deepest ocean!" roars Justin.

"Ah, does my husband need a nap?" croons the lady General, and with a flick of her tentacle knocks him unconscious, against the black prow of the large stealth motor-boat moored in front of us.

"Hey," Ace chips in sharply. "You forgot to say *'I name this ship'*."

"And all who sail in her," Luke adds.

"He gets sea-sick," she excuses him. "Much better that he sleeps on the way."

And she tosses him aboard, like a sack of old spuds. The tentacle abruptly retracts and vanishes, into whatever hellish portal it occupies.

It's nothing like the Great Barge in the Five a.m. Lounge – or even Crispin's own paddle-steamer. This is a stripped-down small Naval ship, a speedboat armed with heavy artillery – is that a Gatling gun in the tower?? Oh dear…

"Carvery gets sea-sick too," I announce hopefully, but nobody hears me.

"It is not licensed for casual passengers," Cutthroat Liss warns. "So long as you are on board, you are considered crew. So if I give you an order, you say: *Yes, Ma'am*."

"Yes, Ma'am," everyone responds promptly.

"*Gooood*," Homer improvises, and she dismisses his impertinence with a wave of her hand.

"*Very* good, Homer. Let's go. Ten a.m. won't wait around for any old body."

"You are coming with us, Corporal Punishment?" I plead. "I think that little book might be relevant to this clockwork hand thing…"

I hold it up under his pierced nose for inspection, the golden bejewelled device still locked around my wrist – and its gemstones still glittering malevolently with acquired Taser voltage.

"Oh, that is very pretty, Miss Bellum!" Corporal Punishment replies. "But no, I do not see it mentioned in the Missing Incantations yet."

"There must be something!" I press him. "Please, you must tell me if there are any clues to what it is and what it is for! Because I think it might hold the cure for…"

"All aboard!" snaps General Lissima.

We fall into line, and shuffle onto the loose gangplank. She chuckles as we pass.

"There's my good little shamblers," she purrs.

"Do you know what a shambles is, Miss Bellum?" Corporal Punishment asks me, under his breath for the first time.

"It's what we are?" I suggest, feeling unusually clever at anticipating some derogatory military remark.

He looks worried.

"I certainly hope not, Miss Bellum," he replies. "It is a meat market for the remains of animal sacrifices, deemed unfit for consumption and prohibited in many religious sects. Incantation Fifty."

"Fifty shambles of gray zombies would be a pretty tasteless meat market overall, I imagine," interrupts Carvery, glancing from Homer to Crispin and down at me. "Drool much lately, Sarah?"

"She's calling us animal sacrifices!" I hiss.

"Maybe she's referring to zombies as being general consumers of sacrilegious meat parts," he shrugs, pushing past and making a bee-line for the gun turret. "Sounds about right to me."

"Waterskis!" Luke cries, and is suddenly hopping up and down in the bows like a kid on Sunset Yellow, a ski in each hand. "Oh, man, I have to try *theeeeese!*"

I'm starting to worry that there isn't anyone here who is taking the situation seriously…

"Mr. Bumgang!" General Lissima hails, and points to the controls. "How's your driving?"

"How's your holding on tight?" Ace grins.

"Then let's make waves, Mr. Bumgang. Time to run the gauntlet!"

The gauntlet? I look down at the golden clockwork hand. But no – still nothing.

Damn it! And – is she *flirting* with him…?

I topple over sideways as Ace steers the boat around in a circle, mid-river, and find myself face-down in a lapful of black wool suit.

"You are in a hurry to perform a closer examination, Sarah *Bellummm*," Crispin intones deeply above my head. "We are not even in private yet."

"No, no – just making sure you were, erm…" I hazard, trying to sit up but finding my hair snagged in his zipper. "Oh dear. I think we might need scissors."

"I will pretend I did not hear that, Sarah *Bellummm.*"

I attempt to coax the strands of hair free from the zip tag.

"You know, Crispin," I say, concentrating fiercely. "You really could be being a bit more helpful."

"You seem to be managing admirably down there," he assures me.

"No, what I mean is…" I tut to myself, as I release one single solitary hair, resulting in making the remaining tangle worse. "This is YOUR hereditary clockwork hand. Made in Switzerland by the finest Swiss watchmakers…"

"Why would I need that as well right now?" He sounds puzzled. "Your own hands are keeping me quite busy enough at the moment. You're not suggesting I need a prostate exam too, I hope?"

"No, Crispin!" I sigh in exasperation, fiddling and fumbling like an amateur acupuncturist. "I mean – why didn't you ever learn anything about it, while your father had it? Why didn't he teach you anything? What is it for? What's its special purpose? And it better not be for better self-prostate examination, now you mention it… stupid thing's been hanging onto all sorts of parts of me when it's not blowing things up or turning them to stone…"

"That certainly does not sound like a necessary range of powers by which to perform prostate exams," Crispin agrees, and sighs in turn, his undead lungs whistling sadly an inch from my right ear. "But you are absolutely right, Sarah *Bellummm.* My father was in mourning for so long over our first brother, that he never shared much of any knowledge value with Homer and myself. We had to try and guess what would earn his approval. Homer as you know, was a little far off the mark."

"*Hoooome,*" says Homer unhappily, seated beside Crispin atop the stocky body of the unconscious Justin Time.

It's so frustrating… I pluck another hair free, trying not to lose my temper and vigorously jiggle the zipper with what would appear to be impatient enthusiasm.

"Why would you spend a lifetime looking for something when you don't even know what it is?" I grumble.

"It is not what it is," he says, patting my head somewhat inappropriately. "It is the hope of what it is, when you find it."

"Bogeys at twelve o'clock!" shouts General Lissima from the prow.

"Don't think we want to go there," Carvery complains. Out of the corner of my eye, I can see him installed in the gun turret, putting on some goggles.

Uh-oh…

"Can we skip the Twelve o'clock Lounge? Or is it compulsory?" Luke queries, one sandal already off and replaced by a waterski optimistically.

"Full speed, Mr. Bumgang!" she snaps. "We will lose them in the Shambles!"

"Yes, Ma'am!"

The boat lurches forward as Ace opens the throttle. With a rip, I topple backwards this time, my freed strands now a frizzy hairball hanging over my right eye.

"What does she mean, the Shambles?" I demand, struggling upright once more.

"A place no-one should see or hear of," Crispin replies, adjusting his fly modestly. "The place where unanswered prayers go to rot, and priests conceal their sins."

"Miss Bellum…" Corporal Punishment beckons me to the starboard.

"What is it?" I join him at the handrail. "Have you found something?"

There is an engine roar approaching low in the skies, and again I see the two flat triangular jets passing overhead.

"The planes are what take up all of our fuel in the Nine a.m. Lounge, Miss Bellum," he tells me. "But they are not unnecessary against the saboteurs…"

Several flying rickshaws burst from the treetops, and I can just see their Six a.m. pilots lighting Molotov cocktails in the driving seats.

"They come to destroy evidence, Miss Bellum," says Corporal Punishment. "Evidence that prayers alone are not the answer."

He points to the riverbank.

Oh, God…

So many corpses…

So many hooves…

So many feathers…

"So many sacrifices, Sarah *Bellummm*," says Crispin, joining us at the side of the boat.

"Oh, Crispin," I say, my heart going out to him. "So many chickens…"

With a clomping of one waterski, Luke shuffles over to see what we are looking at.

His face slowly sets, as the grim scene sinks in.

"I knew it," he mutters. "They all lie! The gods don't want sacrifices! The priests just take your money! And then – they sleep with your wife!"

With that, he promptly throws up noisily over the side.

"Yeah, I love the smell of Guinness in the morning," Ace remarks, from his place at the the controls.

The rickshaw pilots launch their napalm cocktails onto the riverbanks, and the air is filled with the stench of burning feathers and fur.

Corporal Punishment downcasts his milk-white eyes and clasps his hands closed around the little leather-bound book.

"*My place of slaughter belongs to Him who is over the place of sacrifice*," he begins, solemnly. "*I am happy and pleased with the altar of my father Osiris. I rule in Busiris, I travel about on its riverbanks, I breathe the east wind…*"

What is he doing? Is he losing his mind as well??

"Clear a path, Mr. Slaughter!" orders General Lissima.

"Yes, Ma'am!"

…And I just remember to cover my ears in time…

CHAPTER SIXTY-EIGHT: IT AIN'T HALF ARSED, MUM

The surface of the river ahead of us erupts with the gunfire of all three barrels in the speedboat's turret. A rickshaw and its flying carpet making a low pass explodes into splinters, followed by a spitting fireball from its stock of napalm cocktails.

"Get down!" shouts General Lissima.

We hurtle through the fireball as it rapidly burns itself out. Ace twitches at the controls, to dodge a flaming coolie hat as it spins past his head.

The General hefts her own chain-gun, and takes care of another flying rickshaw as it pulls along the port side.

"Behind you…!" I yell, as a third draws parallel on the starboard.

Cutthroat Liss keeps her eyes on her current line of fire, but her apparently independent alien tentacle shoots out backwards, straight through the side of the latest rickshaw, fatally piercing the pilot. Then it cracks like a whip, causing the pilot and his vehicle to disintegrate.

The flying carpet, unleashed, flaps quickly into the sky.

"Stop that rug, Mr. Slaughter!" she yells, as her tentacle retracts. "The flying carpet whisperers will learn of our position!"

"Yes, Ma'am!"

Carvery aims the turret guns upward, and another volley of deafening fire rips the unfortunate magic carpet to shreds. There is a smell of singed wool on the breeze.

"Crispin, those are your grandfather's men!" I say, grabbing his arm. "Why are they attacking?"

"It is a clash of different cultures," he says. "Nothing is personal. When one has alchemy but no technology, and the other has technology but no alchemy – without formal and incorruptible trade management, the world will always lapse into a betterment *Tug o'War.* These are merely the casualties of poor commerce."

"I get it," Ace chips in, steering us around a burning tree-trunk floating downstream. "It's like they're both saying '*Who Moved My Cheese?*'"

"And assuming the other one did it," Carvery agrees, between shots. "Blaming with extreme prejudice."

"Quite correct, gentlemen," Crispin nods sagely, although I have no idea what they are on about.

"And whose side is she on?" asks Luke, jerking his head towards General Lissima, while still strapping on his other waterski.

"Half on my mother's side – a distant cousin, or some such." Crispin waves a hand around vaguely. "The other half – who knows?"

"He means, whose side in the war?" I hiss.

"Oh." Crispin contemplates a moment. "I think the answer is still the same."

"Wheeeeehh!" Luke leaps from the bows of the boat, and is soon surfing energetically in our wake, dodging bullets and flaming cocktails.

"That's the spirit, Mr. Lukan!" Cutthroat Liss approves. "Everyone should be having fun!"

And she blows two more rickshaws out of the sky.

"I am having fun," shouts Carvery.

"Me too," Ace agrees, steering for a moment with his knee while rolling a cigarette. "Especially watching her playing with that watering-can."

General Lissima just chuckles, as she aims the massive chain-gun again. The barrels roll and the muzzles spit bullets relentlessly. The air hanging above the river is filled with smoke, rickshaw sawdust and cut pile.

Corporal Punishment has stopped praying, and joins Crispin and Homer and me as we sit in a row on top of the still-unconscious Justin Time.

"Are you all right?" I ask him. "What was that you were quoting just now?"

"Incantation Seventy, Miss Bellum," he says. "An unnamed spell, but the purpose is clear to all who study them."

I glance in frustration at the dormant clockwork hand, clamped around my wrist. It's like it has a mind of its own. Rather than me being able to control it, I'm starting to worry that its reticent powers could mean the reverse is the case.

"Are you sure there's nothing in that book about this?" I persist. "I'm certain Mr. Dry Senior was implying that they are connected in some way."

"Oh, everything is connected, Miss Bellum," says Corporal Punishment. "You have to recognise that not everyone can be bothered to wait for prayers to be answered, although they still go through the motions for appearance's sake. They go to confession, they make the obligatory sacrifices. But the heavens can wait, they say. Here on Earth, time is money."

"Whffft?" says a muffled voice, and our seat shifts a little. "I knew it! You are selling me for spare parts!"

"Your parts are safe, Mr. Time," Crispin replies. None of us makes a move to get up, and Homer tries to wriggle into a more comfortable spot between the rickshaw pilot's hamstrings. "Except perhaps from Mrs. Time."

"Hah, never marry a virgin!" Justin Time grumbles into the deck beneath his whiskers. "They are always hiding something. A homicidal tendency, a drunken father, a taste for human flesh, a tattoo of *Jedward*, a financially-crippling designer handbag habit…"

"A big alien sucker tentacle?" I suggest, hoping no-one has noticed my burning flush at the mention of tattoos.

"Oh, that not be so bad…" Justin mumbles. "Except she always getting it out in public, like the trollop that she is…!"

"What is she, Crispin?" I whisper, while Justin continues to rant under our collective buttocks. "And your mother, begging your pardon? I mean, I know I'm not a fully-qualified Forensic Anthropologist yet, but I've never seen…"

"I thought you knew, Sarah *Bellummm*." Crispin sounds genuinely surprised. "The Sirens are well-documented."

"Ohhh…" I dredge my memories of early schooling in history and Greek mythology. "I think I recall – but tentacles were never mentioned…"

"Of course," says Crispin. "No-one who came that close survived to describe the tentacles. They traditionally kill their mates after fertilisation. Or sometimes just for fun, nowadays. Civilisation has a little to be grateful for."

"Ah." I gulp.

I glance at Ace Bumgang, wondering if he knows how lucky he is to be alive.

Should I tell him?

No – maybe I'll spare him the horror. For now...

After all, there might be a more opportune moment for him to be thankful to be alive, and in my company...

"It looks like we are out of the Friendly Fire zone," Crispin observes, intruding a little on my own thoughts of future human fertilisation. "We are nearly there."

The sound of gunfire and screaming of rickshaw pilots has ceased. I risk a peek over the side.

"Wheeeeehh!" Luke hollers happily, skipping over the last of the wreckage on the waterskis behind us.

The jungle has thinned out, and thank goodness – the littering of sacrificial corpses on the riverbanks is no more.

Instead, a scattering of rude wooden huts denotes villages, with women in saris beating clothes against flat stones, men in make-do diapers beating bony cattle and elephants with sticks, and children in nothing at all beating monkeys at *Who Can Make The Best Silly Face*.

"They look so peaceful," I remark.

"Yes. The Ten a.m. Lounge is among the most benign," Crispin agrees. "Not exactly neutral, but as close as can be estimated to neutral. The only conflict here is the Cult of Atum, and the renegade General Foramen Winslow."

"Is he dangerous?" I ask.

"He is psychotic," Crispin admits. "But of the type it is best to humour his delusions, for that is the only way to stay alive in his company."

"I will drop you off here," Lissima Domina announces, as we approach another small jetty. "I have to take my wayward husband back to my ship."

"To the mothership?" Ace queries.

"Back to Hell!" screams Justin, and is knocked unconscious again by an alien tentacle-wielded knife-butt.

"Just a regular old ship, Mr. Bumgang," she says, smiling. "I can't be having my naughty spouse running around on dry land. Not even to see his *Playbunny Boy* girlfriend. Leave the controls to me."

Rather reluctantly, Ace and Carvery leave their posts. Luke is also sad that his ride is over so soon, letting out a sigh, his skis sinking below the surface as we decelerate.

Corporal Punishment helps Homer to his feet, and Crispin offers me his arm.

"Shall we, Sarah *Bellummm*?" he says.

We step ashore.

General Lissima's boat turns and roars away again, back downstream into the Shambles.

If anything, it is even hotter here than in the jungle. There is less shade, and the ground underfoot is closer to sand and dust than to mud. A few scrubby shrubs cling to the ground between the huts and shacks, but anything green has been stripped from them, by the livestock and the scavenging monkeys.

"Serves you right," says Carvery, as a chattering, boisterous monkey picks his pocket, and promptly Tasers itself.

Not for the first time, I'm glad I didn't attempt that route.

"This way." Crispin gestures towards a dried-out track, marked out either side with bird skulls on sticks. Their feathers are strung between, on lengths of frayed old string.

It doesn't seem to be a great indicator of this Cult being a peaceable one…

As we trek further, occasionally a piece of coloured paper flutters in the dust, or is caught against the scrub.

Luke picks one up.

"'*The winter of our discontent…*'" he reads. "What is that – some sort of war propaganda?"

I rescue another, caught in a strip of bark.

"This one just says '*Alas…*'" I add.

"They are prompts, Sarah *Bellummm*," Crispin replies. "The discarded notes of Cult sermons."

"Not one of those self-appointed preacher cults?" says Ace. "That's it, I'm not drinking anything they serve here. It'll be a suicide by cyanide cult."

The ramshackle buildings ahead are arranged around a square, the tallest, facing us, shrouded in a heavy red-and-gilt curtain. As we approach, we see an elderly gentleman, in a white turban, totter across the quad with a tea-tray to knock on the door of one of the lower buildings, which has a golden star on its door.

On the breeze, I swear I can hear a piano, and the sounds of someone practising their scales…

"Your early morning call, General Winslow, sir!" says the tea-vala gently, rapping again on the door.

"Early morning call?" repeats Carvery. "It's ten a.m!"

"Do not let them hear you making light of the time, Mr. Slaughter," murmurs Crispin. "They are a delicate sort in the Cult of Atum."

The distant voice accompanying the piano clears its throat, and starts afresh.

"Ta-ra-ra boom-dee-ay! My knickers flew away!"

We exchange looks.

"They went on holiday! They came back yesterday! Ta-ra-ra boom-dee-ay…"

Ace twirls a finger perpendicular to his ear.

The door with the golden star on flies open, and out storms a whiskered, well-built, middle-aged man in a string vest and khaki shorts, sporting a uniform peaked cap, and brandishing a cane.

"I heard that, you naughty boy!" he roars, with an impressive voice that you knew was born to *enunciate*, not just speak like any old commoner. "I also heard you singing your scales with *Doh-Ray-Me-So-Farty!* You are lucky I have not had my first cup of tea or I would be right over there to give you a good hiding, yes I would! Tea-vala! In my cabin now! And bring extra sugar!"

"Right here, General Winslow, sir!" The tea-vala picks himself up from behind the door, having kept the tray and its contents miraculously upright, and follows him back inside.

"We are fortunate," Crispin remarks. "It looks like a regular rehearsal day. On *matinée* performance days, the General has been known to execute both leads and their understudies before brunch."

"Ah, maybe that's what this is for," Luke remarks, handing over another of the slips of paper he has been collecting as we walked. "'*Casting for female lead and understudy. Must have good legs, high-C, and dance*.' What is a high-C?"

"It's what Homer's got, since the operation," Ace points out.

"You could audition, Homer," Carvery suggests. "Then we'd have a man on the inside."

"They'll be none the wiser to that," Luke agrees. "So long as they don't look too closely at his high-C."

"*Goooood.*" Homer hops up and down excitedly, and turns begging eyes on his brother.

Crispin's manly shoulders sag.

"Yes, yes," he sighs. "We can play along, Homer. It may buy us a little time in which to find out if they have any real intelligence on the river-god Atum's recent actions, or if the Cult is merely a front for the General's Broadway ambitions."

"Did somebody say Broadway?!"

We turn around. A skinny young woman, with chestnut-red braids, clutching a cello case, looks at us like one big hopeful question-mark. She wears big honest spectacles and a very Amish-style pinafore dress, a cross between *Anne of Green Gables*, and Corporal Punishment's dream librarian pin-up.

"Are you talent scouts?" she breathes. "Is this *The Jungle's Got Talent, Get Strict With Me* audition tour?"

"Ah, now I see how the General finds his recruits," Crispin remarks. "Where are you from, Miss…?"

"My name is Summer… well, it's the name I've chosen since I ran away from the nunnery on the mountain, where I was called Sister Jaundice. And the best I got there was second fiddle in the nuns' orchestra, for the children's Sunday school choir. What I really want is to play on Broadway, join a conservatory, study at Juilliard, perform under Andrew Lloyd-Webber…"

I feel my hackles rising, catching me unawares as the bespectacled drama shrimp makes big eyes at Crispin's expensive black suit.

Am I… am I getting *jealous…?!*

"I think you've come on the wrong day, my friend," Luke interrupts, patting Homer reassuringly on the back, and I realise I'm not the only one feeling threatened. "Today we are auditioning for dancing girls."

"Oh." The big blue eyes resemble Shubunkins lost in goldfish-bowls. "I can tap-dance…"

"Strippers," Ace cuts in.

"And *Playbunny Boys*," adds Carvery.

"Ohhhh…" Now, Summer Jaundice looks decidedly less hopeful. "Don't dancers need musicians?"

"We've already got a pianist," I say.

"*Gonnne*," says Homer, looking down at himself through the grass skirt, wistfully.

Luke pats him on the back again.

"Man, that's something you dead white boys just gotta learn. Use it, before you lose it."

The invisible pianist in question starts up on cue, with an off-key rendition of *'Anything Goes'*… but by the reaction from the General's cabin, it is quite clear that *Anything* definitely does not *Go* as far as musical talent is concerned.

"That is one of my favourite songs and you has just ruined it, my lovely boy!"

The General bursts out of the gold-starred door again, this time armed with a revolver, his other hand holding a half-finished mug of tea. He marches across the square to the far side, kicks open the door to the dormitory opposite with his 13-hole Army boot, and empties the gun into the unseen room beyond.

The chorus of *'Anything Goes'* ends with an open-ended B-Flat, by the sound of it struck heavily with the forehead.

"Wow," Summer Jaundice gasps. "The judges are really harsh!"

"We still have a pianist." I catch hold of Crispin's arm possessively, remembering his *Franz Ferdinand* in the restaurant last night, and what nearly happened on that piano before the power-cut…

"Not dropped off yet, Sarah *Bellummm*," Crispin confirms, coughing modestly.

A second door in the dormitory opens, and a completely different figure steps outside to light a cigarette, her blonde tresses in big rollers, wearing only white stockings and an oversized khaki shirt.

"Now that's the competition you've got to worry about, Homer," Carvery remarks.

The strange woman turns and stretches, revealing a *Playbunny* tattoo on one lithe hip.

"I hope you has been rehearsing, Miss December!" snarls the General, sipping his tea and scowling.

"Cynthia," she corrects him. "Only creeps call me Miss December. Creeps and creepy boyfriends, anyway."

"We has got a big day coming up! Entertaining the troops! I will not be having you lazy boys and girls spoiling it by sloppy rehearsals and coming down with the mumps and all turning up dead like last week! Poor old tea-vala spent the intermission sewing arms and legs back on instead of serving the tea! And Miss February has already cried off sick with the jungle bottom and called her agent to pick her up and still makes my life a misery with the long-distance phone-calls about her luggage not being returned! Now – what has we got here then?"

And the scary General turns towards us, and strides over.

Instinctively, we all salute.

"Here to audition, sir!" pipes up Summer, as foolhardy as she is desperate, apparently.

"Has you got a bikini in that cello case?" the General barks.

"Just a cello, sir!"

"Then I hopes you is good at ironing shirts and peeling spuds!" he shouts. His eyes move on to me, looking at my back-to-front field hospital scrubs. "What has happened to you, Sonny-boy? Did they sew your head on backwards?"

"No, sir! Got dressed in the dark, sir!" I'm too scared to correct him as to my gender.

"Well, at least you is honest as well as dimwitted. We can always use more medics. Can you tell a hand from a foot?"

"As long as it is not on a monkey, sir!"

"Good!" His gaze crosses over to Ace and Carvery. "What is up with you two Pansy-boys? Run away from the Navy, have we? Fancy a bit of singing and dancing instead, do we?"

"Oh, the uniforms…" Carvery looks down at his. Ace is still shirtless. "We're not absconders."

"Nah," Ace joins in. "We're strippers."

I swear, my lungs contract all by themselves. I so do NOT need that image in my mind while trying to stand to attention in front of this terrifying and allegedly deluded man…

"Ah," the General muses. "Chippendales, eh? Well, I hear there is some market for that, especially among the other lovely Pansy-boys we has got here. And I see you has brought along some exotics. Something for everyone, whether they is into spear-chucking or limbo-dancing, no doubt. Looks like we can put on quite the variety show with all of you circus freaks here today…"

…And then his eyes level with Crispin's.

For a fleeting moment, there sees to be almost a spark of recognition – of FEAR – in the General's eyes…

But then just as quickly it is gone, and the glassy stare of madness returns.

"And what is you, errand-boy?" he growls. "A looky-likey act?"

"Yes, General," says Crispin, smoothly. "A look-alike act."

"Who plays the piano," I squeak, before I can stop myself.

Fortunately, the General has priorities other than insolence.

"Good," he says. "I believe I has an opening for an ivory tickler."

And he turns away, heading back for his cabin.

"Yes," Corporal Punishment remarks, as the rest of us all breathe freely again. He strokes the long carved bone inserted through his nose thoughtfully. "I can see his opening from here."

CHAPTER SIXTY-NINE: CHYME BANDITS

The cello-toting ex-nun, Summer Jaundice, is already strolling over to the dormitories on the far side of the square.

"Hello," she says to the *Playbunny*, Miss 'Cynthia' December. She sticks out a pale hand, attached limply to a very bony wrist. "I'm Summer."

The calendar girl squints down through her cigarette smoke.

"Wearing a lot of clothes for summer," she remarks. "Where you from, the Himalayas? I bet you kick ass on the catwalks there."

"What's the plan?" Ace asks, while Carvery merely watches the two women talking, as if wondering if they'd both fit into the same pre-dug hole in the ground.

"We had better start acting like professional thespians," Crispin advises quietly. "The General likes to hear music while performing his morning ablutions. I will practise some melodies on the piano, and you two – I don't know, look like you are warming-up and stretching… Homer – well, of course, we don't need to worry about him or her…"

Homer is already twirling artfully around the supports of the long porch spanning the length of the dormitory building, flapping his striped woolly scarf like the feather boa from earlier.

"…Mr. Lukan, do you have any skills? Any juggling or balancing tricks besides the waterskiing which could be put to good use?"

"No, sorry." Luke sighs. "I can sing a bit, I guess… ahem… '*When I fall in love, it will be forever…*'"

Our jaws drop.

"Holy cow, dude," says Ace. "You sound like Old King Cole."

"Nat," says Carvery, glancing my way as I stare at him in turn, and he slaps me sharply on the forehead. "There – gnat. Wouldn't want your head swelling any bigger."

"Oh." I dazedly glimpse the squashed bug on the palm of his hand, before he wipes it on his trousers. "Cheers."

"I was aiming more for Louis Armstrong…" Luke grumbles vaguely. "Do you think he'll fall for it?"

"I don't think you will have any problem fooling him, Mr. Lukan," Crispin assures him. "That leaves Corporal Punishment and Miss *Bellummm*, who has already been mistaken for medical staff…"

"*Nearly* a qualified Forensic Anthropologist, you know," I say, a little hurt.

"I think you two will be the safest to explore the camp and see if any intelligence on the river-god Atum is being kept here," Crispin continues. "Corporal Punishment has the relevant knowledge, and Sarah *Bellummm* has the clockwork hand to protect her…"

"Well, I…" I say, bashfully, not entirely sure it's picked me for that reason at all – but Crispin is decided on the plan.

"We will rendezvous backstage," he announces, pointing towards the tall building swathed in impressive drapes. "If you hear the music stop, or anything else alarms you, take the northernmost path into the hills, beyond the main theatre. Do not wait for anyone. Is that clear?"

We all nod.

"Excellent." Crispin straightens up, and turns towards the dormitories. "Would anyone care to join me for a little light rehearsal in the piano-room…?"

Ace, Carvery and Luke follow him into the building.

Ace and Carvery re-emerge, only briefly, to dump a dead body on the porch. Possibly of the previous pianist.

Some notes strike up. Homer carries on dancing regardless.

"Honey," Miss December says to him, as he pirouettes past her. "You're really working that woolly scarf."

"This way, Miss Bellum!" Corporal Punishment urges. "I have long awaited the opportunity to investigate this cult!"

I follow as he leads the way around to the back of the building housing General Winslow's cabin, checking doors and windows.

The subject of cults has been touched upon at University, certainly – from a Forensics viewpoint, usually regarding the best way to preserve the crime scene and identify all of the bodies…

I catch myself sighing again, thinking of Mr. Wheelie-Bin back at the Body Farm. If only I'd said 'No' to my housemate yesterday when she'd asked me to go to the interview in her place. I could be sitting under that silver birch tree now, doing my own homework, with a thermos of Mochaccino and a Rich Tea biscuit, catching up on one of our comfortable heart-to-hearts.

Such a good listener… and of course, is *never* jealous when I talk about waiting around for Ace Bumgang outside the breaker's yard with a Chinese Meat Feast pizza…

And then I give a little squeak of pain.

The clockwork hand *pinched* me!

It's as if it knows exactly what I'm thinking!

"I believe many of the General's recruits are buried here, Miss Bellum!" says Corporal Abandon Hope All Ye Who Enter Here Punishment.

"What makes you say that?" I ask.

"All the burial mounds, Miss Bellum!"

I look to where he points.

The ground out back of the buildings is a giant molehill paradise. Some have little makeshift crosses or stones arranged on them. Here and there, an Army toecap sticks out, or a skeletal extremity.

Some are even decorated with the dead stems of floral tributes (the flowers, I assume, having been eaten by monkeys long ago), and the occasional stage prop, such as a moth-eaten top hat and cane…

The Corporal cups his hands to a grimy window.

"It looks like a store-room, Miss Bellum!" he hisses. "What do you think?"

I try to clean the greasy glass with my sleeve, before peering in.

"Maybe theatre props?" I suggest, prompted by our ghoulish backdrop. "Look, I'm sure that is a suit of armour in the corner."

"We will investigate!"

He produces another carved bone from somewhere in his uniform, and uses it to pick the lock on the door. As quietly as possible, we slip inside.

"It does look like props…" I remark. "Look, a treasure chest – some maps – and it *is* a suit of armour…"

Corporal Punishment picks up one of the scrolls and unfurls it. After a second, he produces an eyeglass and screws it into his eye socket for closer perusal.

"These are not props for the theatre, Miss Bellum," he says, grimly. "These are genuine. They are the spoils of war."

"What?" I gasp.

I look around the room. All this treasure – and even edged weapons, dating back to Medieval times…

"The General has been keeping the property of his unwitting recruits, it appears," says the Corporal. "I see a Morningstar from the Elevensies Lounge in the corner there…"

"Oh," I look, but I don't see the newspaper. "Are they Communists in the Elevensies Lounge?"

"No, Miss Bellum," says Corporal Punishment patiently. "Besides the point, but – the spiked iron ball and chain attached to a club. A Morningstar. A cultural weapon of the Elevensies Lounge."

"Ah." I try not to look too long at the bloodstains, and the remains of desiccated brain matter. "Crispin did tell me they are very cultured there."

"Extremely, Miss Bellum."

The Corporal continues poking around, looking for more academic material. Idly, I go to examine the suit of armour. It has some rather nice engravings and embellishments.

"It must have belonged to someone quite important," I remark. "A pity, there are some parts missing. It only has one arm, and no stopcock."

"A suit of armour with plumbing, Miss Bellum?" The Corporal sounds impressed. "That is technology unknown to me, I must admit."

I peer into the empty shoulder-socket.

"How very curious…" I muse. "It seems to be equipped for attachments – on the inside…"

"Let me see, Miss Bellum!" Corporal Punishment is suddenly behind me and breathing right down my neck, giving me an unexpected thrill, and I step away obediently.

Goodness… all of the little hairs on my nape are standing upright…

"This is bad, Miss Bellum," he announces.

He's not kidding. I don't think there is room in my diary for any more male fantasies.

"General Winslow might not know what he has here, or he could be holding it to ransom," the Corporal mutters, half to himself. Gosh, he is *very* attractive when he is thinking aloud... "You know the story of the mad man, he runs around like a headless chicken shouting *Wolf! Wolf!* All day every day... until a wolf shows up, but nobody listens... it is also true of the cult-leaders, they preach much nonsense, but sometimes in the nonsense is an invisible truth..."

"Is this something to do with Atum?" I ask, wondering how a huge carved bone through the nasal septum would affect potential intimacy.

I will have to Google that, when I get home...

"It is somewhat relevant, yes," says the Corporal. "Like I was saying, to those who would not bother to wait for prayers to be answered. I hope the General does not know what it is – unless he has the rest of it as well – because then the world is in very great danger!"

"Ohhh..." I look it up and down, under its patina of dust. "Could we steal it from him?"

The Corporal's pearly white eyes focus and re-focus, as his great academic mind grapples with the suggested solution.

"Um," he ponders. "Well, er, that would certainly... yes... Yes! Find something to wrap it in! And quietly!"

We emerge again into the quad nonchalantly, the Corporal's stride a little stiff, while I'm now feeling decidedly reinforced around the chest and corset regions. The rest of the parts are rolled up in a small ornamental rug, which despite much whistling and coaxing seems to be of the Lesser Wiping-Footed variety, not the Great Flying Carpet sort.

And I swear the clockwork hand is getting impatient. It gave me at least one Chinese burn and pinched me several more times while we were packing up the suit of armour...

But I'm quickly distracted by the sound of the piano accompanying Luke's impressive tenor, and – is that the *cello* playing along?

I can feel my ears burning already, as the thought of Crispin seated at the piano with another woman invades my mind...

And then the General himself appears briefly on his own porch, a pink towel on his head and a white fluffy bathrobe wrapped around him, cooling himself with a rice-paper fan.

"That is not bad, my lovely boys and girls!" he shouts. "But let's see if you is any good at putting on a dress rehearsal! All of you on stage in one minute, chop-chop! Get moving!"

The quad is suddenly a hubbub of activity, as hitherto unseen occupants of the theatre camp hurry out of various dormitories, setting out chairs and working on winching up the enormous curtains.

A white grand piano is wheeled out onto the middle of the stage.

"Homer, honey!" I hear Cynthia's voice calling. "Help me with these rollers!"

"Backstage, Miss Bellum!" Corporal Punishment reminds me. "Quickly!"

Although there's not much that's 'quickly' about it for the pair of us, we waddle over uncomfortably, and clamber the steps into the wings.

"What do you mean when you say, people who won't wait for prayers to be answered?" I whisper, as more stage-hands hurry back and forth. "Have they learned of the Shambles too?"

"They have taken advice from the Incantations, but interpret them differently," the Corporal replies. "From Incantation Seventy-Seven, One Hundred and Fifty-One, One Hundred and Seventy-One, and possibly others. They have replaced faith in the gods with science and technology. Even in planning for the afterlife, Miss Bellum!"

"Why? It's not as if they can take it with them…" I begin. A large scenery cut-out of the Great Pyramids is wheeled past me. "Who would be silly enough to think they'd need technology in the afterlife?"

"You may have noticed, Sarah *Bellummm*," that other voice joins us, and my quadriceps melt. "The afterlife is not something anyone can take for granted."

"Of course, Crispin," I murmur apologetically.

For some reason, I'm glad to see that both he and the former Sister Jaundice are still in their regular clothes as musicians… Luke is looking very groomed, in a suit and bow-tie, very appropriate for his skills… and Homer, perhaps also appropriate for his own, is now sporting a cheerleader's outfit and another blonde wig, matching Miss December's quick change into her *Playbunny* cheerleader costume. Ace and Carvery, however…

…Here my patellas completely lose it, and try to run away down my legs, past my metatarsals and out through my phalanges…

Both are dressed as cowboys. Well – the ripped denim jeans, boots and Stetsons are recognisable, although there's rather less going on in the shirt department. Carvery seems to have on the remains of a white muscle-back vest, while Ace has donned an open leather waistcoat.

"What have you two come as?" I try to sound cool and sarcastic, while worrying far too much about them both wearing gun-belts, and whether or not the weapons holstered are merely props.

"*Lunchbox Mountain*," says Ace. "Look, I've covered in glitter as well…"

I try not to make eye contact with his flexing biceps and deltoids. Carvery still has the shotgun with its last cartridge, and most likely has the Taser in one of those riveted pockets…

"If this makes more money than paving and concreting, I'm throwing out the cement-mixer," he remarks.

I realise that Crispin and Corporal Punishment have been whispering. *Damn!* Why wasn't I paying attention? Damn my traitorous hormones for distracting me!

We notice as a deathly hush falls across the quad. The General has emerged from his cabin, followed by two turbaned attendants – one of whom is carrying the tea-tray, the other a large wicker fan.

Now finally dressed, in a khaki uniform, the General inspects every detail of the scene as he approaches.

"Not bad, not bad, lovely boys," he rumbles. "Sweep up that monkey do-do in the aisles, that's right, chop-chop! Now let's see what you band of vagabonds is hoping will entertain the troops! I want big smiley faces and jazz hands on the lot of you!"

Oh, dear. I can't imagine any one of our surly troupe meeting those expectations. Except for Homer, of course…

Fortunately, Homer and Miss December are first out onto the stage, as Crispin plays a rousing introduction on the grand piano. Sister Jaundice is installed nearby, the cello wedged between the long skirts covering her bony knees, like a musical hydraulic jack.

"So," I hear Ace mutter to Carvery in the wings beside me. "How come neither of those two…?"

"Well, one of them's Miss Plastic Fantastic," Carvery replies. "And the other one is as deluded as this one."

"Are you referring to me?" I whisper, annoyed.

They look at me irritably.

"No," says Carvery. "Your dead housemate bitch, back in the Five a.m. Lounge."

"Why do I get the feeling you want her to stay that way?" I demand.

"One less mad woman in the world," Ace shrugs.

Ah, okay. He does have a point… I've had to live with her, after all.

Homer, of course, gives a stellar performance with his pom-poms, and his high-kicks are far superior to Miss December's tassel-jiggling. I just find myself hoping it's all to the General's taste. His reaction is inscrutable, sipping his tea through his waxed moustache, the peak of his cap pulled too low to read his expression.

Luke launches smoothly into *'Me and My Shadow'* after his introduction by the two cheerleaders, and Sister Jaundice joins the piano-backing by scraping away enthusiastically at her cello-strings, trying to throw in the occasional jazz hand between strokes.

The General is still immovable. I'm glad I didn't volunteer to wear the bottom half of the stolen armour under my hospital scrubs, because with this sort of nervous tension, it might be in danger of going rusty, the longer I stand here…

CHAPTER SEVENTY: THE WONDERFUL WRISBERG OF OESOPHAGUS

General Winslow's response to the performance is a slight nod, at which the rest of the encampment applauds politely – if somewhat nervously.

"That is not too shabby, lovely boy," growls the General. "But I does not want you pandering to that old tea-dance black-and-white minstrel image. We is not the occupying hordes anymore, we is culturally integrated now! How about something exotic? Something what harks back to your roots in the Sahara Desert?"

"Sahara Desert?" I mutter. "'*Working legally as a taxi-driver since 1971*'?"

"That means an encore, Mr. Lukan!" Corporal Punishment hisses. "Be careful not to overstrain your voice! The General is – *very* demanding!"

Luke beams and turns to Crispin at the piano for a musical prompt, whose shoulders are slumped, at a loss.

"Toto?" Luke suggests.

"Where?!" Sister Jaundice shrieks, looking down and snatching her feet up off the floor either side of the cello, and unwittingly displaying her striped woollen nunnery stockings, under the long skirt.

Crispin nods, flexes his hands, and launches into the opening bars of *'Africa'*.

Oh, dear. I hope all the keyboard exertion doesn't wear down those talented undead fingers of his…

"More like it, more like it…" mumbles the General, and the rest of the audience heaves a collective sigh of relief.

A sudden breeze flaps the stage curtains, and the scenery-hands hurry to secure them.

Funny… I didn't think the audience sighed THAT hard…

Homer and Miss December sway rhythmically beside the piano, taking up the backing vocals.

"Corporal Punishment," I whisper. "What were you just saying to Crispin?"

"A family matter, Miss Bellum," replies the Corporal gravely. "The discovery of the armour here potentially solves an old mystery."

"What mystery?" I ask. I'm all too aware of the chafing inside the stolen breastplate, under my medical scrubs.

"The mystery of what happened to the last person wearing it, Miss Bellum."

"What…" I begin, but then I remember the rows and rows of burial mounds beyond the cabins. "Oh, dear…"

"Yes, Miss Bellum."

"One of the Dry family?" I venture.

"The finest Swiss watchmaker, Miss Bellum."

I gasp. No wonder the clockwork hand had been pinching me, and wringing and squeezing so painfully! With the body of its maker lying right here – somewhere…

I wonder what horror and torture the poor watchmaker had endured here in the Cult of Atum, under General Foramen Winslow's ruthless regime – whether he was forced to sing himself hoarse, tap-dance to death, strip-tease down to the bone…

My bladder shrinks another two centimetres, as I glance at Ace and Carvery in the wings beside me, dressed in their Chippendales' cowboy outfits.

Suddenly, I feel as though I now know the meaning of the phrase '*Danse Macabre*'…

…And I don't even speak Swiss…

"You!" the General is shouting, over the music. "Sister Bandy-Legs! Is you playing a cello or trying to light a fire?! Stop sawing away like a lumberjack! Put some soul into it, damn you!"

Sister Summer Jaundice blanches, and tries to sit more elegantly.

"I imagine it's not an easy task, with two feet of wood wedged between your legs…" I murmur.

Ace and Carvery look at me.

"No different from riding a horse, Miss Bellum!" replies Corporal Punishment.

"That's what I always tell them," Ace remarks.

"No point telling them," Carvery says. "They're usually too busy screaming to listen. Just wear ear defenders instead."

"If the General had ear defenders, he wouldn't know if she was playing along badly or not," Ace agrees.

"Exactly."

General Winslow glances down at his wrist, and I note the ornate watch he is consulting. *Stolen*, the indignant thought occurs to me…

The wind springs up again, yanking one of the curtains free from its ropes. The nearest stage-hand leaps to tame it, and ends up swinging ineffectually on the end of the gilt cord against the rising gale.

"That's quite a dust devil," Ace grimaces, holding onto his Stetson.

"It is no dust devil," says Corporal Punishment. "It appears that Mr. Lukan is hitting the right notes."

The General is rising slowly to his feet, as Luke starts the chorus.

"That's right, my boy…" murmurs General Winslow. "Keep singing…"

Behind him, on the horizon, I see a gyrating whip-like shape also rising out of the dust, gradually gathering mass and speed, as it approaches the river – directly towards us.

Distant trees and shrubs are torn from the ground in its wake…

"It's a cyclone!" I cry. No-one in the audience seems to be taking notice. "We have to get to shelter!"

Corporal Punishment stops me, with a hand on my arm.

"What are you doing?!" I demand. "Are you mad?"

"No, Miss Bellum," he tells me. "Wait and see…"

He's crazy… but I stand firm – or as firm as my jelly-legs permit – while the weather phenomenon towers above us, blotting out the sun.

I look in utter frustration at the clockwork hand clamped around my own wrist.

"Now would be a good time!" I shout at it.

But it merely glitters, and does nothing.

The scream of elephants and braying of cattle is barely audible above the roar of the twister, as it hits the far riverbank and forms a waterspout…

…Where it remains, the muddy waters of the river raining down on the stage and the audience, along with the occasional monkey limb.

The rearmost four rows of seats in the audience are decimated by a falling bullock.

"Keep playing!" orders the General. "Louder!"

Luke closes his eyes, and opens up his lungs.

The cyclone's rotation gathers speed in its static position mid-river, like an upright washing-machine entering the spin cycle.

And in the hellish darkness at the centre of the waterspout, glimmering through the murky rush of water, a giant Eye slowly ascends…

"Atum…" I breathe.

"It is a Summoning!" Corporal Punishment shouts in my ear, as we cling to the side-supports of the stage, against the buffeting wind.

The gigantic river-god rises higher and higher inside the water-spout. There is a strong smell of brine, and a barnacle the size of a saucepan ricochets off the hidden breastplate under my clothes, knocking all the air out of my chest.

"Keep playing!" the General yells. "Even you, Bandy-Legs!"

Sister Jaundice leaps to her feet, tossing aside the cello, which concusses Miss December.

"My legs are not bandy!" she screams, pointing at the General with her bow, her eyes flashing angrily.

And I mean, literally flashing… green, like traffic-lights…

Almost apologetically, the clockwork hand opens from its death-grip around my wrist.

It's too late, I hear myself thinking before I can grasp and level the illuminated clockwork hand, as the line of green fire from Sister Jaundice's eyes crawls down the bow, and leaps straight into the General's heart.

There is a bang, and a puff of green smoke and glitter, quickly washed away by the rain from the tornado.

There had been neither a shout nor a scream. No reaction at all to the sudden transformation of the skinny, bespectacled, cello-playing ex-nun.

All that remains of General Foramen Winslow are his boots and hat.

Crispin is still playing – and the others are still singing, eyes closed as if in a trance.

The clockwork hand only uncurls those deadly fingers as she aims the bow a second time – towards the river…

…*Too slow*, I'm thinking, as I see the line of green fire moving down her arm again…

"I hate musicals," she glowers. "And I hate crazy megalomaniac Generals. But I really *REALLY* hate giant, omnipotent snake-gods…"

Then I remember the last thing the clockwork hand absorbed, as Carvery reaches for his Taser and shakes his head, hesitating.

"Can't mix water and electricity," he grumbles, stamping into the considerable puddle on the stage.

As a last resort, I look upwards into the sky desperately – *yes* – and point the clockwork hand straight up above my head.

"First rule of home D.I.Y…" Carvery mutters.

"There's no place like home!" I scream.

The massive bolt shoots from the clockwork hand, lighting up the sky, turning the entire landscape white – except for the witch-nun Sister Jaundice and her green fire, poised to strike the river-god in his watery prison…

There is a deathly nanosecond of eternal waiting…

A blackened village hut comes crashing down onto the stage, its grass roof smoking ominously. Cello splinters and imploded green glitter fly everywhere.

"Aw, Sarah," says Ace, brushing himself down. "Did you have to squash Miss December as well?"

"That's almost two full sets of human organs you owe me," Carvery adds, extracting a nipple-tassel from his ear. "And a few extra pounds of silicone butt and boobage."

The door of the burned hut swings open with a creak, for a dazed elderly villager to emerge, his make-do diaper around his ankles.

"Jeez…" says Carvery, organ repossession quickly forgotten.

"Someone get this man a nice big leaf!" hollers Ace.

Ribbet... croak... *ribbet*...

I turn to see a webbed forefoot reach up out of the General's right Army boot, and a batrachian amphibious brown warty face with a waxed moustache follows, burping imperiously.

Crispin's hands hesitate over the piano keys, and his eyelids flutter over his jet-black eyes. Luke's voice fades uncertainly. Homer stops swaying, and looks around.

"*Hoooome!*" he squeaks, pointing at the pom-poms sticking out from under the lightning-stricken village hut.

As soon as the last note of the tune echoes away, the storm abruptly ceases. The cyclone and waterspout silently collapse, and for one split second, the river-god Atum is looking down at us accusingly, with his all-seeing alien Eye.

Then he is gone, with a serpentine flick, back underwater. A never-ending tidal ripple follows.

"He looks really pissed off," I observe, as the last few raindrops fall, and the broiling sun returns.

"Well..." Carvery ponders, and then shrugs. "He's just been sucked up out of nowhere... and then the witch tried to blow him out at the last minute. Where do I even begin?"

The tea-vala has picked himself up from where he was sheltering under his tea-tray. He surveys the scene briefly, and claps his hands.

"Strike camp!" he cries. "Moving on after lunch – Frog Leg Soup!"

The former General makes an optimistic leap for freedom, straight into an awaiting silver samovar. The lid clatters down, drowning out his final, outraged *ribbet*.

I hurry to Crispin's side, as fast as the top half of the stolen armour encasing my body will allow me. The clockwork hand has immediately clamped around my wrist again, like a mechanical Chinese Burn torture device.

But it's not the first concern on my mind any more.

"Crispin," I say gently. "Are you all right?"

He looks my way, but doesn't seem to focus.

Please don't say it, I think. *Please don't say*...

"*Braaainsss*," he groans, blinking, and my heart plummets.

His hands, weakened and groping, reach up to my shoulders, as my own eyes fill up with tears.

We've come so far… why did it have to be while he was playing music? This wasn't the piano-related fantasy I was having at all…

"*Braaainsss*," he repeats, his voice getting louder.

"No, Crispin," I cry. "No, no…"

He heaves a sigh, both leaky lungs whistling in harmony.

"You used your *braaainsss*, Sarah *Bellummm*," he says. "I couldn't be prouder of you."

The tears pour down, and if it wasn't for this stupid armour holding me rigid, I would have collapsed into his arms in relief.

"Be careful," he warns. "You will go rusty under there."

Of course – he knows about the armour…

"The watchmaker?" I query. "Was he related to the Dry family?"

"No time," he shakes his head. "We must hurry. Our ride to the Elevensies Lounge will be early, in the wake of the tornado."

I move to help him to his feet, but he brushes off my assistance, his strength returning.

Thank goodness…

"What happened?" Luke is asking, squinting into the ten a.m. sunshine. "Did I get the part?"

"You sang up a storm, bro." Ace claps him on the shoulder.

"Yeah, you slayed 'em," Carvery adds, retrieving his cowboy hat from inside the grand piano and putting it back on. "Let's go. Where are we going?"

"The yellow road to the north," Crispin tells us, pointing beyond the stage. "To the hills. We have a hot-air balloon to catch – to the far side of the world."

"Sounds familiar," says Luke, vaguely, evidently still a little worse for wear. "Wasn't there a tune, or something – *Around the World in Eighty Days of Yellow Brick Road?*"

"Closer to eighty minutes, I hope," Crispin tells him. "No, Homer, leave the pom-poms. Keep the shoes, if you must. Will you be joining us, Corporal Punishment?"

The Corporal salutes stiffly.

"There is much work to be done here, Mr, Dry!" he snaps. "Stolen property and Missing Persons to identify! Lots of filing and documenting!"

"In that case, I look forward to your report," Crispin acknowledges, and returns the salute formally.

The Corporal remembers something.

"Take these," he says, and pulls the lower half of the armour and the little leather-bound diary out from under his trousers. "I will inform you the moment I have any further intelligence on the fate of the finest Swiss watchmaker!"

I pocket the tiny book and accept the rest of the armour on Crispin's behalf, tucking the parts under my arm.

"I shall miss you, Corporal Punishment," I say, sadly. "Won't you, Crispin?"

"Corporal Punishment is never far from my thoughts," he admits.

My heart swells hopefully. He really is a family man under that hard, undead exterior.

The Corporal shakes hands with the others.

"Mr. Slaughter," he says politely.

"Abandon Hope All Ye Who Enter Here," Carvery nods.

"Mr. Stig – I mean, Bumgang…"

I rattle a finger in my ear, uncertainly.

"Cuz," Ace winks at him.

"And Da… I mean, Mr. Lukan…"

"Good to meet you too, son," says Luke, gripping the Corporal's hand in both of his own. "You will make a mighty fine librarian one day."

"*President*," Crispin corrects, with a sniff.

Homer, of course, will only settle for a hug. The Corporal graciously accepts, before saluting again sharply – and then scampering away, like an eager meerkat.

The six of us remaining turn to face the hills, and step onto the yellow dirt road.

"What will happen to the Cult of Atum without General Winslow?" I ask. "Will they disband now, and return to their homes?"

"In my experience," Crispin divulges, as we fall into an easy, if brisk pace. "They will have a four-day holiday with much feasting and dancing, and enjoy themselves so much that they decide to celebrate annually in order to remember the day of their freedom – requiring a committee, and a calendar of events and organisation. Leaders will be appointed, and much of the year will be invested in rehearsing – so I think, over all, the answer is no."

CHAPTER SEVENTY-ONE: SCARDUSK

Mist gathers on the yellow dirt road as we ascend to higher ground, and the air noticeably cools, a relief from the relentless sun. I notice Crispin looking up at the scudding wispy clouds, worried.

"There is a short cut to the top," he says. "But it is guarded, as a strategic outpost. With this fog, we could be at risk."

"We could be at risk IN this fog," Luke points out.

Shifting shapes are already forming on the path up ahead, and I hear a faint dragging over the stony ground, akin to the noise of a heavy suitcase hauled by a weary traveller.

"*Ahhh,*" Crispin muses. "These people are usually of the least concern, to most visitors of the Ten a.m. Lounge… but taking recent events into consideration, perhaps avoiding them should be noted as advisory."

"Who are they, Crispin?" I ask, while Homer skips ahead foolishly.

Through the wreaths of mist, dark robes flutter.

"They are the Sisters of Tolerance and Forgiveness, from the nunnery in the mountains," Crispin replies. "By the look of things, the orchestra, taking a morning stroll."

A bass drum with a large hole in it rolls down the path right past us, trailing green smoke. It strikes a rock on the way, and a disembodied gray head bounces out of it, shedding wimple and spectacles.

"I get the feeling Sister Jaundice didn't like orchestra practise much either," Ace remarks.

Green eyes glow dimly through the fog, as the undead Sisters move gradually closer.

"I don't think I've ever been less pleased to see a bunch of virgins," says Carvery. "Present company excepted, Sarah."

"Glad to hear I'm still your *Pubic* Enemy Number One," I mutter.

The ground at their feet seems to bubble in an unearthly fashion, preceeding their approach – but then I hear the croaking, and the tide of panic-stricken frogs bounds ahead, parting like the Red Sea as they pass by our own little group.

"Where is this short-cut again, Crispin?" Luke asks brightly, as the nearest nun lurches in his direction, dragging an acoustic guitar behind her. "Before I'm Tolerated and Forgiven with Extreme Prejudice?"

And then the guitarist nun's head explodes, scattering glittering green slime. A set of false teeth clangs off my breastplate.

"I thought you were saving that last cartridge?" Ace says to Carvery.

"Wasn't me," Carvery shakes his head.

"The Hill-Dwellers," Crispin points up into the trees.

We look. The next movement I see is small and fast – and a feathered spear skewers the next two nuns, like a shish kebab.

"They're children!" I exclaim, spotting several small, round, black-eyed faces in the ferns. Two are blowing raspberries, and one turns around and drops a farting moony.

"Otherwise known as the children's Sunday school choir," Crispin says apologetically, as a volley of water-balloons slows the encroaching nuns down a little.

"Let me guess – they hate music practise too?" says Ace.

"How dangerous are they?" Carvery asks. "On a scale from *Ewok* to *Chucky?*"

"I would say, *Mad Max III: Beyond ThunderGoonies…?*" Crispin hazards, waggling a hand uncertainly.

"Then let's go," Carvery says. "Rather the *ThunderGoonies* than Sisters *Silent Order Hill*."

And we leave the yellow dirt path, scrambling up into the bracken underneath the trees, while the occasional twang of catgut and honk of brass section behind us punctuates the stand-off between orchestra and choir.

The forest is steep, and carpeted with slippery pine-needles. More than once, Homer has to be rescued from holes among the tree-roots, and his blonde cheerleader wig is lost in the brambles.

"Seen a few booby-traps," says Luke, pointing out a net high in the branches as we pass under it. "Resourceful, aren't they?"

"Getting out of Sunday school requires some cunning, Mr. Lukan," Crispin agrees.

Ace and Carvery navigate the uphill rocks and fallen tree-trunks with the same ease that Ace demonstrated on the rooftops of the citadel in the Eight a.m. Lounge, hopping, skipping, jumping and somersaulting from one foothold to the next. I trail behind, lugging the rest of the Swiss watchmaker's armour wrapped in the small and useless rug.

If only it was a *flying* rug – I'd be up this cliff in no time…

"Pity I don't know how you really work," I mutter to the dormant clockwork hand, clipped around my wrist as usual. "I'd make you enchant this rug to fly…"

I blink. One of the gemstones in the clockwork hand *winked* at me. Glittery green, like the magic from Sister Jaundice's cello-bow.

I should have known it would absorb some of that…

"Nah…" I say aloud, warily. "By the look of things, her magic only does frogs' legs and zombie nuns. I don't think I fancy it."

"You are referring to the witchcraft," Crispin says, overhearing me, as he and Luke help Homer over another tree-stump. "You are right to be cautious. Channelled through the clockwork hand, I have no idea how it would be magnified."

I gulp. He's got a point. Everything that the clockwork hand has absorbed so far has been regurgitated at a magnitude many thousand times over.

And if the spell Sister Jaundice was about to cast had been intended to destroy Atum, what that small glittery green glimmer in the works of the clockwork hand could do now is anyone's guess…

"She seemed nice," I say, and he shoots me a quizzical look. "At first, I mean. Not evil at all."

Liar, my conscience pricks me. *You thought she was competing with you for Crispin!*

"Her career ambitions may have been genuine," he says, generously. "Perhaps she had a small problem with constructive criticism."

"Oh." This hadn't occurred to me. "So you don't think it's unusual that a witch would join a nunnery?"

"Not at all, Sarah *Bellummm*," he replies. "Judging by her reaction to the unfortunate General Winslow's remarks, I imagine she joined the Sisterhood to avoid the stress of romantic disappointment in life."

I suddenly feel quite cold all over. Yes… and judging by her reaction to the snake-god Atum, and what I've recently heard that HE represents, I expect she had rather a large bone to pick with romantic disappointment…

More pity the poor nuns, I think. The sound of an explosion behind us, and the whooping of the junior Sunday school choir, makes me think it's probably not a good day to be a nun, all in all.

"But you have nothing to fear there, Sarah *Bellummm*," Crispin continues. "I think that your self-control in her shoes would have been admirable."

What? What does he mean by that?

My reaction to *romantic disappointment* in life?

Or my possession of a deadly spell-casting ability?

"Er…" I say, but I don't know where to begin on that one. "Thanks."

Crispin looks satisfied, anyway – but I… I can't put my finger on it. What is he suggesting?

"Whoa," I hear Ace's voice, ahead of us. "Is this it?"

We hurry to catch up, and emerge on a hilltop clearing. It ends abruptly, with a sheer drop of eroded cliff-face. The end of the winding yellow dirt road can be seen curving up to it, around our short-cut through the wooded hillside.

A gangplank is installed over the precipice.

"Our ride should be here." Crispin produces his little opera-glasses, and scans the horizon. "The wind has been brisk, and they will have been in the slipstream of the tornado…"

"Perhaps they were IN the tornado," Carvery suggests.

Then the view abruptly vanishes, as a colossal shape rises silently out of the gorge before our feet. Ropes restraining a multi-coloured silken aeronautical envelope loom above us, creaking a little.

"My apologies for sneaking up on you, Mr. Dry!" a voice hails from the deck of the wooden barge suspended underneath the balloon. "We had to sail in beneath the mist. Very poor visibility today. You are on foot? Where is the Diablo?"

"I had company instead this morning," Crispin replies. "We have taken a stroll via the scenic route."

"The boys in charge of valet servicing will be disappointed!" The side of the airship lines up with the gangplank, and figures on board secure it with ropes before opening the gate.

"Permission to come aboard?" Crispin asks, formally.

"Permission granted, Mr. Dry."

We file across the plank. I do my best not to look down.

"Captain Dartos," Crispin greets the pilot of the airship. "May I introduce Mr. Bumgang, Mr. Slaughter, Mr. Lukan, and Miss *Bellummm*. Homer, of course, you know…"

The swarthy Captain, in the shiny black cap and navy-blue fisherman's sweater (with leather elbow-patches) gives us a little nod.

"A pleasure to fly you," he says, as the crew untie the ship. "Make yourselves at home. Homer, show Miss Bellum to the Ladies' cabin, so that she may rest and freshen up if need be."

Homer eagerly complies, and I find myself hustled to the far end of the deck and through an oak door, inlaid with Mother-of-Pearl.

On the far side is an elegant suite furnished with *chaises longues* and mirrors, with leaded windows to make the most of the view. I take a last look out at the Ten a.m. Lounge, where the retreating hillside is smoking, punctuated by flashes of burning green glitter as the Sunday school choir continue to negotiate their singing class grades with the charmed zombie nuns.

Homer bounces around the cabin happily, finding a giant powder-puff on the large dressing-table, and coating himself liberally with talc. *Herself*… I'll get it right at some point.

I head for the washroom, and the mirror describes pretty much what I expected. More mud and green slime than Sarah Bellum. I shed the medical scrubs, and prise off the armoured torso underneath before helping myself to the hot water and scented soap.

Homer bursts in wearing a pink frilly housecoat and a new *Cher*-style long red wig, and drops a great heap of things on the floor.

"*Goooood*," he says, before exiting again.

I'm not so sure that 'good' is the word I would have chosen… I pick up the first item, which turns out to be a fuchsia pink patent leather thong with a front zip opening, and gulp.

Why do they keep all this stuff on board? Is it Homer's? Is Crispin into this sort of thing? How will neon-coloured pigskin undergarments increase my chances with men generally? Of course, I don't want to end up like Sister Jaundice – repressed, unfulfilled, frustrated, angry, blaming the gods, and squished under a falling house…

And of course, there's all this armour belonging to the unfortunate Swiss watchmaker to haul around as well… perhaps I could tie it all together with something in that little rug? I sigh, and rummage in the heap of clothing further.

The clockwork hand winks repeatedly at me from my wrist, with its green glittery potential to do harm.

"Homer," I grumble to myself, holding up a *Wonder Woman* outfit. "You have got to be kidding."

I straighten up and shake my head, tossing it back onto the pile.

"You want to do something useful with that magic?" I ask the clockwork hand, as it sparkles away on my arm merrily. "Turn this heap of junk into something suitable to wear…"

There is an obliging puff of green smoke, and I jump, at a bang no louder than a champagne cork.

Hmmm – maybe it didn't absorb as much of that nasty magic spell as I thought?

When the smoke clears, a neatly-folded pile of cream silk and cashmere appears, complete with elegant footwear and understated underthings.

…Wow. And then I catch sight of myself in the mirror, and get a bigger shock.

It's even done my hair and make-up! I look like the actress out of *Some Like It At Tiffany's*, or whatever it's called.

I take it back – that was a LOT of magic…

But that's not all.

Where the segments of Swiss suit of armour and the dismal small rug were lying, there is now only a tapestry clutch-bag, and a gold charm necklace.

I pick it up curiously, and dangle it in the light.

The single charm is, of course, a tiny, one-armed suit of armour.

"At least it's better than frogs and zombie nuns," I concede, immediately transferring the little leather-bound diary into the clutch-bag, and pull on the enchanted attire. "Hmmm. It might *look* like *La Senza*, but it still chafes like pink plastic pig thong…"

Pushing the discomfort to the back of my coccyx as well as my mind, I finish dressing, and clasp the necklace around my neck. Fortunately, the suit of armour as a charm doesn't weigh the same as a suit of armour at full size.

I pick up the clutch, and step out of the bathroom.

"Goodness, Homer," I greet him. "Ready for the prom?"

He gives a coquettish twirl of full-length peacock-blue satin, fanning himself like a débutante.

There is a knock on the door.

"Are you girls decent yet?" Ace Bumgang's voice calls through, and my heart responds like a hamster in an exercise-wheel. "If not, hurry up. Got another *situation* out here."

"Just coming!" I reach for Homer's hand, who totters along behind in sequinned slippers, as we hurry back outside.

Ace is already heading back towards the others, who are looking over the side of the wooden air-ship when we emerge. Leaving Homer straggling, I try to catch up with him.

Only Crispin spares my new turn-out a second glance when I join them.

"Very fetching, Sarah *Bellummm*," he whispers, giving me a dark thrill.

Ace and Carvery are still in their cowboy outfits, and I'm aware of feeling a little resentment that my own sartorial efforts don't have the same effect on them as theirs are having on me.

…Which could be due to the issue of the zombie nuns hanging onto the ballast underneath the air-ship, I note, as I peek over the edge.

"Can't we cut them loose?" Carvery asks.

Through the clouds below, it's clear that we're now over open sea.

"We are already ahead of time, Mr. Slaughter," Captain Dartos tells him. "If we drop the ballast, we will jump forward even further, and lose our place in the schedule completely. The timetable will be totally awry."

One of the glowing-eyed nuns tries to crawl higher. A trombone is bent around her oddly-angled neck, hindering progress slightly.

"Maybe they just want to put on a little concert for us?" Ace suggests. "Spread the word of the Lord."

"Well, I didn't think they wanted to join the Mile High Club," says Carvery sourly.

"You hope," Luke adds. "Might be the best opportunity to get your hands on a set of virginal organs for your girlfriend."

"I don't think she plays the keyboards." Ace shakes his head.

A liver-spotted, wrinkly nun-hand reaches up the side of the ship, grasping the air for another handhold.

"Virgin or not, I think they might be a bit past their *Use By* date," Carvery remarks.

A set of bagpipes drops out of the skirts of the nearest nun as if to illustrate, braying as they fall towards the ocean below.

"*Hooome!*" Homer clutches himself in sympathy.

"Behind you, Sarah *Bellummm!*" Crispin shouts.

I turn, just as a double bass is raised over my head, blotting out the sun, and I open my mouth to scream…

…But it appears that the zealous elderly nun has overestimated her super-human zombie strength, as the weight of the instrument reaches its zenith and continues its momentum, toppling her slowly over backwards with a look of undead surprise. Captain Dartos runs in with an indignant cry, and more helpfully, an axe.

The look of surprise and disappointment on the nun's face is still evident as her head is sent flying over the side, off the steel toecap of his boot.

More disappointment is evident from the groans of her Sisterhood, as they remain clinging to the ballast.

"We cannot introduce this metaphysical type of infection to the Elevensies Lounge," the Captain says, holstering his weapon.

Ace and Carvery haul the rest of the nun's body over the side, managing to knock another doomed groping climber loose in the process, and Luke does the same with the abandoned double bass. "If they cannot be stopped, Mr. Dry…"

"A detour. I understand," says Crispin, grimly.

"What do you mean, a detour?" I ask.

But his expression is cold and distant. A scream from one of the crew alerts us to further hostile presence already aboard our ship.

"Where's that Sunday school choir when you need them?" Luke mutters.

"Oh, that would be chaos, Mr. Lukan," Crispin replies. "They get terribly air-sick, require more clean underwear for a single journey than the luggage allowance permits, and are always asking to stop for chicken dunkers and ice-cream."

"There is only one solution," Captain Dartos continues, while the others seize more axes from the emergency points by the ballast ropes, to arm themselves in turn. "The logical solution!"

"Do what you have to, Captain," Crispin agrees. "We will cover you."

The Captain runs to the helm, leaping up the stairs four at a time.

"What's happening?" I ask as Crispin hands me an axe, which I nearly drop straight through the deck at my feet, scuffing a satin-covered toe. It's far heavier than I expected.

"Change of course, Sarah *Bellummm*," he tells me.

I look up in time to see the Captain already spinning the tiller, and the great air-ship tilts.

The door to the Ladies' cabin at the far end of the deck swings open, and several nuns shuffle out, groaning and trailing musical instruments, entangled with neon Lycra hen-night party-wear…

CHAPTER SEVENTY-TWO: THE TOURNIQUET

"Change of course?" I repeat, while the crew rush in with their axes raised. Bits of violin and spangly nylon underwear fly around wildly. "Can we do that?"

"We can, Sarah *Bellummm*," Crispin says, as a nun's head bounces across the deck between us, a beaded thong caught over one ear. "What do I own in Paris, Captain Dartos?"

"Everything below sea-level, Mr. Dry!" the Captain calls out, from the helm.

A flute whistles by, embedding itself in a life-preserver strung from the wall.

"Perfect," Crispin nods, curtly. "Behind you again, Sarah *Bellummm*."

I turn quickly, and just see the tuba arcing overhead before everything goes dark and echoey.

I can't even lift my arm to swing my own axe.

Great, I think. Sarah Bellum dies, trapped by a bell-end.

I'll never hear the end of it at University…

"Help!" I shout, but only succeed in half-deafening myself inside the brass convolutions. "Let me out!"

A *clanggg* from the outside denotes the expiry of another set of sisterhood false teeth. Eardrums already numb, I let out another scream as I'm lifted bodily from the deck, inside the giant tuba.

I manage a glimpse down past my feet as I feel the instrument swaying, only to see the upturned gray faces of clambering zombie nuns with glowing green eyes, scudding clouds, and beyond, the ripples of distant blue sea…

"Help!" I scream again, picturing a subsequent plummeting to a watery grave. "Pull me back in!"

The tuba lurches, and I fill my lungs, trying to increase my body area in contact with the surface…

And then it is shaken abruptly, and I shoot out backwards with another yell.

"Sorry," says Ace, as I tumble heels over head, back onto the deck. "Thought you were a nun."

"In all senses but the religious," Carvery says, elbow-deep in another zombie. "...She is."

"Any luck with those organs?" Luke asks, holding a clarinetist at bay with the loops of his axe.

"Not a sausage," Carvery sighs, shaking the drips off. "Whatever spell Sister Jaundice used on her Superiors, it only did a Green Slime Reduction on their old carcasses. Crispin, wherever we're going, I hope you have a REALLY big hole in the ground ready and waiting."

"I am indeed ahead of you there, Mr. Slaughter," Crispin replies.

The air-balloon progresses at speed, whipping tears from my eyes, while the crew adds to the pile of musically-inclined gnostic zombie corpses amidship. But undead members of the elderly orchestra keep coming, scrambling over the sides.

I shouldn't have wasted the magic in the clockwork hand on changing this stupid dress.

I try to wipe green smears off the silk, and struggle back onto my feet. I could be standing here in a cheap cosplay *Wonder Woman* outfit, an itchy pink patent thong, half a suit of Swiss watchmaker's armour, and be turning all of these zombie nuns into...

I glare at the clockwork hand, hanging onto my wrist.

"Not even one speck of magic left?" I demand of its dull and inert gemstones. Nothing. It might as well be a bangle. "Nothing of any use at all? Wow, sometimes, you really..."

A shadow falls across me, and I look up into the glowing green eyes of what I can only assume was the Mother of all nuns. Mottled, wrinkly and warty, and raising her conductor's baton. She opens her mouth, like Donald Sutherland in the final scene of *Invasion of the Body-Snatchers...*

Ribbet, she says.

"...Suck!" I continue angrily.

The baton strikes, gashing my forearm – as the gemstones in the clockwork hand open, and the green glow pours into it from all sides…

With a banshee-like scream, the enchanted undead life-force drains from every remaining nun, shaking and vibrating them right off their feet. Black robes smoking, they shrink and shrivel alarmingly.

The gemstones close with a *whoosh*, now illuminated like evil radium.

Suddenly, the deck is hopping mad.

"Well done, Sarah *Bellummm*," Crispin approves, lowering his axe and moving quickly to attend my bleeding arm, thoughtfully tying a monogrammed, embroidered handkerchief around the wound. "Frogs go down a treat in Paris. Easier to explain than nuns turning up in the sewers, too."

The crew exchange their axes for buckets, and are soon scooping up frogs left and right.

"The nuns *were* frogs!" I gasp. I look down to check my clothes. Phew – still silk and cashmere… perhaps the clockwork hand can only do one thing at a time… "I mean – before they were nuns! I didn't cast a spell! It sucked the magic out of them!"

"Ah." Crispin picks one up and dangles it thoughtfully, while it blinks a benign yellow-and-black eye. "Then let us consider ourselves fortunate that you have already dealt with Sister Jaundice, the witch. I will make a note to have the nunnery in the mountains investigated, to see what else may have occurred there."

"No wonder the organs weren't right." Carvery wipes his hands on his cowboy denims. "Nothing but out-of-date frogspawn."

"No wonder they never stood a chance against the Sunday school choir," Ace grunts.

"Be careful with that power, Sarah," Luke whispers to me, as I try to cover the glow around my wrist with my sleeve. "You don't know what the witch was practising. Turning a man into a zombie is one thing. All that takes is low wages and a bad marriage. Just ask my wife! Turning other living creatures into zombie folk? That's amassing a cheap Army."

I glance at the zombie entrepreneur Crispin Dry, as he drops the frog into a passing bucket and wipes his gray fingers on another monogrammed handkerchief, embroidered with a cockerel.

"Yes," I agree. "We wouldn't want that sort of thing to catch on…"

"Approaching the *Seine*, Mr. Dry!" Captain Dartos reports.

Ooh – I hurry to look over the side. White clouds part, and a river sparkles as it divides the Most Romantic City on Earth…

"Well done, Captain," Crispin announces. "Prepare to offload cargo of nuns… sorry, frogs…"

"Can we stop here?" I ask. "I know it's not the Elevensies Lounge, but – I've never been to Paris…"

"That's because if you set foot here, the city's reputation for love and romance would drop too far below average for the tourist industry to survive," Carvery tells me, resting his elbows on the railing to my left.

"Oh, I don't know," Ace muses, appearing at my right. "It'd be like allowing the World's Biggest Loser into a casino. Suddenly everyone else feels marginally luckier, regardless of how they're actually getting on…"

All I know is I'm currently flying over Paris, with two fit guys dressed as cowboys standing either side of me. Meaning regardless of what they're actually saying, all I'm hearing is *Non, je ne regrette rien...*

"No – I quite agree," Crispin's voice joins us. "It may not be the Elevensies Lounge, but there are parts of the city I will be happy to show you, Sarah *Bellummm*. A small diversion. We will be taking one of the lifeboats, Captain Dartos! And after you have dropped us off – perhaps check the nunnery, in the mountains…?"

"Right you are, Mr. Dry, sir!"

I try to gird my excitement as we climb into the smaller boat suspended from the side of the air-ship, only slightly dampened by the buckets full of anxious frogs surrounding us.

On the Captain's orders, the ropes start to lower us steadily towards the surface of the river.

Oh my God – I'm in Paris!

And not to deliver a pizza!

"Is it true that you shouldn't drink the water here?" Ace asks.

"How much water do you usually take in your alcohol?" says Carvery.

...I'm in Paris! With Ace Bumgang! My innards are knotting like voluntary sausage-skins. Not to mention the undead heart-throb Crispin Dry... and even more darkly and reluctantly, Carvery Slaughter... *stupid traitorous hormones*... if I had to pick one man, for my currently-overloaded fantasy, it should really be the one I'd survive longest in the company of...

"*Goood*," Homer approves, opening a lace parasol against the balmy sunshine.

Luke and Crispin free us from the ropes, and Ace starts the small outboard motor.

"Where are we dumping the Sisterhood of Tolerance and Frogs' Legs, Crispin?" asks Carvery, nudging one of the croaking buckets. "Right here?"

"Not yet, Mr. Slaughter," Crispin replies. "You will see a large overflow ahead at the second bridge, Mr. Bumgang. Take us to it, if you please. We will release them there."

I soak up the view across the rippling water. Other boats chug along, some carrying tourists – *real* people! Not Lounge-dwellers... we pass under the first bridge, where on one bank, a great iconic structure looms.

"The Eiffel Tower..." I breathe.

"Yup," Carvery affords it a glance, and sighs. "Reminds me of Las Vegas..."

"Er, Crispin," Luke interrupts any mood of romantic reverie. "Some weird-looking guys over there seem to be taking an interest in us..."

We turn to look at the other small boat in our wake. Four occupants pretend not to notice, swathed in scarves under their trilby hats and dark suits with gloves, no doubt to protect their sensitive green and purple-marred skin from the daylight...

"I've seen someone like that before..." I recall aloud. My adrenaline surges, much to the annoyance of my kidneys. That head, as it rolled across the floor of *Casabladder*... "Yes! In the Eight a.m. Lounge, Crispin! Looking for *you*...!"

"Try not to make it look as if we are spooked, Mr. Bumgang," Crispin suggests. "But perhaps a little faster..."

Our boat burrows into the water and glides ahead smoothly. The shadowy pursuers accelerate in turn, to follow.

"Who are they?" Luke asks.

"Caterers, Mr. Lukan," says Crispin. "I am afraid they take issue with the existence of vending machines in the workplace."

I knew it! I knew he couldn't be in debt – it was just a jealous food-industry rival!

"Oh, they reckon you're stealing their business," Carvery remarks, thinking alike. "I get that from turfers, lawnmowers and landscape gardeners all the time."

"And divorce lawyers and undertakers?" I query.

"The overflow," Crispin repeats, as we approach the second bridge. "Take the exit straight into the tunnel."

"Into the sewer?" Luke exclaims.

"What?" Ace scoffs at him. "You never rode the poo flume before?"

We turn sharply, and the daylight is replaced by darkness and dankness. Homer closes his parasol and produces a fan instead, fluttering it delicately under his nose.

"Are they following?" I ask.

Ace looks over his shoulder.

"They've slowed down a bit," he reports. "But yes."

"Keep going," Crispin orders. "There is a corner ahead – once past it, we can release the frogs. It may hinder them a little further."

Ace pulls on the rudder, and as we complete the turn, the rest of us each grab a bucket of Paris-ready *Jambes de Grenouille*.

My sleeve hikes up, and the green gemstone glow from the clockwork hand illuminates the dark tunnel eerily.

"Good luck, Sisters," says Carvery, tipping his bucket-load over the side. "You'll need it."

"*Bon appetit,*" Luke adds.

The fetid water burbles and plops, as I add my contribution to the endangered French batrachian population.

"*Hoooome*," says Homer sadly, releasing his own.

"Straight ahead, Mr. Bumgang," says Crispin, once the last frog is liberated onto the subterranean streets. "Let us hope that the harvesting of delicacies is enough to distract vengeful caterers…"

I look down at the clockwork hand.

I suppose, if not – those delicacies could soon be turned back into rabid zombie nuns…

…But remembering Luke's words, I pull my sleeve back down again firmly.

Besides – it's *Paris.*

I still might get a *proper* date here, one day. And I know what I'd rather see on the menu, next time I visit…

CHAPTER SEVENTY-THREE: CHYLE & THE CHOCOLATE FASCIA

Behind us, the caterers' boat slows even further as it happens upon the unexpected tide of frogs. We wait, the tension unbearable, to see the fate of the re-introduced creatures.

And then there is a loud, resentful *Ribbet.*

The rest of the batrachian Sisterhood take up the call, and the uncertainty of the advancing caterers becomes clear. A first brave frog hops onto their bows, and a gloved hand reaches out to knock her aside.

"Should we do something?" Ace asks.

A long adhesive tongue lashes out and attaches to the caterer's wrist.

Which detaches with a pop of carpal bone, followed by an unearthly scream…

"Yes," Crispin replies. "Full speed ahead, Mr. Bumgang! Try to avoid the stalagmites of frozen poop!"

Ace opens up the throttle of the outboard motor and we beat a hasty retreat along the tunnels, to the backing music of empowered frog song, and dismembered catering competition.

"I hope that is the last we see of them," I breathe at last.

"The frogs, or the caterers?" Luke asks.

"Both," I answer.

The words of the caterer I had encountered in the Eight a.m. Lounge are branded into my brain…

'You are a secretary for Crispin Dry at Dry Goods, Inc, and a traitor… More fast-food delivery boys and girls have disappeared before you than you can possibly imagine…'

"Why are they so hostile towards you, Crispin?" I ask. "I thought business competition was healthy for the economy?"

"That is what is generally taught, indeed," he replies.

"By your father?"

"*Ahhh*," he muses. "My father – had some very strange notions of everyday business. The munitions business was his forte, which meant fuelling and arming the most inflammable of business competition. Sadly he did not share the concept of 'healthy competition' – like our unfortunate rickshaw pilot Mr. Time, he felt there was no profit in co-operative peace treaties… so I was forced to find my own way in such troubled waters. Only to find myself accused of monopoly."

"Surely not?" I remark, shocked.

"Vending machines of high quality are in demand by the consumers, but they annihilate employment in the food industry," Crispin sighs. "That is why I always have to be on the look-out for saboteurs, and vandalism – those cut-price pirates who supply sub-standard stock to the users, accessing my machines without permission…"

"The food poisoning at Cramps University?" I conclude, horrified. "Sabotage by catering staff?"

He nods, in his endearing lopsided fashion.

"*Yesss*, Sarah *Bellummm*." He spares me a sad, wonky smile. "I knew you were an intelligent woman."

But what has this got to do with a pizza delivery girl? *What was the caterer trying to tell me?* My paranoid subconscious rants, but I cannot put it into words.

Probably just further propaganda by an embittered competitor, I tell myself…

Crispin claps his hands twice, and pink lighting illuminates the sour-smelling tunnels, as we speed ahead.

"I think we may have taken a wrong turning," he ponders. Adjoining exits whisk past, as myriad as a honeycomb in either wall. "We have gone back on ourselves."

"How far back?" Carvery asks. "We're still heading downriver from what I can tell."

"Several hours, Mr. Slaughter," says Crispin. "It is a junction, as we encountered earlier beneath the Eight a.m. Lounge…"

"So we could end up in any of the Lounges?" Ace asks. "Wouldn't be too bad – I think I left my keys in *Madam Dingdong's Sauna and Spa* at the Six a.m. Lounge."

"I'm not sure I fancy the Seven a.m. Lounge again," says Carvery. "Bunch of flower-selling crazies."

"I was looking forward to the Elevensies Lounge," says Luke. "A nice cup of tea would be just the thing right now."

Having already seen what the Elevensies Lounge considers to be a cultural weapon, I'm not convinced of that myself…

"There is no knowing. Hang on," Crispin warns. "We are about to hit the Flume…"

"*Goood,*" says Homer, bouncing up and down excitedly in his seat.

I grip the side of the lifeboat, just in time, as we hit the brink of a fall, and plummet…

The lifeboat spins, out of control, hurling us deeper into the Earth, and the strobing pink darkness.

I can still make out the various exits as they flash past, some of which are even signposted:

Cold War.

French Revolution.

War of Independence.

McDonalds v. Wimpy...

"Oh, Crispin," I murmur, reaching out to squeeze his hand.

"*Yesss,*" he agrees, distantly. "My father kept his business channels open…"

"What the Hell is that noise?" Carvery asks.

I strain my ears. Over the rushing of the water, an electronic tinkling can be made out, a tootling and parping, oddly familiar and yet out-of-place.

"My apologies," Crispin coughs, clearing his throat. "One of my father's major sponsors was *The Library of Elevator Muzak.*"

"Psychological warfare?" Ace scowls. "That's below the belt."

"Does anyone even know what a *Samba* is?" Carvery scoffs.

"The lion king?" Luke squeaks in terror, trying to hide behind Homer's prom skirts. "Where?"

We experience the G-forces as we hit bottom and level out, still rocketing forwards. My stomach is informing me that travel-sickness is imminent, and I wish I had a boiled sweet handy.

Maybe one of those pink ones…

"Here, Sarah *Bellummm,*" says Crispin, appearing to sense my discomfort, and he hands me a chocolate-coated cinder toffee bar from inside his jacket. "One of my vending machine empire's most popular snacks."

"Thank you." I tear the wrapper eagerly and bite into the crisp sugary centre, salivating with relief. Mmmm – so crunchy and delicious…

"As I recall, you liked your nibbles crunchy," he hints in a low voice.

Ohhh, my…

"Is it far now?" Carvery asks.

"If it's a pee break you want, we're sliding down the biggest toilet in the world," Ace tells him. "Go over the side – I just did."

We're not showing any sign of slowing down.

War of the Roses.

Falklands Conflict.

Safeways v. Morrisons…

"Look for an exit marked in red, Mr. Bumgang!" Crispin shouts.

"We just passed *Woolworth's…*" Ace reports. "I see it – *Strategic Occupation of Atlantis?*"

"That is the one, Mr. Bumgang!"

And the lifeboat lurches again, meaning I nearly see the snack bar twice…

CHAPTER SEVENTY-FOUR: TOMB BATHER ~ CRADLE OF AFTERLIFE

The pink glow becomes red as we take the exit almost on our side, and we remain at an acute angle as the chute becomes a twisting, accelerating Helter-Skelter downwards, pressing us back into our seats on board the boat.

Just when it seems like the hull is about to disintegrate, screaming in protest, we fly out of the far end, and plop neatly into a still, subterranean pool. The jolt almost knocks us overboard.

The high roof of the cave glimmers with surface reflections from the cool – and thankfully clear – water.

"Are we in another Lounge?" Carvery asks, leaning over the side to squint down into the depths. "Looks like it's seen better days…"

I follow his glance. Far below us, I can see walls and pillars, even broken statues and stone stairways, relegated to an underwater tomb. Small shoals of pale pretty fish dart between the wreckage.

"My father did not frequent the Lounges," Crispin replies, his zombie monotone echoing hollowly around the cave walls. "He was not a man of leisure, and only visited what he knew as the *Boardrooms*. Where munitions business was conducted."

"Doesn't seem to have helped these guys," Ace remarks.

"Rumour has it that the Atlanteans declared war on Atum," Crispin shrugs. "It was foolhardy of them, to say the least. I know my father spent many years trying to analyse their plans, trying to distil what they imagined would work – but of course they never stood a chance. One tiny earthquake, and they vanished without trace."

"Why would they declare war on a god?" I ask, curious.

"Atum represents unfinished business in the creation of the world," Crispin reminds me. "An advanced culture that wants to stay ahead of the game does not want to see progress elsewhere."

"Like running a monopoly," says Luke, darkly.

"Quite, Mr. Lukan." If Crispin has taken offence at the remark, he doesn't show it.

It's rather melancholy, looking down into the ruins of the ancient city. I wonder if there were any undead survivors, and how they would exist for all these centuries…

A flash of silver tail and snake tattoo behind a pillar causes me to choke on my own tongue.

"I saw something!" Ace announces, before I can speak. "Like a shark!"

Did I imagine it?

"There should not be any danger, Mr. Bumgang," says Crispin. "But we will have to swim our way out…"

"Not more Hermit Squidmorph eggs?" I say, warily.

"No, they are not indigenous to this region," Crispin reassures me. "The fully mature adults are too big to nest here. They need direct access to the Deep Ocean Trench."

"*Gooood,*" Homer approves, obviously as relieved as I am.

"The best way out is from the feeding sites of the Great Flatulent Clams," Crispin continues. "They come to filter microbes from the underwater lichens, which is why the water here is so clear. But they return to the shallow seas to convert the dormant chlorophyll to sugars in the sunlight. If we catch them at the right time, we should each be able to hitch a ride out of here."

"Can I be the one to say…" Carvery begins. "…*Flatulent?*"

"They continuously emit bubbles of oxygen, Mr. Slaughter," says Crispin. "Which is how I imagine you will all breathe underwater, without scuba apparatus."

We exchange looks.

"Follow me," he says, and steps ashore, onto a rocky outcrop.

Nervously, I follow.

There might be no sharks down there… but there *might* be a harpoon gun-toting fishtailed man-babe, whose motives are not as clear as the water is…

"Hey," Luke says, as we pick our way over the rocks, around the perimeter of the cave. "Do you think there is any Atlantean treasure lying around? Anything of archaeological value?"

"If there was, I'm betting that the Dry family beat you to it," Carvery replies. "You're more likely to find it buried back in that dusty old mansion of Crispin's, than anywhere here."

It does look as though what remains of the great city is now just bare stone foundations, and the occasional ruined statue. Not so much as a broken urn or piece of crockery is visible.

I don't know what Luke was expecting to discover… brass-bound chests? Giant pearls? The kind of thing you see in a dental surgery waiting-room fish-tank… well, the diving-suit would be useful, come to think of it.

"We will have to climb the wall here to the next part of the caves," says Crispin, pointing up towards a narrow gap near the roof, where a rock-fall has divided the underground air-space. "Homer – jump onto my back, and hold on tight."

"*Hooome*."

"Yes, Homer – eventually…"

The rock wall gives Ace and Carvery no issue at all, and even with Homer piggybacking along in his peacock-blue prom dress, Crispin navigates the handholds deftly. Luke grumbles about the prospect of arthritis.

"I'm not as young as I look, you know," he says, as his slipping foot finds my ear for the second time.

"*Working legally since 1971?*" I remark, recalling the chase across the rooftops of the Eight a.m. Lounge. "From that, I'm guessing you can bend the truth in more ways than one."

Somehow I keep up, my fingers blistered and bleeding, and crawl after the others through the vertiginous gap, to the far side.

"Down there," Crispin points, to where a slight bubbling is visible on the surface of the water. "We are in luck, Sarah *Bellummm* – the clams are grazing."

We scramble back down the rock-fall to the water's edge. I find myself scanning the depths, looking for any sign of tattooed, silver-tailed merman – imaginary or otherwise…

"They are quite safe to approach," Crispin is saying. "The oxygen is emitted from a clear respiratory tube near the hinge of the shell. You should be able to grip either side. When they decide to move, allow them to lead. They always take the shortest route to the open sea outside."

As if to demonstrate, Homer wades happily into the shallows, fully-dressed, and disappears beneath the surface.

Okay – at least it doesn't look as though clothing will be a hindrance this time. I glance regretfully at Ace and Carvery, who have only rolled up their Stetson hats and shoved them into their boots.

Then I swallow the ball of nerves and bile threatening to rise up the back of my throat, and follow Homer into the water.

The weight of my clothes soaking through drags me down easily, and I blink, into depths which are remarkably clear. I can see Homer hugging a great frilled bivalve, and I paddle my way forward to the next, following the trail of bubbles.

The respiratory tube looks remarkably like a snorkel mask, pointing slightly upward of a shell about three feet wide. I find handholds in its ridges, and tentatively move my face near to the tube's outlet.

I get a shock, as it strikes out, clamping to my face. Suddenly I'm breathing pure air, deep underwater.

Maybe they need the carbon dioxide to activate the chlorophyll in their diet? It's most bizarre. I feel as though I've been attached to an artificial lung…

One by one, I see the others joining us, and just after Crispin enters the water, I feel my ride twitching, and pushing off from the bottom.

Here we go, I think. Should I close my eyes? Kick my legs? No – let them lead, Crispin said…

Homer overtakes me, his fatter mollusc pumping out a jet of water to propel itself through the caves, and we leave the rocky ledge and head deeper.

I can feel my panic rising up again. This can't be right – not deeper underwater, surely?

What if it's a trick? What if they're dragging us back to a nest of hatching Squidmorphs?

Out of the corner of my eye, I swear I see the flash of silver tail again…

We enter a tunnel of pitch darkness, and my fear is now on full *Red Alert*. I'm already imagining tentacles emerging from every crevice. I shake my sleeve upward a little, so that the glow from the clockwork hand around my wrist gives out some reassuring light to see by.

Even worse, my Flatulent Clam seems to be flagging…

Breathe, I will it along. But it starts to slow to a drift, and worse – the air-flow drops.

Damn! Just my luck to pick one that's on a diet!

And then I feel it hiccup – with a definite waft of Sloe Gin Sling.

Oh God – I'm the first human to get a Great Flatulent Clam drunk, on my own breathalyser-breath!

I can see daylight at the far end of the tunnel, and both Ace and Homer now way ahead of me. Luke shoots by, a trail of seaweed flying from the side of his buff clam, as it jets past smoothly.

I kick my legs desperately, but then even the adhesion of the respiratory tube fails, and my ride is suddenly a dead weight.

Holding my breath, I have to let it go, and try to swim forward on my own.

Without the clam's propulsion, it suddenly seems like a very long way indeed. And the enchanted clothes I'm wearing feel like ballast, dragging me down and holding me back. I close my eyes in defeat.

I'll never make…

…An arm locks around me abruptly, knocking the last of the air out of my lungs, and I shoot forward once more.

How?? Not – the merman…?

I feel a respiratory tube pushed in front of my face, and take a blessed gulp of air before it moves away. My hand is guided to grasp the back of another clamshell. Has the mysterious merman brought reinforcements…? But as I turn to look at my rescuer, the shock is even greater than that.

Carvery Slaughter??!

I almost cry out all of my precious breath again, and looking irritated, he gives me another slug of oxygen from the respiratory tube. I take one, and push it away quickly, knowing the fate of my last steed to be my fault.

I'm *never* drinking again…

Fortunately, Carvery's bivalve is a speedy one, and we quickly exit the tunnel.

A few exchanges of air-supply later, we break the surface of the sea, as the clam arrives at its basking-beds, in the shallows of an idyllic shoreline.

I can't even look at it, backing away from Carvery in the waist-deep water, in shock.

"The word you're searching for is *'Thanks'*," he prompts me, pulling his cowboy hat from his boot and straightening it out, shaking the drips off before putting it back on.

"What?" I gasp. "You can't stand me. Why did you save me – again?"

"Do you want the honest answer?" he says. "For later. The only set of spare female donor organs we seem to be able to hang onto around here is inside you. Keeping you alive is the best way of keeping them fresh."

I take it back. I'm going to drink and drink until my organs are pickled…

"Good, we all made it," Crispin's voice interrupts our awkward stand-off, before I can threaten to tear up my donor card. "We should head inland, where we will be less exposed."

"Exposed to what?" Luke asks. "Where are we?"

Up on the rust-coloured sandy beach already, Ace Bumgang points.

"Look," he says. "The Five a.m. Lounge."

We all look. On the horizon, the unmistakeable outline of the pyramids is jutting heavenward, like an omen of our future.

"The time-line has been corrupted," Crispin says. "Potentially, we could encounter anything…"

CHAPTER SEVENTY-FIVE: COWBOYS AND ILEUMS

Not wanting to encounter Hermit Squidmorphs again being the first on my personal list, I hurry out of the bivalve basking-beds in the surf. I don't stop hurrying until I'm a considerable distance from the shoreline.

"That's where we should be heading anyway," says Carvery resignedly, wading out after me. "Got to pick up a Pumpkin, before she turns back into fertiliser."

"But we don't have any spare parts," Ace replies, shaking water out of his own Stetson, and putting it back on.

"I can see two sets, from where I'm standing," Carvery remarks, looking from me to Homer and back again. "I'm sure between them, they could manage on fifty percent each. Sarah's never going to use half of hers anyway, and Homer only wants to look good in a thong."

"You are thinking very practically, Mr. Slaughter," Crispin concedes, to my annoyance. "But it may not be necessary. Our mother keeps many spare parts preserved in ceramic jars aboard her Great Barge, as is traditional. If Sarah *Bellummm* can summon the powers now within the clockwork hand, which appears to be favouring her, I'm sure those organs could be restored to full working order."

Gosh – I don't know if I'm capable of that. The clockwork hand still seems to be very much under its own command. But the idea is preferable to donating my own…

"Good idea," says Carvery, apparently thinking likewise. "Wouldn't want Sarah thinking her innards were about to see any action. Whether she's attached to them at the time or not."

It hadn't crossed my mind, but I blush anyway. *Damn.* I wonder if it's too late to volunteer?

"Do you hear that?" Luke cuts in, interrupting my thoughts of loss of virginity by proxy. "Something's coming."

We strain our ears. I'm sure I pick up on a distant roaring noise.

"Sounds like the Nine a.m. fighter jets," says Ace.

"We should make a move," says Crispin. "We would not want to be sitting targets, for whatever approaches."

The thought is mutual. We head further up the beach into the shade of the date palm trees, only slightly startling some donkeys, who are cooling themselves out of the sun.

"*Hooome*," says Homer, pointing at them.

One reaches out obligingly, to sample the tip of his finger.

"This might be a good time to practise your sidesaddle indeed, Homer!" Crispin agrees, as the donkey masticates the fingertip lethargically. Embarrassingly, my stomach growls in empathy. "It is no harder than riding a camel. Everyone, find a mount."

I find a docile-looking albino donkey that regards me guilelessly from under its white lashes, and after falling off the far side only three times, I manage to scramble aboard, and stay upright.

Crispin is the last to clamber astride, and the patchwork herd as a whole, even those without riders, sets off in the direction of the pyramids. Their conical, hairy ears have a life of their own, waggling and signalling and rotating independently, like little radars.

I'm missing Paris already, and its soothingly clement weather. Another dose of desert heat is not what I needed today, even though my wet (and still enchanted) clothes are already drying to a crisp against my sore skin.

"They're circling way out over the sea," Luke reports, looking behind us, as we proceed at a lumpy jog across the equally patchy desert. "What are they doing so far offshore?"

"Maybe they've spotted a flying rickshaw," Carvery suggests.

There is the barest hint of a shadow passing over the sun, and the fat gray donkey plodding along to my right is suddenly gone. I can hear the echoes of its braying on the breeze.

"What was that?!" I shriek, staring back at the spot where its hoof-prints in the sand abruptly end.

The second time I feel the rush of air, and hear a *clack-clack-clacking* sound, before another donkey vanishes skywards.

"You know what you said about sitting targets, Crispin?" Ace begins, as the donkeys, panicking, start to run.

And this time I see the shadow clearly, spreadeagled on the sand as it approaches, and hunch myself low over my brave little donkey's neck, as she accelerates to a full bolt.

"Do not worry, Sarah *Bellummm!*" I hear Crispin calling out to me, my ears full of donkey-mane. "There is no methane here! The Pterodactyls will be unable to ignite a flame!"

"You're not riding behind Homer!" Luke shouts back at him. "There's enough gas emanating from his mule to light up Miami!"

As if on cue, Homer squeals as his mount leaves the ground, tail-end first. He topples forwards over its ears, with a rip of peacock-blue satin – landing rather neatly across Luke's lap on the donkey behind.

"Geddoff!" yells Luke. "My feet are almost dragging along the ground already…"

Ace draws up alongside and grabs Homer by the bustle, hoisting him off Luke's overloaded and short-legged ride, and tossing him unceremoniously onto the next available mount.

Again – I can't control that feeling of envy at being manhandled by Ace Bumgang. Why is it, whenever I need rescuing, I get the psychopath with the donor-organ-harvesting fixation?

Well, at least he's efficient, I think – as Carvery catches up and sideswipes my donkey hard, so that the nose-diving Pterodactyl I hadn't seen coming misses, and ploughs into the dust with an almighty crash, right where I would have been.

Maybe he's got a killer's ego. Nothing is allowed to do it better than him…? I should have paid more attention to research during the Criminology module of Forensic Anthropology, instead of playing *Draw My Thing* online…

The stampeding donkeys trample the fallen Pterodactyl thoroughly as we make our escape. The roar of a Nine a.m. Lounge jet hits us instead as it cuts across our path, banking sharply, and another Pterodactyl is gunned down out of the sky.

"Is this what they mean when they say 'Everything happened at once'?" Luke calls out.

"Quite literally, Mr Lukan!" Crispin replies. "All at the same time!"

"Everything is *not* happening at once!" I shout back irritably, spitting out bits of flying mane as I cling to my donkey's neck. "I am still a virgin, you know!"

"Glad to hear it, Sarah *Bellummm!*" says Crispin.

Oh, yes. I'd forgotten about *his* ulterior motives…

"We should dismount," he announces. "Before the fighters begin carpet-bombing."

"But," I puff, trying to slow my juddering and panting donkey down. "We don't even have a carpet with us at the moment…"

The jet banks again over the beach behind, looping around for another pass.

"That's not what it means, Dumb-Ass," Carvery warns, jumping from the back of his steed without stopping. "And it doesn't mean they're about to deliver one, either."

"Better pray they don't have napalm yet." Ace follows suit.

From the belly of the approaching aircraft, a thin blazing line drops silently to Earth.

"Too late," says Luke.

Hypnotised, I watch as the glowing ribbon falls – and where it strikes, the dust explodes, in incendiary plumes of yellow and gold burning death…

The trampled Pterodactyl erupts, its carcass rising up briefly like a phoenix, before it disintegrates and disperses throughout the fireball as black ash.

I'm dimly aware of Crispin's hand reaching out to seize my ride's mane as he gallops past, yanking us out of the flight-path, and over the edge of a large gully into an incredibly muddy river…

Above us, the trail of meltdown destruction continues until the jet peels off and doubles back, leaving a vapour-trail across an azure sky already filling with black smoke.

"That was close, Sarah *Bellummm*," Crispin's voice says.

I realise my teeth are chattering, and I'm not the only one. My albino donkey, still clamped between my terrified legs, is now a grayer shade of mud and trembling with shock.

"You know what this means, don't you?" says Ace.

"What?" asks Carvery.

"Everyone in the Six a.m. Lounge is now off their tits on Guinness ambulance fuel." Ace waggles his hand, as if holding a pint glass. "Drunk rickshaw pilots galore, and goat curry on the menu."

"Justin Time must have leaked," Carvery muses. "I would, if I was married to that trigger-happy ho. Everywhere."

Homer is looking down at his ruined prom dress and crying like it's the end of the world. Luke is undoing his bow-tie and cuffs, evidently feeling that the time to be in formal attire is well and truly over.

I remember what Crispin's cousin Sandy said to me, about the Nine a.m. Lounge…

'They look forward to the day they believe that the taxmen and regulators will flatten our haven of peaceful business…'

What if they can't wait any more and have decided to hurry things up, now that they have the fuel as well as the the firepower?

I look down at the glowing clockwork hand, clamped around my wrist. Full of rabid zombie nun spell.

Probably not much use against napalm.

"Crispin," I say, seriously. "I don't think this is just fun and games anymore."

He looks solemn.

"I believe you are right, Sarah *Bellummm*," he says, heaving a sigh. "There has not been a full-scale conflict between the Lounges in my lifetime. But the signs are hard to ignore."

"You think?" I reply, trying to rein in my distress. "The occupants of a gun-toting war-zone get the recipe for unlimited fuel and napalm, and you're considering that they might just sit happily in their jungle with ambulances that work and functional oil-lamps that don't smell of Guinness?"

"Not to mention that you've now got a megalomaniac undead elderly relative with a fort full of piss-drunk military on his hands," Ace chips in. "They could declare war on just about anywhere – and not even remember doing it by tomorrow morning."

Crispin stands up, and his darkened face is unreadable against the sun and the backdrop of burning napalm.

"This is why not all business competition is healthy!" he roars, and my donkey jumps, its nerves in almost as bad a state as my underwear. "Without regulating, people just run about doing as they please, manufacturing anything they like! Recreational alcohol that contains no recreation! Junk food items that are all junk! I will not have it!"

And he stamps off upriver, like a toddler who has had his last balloon burst on his birthday.

"Monopoly," Luke repeats under his breath.

"Maybe you shouldn't have said that about his Grandpappy, Ace," Carvery remarks.

"What?" Ace turns his palms skywards. "He *is* old, *and* undead."

"*Hooome*," says Homer, pointing after his brother sadly.

Crispin is already a grumpy black silhouette, against the distant pyramids.

"Yes, let's go," I agree, and move to help the bedraggled Homer to his feet. "We'll go and find some of your mother's nice clothes for you to change into."

Homer has to be helped onto the back of my surviving donkey, too distressed to walk, and I coax it along the river bank gently, while he whimpers, with not one mention of anything being *Goood*.

Ace, Carvery and Luke trail behind.

"I'm getting a really weird sense of *déjà-vu*," says Luke, thoughtfully. "Aren't you?"

"Nah," Ace grunts. "You mistake me for a wise man, Luke."

"The only *déjà-vu* I'm getting is one about a big alien sucker tentacle," says Carvery, and I glance back to see him taking out his Taser and squinting at it. "I think this might be out of charge…"

"Still got one cartridge, though," Ace points out, indicating the shotgun strapped to Carvery's back.

"Yeah, saving that, though," Carvery reminds him, loud enough to remind me at the same time. "In case those donor organs up ahead try to run away."

I scowl at him. Before I can turn around again, behind them I spot the distant dot of a jet fighter as it drops from its stacking loop in the skies above the sea, and dips for another approach up our muddy gully…

"Like now?" I reply, as the advancing engine roar meets our ears.

The others turn to look, and swear.

"Fuck," says Carvery. "Everybody down!"

Homer gives an indignant squeal, as I push him off the donkey back into the water.

Still on my feet, I wrench angrily at the stubborn clockwork hand, but it won't budge from my arm.

"Do something!" I shout at it. "Anything!"

"Get down, Fuckwit!" Carvery is shouting at me in turn.

This time, there is no line of liquid fire as the aircraft bears down upon us. Worried, I turn and look to where Crispin is trudging onwards, up ahead.

Maybe *he's* the target…

"Crispin!" I yell in warning.

But he ignores me – or can't hear me…

The stupid clockwork hand just glows in a radioactive fashion, but does nothing.

"Even if you can only do zombie nuns!" I beg of it. "Do something! Blow something up! Change something! Stop acting like costume jewellery!"

A metallic twang slices through the air, and there is a scream behind me.

I look upwards just in time to see the jet soaring away, carrying off our taxi-driver Luke – on the end of a long, barbed steel cable.

CHAPTER SEVENTY-SIX: FRANKENMINKY

"Luke!" I scream, but the jet vanishes all too quickly over the blue horizon.

Desperately, I look ahead – Crispin is barely a speck in the distance, against the pyramids. And he looks like a bad-tempered speck too…

"What would they want with Luke?" Ace asks, as he and Carvery pick themselves off the riverbed, catching up with us to help the now hysterical Homer back out of the mud, and onto the donkey once more. "The dude's harmless. I've seen more evil bones in a bagel."

"Maybe they still think he's a treasure-thief," Carvery speculates. "They don't take too kindly to that sort hanging around near their ancient tombs."

"They don't seem to be taking too kindly to anyone much at the moment," I remark, looking up at the top of the gully.

Outlined against the smoke-filled sky, faces are appearing, peeking down at us over the edge. Gray faces, attached to lanky gray bodies in little more than loincloths. Five becomes ten, and ten rapidly becomes twenty…

"I don't suppose you fancy giving them a bit more of the old *Moulin Gris*, Homer?" Ace suggests, as the ranks of slave zombies lining the river increase exponentially.

"I don't think they'll fall for that one again," Carvery replies, as Homer looks thoughtful. "Even if he does have the right qualifications now, under that dress."

Behind us, some of the slave zombies slither down the steep ochre bank, and form a line across the shallow riverbed.

"Guess we keep moving," says Ace. "I hope Crispin knows what he's doing."

That's what's worrying me – but I don't mention it. The last time I upset Crispin, we all ended up chained to grubby bathroom fittings in an underground cell…

Herded by the surrounding gray zombies, we head further inland towards the pyramids, and to where our mud-filled trench adjoins the main river.

Lady Glandula's wooden-hulled Great Barge is even bigger and more imposing than I remember. But that's not all, currently moored on the riverbanks.

A giant steel aircraft carrier is now anchored alongside, almost parallel in size – and a row of Nine a.m. Lounge fighter jets are stationed along the runway of its upper deck.

"I don't like the look of this," I remark to Homer, and my exhausted albino donkey. "From what I've learned about inter-Lounge relations so far, I don't think they're here to borrow a cup of sugar."

The aircraft carrier has already seen some action, by the appearance of things. Shattered dinosaur corpses are piled up at one end of the runway, and an industrial-sized fishing net full of captive flying carpets flaps helplessly on the end of its restraints.

"They've been busy, since getting their hands on moonshine fuel and napalm," Ace observes, as he and Carvery catch up with us.

"Pity the other Lounges," Carvery agrees. "Hey, maybe they've already neutered Lady Glandula de Bathtub. That would be a bonus."

"Save you the trouble," I remark absently.

Prodded onward by the slave zombies, we ascend the gangplank onto the Great Barge. Greeted by more of Lady Glandula's attendant zombies from earlier, in their red leather chaps, we are escorted again into the huge wooden torchlit pyramid.

But instead of featuring Lady Glandula de Bartholine as a statue on the imposing pedestal as the centrepiece, there is the far more recognisable – and apparently still deceased – body of my housemate, Whatserface, supine on the wooden plinth at its base.

"Crap," says Ace. "They found her already."

"Not exactly, Mr. Bumgang," says a familiar voice, and an equally familiar figure lurches into view, from behind the gory display. "We are just preparing for the Rejuvenation ceremony. Glad you could all join us."

"Crispin?" I gasp.

He looks so different…

Instead of the expensive black wool suit I've only seen him in thus far, he has changed – into something far more traditionally *undead.* Ragged, bloodstained denim jeans and a torn grubby shirt hang casually off his masculine zombie frame, in a way that short-circuits all of my mental strength and resistance.

It's so deliberate… it's so undeniably…

...Like your Mr. Wheelie-Bin, I hear his voice taunting in my brain, brutally.

"Who's 'we'?" Carvery asks him, warily, while my mind reels from the unexpected visual assault. "Is your Mum here?"

"No need to rush things, Mr. Slaughter," says Crispin, calmly. A pair of zombie attendants are arranging earthenware pots of various sizes alongside Thingummyjig's inert form on the plinth. "We are a few organs short, but I believe that suitable replacements are on the way. Sarah *Bellummm?*"

"Hmmm?" I respond, still in shock at his change of turn-out.

He smiles lopsidedly, knowing he's delivered a blow below the belt.

How dare he? Knowing that I've got a soft spot for all those poor bodies, naturally decrepitating on the Body Farm…?

"You have assisted in surgery once already," he reminds me. He moves towards the plinth and unrolls an embossed leather case, and I see the array of shiny hooks and blades glinting within. "Would you reprise your position on this occasion? Or would you prefer a more… *passive* role this time?"

I look from my housemate's pale, waxlike body, to the golden clockwork hand clamped around my arm. Dreading to think what sort of impact zombie-frog-nun magic will have on her – organs or no organs…

"We can try," I say loftily, pulling myself together. "If Carvery has enough charge left in his Taser to help resuscitate…?"

I glance at Carvery, but he shakes his head.

"I'm sure you can find a way to channel the power of my father's right hand," says Crispin, confidently. "If not – we have other resources here…"

"You are not sterile!" says a booming voice, and suddenly I'm drenched from head to foot. "That's better!"

Blinking away the effect of the uninvited bucket of lavender-scented water, I can make out a huge shape waddling past me, from behind the taller pedestal in the centre of the pyramid. She resembles a fertility goddess in all the most generous ways, not so much *wearing* bright colours and patterns as swaddled and pleated into them, like a fat and jolly Christmas cracker, covered in ribbons, bows, tinsel and beads.

"My cousin, Beneficience Vassally Dry," says Crispin, a hint of pride in his voice. "Beneficience has spent her life researching the phenomenon of witch-doctors, and their powers of suggestion on the superstitious mind. As well as raising the orphans she has rescued from their clutches…"

Corporal Punishment – *of course…*

"…Should all other technology and magic fail, Beneficence assures me that the old traditional methods still have their uses."

Beneficience is setting out bunches of dried herbs and flowers around my housemate's corpse, flicking infused oil over her from a small ceremonial flail, and scattering citrus peel alongside.

"Traditional methods of what?" Ace asks, quizzically. "Barbecue marinade?"

"I'm still full," Carvery adds. "I had chilled monk brains for breakfast."

"Speaking of *braiiiinsss…*" Crispin remarks. "Our remaining organs seem to be arriving. Just in time."

We look round, and do indeed see Justin Time entering the pyramid. At zombie Naval officer gunpoint, pushing a small wheelbarrow.

"This is all that was recovered, on your instructions," the captive rickshaw pilot grumbles angrily. "That old man, he was a very mean haggler. He wanted a new house with full indoor plumbing!"

"I'm sure it was worth it," Crispin muses, as the wheelbarrow squeaks to a halt beside me. "Yes – these seem to be intact…"

"Oh, no, Crispin…" I murmur, in horror. "Not THOSE brains…"

The donor organs are entangled in a mass of Sister Summer Jaundice's striped nunnery stockings, and bits of splintered cello.

"It is a fifty-fifty chance, Sarah *Bellummm*," Crispin announces, detaching a cheerleader pom-pom from the mess. "Miss December very kindly signed her donor card as well."

"And you owe me a new girlfriend!" Justin Time spits, receiving a sharp nudge from the muzzle of the officer's gun.

"Now, now, Mr. Time," says Crispin, while Homer slides off the donkey and homes in on the rescued pom-poms. "There are eleven more months on the calendar. I'm sure you will find one to your taste before your wife obliterates them all. Um. Are these necessary for female resuscitation, does anyone know?"

"God, don't give her those," Carvery groans, as Crispin rummages in the wheelbarrow and holds a pair of silicone implants aloft. "She'll never stop talking about them."

"Mother might find them amusing…" Crispin ponders, but catches his cousin Beneficience's disapproving eye. "Perhaps not. Sarah *Bellummm*, would you identify and prepare the heart and *braiiinsss* from this mélange?"

Reluctantly, I scoop the required replacements from the wheelbarrow and transfer them to silver dishes, plucking out chips of wood and strands of tinsel.

If only there was a way of telling if it is the musical witch's heart or brain! Someone has to pay their share of the rent… but I don't think I want to live with a housemate whose solution to disagreements is to turn the opposition into frogs. Or nuns…

But the sad soggy lumps of inactive tissue give me no clues at all. No puffs of green smoke, no flashes of glitter. Not even when Beneficience Vassally Dry wafts a stick of burning sage over them, mysteriously humming *Follow the Yellow Brick Road* to herself.

"Now, Sarah *Bellummm*," Crispin says darkly, taking up the largest surgical knife. I gulp. "Shall I insert, while you stitch up?"

Homer twirls past with Miss December's recovered pom-poms, and Beneficience continues her humming and chanting and air-smudging with the sage, as we commence work on Miss Frankenminky once more.

"What are you hoping for?" Ace asks Carvery, as they stand by and watch, with the armed guard and the still-grumbling Justin Time. "Boy or a girl?"

"I don't think it matters," Carvery replies. "I won't be touching it."

Within a short interim, once again Crispin and I are facing one another over the watertight – if still dead, and this time partially pickled – corpse of my housemate.

"Now," says Crispin, wiping off his hands on those mind-numbingly ragged jeans. "To resuscitate her…"

"Oh," I snap sarcastically. "You wanted her alive?"

"Well, of course *ALIVE*, Sarah *Bellummm*," he echoes, without a hint of irony in his tone. "Mother is quite specific about that requirement. We can try some of your earlier suggestions… invoke a special god, say some magic words – we are already in a forbidden temple, obviously. Oh – and sacrifice an illegal immigrant. That was an excellent idea."

A creaking sound reaches our ears from the ceiling above, and a dark shape begins to lower from the apex of the wooden pyramid.

"A very suitable idea," Beneficience Vassally Dry concurs, in her bass rumble.

The shape appears in the torchlight as a large wooden cross, affixed to a wheel suspended by chains from the darkness overhead.

Bound to the cross, bleeding, but still breathing, is…

"Luke!" I cry out, before I can stop myself. "No!"

"Beneficience is quite sure that the ceremonial sacrifice method could work," says Crispin. "Unless you have found a better way to control the clockwork hand, Sarah *Bellummm*."

Our taxi-driver tries to raise his head from his chest, but is either unwilling or unable to acknowledge us.

I try to wrestle the clockwork hand from my arm, pressing on the gemstones, attempting to lever up the fingertips.

Nothing…

"What?" Beneficience explodes, snapping the building tension in the room, like a ripe carrot. "Crispin! You promised! I have waited since nineteen seventy-one!"

"Not now, Beneficience…" Crispin mutters.

But his rotund cousin is fuming.

"Not only did he leave me deserted, a virtual widow, he has made a mockery of my mission – by fathering bastard children to every witch-doctor he can find ever since! Sometimes even seducing them with a fish-and-chip supper! My favourite!" Beneficience throws her sage-stick to the ground, and jumps up and down on it petulantly. "You promised! *You will have your revenge*, you told me!"

"See?" Justin Time says triumphantly, slapping Ace on the back. "Perfectly normal! I told you, no-one is worse than *my* wife!"

"I'll take yours any day," Ace remarks. "Seriously."

"I think Mr. Lukan found your methods of obtaining marital sympathy from the local elders and priests objectionable, dear cousin," Crispin says, soothingly. "You will know your vengeance, as promised. But for now, negotiations take priority."

"I'm doomed either way, Sarah," Luke's voice croaks, and I look up at his miserable limp form on the cross. "Don't do it. It's for the Queen..."

"How dare you! Runaway husbands should be seen and not heard!" Beneficience grabs an olive branch from the altar, and beats him soundly with it.

"Well, Sarah *Bellummm?*" Crispin prompts me, to the background noise of thwacking olive branch and shaking pom-poms. "How shall we proceed?"

How indeed... I give up on trying to activate the clockwork hand, my fingers blistered and raw.

And what did Luke mean...?

Before I can summon an answer, there is a flash overhead.

A lightning bolt appears from nowhere – inside the pyramid – and strikes out, earthing itself on every available downward surface. The pedestal, the chains suspending Luke's wooden cross, the plinth with the body of my stitched-up housemate, which arches and contorts inhumanly... and finally, the floor.

Throwing up sparks, with the smell of scorched cedar.

Three flapping figures descend the bolt in a huddle, their coolie hats and chain-mail masks all too recognisable, landing with a resounding thud.

The lightning fades as they turn to face us, swirling their capes outward, and folding their arms in an attitude of intimidating attention.

Oh, God – Higham Dry Senior's Six a.m. Lounge bounty hunters…

A small white billy goat skids out from amongst their armoured legs abruptly, belches a large Guinness burp, and runs to hide behind our donkey.

"Damn, I nearly had him that time!" shrieks a wizened and familiar voice, behind the first bounty hunter's cloak. "Er, help an old man up, somebody. Stupid knees only bending one way these days."

CHAPTER SEVENTY-SEVEN: IRON MANDIBLE

Ace and Carvery are the first to respond to Higham Dry Senior's call for assistance, untangling him from the bounty hunters and dusting him down. Beneficience Vassally Dry wrings her hands and cries in between beating Luke on the cross, and Crispin just looks embarrassed, like a seven-year-old caught playing in his father's shed.

"What did I miss?" demands Higham Dry, straightening his robes and coughing like a chimney-sweep. "Is the old trout awake yet? Ah, Justin Time, still alive, I see. We will have to do something about that as well."

"Mercy!" yells Justin Time, throwing himself prone onto the floor. The billy goat, who had been loitering nonchalantly behind him, bleats in panic, and dives beyond a pillar.

"Grandpappy," says Crispin, clearing his throat bravely. "You know it has to be done."

"Pooh!" grouches the old man, and beats his hacking chest a few times. A clockwork cuckoo appears from his breast pocket and squeaks out a chime, along with a few centuries' worth of dust. "Nobody care anymore, my boy! They all either drunk or blowing stuff up! No place in the world for fancy women now! The only thing they good for the curing, is of being teetotal and pacifist!"

"Hear, hear!" Luke and Justin burble, in unison.

"*Ouuuch*," Homer agrees sadly, looking down at the remains of his prom dress.

"But, Grandpappy," Crispin continues, while Higham Dry Senior hobbles over to inspect the body of my housemate, Twatface, displayed on the wooden altar. "If a reconciliation could be made and the undead curse lifted, there would be no more fighting. Just good trade routes for business."

"You live in rose-tinted goldfish-bowl, Crispin." Higham Dry prods my housemate's body with his carved bone walking-stick. "All work and no play make a dull criminal record! Why you so loyal to your mother? Let her rest in pieces like the others! Make your own new friends and playthings. No room in the world for dead old hoarders and their *fancy-schmancy* loot. I told you when you little, growing boy need to eat more fish and seafood. Grow your own *braiiinsss*."

The elderly zombie puffs his way over to me, nodding more approvingly – or perhaps just arthritically.

"You still looking for your first time, young lady?" he enquires, his eyes bright with insinuation. "Don't waste it waiting for young Crispin. He only interested in unsound medical advice."

And he pats my arm, reassuringly. For a second I imagine the clockwork hand has responded to his touch – but as I look down at it – still glowing, and still nothing.

"I will prove *or* disprove those theories, Grandpappy," says Crispin, obstinately. "But not by harbouring fear of the unknown. Only the brave succeed!"

"*Harrumph*," says Higham Dry Senior, unconvinced. "Only succeed in catching all diseases known to mankind – and discovering new ways to die, not even tested out on Justin Time yet…"

"Mercy!" Justin Time chews on the planks beneath him, sobbing.

Crispin gestures to the attendant zombies, who pull levers on either side of the tall pedestal. The upper part splits vertically, and opens.

As the wooden panels retreat into the pedestal, there above us, in all her frozen black onyx stony glory, is the dreaded Lady Glandula de Bartholine – Crispin and Homer's mother.

Still beautiful – but now, still more evil.

"Do you know what?" Ace remarks. "I don't think I fancy it a second time."

"I agree, she looking quite dusty now!" Higham Dry cackles, and points to my housemate on the altar below. "No wonder she looking for a new body to park her fat old tentacle in."

"What?" Carvery demands. "She's planning on moving in there? No fucking way!"

"Oh, you didn't know? She been hanging on to this one for a long time. It *waaaay* past its *Use By* date," Higham Dry nods. "Hermit Squidmorphs don't usually live so long in one body, but she pick up this old Dry family carcass from the tombs of Ancient Egypt. They famous for hanging onto afterlife indefinitely. I think her Incantations run out though. There were some missing already, when this body discovered. Without all of the spells, eventually the Shades of the Dead run you to ground and you neither live forever nor pass into the Field of Reeds. That means heaven, for all you heathen breathers."

"Ace," says Carvery. "I told you, you did a zombie Queen with one up the spout already."

"Get used to the idea," Ace tells him, indicating Miss Fuckwit's currently-vacant body on the altar. "You're up next."

"Crispin said she was a Siren!" I gasp. "Not a Squidmorph!"

Higham Dry shrugs.

"Same difference." He waggles his hand back and forth, ponderously. "They start out small and pink with little hooks – then grow big and ugly with suckers… beautiful singing voices. Make your nose bleed." He sighs and looks misty-eyed for a moment – or it could just be the cataracts. "Of course, no-one ever survive encounter with Sirens in the old days to describe the tentacles. Crispin probably tell you that already. He probably not tell you about the Squidmorph part, in case you the only spare body handy when you get back here. His mother very fussy, but any port in a storm… Pretty soon she get too big for human host anyway. Have to start looking for next size up."

I can't believe it. First Crispin thinks my virginity is a likely cure for zombification – and now it sounds like his *Plan B* was to turn me over to his own mother, as a potential evil Squidmorph host! Maybe even both!

My stomach lurches horribly. I don't even know where to begin, with all that's wrong with this picture…

Prompted by Crispin, one of the attendant zombies in the backless red leather chaps approaches me, and with one deft twist, unclips the bejewelled clockwork hand from my arm.

"No!" I shout, as he marches away with it, towards the altar. "That was given to me to look after!"

"No!" shouts Beneficience Vassally Dry. "Sacrifice first!"

"Ooh…" Higham Dry Senior leans over, suddenly distracted, to peer intently at my cleavage. "You find finest Swiss watchmaker! He make all of old man's innards, you know!"

"Excuse me?" I reply, startled.

I look down, to see the Swiss watchmaker's armour, shrunk to the size of a gold charm, still suspended on the enchanted necklace around my neck.

Why *did* I waste that magic earlier?

"See?" he says excitedly, prodding the articulated charm on the golden chain. "No stopcock! That where *Mister Whizz* goes!"

The zombie attendant has already opened the gemstones on the clockwork hand, and a green illuminated fog is bathing the body of my housemate, rolling heavily down the sides of the wooden altar, and out across the floor of the pyramid.

"Pity it not the real thing," says Higham Dry Senior, sighing like an old cellar door. "It be like upgrading the old man from wooden spoon to *Moulinex*…"

"But it is the real thing," I reply.

High above us, on top of the pedestal, the surface of the statue of Lady Glandula is starting to swirl again, with those fractal oil-slick patterns – as she gradually emerges from her stony slumber…

"Wow, my eyesight *really* bad today," says Higham Dry, squinting closer at my bosom. "Either that, or it much further away than it looks."

"It's cursed," I sob, and reach into the nearby wheelbarrow for a splinter of Sister Jaundice's cello-bow, waving it around to illustrate, trailing a shred of catgut. "It's been shrunk by an enchantment. So I could carry it more easily."

"*Ohhh*," he nods. "What did you wish for?"

"Something suitable to wear," I admit, wretchedly.

"Maybe you just need repeat same wish," he suggests. "Magic still in clothes. Only circumstances to which suited now different."

I look down at the stupid muddy *Audrey Slapbum at Tiffany's* style silk dress, which used to be a neon Lycra *Wonder Woman* outfit and some impractical underwear, before I put it on earlier.

Either way, I'm already on a losing fashion streak today.

"I wish I wasn't pretending to be something I'm not," I grumble, without thinking.

The shard of cello-bow flashes green in my hand, and I drop it in shock. It burned me!

It continues to burn, until nothing but a tiny strip of black charcoal remains.

A split second later, the Swiss watchmaker's armour clatters heavily to the floor, and a small innocuous rug flops apologetically on top of it, where previously there had been a tapestry clutch-purse.

I immediately check my lower regions, expecting a draft and an itchy pink thong – but instead, all I find myself wearing are my old jeans, and my *Pizza Heaven* delivery-girl work fleece.

What the Hell?

"Clever girl," Higham Dry Senior approves, as the bounty hunters recover the armour from the floor. "Look very suitable. Now, boys, put him together the right way up this time…"

By my feet, Justin Time grabs the small rug, and buries his head underneath it. Something bounces off my toecap from within, and I pick it up.

The little leather-bound diary – the missing Incantations!

"Really, Crispin," that imperious female voice echoes down on our ears, from atop the pedestal. "Is this still the best you could do? It all looks very sordid…"

"With new replacement parts, Mother," Crispin replies, reproachfully. "Guaranteed virginal – or at least, surgically virginal. Some might even be magically-inclined."

Lady Glandula quirks an eyebrow, but otherwise gives nothing away. The steps are still emerging from the pedestal, and the attendant zombies hurry to flank her path.

"What is the alternative?" she enquires, and her icy gaze visits me briefly as she descends. "The scrawny fast-food delivery girl?"

"I was still seeking your approval for myself, there, Mother," Crispin reminds her.

"You know these things aren't that simple, Crispin," she says. "I can't just hop into any old body and hope it lasts. It's like a traditional wedding. Or a Broadway musical. There has to be an understudy on standby – in the event of the worst case scenario…"

"What if there was an alternative?" I butt in, breathlessly.

Everyone turns to look at me. I feel like the rotisserie chicken that has decided to stand up for itself, one plucking and basting later than usual. The only sound is the clanking of the bounty hunters, as they try to assemble the legs on the suit of armour, chivvied along by Higham Dry.

"An alternative to the alternative?" Lady Glandula muses. "I cannot imagine what *you* might have to trade."

"How about keeping the body that you've already got?" I hold up the little leather-bound diary. "With all of the Incantations you'll ever need. For ever."

She stares at the little book, but again, her sly poker-face takes over.

"My dear, if there's one thing I learned from marrying Crispin's father, it's that you can never trust a man to write absolutely everything down," she smirks, a little smugly. "I imagine there is no more in that diary than I haven't already found out for myself."

"I'll exchange it for the clockwork hand," I suggest, taking a chance on her bluff. "And my housemate – er… Frankenminky. Someone has to pay their half of the rent. Otherwise – I'll burn it, and you'll never know."

Snatching a torch from its bracket, I hold the little diary over the flame, singeing the knitted cuff of my fleece.

"Do you really believe," she begins, as the sinister tentacle emerges out of the darkness and uncoils almost lazily towards me. "That you have any powers over what I choose…?"

"Mother!" I hear Crispin's shocked voice protesting. "No! Not the understudy!"

As the suckers in front of my face threaten to blot out the view permanently, a metallic *clanggg* stops the tentacle's advance abruptly.

"You were saying?" a strangely mechanical version of Higham Dry Senior's voice interrupts.

My terrified vision swivels along the gleaming golden arm that has intercepted the Queen's extraneous limb, to meet an armoured faceplate, with glowing red slits for eyes.

"You are too late, old man," Lady Glandula laughs, while trying ineffectually to extricate her tentacle from his iron grip. "In a fresh body, I will be ten times stronger than your cheap old clockwork sarcophagus-suit!"

"Over *my* dead body," Carvery remarks, and giving me one last regretful glance, levels the shotgun with its final cartridge…

…At my housemate!

Lady Glandula cries out an indignant warning, and the attendant zombie with the clockwork hand whirls around, raising it defensively.

The hardening – the blackness – the freezing of stone…

Where Carvery had been standing, is now a Carvery Slaughter statue in black onyx – black onyx shotgun poised to fire.

CHAPTER SEVENTY-EIGHT: TRANSMOGRIFIERS

"Quite a nice patio ornament," says Crispin, mildly.

"That's if you make it as far as the new body," says Higham Dry Senior's voice, from within the impressive exoskeleton of finest Swiss watchmaker's armour. "Without becoming *tapas*!"

Only one of his arms armoured in the incomplete suit, he gives a yank on the captive tentacle, overbalancing the zombie Queen, and upsetting Beneficience's careful dried floral display around my still-inert housemate.

Crispin's cousin loses her tether, tosses aside the olive branch, and seizes a large knife from the altar, advancing on her restrained husband, Luke.

"Is it too late to agree to mediation and couples therapy?" Luke suggests, as she raises the knife.

"No!" I shout, and am dumbfounded, as Crispin echoes my cry.

Both of us dive to Luke's salvation, with differing agendas.

"Murderer!" I shout.

"Not without the formal ceremony!" Crispin hollers.

While Crispin wrestles with his cousin for possession of the knife, I thrust the burning torch at the attendant with the clockwork hand, before he can intervene again. He dodges to the far side of the altar, causing me to collide with the body of Miss Air-Head, as I struggle to reach him.

"Give that back!" I squeal at him, digging into Whatsername's ribcage with my elbow as I flail forwards. "It was given to me to look after!"

A hiccup beneath me almost goes unnoticed.

"Sarah…" says my housemate. "What's going on? Where's Carvery?"

Oh, God – not now!

"Get down, get down!" I hiss at her, pulling her clear of the plinth. "Sshhh! They want to use your body as a zombie Queen Squidmorph host! They mustn't know you're awake!"

"That queen over there?" She points over my shoulder.

"No, no – that's Homer. Remember? He just wants to be a prom queen," I reassure her. "That one, over the other side. Being dragged around by her tentacle, by the big angry cyborg. Long story."

"Why is there a goat and a donkey watching?" she asks. "And who is that man with his head under the rug? Where is Carvery?"

I really don't know which of those questions I'd rather answer least.

"I have to get the clockwork hand back, and try to get us home!" I whisper, hurriedly. "Ace is here somewhere…" Oh, yes. I spot him surreptitiously attempting to untie Luke from the wooden cross – while Crispin and Beneficience fight over his potential as a sacrifice – kicking out at any attendant zombies who interfere. "The man under the rug is…"

I have a brainwave, and hurry over to Justin Time. He is pinned to the floor by the booted feet of two of Higham Dry's bounty hunters upon his driving cape, and still at gunpoint by the Naval officer, resolutely hiding his head under the small mat.

I lift up one corner, and he screams.

"Justin," I greet him. "Can you summon the rickshaw?"

"My wife smash all of them up already!" he rages. "I am grounded!"

"But I've seen rugs, captive on the aircraft-carrier outside…" I begin. "Is that your wife General Lissima's boat? The big Naval ship? Could we get away from here on just a flying carpet?"

"You should be so lucky!" Justin scoffs. "You never sneak one past her! Believe me, every day I have tried! Sometimes four, no, six times a day!"

Lady Glandula is using her attendants as ammunition, seizing the poor helpless zombies by the legs and battering them against Higham Dry Senior's armoured hull. He deflects them effortlessly, scattering spare parts. My housemate screams as a dusty skull rolls over her foot.

"Perhaps *you* should be the one thinking about mediation and counselling?" Higham Dry's robotic voice chuckles, as he gives her tentacle a whip-crack, causing her to drop the enormous urn she had been poised to throw.

"The gods and I do not see Eye-to-eye!" she spits.

"Shouldn't have declared war on him while you were alive, then, should you?" Higham Dry replies, winding her tentacle around a pillar to deliver a body-blow. "You wouldn't have had to run away to Egypt in the first place. Or had the most important Incantations taken away from you."

"Atum took everything!" she roars, and the pillar crumbles as she contracts the tentacle, breaking free. "To the bottom of the ocean! Everything that was mine! My country! My culture! My business! My empire!"

"I can see where Crispin gets his monopoly fixation from," Ace's voice joins us.

"Ace!" I gasp. "Where's Luke?"

"Said he was going to sort out his marriage." Ace looks dubious. "I hope that means he's got a bigger knife than she does."

I look across at the altar. Crispin and Beneficience are still tussling with the sacrificial tools. Having disarmed one another several times already, they are now down to the hooks and the leather belt-roll, in a stroppy *Tug o'War* that I can clearly see harks back to their childhood as merely playful cousins.

Of Luke, there is no sign.

"I need to get the clockwork hand back," I say. "I think it might be able to stop them…"

"I have a better idea," says Justin Time's Naval officer guard. We look up in surprise, and she pulls off her dark peaked cap. Before I can react, she has twitched the little leather-bound diary out of my hand. "How about you all wait here with Higham Dry Senior's men, and *I'll* get the clockwork hand back?"

"General Lissima!" I cry out. *No!*

"I told you," Justin Time groans into his comfort-rug, as his wife runs off with the precious diary, grinning. "I try to sneak one past her many times! She always one sucker ahead!"

Over by the pedestal, Crispin and Beneficience knock the remainder of the floral display off the altar, and roll around inelegantly on the floor.

"Mine!" shrieks Beneficience, currently on top, with Crispin compressed beneath her suffocating bosom.

"Yield!" Crispin manages to blurt out, before his head disappears again under an enormous polka-dot corsage.

"Play nicely, kids," Ace remarks, a statement which does something else weird to my ovaries. "Should we do something?"

Oh, yes, I'm thinking – but it's probably not appropriate right now.

"I wouldn't even know whose side we're on at the present moment," I admit.

"The one where none of us ends up with more alien squid tentacle butt-plugs than we started out with," Ace reminds me.

I glance up at the three bounty hunters guarding us, wishing I knew what their weaknesses are…

"'When I fall in love, it will be for ever…'"

The tussle at the foot of the pedestal becomes a frozen tableau.

"'Or I'll never fall in love…'"

Beneficience raises her head uncertainly.

"Gaylord?" she snaps. "Is that you?"

Homer, ever vigilant for a song and dance number, hurries to the foot of the steps leading up the pedestal, and gestures upward with his pom-poms.

At the top, his bow-tie and cuffs straightened, a single dead rose from the altar clutched between his hands, Luke is singing to the rafters.

"Ooh, that lovely!" Higham Dry Senior the cyborg approves, windmilling an unfortunate zombie attendant in each hand like a *nunchaku* expert. "It take a hard woman to reject a man with great big lungs like those!"

Crispin struggles free from beneath his plus-sized cousin, and looks wildly at the vacant altar and suspended wooden cross of torture.

"*Nooo!*" he cries, pitifully. "The ceremony – all ruined!"

"No!" screams Lady Glandula, now using her tentacle to defend against Higham Dry's attack. "Make him stop!"

"*Yesss*," hisses another voice, and I look in its direction to see Mrs. Time, General Cutthroat Liss, clockwork hand in her grasp and stripping the flesh from the zombie still hanging onto it with her own tentacle.

The gray skin and connective tissue slides off the bones easily, like a well-cooked spare rib.

I don't think I'll ever be able to watch *Man v. Lunch* again…

"I'll go after the General and the clockwork hand," says Ace, close to my ear. "You stay here with Whatserface and find a way to distract the bounty hunters."

"How?" I demand, looking at my useless companions.

Justin Time with his head still stubbornly under the pointless rug. My housemate Shithead, huddling up between the drunk billy goat and the albino donkey. And an even less helpful Carvery Slaughter – turned to stone. My heart sinks.

I don't think you can retrieve DNA samples from stone… what a waste…

"Oh, Gaylord…" says Beneficience, a tear in her eye and clasping her breast, as Luke sings on. "Can you forgive me?"

The panels in the great wooden pyramid start to creak, and slide apart, allowing bright shafts of sunlight through. Slowly, the structure retracts into the deck of the giant barge.

"You'll think of something," Ace assures me.

I give up. What do Higham Dry's bounty hunters *really* want…?

As a last resort, I snatch the rug from Justin Time's head, and spin it away across the deck as he scrabbles to retain it.

"Justin Time is escaping!" I yell. "Trying to steal that doormat! Stop him!"

It works – the three bounty hunters launch themselves after the errant rickshaw pilot, and pin him to the floor. Ace dashes off in the other direction.

"It's nothing!" Justin Time protests, struggling. "A trinket! A souvenir! Nothing special! Not prototype, or anything important like that!"

The last of the panels is now flush with the deck, and my housemate squints up into the daylight.

"Oh, no," she moans vaguely. "It's going to rain."

"Pop Quim, hopscotch!" says Higham Dry, throwing another unlucky zombie, javelin-style, at Lady Glandula. "If a man sing up a storm, who remember to bring umbrella?"

"*Nooo!*" she shouts. "Make him *stop singing!*"

I look up at the sky, into a gathering funnel of gunmetal-gray cloud. The Great Barge, usually as steady as a rock, begins to quiver.

"Not bad, lovely boy..." I echo. My voice is barely audible, even to my own ears. "Louder..."

CHAPTER SEVENTY-NINE: PROSTATES OF THE CARIBBEAN

We start to slide across the deck as the Great Barge tilts. Alongside, the Nine a.m. Lounge aircraft carrier also leans inward, with the centrifugal pull of the vortex appearing, mid-river. The heaped-up dinosaur skeletons take a dive from its upper deck into the abyss, followed by one of the jets, parked too close to the edge.

"Hold on!" I shout at my housemate, halted as my legs entangle with the billy goat. Apparently, it could remain upright on a sheer drop. "Grab onto something!"

The *something* she finds, with her groping clumsy hands, is Justin Time under his heap of bounty hunters. Justin squeals indignantly.

"I am a married man, Madam!" he yells, playing his loyalty card as it suits him.

Lady Glandula lashes out with her tentacle, anchoring herself to the main mast. Higham Dry Senior clamps onto her with his one mechanical-armed grip, trying to drag her away.

"You don't want a little reconciliation with your god?" he says, gesturing over the side with his other scraggy zombie arm. "Surely it's nothing personal… just good for business!"

Below us, in that watery whirlpool, the gigantic Eye is rising, scattering the sunbathing crocodiles.

For the first time, I see genuine panic cross the zombie Queen's face.

"No!" she cries. "I will not enter the limbo of Darkness and Shades! Give me the rest of the Incantations!"

"Only your frail human form is in debt to Atum, Mother!" I hear Crispin shouting, but I don't see him. "Let it go! Take a new body!"

"Frail?" Higham Dry grumbles, straining on his cyborg chassis. "She is testing the limits of *WD-40* here, I tell you!"

"This frail human form is what gave birth to you, Crispin!" she yells.

"Exactly!" says Higham Dry. "The rest is just indestructible hermit *calamari!*"

Over by the ravaged altar, Beneficience is on her ample knees, sobbing. Luke reaches her with his hands outstretched in supplication, still singing, like a taxi-driving absconding angel.

And beyond, General Lissima has finished dismembering the attendant zombie from its grip on the clockwork hand. She snatches a long-bladed knife from the altar in the tip of her tentacle, and turns her attention to the struggle between Higham Dry Senior and Lady Glandula de Bartholine.

"Hey, folks!" she taunts, waggling the golden clockwork hand, and the leather-bound diary. "I have something you want! Who is the better haggler?"

And she leaps quickly aside, laughing, as they both lash out covetously.

"Give me those Incantations, witch!" shrieks Lady Glandula.

"You going to feel Higham Dry's foot in your barnacled bottom, young lady!"

Damn – where is Ace?! And what about Crispin…

Suddenly I have no need of concern with the latter, as an arm in a torn bloody shirt loops around my shoulders from behind, extracting me from the billy goat's legs.

"Thank goodness you are all right, Sarah *Bellummm!*" he greets me. "I believe we still have time…"

"Yeah, he's right there…" I say, pointing at Justin, under the increasing heap of bounty hunters, my housemate Miss Numbskull, albino donkey and inebriated billy goat. "Do we need him to get us home?"

"Not *Mr.* Time," Crispin corrects me, pulling me to my feet. "*Time* in which to perform the ceremony. Before Atum recovers his dues."

"What?" I ask, and find myself being dragged over to the altar.

General Lissima evades capture by Higham Dry Senior and Lady Glandula, sliding on her knees under their flailing limbs like a breakdancer under a limbo-stick, making it look effortless and elegant as she leans back almost parallel to the floor.

The second she is clear, she pivots sharply into a kneeling stance, and unleashes one devastating strike with her own tentacle. The knife-blade flashes – and Higham Dry's exposed zombie hand flies off, severed halfway up the radial bone.

"Who is your Daddy now, old man?" she grins, back-flipping upright and twirling the sword into a blur on the end of her tentacle, like a *Wild West* gunslinger. "Bet this clockwork hand looks even more attractive to you, hmmm?"

"Quickly, Sarah *Bellummm!*" Crispin sweeps the remaining artifacts and accessories from the surface of the wooden plinth. "Lie down on here."

"How about no!" I gasp. "I haven't signed a release form for any elective surgery!"

"I have to save my Mother," he states, obstinately.

"It won't be your Mother!" I shout back. "It'll be me, Sarah Bellum! With an ancient evil zombie squid parked up her!"

Crispin picks up a knife, and advances.

"That's the only Mother I remember," he says sadly.

I back away, around the altar. Who'd come to Sarah Bellum's rescue? I look all around, desperately. No sign of Ace, damn it... Homer is still hanging for dear life onto a pillar, looking like a cheap date at *Peppermint Hippo*. Luke and Beneficience are lost in one another's attention, for the first time since 1971. My housemate, struggling on the floor with the bounty hunters and Justin Time, is probably at less risk than she ever was in the company of Carvery Slaughter – who is still a black onyx stone statue.

I sigh. Judging so far, Carvery would have been my best bet for salvation. Even if he'd used that last shotgun cartridge already, I'm sure he'd have found another way of putting me out of my misery before I became a deadly Squidmorph cavity...

If only I could get hold of the clockwork hand – perhaps I could turn him back?

But otherwise, I don't see any point in crying for *'help'*. The mathematics just don't seem to be in my favour.

I just remember to sidestep in time, as Crispin makes a grab for my arm.

"I thought you wanted me for yourself, Crispin?" I try reminding him. "The old cure for zombies you wanted to try? Sleeping with a virgin?"

Crispin hesitates, and my hope flares.

"I am glad you are willing, Sarah *Bellummm*," he remarks. "But…"

"But what?" I try an eyelash flutter, for the first time, and only succeed in making myself dizzy.

"Present requirements are more pressing," he says, regretfully. "And virgins are not too hard to come by. Especially in the fast-food home delivery business."

"I beg your pardon?"

"I am sure your replacement at the *pizzeria* will be equally inexperienced," he adds, with a wink.

The nerve of him! As if I'm as disposable as… as… a burger carton!

Now only clamped onto Lady Glandula with his armoured fist, Higham Dry struggles to remain upright, and the mast creaks with the strain.

"I am waiting…" hints General Lissima. "Nobody want to make me an offer? Atum looks like he got all day, but I don't."

The giant Eye of the river-god is rising slowly out of the whirlpool in the river, gradually blotting out the misty sun in its veil of storm clouds. Crocodiles who weren't quick enough to escape the vortex tumble down his sides into the depths.

As I dodge another grab by Crispin across the altar, General Lissima sighs impatiently, and with an impossibly high leap onto the mast, strikes downward with her sword.

The very tip of Lady Glandula's tentacle is sliced free, with a terrible scream.

"Mother!" Crispin shouts, as Lady Glandula and Higham Dry Senior hurtle past down the sloping deck, still entangled. "Grandpappy!"

"*Hoooome!*" cries Homer, hugging his pillar, like a cheap floozy.

General Lissima laughs, and scuttles after them, jumping over her husband and the bounty hunters *en route*.

"So keen to walk the plank!" she squeals happily, as Lady Glandula's injured tentacle halts them at the railing right where the crocodile-feeding platform is attached, high above the swirling abyss. "Now, who wants to negotiate? Who wants to swear loyalty to the Nine a.m. Lounge first?"

"Never!" spits Higham Dry, clinging to the platform with his remaining mechanoid arm, cradling his stump protectively.

"No great loss," General Lissima shrugs. "All you boys over at the Six a.m. Lounge interested in is beer and sauna and clean socks. And persecuting my husband, which is very naughty."

"The Incantations!" cries Lady Glandula pitifully, her terror at the proximity of Atum evident, while she scrabbles to hold onto the side of the barge. "Give them to me!"

"Hmmm, but what are they worth, Lady Bathtub?" the General muses, twiddling the little book between her fingertips. "I already have a ship. Don't need yours. What else have you got? And don't try to fob me off with any of your undead pets. I have plenty of those too."

Luke reaches the end of his song. But this time, Atum remains, his all-seeing omnipotent Eye taking interest in the proceedings as they unravel below his gaze.

Beneficience takes Luke's hands in her own and sobs into them.

"Forgive me!" she beseeches him, still on her knees at his feet.

"My dearest," he says gently. "I am so proud of you, in spite of our differences… You have done such a good job with Corporal Punishment…"

"He is your son!" she blurts out. "I raised him – for you!"

"I know, my dearest," he says soothingly, and pats her a little awkwardly on the gilt-frilled turban.

In the touching moment of distraction, Crispin vaults over the altar, and seizes me by the hair.

"Now, Mother!" he shouts. "While there is still time!"

"No!" I scream, and flounder for a good excuse to delay things. "I'm not sterile!"

"I don't think you have anything I want, do you?" General Lissima smiles down at the crocodile-feeding platform, and twirls the sword again, preparing to strike.

There is a *swisshhh* through the air overhead, and one of the blood-red sails on the mast abruptly furls, lopsidedly, its rigging pulled sharply by a swinging counterweight.

"Gotcha," is all Ace says, as he plucks the General neatly from the deck, too fast for her to react – and then, on its outermost swing, he lets go of the rope.

I gasp, as the two of them vanish over the side, into the boiling darkness below.

Again, with the jealousy problem… Why not *me*, Ace Bumgang??!

Ow – I wince, as Crispin twists my hair in his fist, holding me captive.

"Mother!" he calls out again.

Lady Glandula drags her despairing gaze from the bottomless depths beneath her, and seems to focus once more on her last chance of salvation. A new body…

Mine!

"*Yesss*, Crispin…" she croaks, and starts to haul herself back onto the deck.

Higham Dry Senior looks on, helpless, and apparently weakening inside his special clockwork armour. The red glow in his eye-slits looks as though it is fading.

"Nobody want to help an old man?" his mechanical voice echoes, wryly.

"Nobody want to help a pizza-delivery girl?" I mutter.

Atum's giant Eye blinks.

Waiting.

"Sing it again, Gaylord," says Beneficience, breathlessly. "Sing it – like you used to…"

Luke smiles benevolently down at his wife.

"'You must remember this…'"

Beyond the crocodile-feeding platform, something flashes upwards out of the water, with barely a splash of foam.

"You are very *scrawny*," Lady Glandula hisses at me, as she slithers over the railing.

I see the metallic twinkle and the blur, whirring in the air, like something out of the *Wild West*.

"Yes," I agree, bravely. "I am a fidget."

The zombie Queen opens her mouth to respond to my insolence, but only silence emerges.

The silence unrolls across us all like a deathly flood.

"'As time goes by…'" Luke's heavenly voice croons.

Lady Glandula was never destined to hear it.

Her human body crumples onto the floor.

The head rolls slowly backwards, and plummets from the end of the platform, alongside the retracting, sword-wielding tentacle that had finished her.

I swear an echo of the General's laugh flits upward, snatched away in turn by the breeze.

"Typical Nine a.m. Lounge mercenary!" Higham Dry grumbles. "Rush off leaving job half done! There still a dirty great big squid up here, young lady!"

CHAPTER EIGHTY: THE RIDICULES OF CHRONIC

He's not wrong about that. Lady Glandula as a human zombie Queen was intimidating enough. Minus the corporeal shroud of Crispin's mother, into which her mantle had somehow been squeezed, she's just a giant evil-looking cephalopod.

Its purple iridescent eyes seem to zoom in on me as it slides back onto the deck, crushing the already-rotting remains of its former human hermit-shell unheeded, leaving a trail of vile slime.

"Yuck!" I struggle, trying to free myself from Crispin's grip on my hair. "Crispin, that's not your mother! It's a Squidmorph!"

"She has been my mother as long as I can remember," he says distantly. "I have to save her."

"Well, why don't *you* volunteer?" I suggest, and managing to free an arm, flap around wildly until my hand closes around the hilt of the last, smallest knife on the altar.

Yes! Even though it'd barely core an apple…

Reaching behind my head, I make one desperate slice.

My ponytail of hair bunched in Crispin's grip shears off. Suddenly released, and sporting a new asymmetric bob, I run.

The giant Squidmorph moves to block my path, and I jump over Justin Time and the bounty hunters – far less nimbly than General Lissima did, getting a groin full of billy goat forehead for my efforts – aiming for my one and only hope.

"Higham Dry!" I call out, finding the elderly zombie in his clockwork armour still suspended from the crocodile-feeding platform. I grab the railings in one hand and reach out to him with the other. "Let me help you!"

"That very sweet of you, young man!" says Higham Dry, his bionic transformation evidently stopping short of improved optometrics. "Crispin still making crazy philanthropist talk up there? Trying to *Save the Squid*, and not for dinner?"

"I'm afraid so," I reply, straining my arm to reach him.

I risk a glance over my shoulder. The Squidmorph, lumbering and ungainly without its human carrier, slithers towards the altar, where Crispin is waiting to greet it with outstretched arms.

"She won't last long without a body," Higham says, coughing. "But they get very angry the longer they wait. Pump out lots of adrenaline, move like bolt of diarrhoea! Better to run away first. Not have to outrun squid – just have to outrun all of your other enemies. Any port in a storm for squid!"

"You can help!" I plead. "Crispin is your grandson! You can talk some sense into him!"

"You flatter an old man, my boy…" Higham Dry Senior's robot grip slides a little – the wrong way. "But sense is all just a matter of perspective."

He looks down into the swirling darkness.

"No!" I shout.

Too late.

The golden armoured figure vanishes silently into the abyss.

I look up angrily at Atum, blotting out half of the sky.

"Why don't you do something?" I yell. "You're a god! I thought gods were omnipotent!"

Under his alien gaze, I feel very small indeed.

It occurs to me that the meaning of *'omnipotent'* is not necessarily the same as *I'm important…*

"Screw you!" I snap, and turn to size up my chances.

One giant hermit squid – check; one Oedipally-fixated zombie entrepreneur and his pole-dancing transvestite zombie brother – check; one formerly-estranged and now reconciled couple serenading one another (*aahhh*) – check; one housemate, name as yet unremembered – check; one renegade rickshaw pilot coveting a doormat – check; three bounty hunters that it would be unwise to touch without rubber boots on – check; one drunk billy goat – check; one albino donkey – check; one girlfriend-battering psychopath turned to stone (*damn it*) – check…

I look down to see what I'm armed with. A knife that wouldn't give blade envy to a teaspoon. A *Trevor Baylis* wind-up torch in my pocket. No clockwork hand, and no little diary full of special symbols. They both went overboard, with Ace and General Lissima.

"Do not worry, Mother," I hear Crispin telling the Squidmorph soothingly. "She will not get away."

Both look at me, and my grip tightens on the knife.

They must have a weak point – an Achilles' heel…

I wish Ace Bumgang was here. He'd know. He seems to have time to spare, looking up strange wildlife on *Wiki*.

I look sadly back down into the bottomless whirlpool, and across at the Nine a.m. Lounge aircraft carrier, tilting in towards us on the far side. Another fighter jet slips off its chocks on the upper deck, pitching into the blackness below. A brief fireball denotes its demise before it is swallowed up.

My foot slips on the Squidmorph's trail of slime, and I glance back again to confirm, seeing Crispin chanting and splashing her with water from a terracotta jug, evidently to ensure she doesn't dry out before finding a new host.

They need access to the Deep Ocean Trench... We just have to ensure the first thing the young squidling sees is the ocean... Maybe these tentacle chicks have something against dry land...

Nothing. I'm getting nothing from this. No ideas at all…

"You had better come here, Sarah *Bellummm*," Crispin calls. "You will require lubricating as well."

"Yes," I agree, absently. "A large Guinness *WD-40* would be about right…"

I look at the aircraft carrier. No longer running on Guinness.

Running on *napalm*.

I take out the *Trevor Baylis* torch and wind it up. Is it dot-dot-dot, dash-dash-dash? Or the other way around? I flash the light a few times at the other ship, half-heartedly.

Still nothing. The net of captive flying rugs on its deck flaps, trying to escape.

"Hey – Justin!" I call out.

"I never touched it!" Justin Time cries, slightly muffled under his captors and my housemate.

"How do you declare war on another Lounge?"

"Oh, that easy!" His nose appears from under the crush, his coolie hat somewhat crumpled around it. "You just make first pre-emptive strike!"

Fuck… not the easiest thing done from a wooden barge with apparently no firepower. I need something to make the occupants of that dirty great military ship angry…

"As you wish, Sarah *Bellummm*," Crispin's zombie monotone alerts me again. "But it will be much more painful this way."

A tentacle lashes out towards my foot, and I jump. Higham Dry was right about something else.

They DO move damn fast when they're desperate…

"Do not exhaust yourself, Sarah *Bellummm!*" Crispin cries, while I do laps of the deck of the Great Barge, dodging the slapping and groping tentacles. "You must conserve energy to survive the transition!"

"Not number one on my list of priorities!" I shout back.

"You will see immortality through her eyes!" he adds.

"She's going to see tempura batter and hot chilli dipping sauce through mine!"

The giant Squidmorph lassos itself around the mast and tries a belly-flop from a great height, scattering the remaining zombie attendants – and eating one or two which get too close.

I only avoid her by grabbing part of the sail rigging Ace had swung from earlier, and slashing it with my little knife, so that the rapidly-ravelling rope hoists me up into the air, as the sail unfurls again in turn.

Swinging from my new perspective on things, I spot something down on the deck of the Great Barge that I had completely forgotten about…

I look out over the crocodile-feeding platform. Ace's own rope still dangles there.

As the Squidmorph lunges up the rigging and hauls herself higher up the mast once more, I let go, and try to land in a professional stuntman's tuck-and-roll, only succeeding in getting one of my feet caught around my ear. Meaning I scrabble, strained and crabwise, across the deck towards Justin Time and the others.

"Help!" cries my housemate. "This donkey keeps eating my hair!"

"Jolly good, carry on, Dobbin," I pant, and snatch General Lissima's peaked Naval officer cap from the floor.

"Um, Sarah…" she asks, managing to angle her head under the tussling heap so that she can see what I'm doing. "Why are you stabbing that hat?"

I thrust the tiny knife into the crown as many times as it takes to make a deep, ragged rip.

"I am declaring war!" I announce.

And just as the Squidmorph hits the deck again behind me, I run for the railings, and jump onto the crocodile-feeding platform.

My momentum means I skid the rest of the way, and have to make a desperate, split-second leap – grabbing the rope…

…I pirouette outward, over the yawning, watery abyss, and I judge the apex of the swing – the point of zero acceleration in either direction – then spin the General's ravaged officer hat across the gap.

It flies – and as I swing backwards, it dips. My heart sinks in unison.

Atum moves, turning to watch its progress.

Just as the backs of my heels crack painfully back on the crocodile-feeding platform, a sudden updraft of air from the whirlpool lifts the declaration of war just high enough – to skim over the railings of the Nine a.m. Lounge aircraft carrier, and vanish aboard its upper deck.

Either they'll respond – or I guess they might celebrate. Hopefully with fireworks.

Depending on how popular she was.

"I don't understand your reluctance at all, Sarah *Bellummm.*" Crispin is rolling up his shirt-sleeves – although I don't see the point, they're already stained beyond *Cillit Bang* guarantees. "You looked so at home in Mother's clothes earlier today…"

Oh, boy. Does *he* have issues…

"*Hoooome,*" says Homer indignantly.

"Yes, yes," Crispin replies, exasperated. "They suit you too, Homer… but no matter. There is still the first option."

The first option? What does he mean?

"Help!" shrieks my housemate again, as a tentacle latches around her ankle and tugs.

Oh – *crap.*

I vault back over the railings from the platform, and dive across the deck, catching hold of her wrists.

"Let her go!" Justin Time snaps. "Shameless hussy!"

"I thought you wanted a new girlfriend, Justin?" I huff, trying to brace myself against the donkey.

"Maybe…" he sulks. "But… she need a boob job first…"

"They're in the wheelbarrow over there," I promise, truthfully. "Help us!"

Justin sighs, and kicks out at one of his bounty hunter captors, who promptly delivers a small warning lightning bolt which each of us feels, and makes a real mess of my underwear this time. The donkey brays, the goat bleats, and the Squidmorph squeals, and retracts her tentacle.

"See?" says Justin. "Never mix water and electricity."

"First rule of home D.I.Y…" I echo vaguely.

"Carvery used to say that," says my housemate, looking past me at Justin with admiration.

Blimey, she moves on fast. What happened to *'Where's Carvery?'*

He'd have finished off this fat old squid in a jiffy… so depressing…

The fat old squid in question doesn't seem to be affected by electric shocks for long, and has its tentacle around my housemate's leg again before our own pins-and-needles have worn off.

"Get your suckers off my girlfriend!" shouts Justin Time, as we both make a grab for her arms.

I hear Crispin's voice, now sounding agitated.

"I am sure she will still let you *borrow* them, Homer…!"

The tentacle performs the whip-cracking manoeuvre, and my housemate is wrenched out of our hands.

"No!" Justin and I both shout. The bounty hunters pin us both to the floor.

The Squidmorph dangles the screaming Miss Numb-Nuts triumphantly in the air, high above the sacrificial altar.

"Now, Mother!" cries Crispin, his black eyes strangely aflame.

My housemate is slammed down onto the wooden plinth.

"Ow!" she yells, annoyed. "I bit my tongue!"

Crispin responds by drenching her with another bucket of the lavender-scented water, and while she splutters and coughs indignantly, the Squidmorph appears to coil itself, like a tensing spring…

I can't look – I turn my head away. How could Atum allow this? Or did he already collect his dues, with Lady Glandula's human body?

"Soulless…" I murmur unhappily, and wonder why the sky has suddenly, silently, without warning, turned from gray to blinding white…

The great mahogany-coloured planks of the deck splinter deafeningly beneath us, as the whole side of the barge explodes.

The central mast pitches into the river, every blood-red sail burning like the flags of Hell.

More gun turrets aboard the aircraft carrier swivel to face us after the first deadly assault, across the void.

"Holy ship!" Justin tries to burrow deeper under the bounty hunters. "Who piss the wife off now?"

But even more horrifying is the scream that comes from the altar – but it's not the scream I was expecting.

"NOOOO!!" Crispin shrieks hideously.

Unwilling, I follow the sound of the cry with my scorched eyes, dreading what carnage I might see…

Miss Knobhead is on the floor by the altar, her nose bloody, her consciousness debatable. Crispin is on his knees alongside, clutching his hair in shock. And upon the plinth itself…

What?

…*Homer* – clutching his pom-poms to his nearly concave gray chest. Smiling.

No squid… I look everywhere. Was she indeed blown up, as I had hoped?

Homer sits up slowly, and surveys us all with a regal – slightly smug – air.

"Oh, I see," Justin Time scoffs. "He in too much of a hurry to wait and *inherit* his Mother's wardrobe."

"You mean…" I begin, and spot the telltale trickle of black squid ink down his skinny leg again. "Homer – you *volunteered?*"

CHAPTER EIGHTY-ONE: BIG KNOBS AND BROOM CLOSETS

"No, Homer..." Crispin sobs, as his brother wobbles a little, sliding off the plinth. He gets to his feet, to confront Homer. "You aren't strong enough – you haven't even been a woman that long! Let her take a younger body!"

Homer looks offended, and drawing himself up a little straighter, slaps Crispin across the face.

Stunned, Crispin holds his jaw in silence. Pom-pom tinsel dangles from his ear.

"I think you asked for that, Crispin," I remark.

A projectile from the aircraft carrier takes out the main ornamental pedestal beyond Luke and Beneficience, still lost in their starry-eyed romantic reverie, a leader into the second round of fire.

"I did not ask to be blown up, Sarah *Bellummm*," Crispin says, rubbing his chin.

He already sounds more like his old self.

"You deserve that too," I snap, crawling over to Whatsit, my housemate, and giving her an experimental prod. The resulting whine is more telling than an electrocardiogram result would be. "If Homer wants to be a zombie queen, he's entitled to be the top Queen, wouldn't you agree?"

"*Goood*," Homer approves, but does give his old gray body a rather regretful glance.

"Um, barge is still under attack, people!" Justin Time points out, from under his tenacious captors. "And Atum is still hanging around out there!"

"Maybe he wants a sacrifice..." Crispin ponders, and shrinks as we all glare at him. "I was only going to suggest the goat – maybe the donkey..."

Something golden roars up out of the whirlpool between the two ships, and lands with an almighty *boom* in the middle of the damaged deck.

"What did I miss?" asks the prodigal clockwork cyborg, Higham Dry Senior.

"Grandpappy?" Crispin exclaims.

"Higham Dry?" I cry. "You're alive!"

"Not just alive," he chuckles, like an inkjet printer with the hiccups. "Look what I found."

And he raises his injured arm.

Or should I say, previously injured.

Where there had only been a scraggy, bony stump, there is now a complete and seamless sleeve of golden armour adjoining the rest of the Swiss watchmaker's body of invention, at the end of which is mounted…

The bejewelled clockwork hand!

"Turned out this thing mighty useful," he says, flexing the fingers. His eye-slits gleam red, bright and powerful like lasers. "It grow back rest of armour and everything. Don't even need special key for *Mister Whizz* now…"

Ooh – maybe too much information…

"What happen to dirty great squid?" he asks.

"*Hoooome*," says Homer, patting his belly.

"Really?" Higham Dry strides over for a closer look. His eye-slits change to blue, and scans Homer up and down. Alarmingly, the X-ray effect certainly does reveal the outline of the squid impossibly coiled in Homer's insides. "Wow. Well, you can wear her clothes all of the time now, my boy! She not going to come out and play for a long time after all that that exertion. Hold out your hand."

Homer offers his ragged zombie hand, with the chewed fingertip inflicted by the donkey earlier, and Higham Dry Senior raises the special clockwork hand to meet it.

The tiniest, briefest spark passes between the two.

"*Ouuuuch*," Homer acknowledges.

And then he changes.

The fingertip grows back. His raw wounds close up. His patchy old skin granulates, and unwrinkles. The hollows between his bones fill out, and teeth reappear in the gaps in his jaw. And finally, perhaps more worryingly, his recent surgery apparently prolapses.

"Whoops," says Higham Dry. "Maybe give you a bit too much help downstairs."

"Ah, there's the old boy I remember," Luke observes. "Still doesn't look right on a dead white fella, but I think it suits you better than trying to pull off a high-C, Homer."

Homer shrugs, apparently pleased with the result either way.

Can't say I blame him. He definitely has the Dry family good looks…

"Now you, Crispin," Higham Dry says sternly. "You need to go home and have a good long look at your boots. In the naughty corner."

"Grandpappy…" Crispin begins, and is interrupted by the altar exploding, in another battery of fire.

"Oh yes," I interject, timidly. "I kind of declared war on the Nine a.m. Lounge."

Higham Dry turns, in time to see several large warheads launching skywards from the aircraft carrier.

That doesn't look good…

"Oh, well – no rest for the rickets," sighs the zombie cyborg. "Okay, boys – let's go and spoil their sports. Put Mr. Time down, we catch him again later."

The three bounty hunters get to their feet obediently, leaving Justin spreadeagled, head still under doormat. One by one, they each summon a lightning-bolt, and disappear into the skies, on the trail of the warheads.

"Before I go…" says Higham Dry Senior, and he turns back to face me, unscrewing the clockwork hand.

"No…" I try to stop him – but as it detaches, a new armoured hand grows in its place, out of the sleeve of armour. I can see the tiny cogs and ratchets and springs slotting into place, as it rebuilds itself.

"This belong to other Higham Dry," he says, and an eye-slit flares, in an approximation of a wink. "You remember where you found it, yes?"

"Yes," I say, accepting the clockwork hand once more. Feeling around in my pockets past the *Trevor Baylis* torch on my keyring,

I produce the long-forgotten scrap of felt plush that used to be a toy rabbit.

"That's the one," he nods. He flexes the new hand, as the joints close over the knuckles. "Clever men, these Swiss watchmakers. They succeed where ancient Pharoahs and their old spells fail. Make something that live for ever."

He takes a step away from me, with almost a salute.

"And you boys…" he says, waving vaguely at the zombie Dry brothers. "You clean up this mess before you leave, hmmm?"

Flames burst from his back-plate, and he soars away after the bounty hunters, leaving a glowing vapour-trail.

"You should go on ahead, Sarah *Bellummm*," says Crispin, and seems unable to meet my eyes. "Justin Time can take you both back to the house."

"What about Luke?" I ask. "And…"

I don't even know whether I should mention Ace and Carvery.

"Mr. Lukan has plenty to catch up on with Mrs. Lukan," Crispin assures me.

Already, I can hear how that is getting on…

"If he wants to be a librarian, he can damn well BE a librarian!"

"Over my dead body!"

"Mr Time!" Crispin summons the rickshaw pilot. "Take the two young ladies home, if you please."

Before Justin is even on his feet, the still-burning side of the Great Barge falls away into the whirlpool, dragging the rest of the rigging with it.

"It not that simple," the rickshaw pilot grumbles, hugging the innocuous doormat to his chest. "This only special prototype…"

As I look at him, a harpoon streaks between us, embedding deeply in the deck. Its cable, leading back down into the swirling, bottomless depths, tightens.

The barge tilts even more steeply over the abyss.

"Quickly, Mr. Time…!" Crispin prompts. "There may be an Easter holiday in it for you!"

Over the noise of roaring water and creaking timbers, the sound of an ethereal singing reaches our ears – but it isn't Luke. It's the same singing I last heard in the Well of Our Souls – and other voices are joining in, forming a mysterious and beautiful choir…

"Cover your ears!" Justin Time warns, pulling his torn coolie hat down, and tying it under his chin. "It feeding-time!"

"Crocodile feeding-time?" I ask, pulling my housemate Frankenminky to her feet.

"Pardon?" he says, pointing to his ear, and I mime snapping jaws with my outstretched arms. "No, not crocodile feeding-time. Baby Squidmorph feeding-time!"

I look down at the churning river, to see dozens of thin pink tentacles, like angel-hair, flying up out of the water and attaching to the ruined deck of the barge, with their little juvenile grappling-hooks. The surviving attendant zombies cling to anything still nailed down, in mortal terror.

Justin kneels on the little doormat and beckons for my housemate and I to join him. We squeeze up, in an uneven trifecta.

"Why have they come here?" I ask. "Was Lady Glandula – I mean, the squid part – their mother too?"

"Hmmm?" He adjusts his coolie hat. "Oh no. The babies stay in underwater crèche for years, herded by mermaids. Occasionally with visiting rights by their Daddy."

And he waves a hand upward, at the looming shape of the river-god, Atum.

"Ahhh…" I say. "Now I think I know what her problem was…"

"Put clockwork hand here," says Justin, tapping the middle of the small mat, which has a woven geometric pattern. The deck of the barge lurches sickeningly. "Now – just got to turn it in direction of home…"

The index finger uncurls and the little gemstones light up, as the rickshaw pilot rotates the clockwork hand.

The gray clouds in the sky billow outward suddenly with the distant *whump* of aerial explosions. Either the demise of the warheads, or of Higham Dry Senior and the bounty hunters…

I check Crispin and the others who are remaining behind. Homer has stuffed his pom-poms into his ears against the Squidmorph-song, and Luke and Beneficience have done the same with what's left of the dried flowers from the altar – but it hasn't stopped them arguing. Carvery Slaughter is still an immovable onyx statue – *damn it…*

Crispin is tugging on the harpoon in the middle of the deck, trying to remove it. Unwillingly, I feel the hot guilty blush creeping over me, knowing exactly how a merman Squidmorph nursery-nurse would have got his hands on one of those…

"Ah, that seem to be working!" announces Justin Time, pleased.

I look down at the mat. The clockwork hand is alight, with a full spectrum of colours.

"So pretty!" says Frankenminky. "Like *Somewhere Over The Rainbow…*"

I throw her a suspicious glance.

"Oh," Justin Time nods in approval, as the beam of rainbow light arcs up out of the clockwork hand. "You travel this way before, young lady, yes?"

And we leap into the sky, just as the timbers of the deck fall away beneath us.

I'm aware of passing by Atum's giant paternal Eye, and then we're above the scudding clouds. Distant lightning bolts and vapour-trails show where Higham Dry Senior and his men are still battling any Nine a.m. Lounge fighter jets that have managed to take off.

The little high-speed mat chases the rainbow, as it arches above the Earth.

"So…" Justin says, crossing his legs more comfortably and steepling his fingers. "You come here often? What your name, young lady?"

A passing Boeing jumbo jet aircraft with the *Iron Maiden* logo drowns out the answer. I nearly fall off the mat, as a loud belch in my ear out of nowhere is followed by a friendly nibble on my newly-chopped hair.

"Don't mind him." Justin pats the billy goat, who has managed to join us with only one forefoot on the mat behind me. "Maybe we celebrate with goat curry later!" His face turns hopefully back to my housemate. "Can you cook?"

We dip below the clouds again, once we pass the zenith of the rainbow. Rising up to meet us, I recognise the huge mansion on Crispin's estate – his Cadillac outside – Luke's taxi – and yes!

My little *Pizza Heaven* scooter!

Slightly less reassuring, is the way the rainbow seems to end at one of the chimneys on the crenulated rooftop…

"Hold on!" says Justin. "Turbulence! It going to be bumpy landing!"

Everything is suddenly coughing and spluttering and Guinness-burp scented darkness.

God… how Father Christmas does this five billion times in a night is beyond me… it must be something in the sherry…

We land with a crunch.

"Everybody okay?" says Justin. "We nearly took wrong turning! Old fireplace bricked up back there. Don't want to end up like Santa Claus. Now, where is door?"

I put out my hands tentatively, and feel splintered wooden sticks.

Are we in the kindling store?

"Here it is!" Justin kicks open the door, and the billy goat, now quite sooty and blackened, trots outside happily.

I crawl out into the daylight, onto gleaming parquet flooring.

It's Crispin's entrance hall. Behind me, the door to the vast cellars is locked, alongside our own escape door…

"Oh, look at the poor things!" says Frankenminky, holding up a snapped broom handle, shedding birch twigs.

…The broom closet?

Hmmm. I'm going to have to keep an eye on her…

CHAPTER EIGHTY-TWO: TRUE LICE

"Thank you, Justin!" I remember to say, retrieving the clockwork hand, while he rolls up the little doormat and tucks it under one arm. Although I'm not sure I fancy another stroll through the hen-house, mingling with the monitor lizards again straight away – Higham Dry Junior might have to wait until I've at least had a lie down and several Sloe Gin Slings before getting his toy back. "How can I repay you?"

"Oh…" He pauses and looks thoughtful, and it occurs to me that making open cavalier offers to the rickshaw pilot might be unwise. "I like your little clockwork thing…"

"What?" I was right.

How stupid am I? I can't give him the clockwork hand!

"Yes, with the little sparkly light," he says. "I saw you pointing it at aircraft carrier. Flash-flash. Good for signalling."

"Oh…" Relief bursts inside me. Fortunately, my bladder and everything else in there is empty. "The *Trevor Baylis* torch! Yes, of course…"

I pull it out of my pocket and pass it to him. He gives it an experimental twirl and a click on-and-off, looking very pleased.

"This good for busy air-traffic," he says. "I make special sequence for *'Get out of way, Stupid!'* But not tell anyone else what it is…"

"Phew," I say, holding up the clockwork hand. "For a moment, I thought you meant this…"

"Oh, really?" His eyebrows go up. "Well, if you insist…"

And he snatches it from my grasp, and runs out of the front door.

"You get back here, Justin Time!" I yell angrily.

"And don't forget, your friend promised to cook me dinner as well!" he calls over his shoulder. "Goat curry!"

Damn, damn, *damn!* And as I hurry after him, I hear an engine start.

Oh no – the *Trevor Baylis* torch was attached to my keys!

I tumble down the impressive stone steps, as my poor little *Pizza Heaven* scooter races away down the drive.

"No!" I shout, struggling back upright and spitting out gravel. Already, I'm getting flashbacks of musical push-along cart, and *Old MacDonald Had A Farm.* "No, no, no!"

"Has he gone?" Frankenminky asks, appearing in the doorway. "I didn't even get his number…"

Something nudges me sharply in the behind.

Old MacDonald had a goat…

"Baaahhh," bleats the billy goat, giving me the drunken eye.

"Right," I say. "I've ridden camels, clams, donkeys and doormats today!"

I grab the goat by the curly horns, and lean forward to whisper in its bearded ear.

"We are going to follow that scooter," I tell it. "And in exchange, you will not become my housemate's special, Goat *à la* Soggy Cheerios!"

I just remember to lift my feet off the ground, as the indignant billy goat bolts. We skid at the end of the driveway, and give chase down the main road.

How could I have been so stupid?! I should have learned by now that he isn't to be trusted!

Justin must know we are on his tail, because he takes a short-cut through the park on the way into town. A park full of Saturday morning strollers, duck-feeders, and unwary fairground visitors…

Oh no – so many innocent bystanders…

My billy goat pounds after him untiringly, stopping only to divest a small child of its ice-cream.

The scooter, meanwhile, has become stuck on the Merry-Go-Round between a Cinderella pumpkin carriage and a fibreglass rocket, and Justin finds himself giving rides to children who pull on his whiskers and insist on calling him *Ali Baba.*

"Stop!" I shout, once my goat has polished off a ball of candyfloss and a blue raspberry *Slurpie.*

"Haha!" Justin cries, finally managing to kick the scooter free of the ride, and vanishing into the mirror maze.

We clatter after him, like the proverbial bull into a china shop. A china shop full of incredibly sticky children, and the occasional excitable puppy.

"I know you are in here, Justin!" I shout at my many distorted reflections. I already know what my goat is thinking – it's thinking that maybe that last Guinness was one too many. "I can smell the two-stroke oil! Give back the clockwork hand! That was given to me to look after!"

"Can I pat your horsey?" asks a little girl with Elastoplast covering one lens of her glasses.

"My Dad says your pizzas are always cold," adds her brother informatively, who is wearing a striped jersey with his spectacles, in a typically mean parental act of inferring that their child resembles *Waldo*.

"Well," I say, while the billy goat receives his scratch around the ears magnanimously. "You tell your Dad that when his tips turn out to be legal tender in this country, maybe his pizzas will magically turn up on time."

"Just in time?" says the little boy.

"Where?!" I look all around, but only see more reflections. "Where's Justin Time?"

"Who?" asks the little girl.

"Creepy man, evil laugh, riding a motor scooter." I struggle for descriptions that match First Grade interpretation. "*Ali Baba!*"

Both the children point, to a gap in the mirrors that only small (and possibly bifocally-enhanced) eyes would notice.

I see a flash of *Pizza Heaven* top-box whizzing past.

"Tell your Dad the next pizza is free," I say, and spur my steed to follow. "With onion rings!"

We gallop out of the maze, in time to see Justin and the scooter mount the Helter-Skelter, going up the spiralling slide the wrong way…

I race to the gate, but the attendant blocks my path and tells me my goat isn't tall enough.

"No!" I scream, as Justin reaches the top, revs the tiny engine, and opens the throttle.

The *Pizza Heaven* scooter flies through the air, high above the funfair.

The billy goat butts the attendant out of the way, and we dash for the steps…

In slow motion, I watch the poor little work scooter falling, falling – the poor children beneath running, scattering, as fast as their slippery socks will allow…

…We'll never reach the top before it…

The scooter lands smack in the middle of the bouncy castle, which nearly folds up double. And then springs back up, catapulting Justin Time far over the treetops beyond, and out of sight.

"Jump!" I shout at the billy goat. "He mustn't get away!"

But instead, my billy goat merely joins the queue at the top of the steps, to slide down the Helter-Skelter the more usual way.

"Oh my God, you are such a pussy!" I grumble, once we reach the bottom.

The goat takes no notice, but rewards itself with a bag of popcorn from a passing *Disney* princess.

"Never mind," says the princess's big sister, as she starts to cry. "Look up in the sky – at the lovely rainbow…"

I look up too, and pretty soon I'm crying as well.

CHAPTER EIGHTY-THREE:

DÉJÀ VOODOO ~ FIFTY SHALLOW GRAVES

I wake up eventually. It's already Monday morning.

I can hear my housemate, the newly-christened Frankenminky, singing in the shower. I strain my ears, suspiciously. Is that *Somewhere Over The Rainbow* she's murdering in there? I'll definitely have to watch her…

By the time I had recovered the *Pizza Heaven* scooter, it was covered in sticky finger-marks, candyfloss, bogeys, and several thoughtful parents and dog-owners had used the insulated top-box as a diaper/baggie bin.

It still runs though.

I check my phone, which I've left on charge all Sunday, by the look of things. Holy Hell – a hundred and seventy-one requests on *Draw My Thing?* I don't really have that much of a social gaming problem, do I?

And one voicemail – from Dry Goods, Inc.

Well – he can definitely wait. I have no idea how I'm going to explain the loss of the clockwork hand this time…

I peel myself off the bed, and go to push Miss Nipple-Nuts out of the shower.

I ride to the Body Farm in a blue funk. Passing *Bumgang & Sons' Breaker's Yard* brings my mood even lower. And as for the D.I.Y. store, with its advertising billboard announcing a sale on patio slabs and cement – I can't even look at it.

I enter the code at the gate for the Farm and let myself in, leaving the scooter to trudge up to my favourite silver birch tree, and even more comforting wheelie-bin. Eyeing some of the exposed body tags warily *en route*.

"Hands up any zombies here?" I say, but they're all either asleep, or very good at play-acting.

I lift up a tarpaulin to check. Pooh. Maybe a zombie with a hygiene problem. If it's true where we get half of these subjects from, that wouldn't be unusual. I think we have the highest rate of scrofula victims *per capita* of the entire civilised world, on our little smallholding. Where do tramps go when they die? They get an open-air burial in a different sort of park.

Slumping down under my favourite tree, I take out my sandwiches and unwrap them. The sight of limp white crustless bread and lemon curd makes me want to burst into tears. No chilled monk brains. No cheese made from billy goat. Just plain old bread and sickly sweet yellow goo.

"I'm glad none of you are zombies," I say out loud. "Too damn noisy by half, they are."

I munch on my sandwich, and pull out my phone, with another gaming notification.

ANONYMOUS HAS SENT YOU A CHALLENGE ON DRAW MY THING. CLICK TO ACCEPT.

I tap on the screen, glad for another slicc of reality as I know it.

An inverted triangle appears on the app, covered in scribbles. Five letters.

Dubiously, I count on my fingers. Most likely another illiterate twelve-year-old being rude.

I stick the remainder of the sandwich in my mouth, and send a request for a letter clue.

P appears as the first letter. Ohhhh – maybe they're just really bad at drawing… I enter the letter E, and click on *Send*.

WRONG. GUESS AGAIN.

"Huh?" I try looking at the scribble from all angles. "Illiterate *and* crap at drawing?"

While my mind boggles, the message reminder on my phone flashes up again. Comforted and emboldened by the proximity of my beloved Mr. Wheelie-Bin, I switch to Voicemail to listen.

"I think we have some unfinished business, Sarah *Bellummm*." The sound of Crispin's disembodied voice on my phone still manages to send shivers down my spine. "If you would like to drop by my office at your convenience, we can conclude the interview."

"He's still serious about offering me a job?" I remark, to Mr. Wheelie-Bin. "I have a feeling that losing the clockwork hand won't go in my favour… Mind you, trying to shove a giant squid up my bottom doesn't exactly go in his…"

I look at the *Draw My Thing* challenge again, and to pass the time while considering my options, type in the letter N.

WRONG. GUESS AGAIN.

"It's nice to know he's alive, I guess," I ponder, dubiously. "And that he's checking up on me too…"

I glance in frustration at the game screen, and completely at random, try a letter T.

WRONG. GUESS AGAIN.

"Crap," I mutter, and send a request for a hint. "I mean, it's not every day a girl meets an eligible bachelor – dead *or* alive…"

HINT: LETTERS 3 AND 4 ARE THE SAME.

There is a noise, beside me. I freeze.

Did I imagine it, or did the wheelie-bin just *rattle?*

Putting my phone away, I sidle a little closer.

"Um…" I say, looking around quickly for any other evidence of undead activity or pranks in the Body Farm, but there is only the usual rustling of dead leaves, dead skin, beetle-husks and rotted clothing on the breeze. "Er… Mr. Wheelie-Bin?"

The square plastic garbage container vibrates again, followed by a definite scratching sound from within.

Bravely, I find the longest stick I can (which, being in over two acres of conservation woodland, is pretty long), and use it to poke the lid open.

Nothing… well, I suppose it would be more conclusive if I actually looked inside…

I drop my eight-foot branch, and creep closer, clearing my throat.

"Is anybody home…?"

The smell hits me first. It's… it's… well, I was going to say indescribable, but as it happens, it's a lot like the barracks in the Six a.m. Lounge. Sleeping-bag farts, I think Higham Dry Senior described it. With a hint of coffee and dead thing, whoever said that as well.

It's not as if I'm unused to it. Just that it seems particularly ripe and pungent today – or maybe some of that is me, and my nervous tension…

I'm just about to peer over the edge, when there is a *glooping* sound, and a dark, rancid slime bubbles out and over the side.

"Gosh," I say, politely, looking down into the upturned eye-sockets. "I hardly recognised you…"

Barely holding together at all, the skeleton gropes its way out into the sunlight. A t-shirt hangs apologetically from his twisted torso, and one of his legs seems to be locked into a foetal position from his stay in the bottom of the garbage container.

The only thing that seems to have lasted the ravages of decay and exposure is that wonderful shock of copper hair, hanging from his scalp as it flaps on the side of his battered cranium, and my pity goes out to him.

Domestic violence is a terrible thing. Hmmm. Carvery Slaughter is probably better off wherever he is. Being a garden gnome somewhere, I suppose.

"You're looking well," I say, encouragingly. "In fact…"

I frown, as he lists weakly in the wheelie-bin, like an X-rated, morning-after *Oscar the Grouch*. Or *Davros* on a bad day – in need of a pampering session.

Doesn't his hair look a little too *bouffant* for this stage of deterioration…?

I take out my Cramps University notebook, and flip back through the pages.

Hair – no change... hair – no change... hair – no change...

I look back up at him, in growing disgust.

"Your hair…" I begin, and watch as the breeze has no effect on its uplift and pattern at all. "…Is a wig!"

All this time! *A badly-attached toupée!*

It doesn't even cheer me up that I will be getting an 'A' for my research, that I have spotted one of the mythological corkers that the academic staff like to test out on the Forensic Anthropology undergraduates.

I feel cheated. I feel conned. The rose-tinted scales have fallen from my eyes.

"You, sir," I announce. "Are a liar and a cad!"

And I storm off, head in the air.

I'm not sure what 'cad' means, but I always assumed it was a golfing insult, implying that they weren't good enough to play, just to hunt for the more qualified men's balls. It feels appropriate right now, as fuming, I head back for my scooter.

Perhaps Crispin can make me a better offer, after all…

I recognise Debbie, Brain-Dead Blonde Mk II in the Customer Services lobby of Dry Goods, Inc, but she doesn't recognise me.

I suppose the yucca plant pot on her head, smashed deep into the front desk isn't helping, but her left arm flaps out anyway and buzzes me in, as I ask to see Crispin.

His office door is already open at the end of the corridor when I show myself through.

"Sarah *Bellummm*," he greets me, rising to his feet behind his own desk. "So glad you accepted my invitation…"

But I freeze in the doorway, staring at the opposite wall.

"What is THAT?" I demand.

He looks hurt.

"My art, Sarah *Bellummm*," he reminds me. "*High-Velocity Spatter.* I thought you liked it."

"Not the painting." I point. "That… *him*."

Alongside the painting, is the black onyx Carvery Slaughter, complete with shotgun.

"Ahh – Mr. Slaughter." Crispin gestures for me to sit on the black leather sofa by the coffee table as before. "I rather like him as office décor, don't you? You can hang your coat on him, if you want."

"I got dressed in a hurry," I say, stiffly, taking the seat ungraciously. "This is all I have on. Er, underneath. Just me."

"Intriguing," he echoes, in a low voice. "Would you like anything from the vending machine? Let me get you a coffee. Or – is it too early for a Sloe Gin Sling?"

"Definitely too early," I say, pleased with my self-control, although the nape of my neck is itching in paranoia at sitting with my back to Carvery Slaughter. Stone statue or otherwise. "Um. How is Homer?"

"Having the time of his life, the precocious trollop," Crispin grumbles, hesitating over the keypad of the state-of-the-art black vending machine. "Mother's wardrobe hasn't seen so much action since she posed for the Ancient Egyptian equivalent of *Hello* magazine."

"Er, Crispin," I say, twiddling my keyring in an embarrassed fashion. "There's something I need to tell you…"

"No, Sarah *Bellummm*," he interrupts. "Let me apologise first…"

"It's not that…"

"…Lady Glandula de Bartholine was my greatest inspiration – more so than the munitions business that the male line in my family dominated, as you may have guessed," he blurts out, and turns to face the window, unable to meet my gaze. "I was her star pupil, her brightest hope – and her devoted patron…"

I don't know how much more icky and uncomfortable this monologue is going to get, so I sneak occasional peeks over my shoulder at Carvery, just to check he's still a statue. Still a man-beast, but still a statue.

Mmmm. Pity you can't get DNA from onyx…

"…It was my honour to serve her and keep her in the manner to which she was accustomed…"

If only I hadn't lost the stupid clockwork hand – if I'd known he was going to end up displayed back here…

"…Provision of certain sacrifices, at regular intervals…"

My phone buzzes inside my fleece, with a notification. I pull it out.

ANONYMOUS SAYS: DO YOU NEED ANOTHER HINT?

"…Now with Homer, I imagine those services will become redundant, except for…"

I tap on *YES* to pass the time, and wonder if Crispin has forgotten about the coffee he offered me.

HINT: YOU EAT THIS.

"…At least once or twice a year, usually at the solstices…"

My brain slowly unfreezes as I stare at the app on my phone screen.

Inverted triangle. Covered in random scribbles. Five letters beginning with P. Letters 3 and 4 are the same…

My hand shaking, I feverishly type in the letters I, Z, Z, A after the P, and hit *Send.*

"…Of course, fulfilling the role of secretary would be neatly killing two birds with one stone, if that doesn't sound too selfish of me…"

Before the app can respond, a text message arrives. My heart pounding, I open it.

IF YOU'RE OFFERING, MINE'S A CHINESE MEAT FEAST.

"…You don't need to give me your answer straight away…"

It's from Ace Bumgang.

I squeal out loud.

"Hmmm?" Crispin turns and looks at me. "Are you quite all right, Sarah *Bellummm?*"

"Yes!" I gasp. Both of my hands are shaking now. He's alive! Oh my God! "Er – I think I just need that coffee, Crispin. If you wouldn't mind…"

"Of course, how foolish of me." Crispin turns back to the vending machine. "Cream, sugar?"

"Yes, please." How can I keep him distracted? "And perhaps some fresh air in here? And – do you have anything to eat? Maybe I just feel a little faint."

"Anything my lady wants," says Crispin, gallantly, typing away on the keypad, and reaching for the remote control for the windows and blinds. He suddenly seems very pleased with himself, although I can't think why.

I reply quickly to the text.

MAYBE LATER. AT CRISPIN'S OFFICE. HE'S GOT A STONE COLD CARVERY SLAUGHTER ON DISPLAY. JUSTIN TIME HAS THE CLOCKWORK HAND.

"…I understand you might want more time to think carefully about my proposal," says Crispin, a strangely intimate tone in his voice. "But your knee-jerk reaction has given me great hope already…"

Ace replies immediately.

I'LL SEE YOUR STONE CARVERY, AND RAISE YOU A MRS. TIME. SHE'S KICKING UP A NICE FUSS IN THE TRACTOR TYRE INFLATION CAGE HERE AT THE BREAKER'S YARD.

Ace has General Lissima hostage! And she most likely still has the little leather-bound diary! How did he manage that…?

Actually, not that hard to figure out – if he wanted to take *me* hostage, all he'd have to do is blow gently in my ear…

Crispin sets out a lovely arrangement of coffee and cream-filled strawberry jam scones on the low table, on a tray decorated with a single pink-and-white Oriental lily, reflecting the edible colours of the scones and filling the room with its spicy perfume. But my mind is racing.

Who is the most likely person to track down that thieving rickshaw pilot?

Yes! *His wife!*

And then – we'll have the clockwork hand. And then – I'll figure out how to change Carvery Slaughter back into a human being. Which might be necessary, I justify the idea smoothly, for if my housemate Frankenminky turns out to be a bit too little of Miss December, and a bit too much of Summer Jaundice…

I send a quick reply, under my napkin.

I'LL BRING YOUR PIZZA ORDER AT 5PM.

"…And then, we will take a tour of the premises, so you can find your way around," Crispin is saying.

Ace answers again, promptly.

COOL. BY THE WAY – YOU WERE WRONG. THE ANSWER ISN'T PIZZA. X.

Eh? I frown at the message before closing it, and the app screen pops up again, with its response to my guess on *Draw My Thing.*

WRONG. GUESS AGAIN.

"Crispin," I say, to hide my confusion and images of triangles with scribbles now dancing in front of my eyes – besides, I feel as though I haven't really contributed much to the conversation so far, and should make it at least look as though I was paying attention. "It's my turn to apologise. I'm afraid Justin Time has run off with the clockwork hand…"

"If it's not one thief, it's another," Crispin shrugs, and treats me to his lopsided smile. "And Justin Time is just a great big pussy."

Hmmm… I put my phone away, and sit back to enjoy my nice coffee. Of course, I'll have to accept the job of secretary now – if only to keep an eye on Carvery, and ensure access to him when I get hold of the clockwork hand. I wonder how grateful he might be, if I was the one to save *him* for a change? There's always a chance Justin Time might turn up here too. Negotiating some holiday, or another... But Ace Bumgang is alive! And wants pizza! And – is drawing very rude things on *Draw My Thing!*

'You eat this' he said! I have to hide my blush behind my sticky napkin, and get my phone out to re-read his last text message just to make sure. And I notice the 'X' on the end of it for the first time – and my brain swims alarmingly.

"I think I really should be going," I smile, my mind now just pink fog. "Thank you for a lovely – er – interview."

"Promise me you will consider my proposal carefully, Sarah *Bellummm*," Crispin says, gravely.

"I will," I promise, sincerely, and hope he repeats it at some point soon, so I know what he's so serious about.

But until then – I have other priorities. I drop my napkin into the waste basket, and before I get to my feet, I do a double-take.

All that the waste basket contains otherwise, is a note saying:

TAKE OUT TRASH.

Strange... isn't that what was in his other waste basket, in the cellar...?

I recall the deep cellar under the mansion, and its refrigerated collection.

Dry family members in suspended animation, infected with the zombie curse. Waiting for Crispin to come up with the definitive cure, tested out on Homer – now fully recovered, and Queen of all he surveys... but that's not all the note reminds me of.

What about his supposition that *take-out* delivery boys and girls are a good source of virginal donor organs?

Am I still just potential *Take-Out Trash* to him?

I get to my feet slowly. My brain now feels like it's whirring and clanking as much as Higham Dry Senior's clockwork *braaiiiinsss*.

"Could I start work tomorrow?" I ask, coughing to hide the tremor in my voice. "Shall I turn up for nine a.m? Or is that a bit too – *warlike?*"

"I've always found that the working day is more civilised depending on the company one keeps, not the time of day," Crispin beams, and offers me his hand.

I shake it, but have to resist the urge to snatch my own away too quickly.

As I hurry back outside to my scooter, a glance backward confirms that the seagulls have found some more pickings on the beach, outside Crispin's office window. Looks like he gets through a lot of his own staff, not to mention other people…

I won't be coming back here just to keep an eye on Carvery. I'll be back to watch *him* as well.

Maybe with a shovel, and a plot marked out ready, at the Body Farm.

In fact, now I think about it – there's a nice wheelie-bin going spare. Prime position.

Under the silver birch tree…

ROLL CREDITS:

THIS PARODY OF MANY SCENES WAS INSPIRED BY…

From film & television:
*Secretary; 9 1/2 Weeks; Body of Evidence; Pretty Woman; Star Wars; Phantom of the Opera; Lara Croft, Tomb Raider; Dangerous Liaisons; Batman; Blade Runner; E.T: The Extraterrestrial; Home Alone; The Goonies; Raiders of the Lost Ark; Labyrinth; Romancing the Stone; Disclosure; The Chronicles of Narnia; Stargate; Jewel of the Nile; Return of the Jedi; Queen of the Damned; Pride and Prejudice; The Graduate; Pulp Fiction; Dirty Harry; My Fair Lady/Pygmalion; Death on the Nile; Octopussy; The Magnificent Seven; The Life of Brian; Big Trouble in Little China; The Men Who Stare At Goats; The Lost Boys; Indiana Jones and the Temple of Doom; Crouching Tiger, Hidden Dragon; Shallow Grave; The League of Extraordinary Gentlemen; The Hunt for Red October; Crimson Tide; 20,000 Leagues Under the Sea; Splash; The Empire Strikes Back; Alien Resurrection; National Treasure; Beetlejuice; Harry Potter and the Chamber of Secrets; Lawrence of Arabia; Sex & The City II; Casablanca; District 13; Casino Royale; Saw; Fermat's Room; ParaNorman; Mission Impossible; Journey to the Center of the Earth; A Town Called Panic; Jurassic Park; Death Race; Men in Black; M*A*S*H; Good Morning, Vietnam; Dad's Army; Full Metal Jacket; Apocalypse Now; It Ain't Half Hot, Mum; Time Bandits; The Wonderful Wizard of Oz; Stardust; The Tourist; Charlie and the Chocolate Factory; Tomb Raider, Cradle of Life; Cowboys and Aliens; Frankenweenie; Iron Man; Transformers; Pirates of the Caribbean; The Chronicles of Riddick; Bedknobs and Broomsticks; True Lies; Déjà Vu... and many, many more...*

Books (not filmed or produced for broadcast at time of writing):
Fifty Shades of Grey © Fifty Shades Ltd
The Magician's Nephew © C.S. Lewis

Forever indebted (professionally and personally) to the work of:
Henry Gray F.R.S. and *H.V. Carter, M.D.* ~ for *Gray's Anatomy.*